ARISTOTLE ON SUBSTANCE

Aristotle on Substance

THE PARADOX OF UNITY

MARY LOUISE GILL

PRINCETON UNIVERSITY PRESS

PRINCETON, NEW JERSEY

Copyright © 1989 by Princeton University Press
Published by Princeton University Press, 41 William Street,
Princeton, New Jersey 08540
In the United Kingdom: Princeton University Press, Oxford

Library of Congress Cataloging-in-Publication Data

Gill, Mary Louise, 1950–
Aristotle on substance : the paradox of unity / Mary Louise Gill.
p.   cm.
Bibliography: p.
Includes index.
ISBN 0–691–07334–1
ISBN 0–691–02070–1 (pbk.)
1. Aristotle—Contributions in concept of matter. 2. Matter—
History. 3. Aristotle—Contributions in concept of substance.
4. Substance (Philosophy)—History. I. Title.
B491.M3G55   1989
111'.1—dc19   89-3620

First Princeton paperback printing, 1991

Publication of this book has been aided by the
Whitney Darrow Fund of Princeton University Press

This book has been composed in Linotron Bembo

Princeton University Press books are printed on acid-free paper,
and meet the guidelines for permanence and durability of the
Committee on Production Guidelines for Book Longevity of the
Council on Library Resources

Printed in the United States of America by
Princeton University Press,
Princeton, New Jersey

8   7   6   5   4   3   2

FOR MY MOTHER
Evalyn Pierpoint Gill

AND TO THE MEMORY OF
MY FATHER
John Glanville Gill

CONTENTS

CONTENTS

PREFACE

This book began as a study of Aristotle's theory of matter and evolved into a study of composite substances, with a particular emphasis on the question of how composites can be unities, given their material composition. Actual work on the project began in 1985–1986, when I spent a year on an Ethel Wattis Kimball Fellowship at the Stanford Humanities Center and profited from both the congenial society of the center and the stimulating group of philosophers and classicists in the West Coast Aristotelian Society. I thank the group of students at Stanford who attended a class on Aristotle's theory of substance, whose lively interest spurred me to reformulate many of my thoughts on this topic. I am grateful to the University of Pittsburgh for granting me two consecutive years of leave, which enabled me to finish a project that would otherwise have taken much longer.

My views on Aristotle's metaphysics have developed through presenting them in two sorts of forums—my classes on Aristotle and various colloquiums at which I have read papers to a wider audience. In both contexts I have received helpful questions and objections. Among my classes I single out especially a seminar on Aristotle's theory of matter, which I taught jointly with James Lennox in the winter of 1985 and which gave the project its impetus, one on Aristotle's *Metaphysics* in the fall of 1987, and another on *Physics* VIII taught jointly with J. E. McGuire in the winter of 1988, all at the University of Pittsburgh. Many topics treated in the book have been presented as papers: at Dartmouth College, the University of Pittsburgh, the Claremont Graduate School, Stanford University, and the University of California at Berkeley; at two sessions of the Boston Area Colloquium in Ancient Philosophy, a conference on Matter and Explanation in Aristotelian Science and Metaphysics, the Society for Ancient Greek Philosophy, and the Pacific Division of the American Philosophical Association. These occasions have enriched my understanding of Aristotle.

My greatest debt is to the various people who have read the manuscript. I have benefited from many discussions with James Lennox, and his views have helped to shape my own on numerous topics; I particularly thank him for his comments on the last draft. Tim Maudlin has been an incisive critic, and his constructive suggestions have led me to reexamine questions and to formulate my answers more sharply. Sarah Waterlow Broadie, who read the manuscript for the Press, has offered the rare criticism that enables one to understand an entire problem in a new way; the book as whole is much improved as a result of her suggestions. Challenging criticisms from G. E. R. Lloyd have caused me to rethink and to clarify my position. Michael Frede has, on several occasions, pointed out weaknesses in my view, and although he will doubtless still disagree with my main thesis, the book is much better for my attempt to answer his objections. William Charlton, Alan Code, and Jennifer Whiting have given valuable criticisms. Andrew Miller has offered crucial advice on questions of Greek and matters of presentation. I particularly thank Paul Coppock for his careful reading of the last draft; his astute criticisms have resulted in many improvements.

A number of other people have given helpful criticisms on particular topics: Alan Bowen, David Charles, Sheldon Cohen, Montgomery Furth, Susan Gill, A. A. Long, Julius Moravcsik, Donald Morrison, Johanna Seibt, Chris Shields, and Charlotte Witt. I thank Sanford Thatcher, Craig Noll, and Sterling Bland for their editorial advice, and other members of the staff at Princeton University Press for their assistance.

My approach to Aristotle owes its direction to my teacher at Cambridge University, G. E. L. Owen. Although his untimely death in 1982 deprived me of his sage advice on this project, his work remains a vital source of inspiration.

In this volume works of Aristotle are abbreviated as listed here. Full references to these works and to other classical texts cited appear in the Bibliography.

ABBREVIATION	LATIN TITLE	ENGLISH TITLE
Cat.	*Categoriae*	*Categories*
De Int.	*De Interpretatione*	*On Interpretation*
Pr. An.	*Analytica Priora*	*Prior Analytics*
Po. An.	*Analytica Posteriora*	*Posterior Analytics*
Top.	*Topica*	*Topics*
S.E.	*Sophistici Elenchi*	*Sophistical Refutations*
Phys.	*Physica*	*Physics*
De Cae.	*De Caelo*	*On the Heavens*
G.C.	*De Generatione et Corruptione*	*On Generation and Corruption*
Meteor.	*Meterologica*	*Meteorology*
De An.	*De Anima*	*On the Soul*
De Sens.	*De Sensu*	*On Sense*
De Mem.	*De Memoria*	*On Memory*
De Iuv.	*De Iuventute et Senectute*	*On Youth and Old Age*
P.A.	*De Partibus Animalium*	*Parts of Animals*
M.A.	*De Motu Animalium*	*Movement of Animals*
G.A.	*De Generatione Animalium*	*Generation of Animals*
Met.	*Metaphysica*	*Metaphysics*
E.N.	*Ethica Nicomachea*	*Nicomachean Ethics*
Rhet.	*Rhetorica*	*Rhetoric*

ARISTOTLE ON SUBSTANCE

This book explores the role of matter in the generation and constitution of Aristotelian composite substances. Aristotle's theory of substance has been widely discussed, but attention has focused more extensively on his doctrine of form than on his doctrine of matter. Although matter has not been neglected, the notion remains deeply puzzling. This book will challenge the traditional assessment of Aristotelian matter by arguing that common assumptions about it derive from the misreading of several pivotal texts. I shall examine these texts in chapters 1 and 2 both to call into question these common conceptions and to reconstruct the account of matter that Aristotle defends. On the basis of that reassessment, I shall turn to his probing account of composite substances in the middle books of the *Metaphysics*. On the interpretation of Aristotelian matter that I shall propose, matter seriously threatens the intrinsic unity, and hence the substantiality, of the object to which it contributes.

The puzzle about matter and composite substances lies at the intersection of Aristotle's theory of substance and his theory of change. The problem, which I will call "the paradox of unity," can be stated by appeal to some central Aristotelian themes. Aristotle uses various criteria in deciding what things are primary substances. In the *Categories* the main criterion is ontological priority. An entity is ontologically primary if other things depend for their existence on it, while it does not depend in a comparable way on them. The primary substances of the *Categories*, such as particular men and horses, are subjects that ground the existence of other things; some of the nonprimary things, such as qualities and quantities, exist because they modify the primary substances, and others, such as substantial species and genera, exist because they classify the primary entities. The primary substances are the ultimate subjects to which other things belong as predicates but which are not themselves predicated of anything else.[1] Therefore the existence of other things depends upon the existence of these basic entities; if they were removed, everything else would be removed as well.[2]

In the *Metaphysics* Aristotle preserves the criterion of ontological priority but emphasizes a different criterion: conceptual priority. A primary substance is something that can be understood through itself, without reference to other more basic entities. Entities that are not primary are

---

[1] *Cat.* 2, 1ᵇ3–6; 5, 2ᵃ11–14; 2ᵃ34–ᵇ6; cf. 2ᵇ37–3ᵃ9.
[2] *Cat.* 5, 2ᵇ3–6.

understood through the primary substances. In *Metaphysics* Z.1 Aristotle indicates that the investigation of being must start with the study of substance because nonsubstances depend for what they are on substances.[3] The crucial question, then, is, What things are conceptually primary? Furthermore, are the things that are conceptually primary also ontologically primary? This book will argue that organic composites, such as human beings and horses, are both ontologically and conceptually primary. It is not at all obvious, however, that such entities can be conceptually primary.

An entity is conceptually primary if it is a definable unity, that is, if it is definable simply in terms of itself and without reference to entities that are prior to it.[4] Definable unity can perhaps best be grasped by recognizing the sorts of situations in which it is absent. An entity C is not a definable unity if, in specifying what C is, one must mention an entity B that belongs to an entity A, where A, B, and C are distinct from one another.[5] In cases of this sort, A and B are conceptually prior to C, since C is understood with reference to them. Accidental compounds obviously display this failure. For example, in specifying what a white man is, one must mention the quality whiteness, which belongs to the substance man. Whiteness and man are distinct from each other, and the accidental compound is identical with neither component but with the combination of both. Definable unity fails in numerous less obvious cases. Consider Aristotle's favorite paradigm, the quality snubness. Although snubness does not contain two distinct components, as white man does, the account of snubness must nonetheless specify two distinct entities, one of which belongs to the other. Snubness is concavity (a quality) in the nose (a substance). Snubness cannot be specified simply as concavity because concavity realized in a different subject would not be snubness but something else; for instance, concavity in the legs is bowleggedness.[6] The subject in which the concavity is realized thus contributes to what snubness is.

Examples of definable unity are hard to find because most entities fail to be unified in this way, and many that succeed are problematic. Forms that exist separately from material objects, such as the Prime Mover, are definable unities. The form of a composite body, such as the soul of a human being, is also a definable unity, but its success is not straightfor-

---

[3] *Met.* Z.1, 1028ᵃ20–29.

[4] On definable unity, see *Met.* Z.4, 1030ᵇ4–13; Z.6, 1031ᵇ11–14; 1032ᵃ4–6; Z.11, 1037ᵃ18–20; Z.12, 1037ᵇ10–14; H.6, 1045ᵃ7–25.

[5] See, e.g., *Met.* Z.4, 1030ᵃ2–17; Z.11, 1037ᵃ33–ᵇ7. I owe this formulation to Michael Frede and have profited from reading his forthcoming paper "The Definition of Sensible Substances in *Metaphysics* Z." Since my account of definability differs in many respects from his, he should not be held responsible for the use to which I put his formulation.

[6] *S.E.* 1.31, 181ᵇ35–182ᵃ3.

ward, and Aristotle must argue that the form does not resemble snubness.[7] His standard paradigm of a definable unity is the shape concavity.
Since concavity is a quality, it is not in fact a definable unity because all
qualities—indeed all entities located in categories other than substance—
are defined with reference to something in the category of substance.
Even so, Aristotle uses the distinction between concavity and snubness to
clarify the difference between those entities that are definable unities and
those that are not. Unlike snubness, which depends for what it is on a
definite and perceptible item in the category of substance, concavity depends on something more general, such as surface. Since concavity can
be realized in various sorts of surfaces, its identity does not depend upon
any particular sort. So no particular subject need be mentioned in its defining account, in the way that the nose must be mentioned in the account
of snubness.

Definable unity seems to be possible in either of two cases: first, if an
entity c can be specified by mentioning an entity b that is not distinct in
nature from c and that does not belong to a distinct entity a; or second,
if c can be specified by mentioning an entity b that belongs to an entity
a, where a, b, and c are not distinct in nature from one another. The first
test is satisfied by separately existing forms (which I shall not discuss).
Aristotle treats the immanent form of a living organism as satisfying the
second test and argues that the form can be defined without reference to
matter. Although such a form can be specified either as a b or as a b in an
a, the form is properly definable because b and a have the same nature. I
shall argue that organic composites, which consist of matter and form,
are also definable unities in the second way. The main task of the book is
to show how such definition is possible.

The problem with composites is precisely the fact that they are composites—that they consist of matter and form. The *Categories*, which
treats living organisms as unquestionably primary substances, either fails
to recognize or ignores the fact that its primary objects contain matter
and form. Once the primary substances of the *Categories* are analyzed into
their components, there is a pressing question whether the composite can
be a definable unity or whether, since it consists of matter and form, these
constituents deprive it of strict definability. If matter and form make distinct contributions to the nature of the composite, in the way that, for
example, the bronze and the particular shape apparently make distinct
contributions to the nature of a statue, then the composite has a compound nature, with one part determined by its matter and the other by its
form. If composites in general resemble bronze statues in the way just

[7] See *Met.* Z.11, 1036ª31–ᵇ7.

described, then they will not be definable unities because their account will specify a form that belongs to a distinct matter.

The reason for thinking that Aristotle must accept this conclusion lies in his theory of change. He believes that all changes involve a continuant, something that persists through the change. In typical nonsubstantial changes—changes of quality, quantity, and place—a physical object, of the sort that the *Categories* calls a primary substance, serves as the continuant when its nonsubstantial properties are replaced. In fact, the *Categories* states that a distinctive feature of a primary substance is its ability to survive changes.[8] The *Physics* investigates substantial generation and destruction as well as the three sorts of nonsubstantial changes, and this treatment leads to the introduction of matter and form. Obviously a man does not survive his own destruction, nor does he preexist or serve as the continuant for his own generation. Yet in this case too there is a continuant,[9] and Aristotle calls the continuant matter. An analogy can be drawn between nonsubstantial and substantial changes: In nonsubstantial changes a substance survives the replacement of its nonsubstantial properties; similarly in substantial changes matter survives the replacement of form. Again, in nonsubstantial changes the outcome of the change is a compound of a substance and a nonsubstantial property; similarly in substantial changes the outcome is a compound of matter and form. But if matter survives a substantial generation in the way that a substance survives a nonsubstantial change, then Aristotle faces a difficulty about the resulting generated object.

Suppose for a moment that the product of a substantial generation is a definable unity. The dilemma is, How can the requirement for unity of the continuant *over* time be reconciled with the requirement for unity of the whole generated composite *at* a time? I will call the requirement for continuity through change a demand for "horizontal" unity, and the requirement for definable unity a demand for "vertical" unity.[10] If matter persists throughout the generation, career, and destruction of a composite, thus providing horizontal unity, then the matter has a nature distinct from that of the form whose temporary presence gives the composite its particular identity. But if so, then the composite lacks vertical unity: its nature is determined in two ways, by its form and by its matter, each of which is conceptually prior to it. Yet if composites are primary substances, they must be conceptually primary entities, and so must be vertical unities. Thus, the kind of unity needed to account for change con-

---

[8] *Cat.* 5, 4ᵃ10–21.

[9] *Phys.* 1.7, 190ᵃ13–21; 190ᵇ9–17.

[10] I thank Tim Maudlin for suggestions concerning the formulation of the paradox.

flicts with the vertical unity required of those entities that are primary substances. This is the problem I call "the paradox of unity."

Aristotle could accept one side of the dilemma and reject the other. Suppose that he preserves vertical unity by arguing that the nature of a composite is exhausted by its form alone, with matter making no separate contribution. He then faces an objection that generation is a sheer replacement of entities, since no identifiable feature of the preexisting entity has survived in the product. Although it has been suggested that Aristotle endorses sheer replacement,[11] this proposal is hard to square with his aim of giving an adequate response to Parmenides on the question of change. Parmenides denied the possibility of change because, on his view, for coming-to-be to occur, something must come to be from nothing.[12] Aristotle agrees with his predecessor in excluding such absolute emergence,[13] yet accommodates change by insisting that coming-to-be, although involving replacement, also involves continuity.[14] He thus avoids the charge that, when a change takes place, the preexisting entity simply perishes into nothing and is replaced by a product that emerges out of nothing. Since some part of the preexisting entity survives in the outcome, change is not a sheer replacement.

Aristotle is more likely to adopt the other alternative, that generated composites lack vertical unity. This proposal finds support in *Metaphysics* Z and H and has won the conviction of many commentators, who believe that, in the *Metaphysics*, Aristotle alters the thesis of the *Categories* by demoting the composite to a derivative status and awarding priority to form. Forms, which do not contain matter and need not be defined with reference to matter, are vertical unities; composites, which do contain matter and are defined with reference to it, are not. Thus forms are conceptually primary entities; composites are not.

But *Metaphysics* H.6 suggests a different conclusion. In a celebrated passage at the end of H.6, Aristotle says, "But, as we have said, the proximate matter and the form are the same and one, the one in potentiality, the other in actuality" (1045ᵇ17–19). Nor is this an isolated statement. In *De Anima* II.1, in the course of offering a series of definitions of soul, he says, "So it is not necessary to ask[15] whether the soul and the body are one, just

---

[11] Charlton 1970, esp. 139–41.

[12] Parmenides DK B8.6–21.

[13] See, e.g., *Phys.* 1.8, 191ᵇ13–17; *G.C.* 1.3, 317ᵇ11–18.

[14] *Phys.* 1.8, 191ᵃ23–31, and cf. n. 9 above.

[15] The phrase οὐ δεῖ ζητεῖν at 412ᵇ6 is sometimes translated "it is necessary not to ask"; see, e.g., Hamlyn 1968, 9; Nussbaum 1978, 68; cf. Nussbaum and Putnam, forthcoming, 32. But since the problem of unity is a central focus of *Metaphysics* Z–Θ, and since Z and H.6 apparently offer different conclusions about the unity of composites, it seems doubtful that Aristotle would now exclude the question about their unity. It seems more likely, in light of H.6, that in *De An.* II.1 he thinks that the question need no longer be asked because there

as it is not necessary to ask whether the wax and the shape are one, or generally the matter of each thing and that of which it is the matter; for although unity and being are said in many ways, the strict sense (κυρίως) is actuality" (412^{b}4–9). Although the theory that underlies these unity claims is far from evident, the sentiment at least seems clear. Composites of matter and form are unities, and they are unities in some strict (κυρίως) sense; the components of a composite are somehow identical with each other. These statements also suggest that the doctrine of potentiality and actuality plays a fundamental role in solving the problem of unity for material composites.

Thus Aristotle seems to be committed to the conflicting claims expressed by the paradox of unity. The aim of this book is to show how he solves the dilemma. Some scholars would doubtless urge that Aristotle weakens the demand for vertical unity so that living organisms, which evidently command a special place in his hierarchy of beings, succeed as substances, even if not as primary substances. I shall offer a more radical defense of these entities. Aristotle maintains both the demand for strict vertical unity and the demand for horizontal unity. The critical question, however, is the interpretation of horizontal unity—the persistence of matter through the generation, career, and destruction of a generated composite. Aristotle's decision about material composites thus depends crucially on his theory of substantial generation. Chapter 3 will spell out this theory and contrast the scheme he uses to describe such generation, which I will call the "construction" model, with the scheme he uses to describe nonsubstantial changes, a scheme commonly called the "replacement" model. Aristotle interprets the construction model in different ways on different occasions. According to one interpretation, the matter that accounts for horizontal unity survives as an identifiable ingredient within the generated object. When Aristotle understands horizontal continuity in this way, he concludes that composites are not vertical unities. This is his judgment about composites in *Metaphysics* Z. I shall examine his arguments against the composite and on behalf of the form in chapter 4. The end of chapter 4 will turn to his defense of composites in *Metaphysics* H.6 and will ask what his justification is for this dramatically different conclusion.

Chapter 5 will argue that Aristotle reinterprets the notion of horizontal unity in such a way that matter can account for continuity through substantial generation without depriving the composite of vertical unity. He argues that the matter survives, not actually, but merely potentially, and this single revision within the theory of generation has crucial implica-

is an answer. My translation is given in Hett 1936, 69; Smith (in Barnes 1984, 1:657); and Hicks 1907, 51; cf. Rodier 1900, 1:67.

tions for the status of material composites. Even so, Aristotle recognizes that the potential survival of material ingredients within the composite remains problematic, though not fatally so, for the unity of the generated whole. The main task of chapter 5 will be to explain what Aristotle means by potential survival and to show that the notion, while leaving space for the vertical unity of generated composites, is not enough to explain why the unity lasts. The matter from which a composite is generated, even if it survives merely potentially, has a disruptive effect on the unity of the object to which it contributes. Thus Aristotle needs to explain, not only how composites can be unities, but also how they remain vertical unities. *Metaphysics* H.6, in which Aristotle defends composites, mentions a cause that is vital to solving the problem of unity. I shall argue that Aristotle appeals to a cause precisely because material persistence remains problematic, even on the modified theory of generation. The solution to the problem of unity will finally depend upon Aristotle's doctrine of form as an active cause or, as he refers to the form within his broader theory of potentiality and actuality, an active potentiality (δύναμις) or nature (φύσις). Chapters 6 and 7 will explain how the form as active cause accounts for the continuity of processes and for the persistence of unities that have been generated. I shall argue that *Metaphysics* Θ, which spells out the doctrine of potentiality and actuality and its application both to contexts of change and to contexts of being and persistence, provides Aristotle's defense of the unity of composites claimed in H.6.

My exposition will be closely tied to Aristotle's text, and the larger argument of the book will be built up from an analysis of central, and often controversial, passages. I have chosen this strategy because it is so hard to understand Aristotle's project from our distance in time. Although he often gives remarkably interesting answers to the questions that we, as contemporary philosophers, find important and valuable to ask, the fact that he so often contradicts those answers indicates the risk of approaching the text with the wrong expectations. Since expectations can be corrected by remaining close to the text, this is the strategy that I have adopted. The project has been as much to identify his questions as to determine his answers.

In attempting an interpretation, I make various assumptions. First, I assume that Aristotle's treatises can be read as a coherent whole. Thus I differ from many interpreters who think that Aristotle's writings reflect his intellectual development. Although Aristotle undoubtedly changed his mind on many issues, and although signs of his revisions can be readily found in his writings, we are simply not in a position to decide the date of his various works. Since he makes few historical references by which to confirm an absolute date of composition, interpreters can at best achieve a relative chronology. The problem with the developmental approach is that, in order to determine a relative dating, the interpreter must have a prior conception about the direction of Aristotle's philosophical growth; and a survey of the literature on this topic makes clear that different conceptions can result in quite disparate datings of individual works.[16]

In any case, it is widely agreed that the extant treatises were not written and published for popular consumption but were tools used for teaching in the Lyceum.[17] Even so, Aristotle's treatises are evidently more than mere lecture notes. The attention to detail within particular works and the elaborate system of cross-references between them suggest that they were written not only to remind the instructor but also to be read and discussed by the students. If Aristotle did not publish his works outside the Lyceum but carefully prepared them for the members of his school, then he probably updated them from time to time, combining works originally composed separately, incorporating marginal notes into the current copy, and revising or rejecting earlier arguments. There is evidence of such composition and revision.[18] If Aristotle revised his work, then the extant treatises most likely represent the last stage of his philosophical reflections, and conflicts between various works and within particular works could indicate, not revisions of doctrine on the part of the author, but an order considered appropriate for instruction or for the dialectical strategy that Aristotle so often uses to reach a conclusion that he later denies.

The *Categories*, which regards organisms, such as men and horses, as primary substances, seems at odds with *Metaphysics* Z and is therefore often viewed as an early work. It is arguable, however, that the conflict between the *Categories* and the *Metaphysics* simply indicates that the *Categories* is an introductory work that conscientiously avoids the issues that would lead to the tangles of the *Metaphysics*.[19] I shall argue that Aristotle's view about organisms in the *Categories* is one to which he remains committed. Again, the conflict between Aristotle's treatment of composites in *Metaphysics* Z and most of H, on the one hand, and in H.6 and Θ, on the

[16] E.g., Jaeger 1948 and Owen [1965] 1975. For a helpful critique of Jaeger's approach, see Grene 1963, 26–34. On the problems of dating Aristotle's treatises, see G.E.R. Lloyd 1968, 9–18.

[17] The end of the *S.E.* (1.34, 184^{b}3–8) suggests that at least this work was read aloud; cf. *P.A.* 1.5. For a helpful discussion of this topic, see Zeller, 1897, 1:105–36.

[18] For example, *Met.* Z.7 opens without a connecting particle, which suggests that the three related chapters Z.7–9 were originally an independent work. But a reference to Z.8 at Z.15, 1039^{b}26–27, and to Z.7–9 as part of the work on substance at Θ.8, 1049^{b}27–29, suggest that these chapters were incorporated by Aristotle himself into the body of *Met.* Z. For a helpful discussion of this topic (and an assessment of the significance different from my own), see Frede and Patzig 1988, 1:21–26, 31–33.

[19] Cf. Furth 1988, 36.

other, arguably reflects Aristotle's careful and sustained dialectical strategy, which enables him to develop the full implications of one view about material composites before turning to develop another. He need not have changed his mind on this issue. My first assumption, then, is that Aristotle's works can be approached as an intelligible whole and that his system of cross-references is our most reliable guide in deciding how the treatments relate to one another.

Second, although one cannot ignore the possibility that textual corruption or the interpolation of an editor's marginal notes has sometimes obscured Aristotle's meaning, I assume that a coherent interpretation can be given on the basis of the edited text together with the alternative manuscript readings. Since suspicion about textual corruption can serve as too easy a solution to rid the text of apparent conflicts, proposals for emendation should be a last resort. If it were possible to know in advance what Aristotle wanted to say, then one could decide what he did say and modify the text accordingly, but the text itself is our best evidence in determining what he wanted to say. Decisions about corruption, later compilation, and chronology should be conclusions reached only after making one's best effort to construct a consistent interpretation of the text as it stands.

Third, and most important, I assume that Aristotle had a broadly coherent and interesting account to offer, one well worth trying to reconstruct, and that conflicting claims within the account more probably reflect inadequate understanding on our part than confusion on Aristotle's. Perhaps this is too generous a claim to make on behalf of an author, even (or especially) a great author. Important discoveries tend to be difficult ones, and it would be extraordinary to find any creative thinker who had worked out all the details of a theory or smoothed out all the flaws. I am not suggesting that Aristotle did. But the major obstacle that the interpreter faces is knowing the right questions to ask. The questions that Aristotle thought to be worth posing and answering may not be those that we find important or would think of asking. And our only access to the right questions is Aristotle's text—his answers to those questions and his account of the philosophical tradition to which he was, to a large extent, responding.

My method in interpreting particular texts and in developing the thesis of the book as a whole has been one of trial and error. If a thesis seemed fruitful in the interpretation of one passage but could not illuminate, or seemed irrelevant to, the interpretation of another passage, I have supposed that the most likely source of the trouble was the interpretive thesis. If I could modify the thesis or find another that promoted the understanding of both passages, I have accepted the modification or rejected the first in favor of the second. Thus, my aim has been to integrate Aris-

11

totle's claims about matter, form, and composite substances into a single coherent theory. Although I find two strikingly different verdicts about the status of composites, one pressed through *Metaphysics* Z and most of H, and the other in H.6 and Θ, the two conclusions can be traced to different answers to one question within the theory of generation, namely, a question about material continuity or horizontal unity. The book examines the arguments that lead to the two conclusions, spells out the common theory of generation on which both conclusions depend, and undertakes to explain why the treatment of material persistence is crucial for the status of generated objects.

All translations are my own, and at the expense of elegance, I have kept them as literal as possible, using square brackets to add words that may clarify the translation and including Greek words or phrases in parentheses if the original words may help to explain the argument. Explanatory notes indicate divergences from commonly preferred manuscript readings and other variations concerning translation.

CHAPTER ONE

MATTER AND SUBJECTHOOD

Metaphysics Z.3 is often cited as the text in which Aristotle describes his own concept of matter; in fact, Bonitz in his *Index Aristotelicus* cites *Metaphysics* Z.3 for Aristotle's definition of matter.[1] I shall argue that Aristotle's main target in this chapter is not his own concept of matter but a concept that he rejects, and that the point of the chapter is to clarify the notion of subjecthood, which he regards as a criterion for substantiality.

INTRODUCTION TO *Metaphysics* Z

The project of the *Metaphysics*, which Aristotle calls First Philosophy, is the investigation of being. The *Categories* too is a study of being, and that work classifies it into ten kinds: substance, quantity, quality, and the other categories. In the *Metaphysics* Aristotle argues that the various senses of being must be understood with reference to being in one primary sense, the being of substance (οὐσία).[2] The being of entities in the nonsubstance categories is somehow parasitic on the being of substance, and so, to understand the being of those other entities, one must first understand the being of substance. Hence the primary task of First Philosophy is to investigate the being of substance. Aristotle describes the project in *Metaphysics* Z.1 as follows:

> And in fact the perennial question and perennial puzzle both in the past and now, namely, What is being? (τί τὸ ὄν) is this question, What is substance? (τίς ἡ οὐσία) (for some [of our predecessors] say that this is one, others more than one, and [among the latter] some say that the number is limited, others unlimited), so we too especially and primarily and almost exclusively must investigate, for that which is in this way (περὶ τοῦ οὕτως ὄντος), what it is (τί ἐστιν). (1028ᵇ2–7)

---

[1] Bonitz 1870, 785ᵃ25–28.

[2] I adopt the standard translation of οὐσία as "substance." Although this translation has been criticized (see, e.g., Owens 1978, 137–54) because it obscures the etymological connection between οὐσία and "being," the warrant for the translation can be traced to the *Categories*, where Aristotle claims that a primary substance is an ultimate subject—a ὑποκείμενον—something that "underlies" its properties. A substance "stands under" other things. Since subjecthood remains fundamental to Aristotle's notion of οὐσία, the translation "substance" is appropriate, despite the regrettable blurring of the connection with being. The word also adequately specifies the notion of essence (τὸ τί ἦν εἶναι), since we speak of the "substance of" things to indicate their fundamental character.

Aristotle frames his own question about substance as one that engaged the philosophical tradition before him, and in Z.2 he lists the items that various people regard as substances. He first suggests that substantiality is attributed most obviously to bodies—to animals and plants and their parts; to physical bodies, such as fire and water and earth and things of that sort; to parts of these and things composed out of these; to the heavens and its parts, for example, the stars, moon, and sun (1028ᵇ8–13). He stresses, however, that it is a topic for consideration whether these things alone are substances, or these things together with others, or only some of these, or none of these but quite other things (1028ᵇ13–15). Some people regard the limits of body rather than body as substances, for example, plane and line and point and unit. Some think that nothing besides perceptible things are substances, but others, like Plato, think that other things exist and that the eternal things are more real. Thus Plato lists the Forms and mathematical objects as two substances, and the substance of perceptible things as a third (1028ᵇ16–21). After mentioning modifications of Plato's view by his successors in the Academy, Aristotle concludes that the project is to determine which of the foregoing statements are correct and which not, which things are substances, whether there are substances besides the perceptible things or not, in what sense the perceptible substances exist, whether there is some substance that exists apart from material things, and if so why and how, or whether there is no such substance in addition to the perceptible things. These are questions to be investigated.

The list of candidates in Z.2 is preliminary. In Z.16 it becomes clear that some of the items have not withstood the investigation. For example, the parts of animals, although they seem to be substances, are claimed to be mere potentialities (δυνάμεις) because they cannot exist separately. If they are separated from the things whose parts they are, they exist as matter (ὡς ὕλη) (1040ᵇ5–8). The simple bodies—earth, water, air, and fire—also fail because these are not unities but more like heaps, until they are worked up and some unity is generated out of them (1040ᵇ8–10). Z.2 surveys the candidates that, for one reason or another, might be brought forward as deserving the title "substance," but in order to decide which ones are deserving and which not, the first task is to sketch what substance is (1028ᵇ31–32). Thus, Aristotle returns to the problem stated above in the quotation from Z.1 (1028ᵇ2–7): What does one mean in calling something "substance"?

Aristotle turns to this task at the beginning of Z.3. The question "What is substance?" is answered in four main ways. "Substance is said, if not in more ways, especially at least in four ways; for the essence (τὸ τί ἦν εἶναι) and the universal (τό καθόλου) and the genus (τὸ γένος) seem to be a substance of each thing, and fourth among these the subject (τὸ ὑποκείμενον)" (1028ᵇ33–36). Obviously, if different people mean different things by οὐσία, they will propose different candidates as deserving the title. So to decide which candidates are in fact deserving, one must investigate and assess the alternative ways of understanding the notion and then sort through the possibilities on the basis of that assessment. It may turn out that each alternative is valuable in a different way, or that only some are helpful, or that none is; it might even be necessary to reconsider the question for alternative answers.

The project of *Metaphysics* Z is thus exploratory. Z.2 lists various items that one might regard as substances; Z.3 asks what "substance" means and lists various answers. In the course of the book, Aristotle spells out and examines those alternative answers and often criticizes suggestions that have been or might be put forward. One reason why *Metaphysics* Z resists interpretation is that, given the exploratory nature of the enterprise, it is sometimes hard to determine where Aristotle stands on a particular issue or whether he rejects or endorses a position that he discusses; and the decision one way or another can have large implications for the understanding of his overall project. Furthermore, in the course of the discussion Aristotle sometimes introduces topics whose relevance to the main issues is not always wholly apparent. Yet the text does display a general structure that conforms, more or less, to the expectations aroused in the opening chapters. Three answers to the question "What is οὐσία?" receive explicit treatment: Z.3 focuses on substance as subject, Z.4–12 on substance as essence, and Z.13–15 on substance as universal. The genus receives no separate treatment, but many scholars agree that the treatment of the universal serves as a treatment of the genus as well.[3] Z.16 then reconsiders, in light of the foregoing discussion, which of the candidates from Z.2 succeed as substances, and Z.17 reopens the whole inquiry by suggesting another way to approach the question "What is οὐσία?" namely, substance as cause.

With so much by way of introduction to the project and problems of Z, I now turn to Aristotle's treatment in Z.3 of subjecthood as the answer to the question "What is οὐσία?"

The Project of *Metaphysics* Z.3

Metaphysics Z.3 begins its main discussion by explaining what a subject is. The notion is already familiar from the *Categories*: a subject is that of which other things are predicated but which is not itself predicated of

---

[3] In his summary of *Met.* Z in H.1, Aristotle claims to have shown that neither the universal nor the genus is substance (1042ᵃ21–22). Since the genus is a universal, he may have found it unnecessary to argue separately against the genus, once the universal has been rejected. Cf. Ross 1924, 2:164; and Frede and Patzig 1988, 2:35.

anything else (1028ᵇ36–37). The *Categories* treats something's being an ultimate subject as a test of its being a primary substance, and it regards physical objects, such as a particular man and a particular horse, as the things that unequivocally satisfy the test. But the *Categories* does not treat its primary objects as complex bodies consisting of matter and form, and once these intrinsic features are introduced, there is a serious question whether the composite whole or one of its intrinsic features should count as the ultimate subject. *Metaphysics* Z.3 agrees with the *Categories* that subjecthood is a criterion of substantiality (1029ᵃ1–2) but indicates some uncertainty about what type of entity should count as an ultimate subject. Aristotle mentions three candidates: "In one way the matter is called such, in another way the form, and third that from these" (1029ᵃ2–3), and he clarifies his meaning with a simple illustration. "By matter I mean, for example, the bronze; by form the configuration of the visible shape; and by the composite from these the statue" (1029ᵃ3–5).

Which of the three contenders—the matter, the form, or the composite—has the best claim to be the ultimate subject and therefore substance? Many scholars take the subsequent argument to show that form has the best credentials, and the conclusion derives in part from a preferred manuscript reading at 1029ᵃ6. If the text is read as printed in modern editions,[4] Aristotle says: "So if the form is prior to the matter and more real, it [the form] will be prior to the composite (τοῦ ἐξ ἀμφοῖν) too for the same reason (διὰ τὸν αὐτὸν λόγον)" (1029ᵃ5–7). The central argument of Z.3 (1029ᵃ10–26) concerns the claims of matter to be the ultimate subject and therefore substance, and Aristotle concludes the discussion by insisting that such an outcome is impossible (1029ᵃ26–27). Since separation (τὸ χωριστόν) and thisness (τὸ τόδε τι) are special features of substance (1029ᵃ27–28), both the form and the composite have better credentials to be substance than matter does (1029ᵃ29–30). (The meaning of "separation" and "thisness" will be discussed in the section "Subjecthood" below, but for the moment they can be left as primitive notions.)

On the standard view of Z.3, Aristotle is supposed to conclude that form has a better claim to be a subject, and therefore substance, than the composite does. Given the opening statement, one expects form to have better credentials than the composite for the same reason that its credentials are better than matter's; yet the reason that Aristotle gives for the priority of form he gives as a reason for the priority of the composite as well. Both the form and the composite are said to satisfy the separation and thisness conditions, and both are for that reason said to be prior to

---

[4] Ross (1924) and Jaeger (1957) print the genitive τοῦ of the definite article at 1029ᵃ6, though the nominative τό is equally well attested. See Ross 1924, 2:165; and Frede and Patzig 1988, 2:40–41, for arguments defending τοῦ.

matter. So scholars locate the ground for the priority of form not in the reason that he explicitly gives but in what he goes on to say. He says that he plans to investigate form next. He sets the composite aside on the grounds that it is "posterior and clear" (1029ᵃ30–32), and he sets matter aside for a similar reason. Matter, he says, is "in a sense clear" (1029ᵃ32). But form, the third candidate for substance, is "very perplexing" and therefore deserves study (1029ᵃ32–33). Aristotle does take up the problem of form in the next chapters of Z (Z.4–6), although he apparently undertakes the investigation under a different rubric. Z.4 explicitly treats form as essence; the topic of form as subject seems to be quietly dropped.

This reading of Z.3 is troubling. Aristotle gives a reason why both the form and the composite have a better claim than matter to be substance: each is separate and a this (τόδε τι). So if form is prior to the composite, it is evidently not because the composite fails to satisfy these two conditions. But Aristotle claims at the outset that, if form is prior to the matter, then it is prior to the composite for the same reason. Interpreters sometimes suggest that, because matter fails to be substance in the primary sense, it infects the composite as well.[5] But if so, the inferiority of the composite rests on a different ground from that of its constituent matter. The failing of matter is due to a lack of separation and thisness—conditions that the composite satisfies. So the failing of the composite must result from its containing a component that lacks separation and thisness. Because the composite contains matter, it is "posterior." Thus form wins.

But Aristotle does not say that form wins. In fact, the end of the chapter still specifies all three candidates—the composite, the matter, and the form—as "substance" (1029ᵃ30–33), and this part of the chapter gives no reasons for the priority of form. On the contrary, it gives a reason why form should be the next topic for discussion; namely, while the composite and matter are fairly clear, form is very perplexing (ἀπορωτάτη). Surely Aristotle does not attribute priority to form on grounds of its obscurity.

These puzzles are all avoided if one starts with a different manuscript reading at 1029ᵃ6. The readings τό (the nominative of the definite article) and τοῦ (the genitive) have about equal authority in the manuscript tradition, and τό occurs in Ps. Alexander's commentary.[6] If one reads τό, Aristotle initiates his argument as follows: "So if the form is prior to the matter and more real, the composite (τὸ ἐξ ἀμφοῖν) too will be prior [to the matter] for the same reason" (1029ᵃ5–7). In the central argument of the chapter, he considers a conception of matter and argues that, on that conception, matter cannot be substance. Since separation and thisness are

---

⁵ See Ross 1924, 2:165; Dancy 1978, 412; and Frede and Patzig 1988, 2:51–52.
⁶ *In Met.* 463.24–26.

17

features of substance especially, and the matter described lacks these features, both the form and the composite have better credentials than it has; both deserve priority for the same reason, and Aristotle explicitly states the reason. He then explains why he plans to treat form next: since the composite and matter are relatively clear but form is very perplexing, form will be the next topic. If the alternative manuscript reading is adopted, both the form and the composite succeed in Z.3 as ultimate subjects and therefore as substance according to the subject criterion.

Twice in the early part of Z.3 Aristotle states that a subject is that of which other things are predicated but which is not itself predicated of anything else (1028ᵇ36–37; 1029ª8–9). But on the second occasion he protests, "But it must not be only thus (δεῖ δὲ μὴ μόνον οὕτως); for it is not enough, since this is itself unclear, and moreover, matter becomes substance" (1029ª9–10). Scholars often take the objection to be that the subject criterion on its own is not an adequate test of substantiality;[7] if it were an adequate test, then matter would succeed as substance. A genuine substance must satisfy two additional criteria as well: besides being a subject, a genuine substance must also be separate and a this.[8] And so, although matter satisfies the subject criterion and therefore succeeds as substance in a way, it has a lesser claim than the form and the composite, each of which is separate and a this as well.

It is doubtful, however, that this is the force of Aristotle's complaint. He objects to some sort of inadequacy and indicates that, because of the inadequacy, matter becomes substance. But he also mentions an unclarity, and this mention is odd, if the point is simply that the subject criterion needs to be supplemented by further conditions in order to be a satisfactory test of substantiality.[9] If Aristotle were simply protesting that the subject criterion on its own is a partial test, his aim would be better served by mentioning only the consequence that matter becomes substance. The fact that he also speaks of an unclarity suggests that he has another qualm as well.

Aristotle objects that the subject condition as stated is inadequate because it is unclear, and because of the unclarity matter becomes substance. Separation and thisness, which he mentions later in the chapter, are not

---

[7] See, e.g., Happ 1971, 662; Schofield 1972, 97; Robinson 1974, 185–86; and Kung 1978, 149.

[8] One justification for regarding separation and thisness as criteria independent of subjecthood is *Met.* Δ.8, 1017ᵇ23–25, which mentions subjecthood first and separation and thisness second as two ways to be substance. But even if Aristotle takes the criteria to be independent in Δ.8, he evidently regards them as closely connected at H.1, 1042ª26–31, where he explains the subject criterion in terms of separation and thisness (see below, pp. 30–31).

[9] For alternative suggestions concerning the nature of the unclarity to which Aristotle objects, see Schofield 1972, 97 (cf. Dancy 1978, 393); and Frede and Patzig 1988, 2:41 with 37.

two further conditions in addition to subjecthood. On the contrary, separation and thisness are constraints on the notion of subjecthood itself.
The point is not that to be a substance an entity must be a subject, separate, and a this; the point is rather that, to be a substance *as subject*, an
entity must be separate and a this. The main project of Z.3 is to refine the
notion of subjecthood; once the notion has been refined, Aristotle claims
that the form and the composite both have better credentials than matter
to be subjects.

The central argument of Z.3, the argument devoted to matter, shows
why the subject condition must be refined. In this passage Aristotle does
not discuss his own concept of matter but depicts the ultimate subject to
which a person who accepts the unrevised subject condition should be
committed. Aristotle demonstrates that this ultimate subject is incoherent because the inadequacy of the original criterion entails a strange outcome: an ultimate subject that is nothing at all. This is an impossible notion and a totally unacceptable object on which to ground predication. To
avoid this result the subject criterion must be clarified, and this Aristotle
does by insisting on separation and thisness.

The difficulty in understanding Aristotle's revision is the absence of a
general consensus about what he means by the crucial technical terms
"separation" and "thisness." Given the obscurity of these notions, whatever clarity they bring to subjecthood is not immediately apparent. I shall
return to these notions below, but first I shall defend my reading of Z.3,
in part by criticizing other widely accepted readings.

MATTER AS SUBJECT

In the central section of Z.3 Aristotle undertakes what scholars have metaphorically called a "striptease," an exercise designed to uncover an ultimate subject. Because of the inadequacy previously mentioned—an inadequacy that I have suggested concerns the subject criterion itself—it
turns out that matter is substance. Aristotle then says:

(A) For if this is not substance, it escapes us what else is; for when
the other things are stripped away, it does not appear that anything
remains; for the other things are affections ($\pi\acute{\alpha}\theta\eta$) and doings ($\pi o\iota\acute{\eta}$-
$\mu\alpha\tau\alpha$) and potentialities ($\delta\upsilon\nu\acute{\alpha}\mu\epsilon\iota\varsigma$) of bodies; and length, breadth,
and depth are certain quantities and not substances (for quantity is
not substance); but rather that first thing to which these belong is
substance. But when lengths, breadths, and depths are removed, we
see nothing remaining, unless there is something determined by
these, and so for those who consider the problem in this way, matter
must appear to be the only substance. (1029^a10–19)

(B) I mean by matter what in itself (καθ᾽ αὐτήν) is neither something (τί) nor so much (ποσόν) nor called anything else by which being is determined. For there is something of which each of these is predicated, and the being for it is different from that for each of the predicates (for the other things are predicated of substance, but this is predicated of the matter), so that the ultimate thing in itself (καθ᾽ αὐτό) is neither something nor so much nor anything else; nor indeed is it the negations [of these], for these too will belong to it accidentally (κατὰ συμβεβηκός). (1029ᵃ20–26)

(C) So it follows for those who employ these considerations that matter is substance. But it is impossible; for separation (τὸ χωρισ-τόν) and thisness (τὸ τόδε τι) seem to belong especially to substance. Therefore the form and the composite would seem to be more[10] substance than the matter is. (1029ᵃ26–30)

For convenience I have divided the text into three parts. In part (A) Aristotle undertakes the mental exercise of stripping off the qualities that characterize a body, and then the quantities. But having removed those properties that determine an object as extended, he reflects that nothing appears to be left—nothing, that is, unless there is something of which they are predicated. So, for those who consider the problem in this way, matter seems to be the only substance. In part (B) Aristotle clarifies what he means by "matter," and in part (C) he repeats that matter is substance for those who adopt the preceding considerations. But the conclusion is impossible because separation and thisness seem to be crucial features of substance, and so the form and the composite seem better candidates than matter to be substance. This broad outline should be fairly uncontroversial.[11]

Interpretations of Z.3

One reading of Z.3 takes Aristotle to present his doctrine of prime matter, the doctrine of an ultimate subject with no determinate properties in its own right. On this view Aristotle undertakes the analysis in part (A) to expose his own ultimate subject, an entity he then describes in part

---

[10] The μᾶλλον at 1029ᵃ29–30 could be translated "rather"; the claim would then be that the form and the composite rather than matter are substances. But since the next sentence (1029ᵃ30–33) still mentions matter as one of the three substances, matter has presumably not been wholly rejected; so "more" is preferable. This translation is adopted by Ross (1924), Tredennick (1933), and Furth (1985).

[11] Not all commentators would accept it: Schofield (1972) would reject the outline of part (A) because, on his view, Aristotle strips the subject to nothing in part (A) and presents his own concept of matter in part (B).

(B).[12] The entity uncovered is in itself neither something ($\tau \acute{\iota}$) nor so much ($\pi o\sigma \acute{o}\nu$), nor does it have any other categorial being; nor even do negative properties capture what the entity is in itself: all properties, both positive and negative, belong to it accidentally. Matter is the ultimate substratum that is nothing in its own right, a substratum called by the scholastics *materia prima*. In part (C) Aristotle objects that this entity is not substance, or at any rate not substance in the primary sense, because substance must be separate and a this, and prime matter, although it is the ultimate subject, fails to satisfy these two further tests.

But many scholars deny that prime matter is the special focus of Z.3, and they object for the following reasons. First, when Aristotle introduces the three candidates for subject—the matter, the form, and the composite—he offers bronze as an example of matter. Bronze, according to the scholastics, is *materia secunda*, matter that has been informed to some extent. Since bronze is the only example of matter that Aristotle explicitly mentions, the reader has reason to expect his argument to attack the substantiality of bronze and other ordinary stuffs like bronze. A second point supports the expectation. In part (A) Aristotle takes an object, strips away its affections and other accidents, and then its dimensions, thus apparently removing the object's qualities and quantities. If the object of the stripping is a typical physical object, such as a statue (and the initial illustration suggests that it is), then one anticipates the matter left over once the dimensions have been removed to be, not some ultimate matter, but the matter of the original object. If the object stripped is the statue, then the matter left over should be the bronze.

Aristotle does sometimes envisage a different sort of analysis that would yield an ultimate matter. In *Metaphysics* Θ.7, for example, he suggests that composites can be analyzed at lower and lower levels. In Θ.7 he starts with a box. A box is made out of wood, but wood itself is made out of earth. If earth in its turn is made out of something further, the analysis can be continued. If one reaches something finally that is not made out of anything else, this entity, he says, is prime matter. The entity that Aristotle calls "prime matter" is not what the tradition calls by that name, since the analysis ends with fire, not with a wholly indeterminate stuff. But the importance of Θ.7 is the proposed method—a method of analyzing a composite into its matter and form, known as hylomorphic

---

[12] For this view, see Owens 1963; cf. Robinson 1974, 183–87; and Loux 1979, esp. 10. Happ (1971, 662–67) offers a somewhat different interpretation, arguing that parts (A) and (B) present a two-stage strip, with part (A) removing the nonsubstantial properties and part (B) removing all definite properties, including substantial. Happ calls the ultimate matter of Z.3 "Hyle Prinzip," the principle of pure potentiality, which is more fundamental than prime matter. While prime matter is restricted to the sublunary sphere, Hyle Prinzip is the matter common to both the sublunary and superlunary realms.

analysis—not the specific items that Aristotle mentions at various levels. Elsewhere he suggests that water might be prime matter, if things are made out of water.[13] In these passages Aristotle does not commit himself on the question of what counts as ultimate matter, but he does provide a conceptual method by which to reach it.

But hylomorphic analysis is not the procedure used in *Metaphysics* Z.3. Aristotle reaches the matter immediately, as soon as the affections and dimensions have been detached. He says nothing about taking what is left, once the affections and dimensions have been removed, and stripping it further. Since the stripping in Z.3 differs from the one in Θ.7 and yields the matter directly, many interpreters reject the view that prime matter is the focus of Z.3 and argue instead that the chapter concerns Aristotle's concept of matter, which includes such ordinary examples as bronze.[14] Although prime matter too may fall under the concept, on this second view, Z.3 is concerned with prime matter only in the way in which it is concerned with any instance of matter. Interpreters take the purpose of the chapter to be more far-reaching, to exclude any instance of matter from being primary substance.

On this second reading of Z.3, Aristotle clarifies his concept of matter in part (B). Whatever counts as matter fails as such to have any categorial being, positive or negative, because all properties belong to it accidentally. Commentators insist that this is not to say that bronze *as bronze* is nothing in its own right; if bronze is regarded as bronze, it is treated as a composite, as something that can itself be subjected to hylomorphic analysis. The idea is that bronze viewed *as matter for a statue* is nothing in its own right: the being of matter as matter derives from the object whose matter it is; viewed in itself as matter, the matter has no determinate properties. The thesis is paradoxical.[15] The entity that counts as matter has (with the exception of prime matter) some determinate nature; but the same entity, regarded as matter, acquires its identity from the form of the object whose matter it is. Take away the form, and the entity is, not bronze, but nothing in its own right.

What is the concept of matter whose instances include stuffs like bronze and prime matter? In Z.3 Aristotle says little about what matter is, although he says a good deal about what it is not. Elsewhere, however, he does offer a description of matter that scholars find compatible with the negative account in Z.3. Aristotle often associates matter with potentiality. In *Metaphysics* Z.7, for example, he describes the matter of something

---

[13] *Met.* Δ.4, 1015ᵃ7–10.

[14] See, e.g., Schofield 1972, 100–101; Dancy 1978, esp. 392–408; Stahl 1981; and Frede and Patzig 1988, 2:46–47.

[15] The paradoxicality was called to my attention by Paul Coppock.

generated as its potentiality both to be and not to be,[16] and sometimes he describes matter as "potentially a this."[17] These statements suggest that the being of matter is parasitic on the being of what it potentially is. So, according to this proposal, one can think of bronze as a subject in two ways: first, the subject can be treated as bronze, but then it is regarded as a composite and not as matter; second, the subject can be treated as potentially a statue, and only then is the subject regarded as matter. In his characterization in part (B), Aristotle says that matter in itself lacks all positive and negative properties. Aristotle does not say but is taken to mean that matter is not *actually* something or so much or the negations of these but is *potentially* these things.[18] The account seems to square nicely with the later specification of matter as potential.

But such an account is not a natural reading of Z.3. Let me show why.

Potentialities

There is no indication whatever that the subject discussed in Z.3 retains its potentialities.[19] Indeed, Aristotle explicitly removes the potentialities (δυνάμεις) along with the other accidents in part (A) (1029ᵃ13). Since he explicitly removes the potentialities, it seems perverse to insist that, nonetheless, the subject described in part (B) retains them.

Still, the defense will argue that Aristotle removes only a particular set of potentialities. He mentions the potentialities together with the other accidents (affections and doings), and he removes these before he strips away the quantities—the length, breadth, and depth. So one might contend that there are other, more fundamental, potentialities that withstand the analysis. Yet he claims that the the ultimate thing "in itself (καθ᾿ αὑτό) is neither something nor so much nor anything else (ἄλλο οὐδέν); nor indeed is it the negations [of these], for these too will belong to it accidentally" (1029ᵃ24–26). Although the defense will urge that the potentialities escape the net of "anything else," it seems more likely that the phrase specifies all positive designations, including the potentialities. If the phrase means what it appears to say, the potentialities, too, belong to the subject accidentally, and therefore he removes them along with the other accidents in part (A). If Aristotle envisages the retention of certain potentialities, it is strange that he does not say so. Without sanction to the

---

[16] *Met.* Z.7, 1032ᵃ20–22; cf. Z.15, 1039ᵇ27–31; Θ.8, 1050ᵇ8–28; Λ.5, 1071ᵃ10–11; G.C. II.9, 335ᵃ32–33; and *De Cae.* I.12, 283ᵇ3–5. For further references, see Bonitz 1870, 785ᵃ46–56.

[17] *Met.* H.1, 1042ᵃ27–28; cf. *De An.* II.1, 412ᵃ6–11.

[18] See Schofield 1972, 100; Dancy 1978, 405–7; and Frede and Patzig 1988, 2:49–51.

[19] I thank Paul Coppock for valuable suggestions on this section.

contrary, we should assume that he means what he says—that the potentialities have been stripped away.

What does it mean for a property to belong to a subject "in itself" (καθ' αὑτό) or "accidentally" (κατὰ συμβεβηκός)? Aristotle spells out his theory of predication (which concerns the relations between entities rather than between words) in *Posterior Analytics* I.4 and *Metaphysics* Δ.18. He explains that an entity B belongs to an entity A καθ' αὑτό, in either of two cases.[20] First, a predicate B belongs to a subject A καθ' αὑτό if B, which is predicated of A, must be mentioned in the account of what A is. For example, animal belongs to man καθ' αὑτό because animal is predicated of man and must be mentioned in the account of what man is, since man is a certain sort of animal, a biped animal. Again, line belongs to triangle καθ' αὑτό because line is predicated of triangle and must be mentioned in the account of what triangle is. These cases conform to our ordinary notion of essential predication because the subject depends for what it is on the predicate. But Aristotle also describes a second case: a predicate B belongs to a subject A καθ' αὑτό if the subject A, of which B is predicated, must be mentioned in the account of what B is.

Aristotle's favorite example of the second case is snubness. Snubness belongs to the nose καθ' αὑτό because the nose, in virtue of its own receptivity to various shapes, is the primary recipient of snubness, and snubness cannot exist or be what it is without it. Snubness is concavity in a nose; concavity realized in a different subject would not be snubness but something else. Thus, part of the identity of snubness is determined by the definite subject in which it is realized. Examples of the second καθ' αὑτό relation are interesting because they do not obviously conform to the usual notion of essential predication, since the subject can be what it is without the predicate: noses need not be snub. It is rather that the predicate cannot be what it is without the subject. This second καθ' αὑτό relation will become increasingly important as we proceed, but for now it is enough to recognize that an accidental (κατὰ συμβεβηκός) relation between a predicate and a subject is simply a failure of both καθ' αὑτό relations: a predicate B belongs to a subject A accidentally (κατὰ συμβεβηκός) if B, which is predicated of A, does not turn up in the account of what A is (i.e., B does not belong to A καθ' αὑτό in the first way), and if A, the subject of which B is predicated, does not turn up in the account of what B is (i.e., B does not belong to A καθ' αὑτό in the second way). For example, white belongs to a man accidentally because white, although predicated of the man, is not defined as what it is with reference to man,

---

[20] See *Po. An.* I.4, 73ᵃ34–ᵇ5, cf. Barnes 1975, 113–15; and *Met.* Δ.18, 1022ᵃ24–36, cf. Kirwan 1971, 168–70. I am grateful to Alan Code and Sarah Broadie for advice concerning this distinction.

nor is the man, although the subject for white, defined as what he is with reference to white.

The matter described in Z.3 is not in itself (καθ᾽ αὑτό) any positive or negative sort of being. The being for matter, Aristotle insists, is different from that for each of the predicates (1029ᵃ22–23).[21] Whatever the matter is, it is accidentally (κατὰ συμβεβηκός) (1029ᵃ24–26). Given this characterization, none of the predicates ascribed to the matter is defined as what it is with reference to the matter, and the matter is not defined as what it is with reference to any of them.

But what is the being for matter if it is different from that for each of the predicates? Consider a subject that, however specified, is other than that specification. For example, suppose that the subject is designated as bronze. The being for the subject is other than bronze—the subject is something *else*. Suppose that the subject is designated as not-bronze; again the subject is other than that. It is not simply that in practice the subject cannot be specified; in principle it cannot be specified because, however one indicates it, it is other than that.[22] And what of potentialities? Suppose that the subject is specified as potentially bronze. Either the property of being potentially bronze belongs to the subject καθ᾽ αὑτό or it does not; and if the property belongs to the subject καθ᾽ αὑτό, then either the subject is defined with reference to that property or that property is defined with reference to it. But Aristotle claims that the being for the subject is different from that for each of the predicates, so the subject should be other than potentially bronze. The subject's potentialities, like all its other properties, belong to it accidentally; for this reason Aristotle removes the potentialities along with the other accidents at 1029ᵃ13.[23]

Although someone could still insist that Aristotle strips from the subject only the actual properties and that the potentialities, by withstanding the analysis, characterize the subject essentially, nothing in the text confirms this reading, and the explicit removal of the potentialities in part (A) is a strong indication against it. If I am right that even the potentialities belong to the subject accidentally, then the matter at issue in Z.3 is not what some people call Aristotle's ordinary concept of matter. Nor is Aristotle talking about prime matter, at least as prime matter is tradition-

[21] On the significance of this claim, see Maudlin 1988–1989. Maudlin's proposal, first suggested in a seminar, has substantially influenced my interpretation of *Met.* Z.3.

[22] I agree with Owens (1963, 85–87) that the subject under discussion is unspecifiable. Scholars who reject this view (e.g., Dancy 1978, 398; Stahl 1981, 178; cf. Cohen 1984, 176) seem to ignore Aristotle's claim that the being for matter is different from that for each of the predicates (*Met.* Z.3, 1029ᵃ22–23). He is interested in what the *subject* is whose features have all been removed.

[23] The members of the London Seminar (Burnyeat et al. 1979, 15) entertain the possibility that Aristotle strips even the potentialities for change, but they do not pursue the suggestion, assuming instead that only qualitative potentialities are removed.

ally conceived, because prime matter is supposed to be actually nothing and potentially everything or, at any rate, potentially the simplest bodies—earth, water, air, and fire. The subject that Aristotle treats in Z.3 is entirely bare, even of potentialities. This entity is not Aristotle's own concept of matter but a concept that he rejects.

The Target of Z.3

Scholars have sometimes urged that part (A) presents an argument based on assumptions that Aristotle does not himself hold, and I agree with this assessment.[24] Notice that he concludes part (A) with the claim that, "for those who consider the problem in this way (οὕτω σκοπουμέ-νοις), matter must appear to be the only substance" (1029ᵃ18-19). To be sure, the claim need not exclude Aristotle if he counts himself among those who consider the problem in the manner proposed; but his initial complaint about an inadequacy, the inadequacy that I associated with the subject condition itself, is reason to doubt that he does count himself among the defenders of the argument. On my view, part (A) discloses the sort of subject to which those who endorse the original subject criterion should be committed, and part (C) finds the outcome based on that conception impossible. There too Aristotle indicates that the argument depends on assumptions held by other people, for he says, "So it follows for those who employ these considerations (ἐκ τούτων θεωροῦσι) that matter is substance. But it is impossible" (1029ᵃ26–27).

Since there is reason to doubt that Aristotle counts himself among the supporters of the argument in (A), it is worth asking whose assumptions he does employ. Of course, the argument may not address any particular individual or group, since Aristotle mentions no one directly. Still, he says various things in various places that suggest Plato as a possible target, or if not Plato himself, at least a view of the sort that Aristotle takes Plato to hold.[25]

On one other occasion Aristotle envisages a stripping similar to the one that he offers in part (A) of Z.3.[26] In *Physics* iv.2 he attacks what he pre-

[24] See Charlton 1970, 136–38; Schofield 1972, 97–101; and Maudlin 1988–1989; cf. Frede and Patzig 1988, 2:44–45.
[25] Others have suggested Plato as a target; see Charlton 1983, 204–5; and Maudlin 1988–1989.
[26] Commentators sometimes point to *Met.* B.5, 1001ᵇ26–1002ᵃ14, for the Platonic assumptions consistent with Z.3; see Charlton 1970, 138; 1983, 204; Dancy 1978, 395 and n. 58; and Frede and Patzig 1988, 2:44–45. In B.5 the Platonist is taken to insist that the quantitative dimensions of a body have a better claim to be substance than does the body they quantify. This passage does not seem relevant to Z.3. Aristotle thinks that Plato has two incompatible accounts about what counts as substance in the realm of becoming: some claims in the *Timaeus* indicate that the surfaces of bodies are most real, but other claims

sumes to be Plato's identification of matter and place. Place, on Aristotle's view, is to be identified with neither matter nor form. He says:

> So, for those who consider the problem in this way [i.e., as described just earlier], place is the form of each thing; but insofar as place seems to be the extension of a magnitude, it is matter; for this [extension] is different from the magnitude, and this [extension] is what is surrounded and determined by form, as by a plane and a limit; and matter, that is, the indefinite, is such [i.e., what is surrounded and determined by form]. For when the limit (τὸ πέρας) and the affections (τὰ πάθη) of a sphere are stripped away, nothing is left but the matter. That is why, too, Plato says in the *Timaeus* that matter and space are the same. For that which participates (τὸ μεταληπτικόν) and space are [on Plato's view] one and the same. (209ᵇ5–13)

In *Physics* IV.2 Aristotle considers two sorts of arguments. For those who consider place in one way, place turns out to be the form of a body; but for those who consider place in another way, the place of a body seems to be its matter. Aristotle accepts neither conclusion because neither form nor matter is separate from the thing of which it is the matter or form, but the place can be, since it is a sort of containing vessel that different bodies can occupy (209ᵇ21–32). But Aristotle's doctrine of place is not my topic. In the passage just quoted, Aristotle adopts what he regards as Platonic assumptions and concludes that place is matter. Thus the analysis envisaged is one that he takes Plato to endorse: strip off the affections of a sphere and the limits that determine its extension, and nothing is left, he says, except the matter. The entity that survives the stripping is the subject for properties (τὸ μεταληπτικόν), and according to Aristotle, Plato identifies this subject as matter and space.[27]

In *Metaphysics* Z.3 Aristotle performs a similar analysis by removing first the affections (πάθη) and other qualities of a statue and then its quantitative dimensions. *Physics* IV.2 indicates that Aristotle takes Plato to approve this analysis. And the conclusion of the stripping in Z.3, as in *Physics* IV.2, is that nothing is left except the matter. If Plato is the target in Z.3, then Aristotle focuses on Plato's receptacle, not as place or space,

---

indicate that the receptacle is most real. In *G.C.* II.1, 329ᵃ13–24, Aristotle objects to the incompatibility of the two stories. Regarding both as mistaken, he attacks one view in B.5 and the other in Z.3. *Phys.* IV.2, which concerns the receptacle, thus has greater relevance than B.5 for the argument in Z.3, since B.5 concerns the other view.

[27] Aristotle presumably associates Plato's receptacle with matter because in the *Timaeus* Plato attempts to clarify it by comparing it to gold. Aristotle may in fact have misunderstood Plato's view; for a different interpretation of Plato's actual theory in the *Timaeus*, see Gill 1987.

but as τὸ μεταληπτικόν, a subject receptive of properties; and Aristotle has serious objections to this conception.

In a revealing text in *On Generation and Corruption* II.1, Aristotle treats Plato's receptacle as matter and as a subject (ὑποκείμενον) prior to physical bodies. His chief objection seems to concern Plato's treatment of the receptacle as the subject for accidents. He says:

> The account given in the *Timaeus* lacks precision. For [Plato] has not clearly stated whether the "omnirecipient" (τὸ πανδεχές) is separate from the elements, nor does he make any use of it. He says that it is a certain subject (ὑποκείμενον) prior to the so-called elements, as gold [is a subject prior to] works of gold (yet even this is not well said if said in this way: of things for which there is alteration, it is so, but of things for which there is generation and destruction, one cannot call something *that* from which it has come to be—yet he says that by far the truest thing is to say that each thing is "gold"). (329ª13–21)

In the *Timaeus* Plato compares the receptacle to gold and physical phenomena to shapes in gold.[28] Plato suggests that, if someone molded all shapes out of gold and never stopped changing each shape into all the rest, the safest answer to give, if someone points to any one of them and asks "What is it?" is "gold." This is the point that Aristotle finds objectionable. Although this answer is fine for contexts of alteration, it is inappropriate for contexts of generation.

Why is the answer inappropriate for contexts of generation? According to Aristotle, in cases of alteration, or change of quality, the subject of the change is a primary substance of the sort envisaged in the *Categories*, for instance, a particular man; and the contraries replaced are qualities, such as musicality and unmusicality. Thus, if someone points to the musical thing that results from the change and asks "What is it?" the right answer is "man," not "musical," because "man" identifies what the object is (a certain substance), and "musical" merely specifies how the thing is qualified. Now consider generation. In this case a substance is the product of the change and not what persists through it. If a sculptor makes a statue out of gold and someone points to the product and asks "What is it?" the correct answer in Aristotle's view is "statue," not "gold," because "statue" identifies what the object is (a certain substance), and "gold" merely specifies the material out of which it is made. In fact, in several passages Aristotle indicates that people do not call such products "gold" at all, but "golden."[29]

---

[28] *Tim.* 50a5–b6.
[29] See *Met.* Z.7, 1033ª5–23; Θ.7, 1049ª18–b2; and *Phys.* VII.3, 245b9–246ª4.

This is not merely an objection about linguistic usage. The answer one gives to the "What is it?" question reflects a decision about what counts as substance. As Aristotle understands Plato's argument, the claim made in the gold analogy indicates Plato's decision about the status of the receptacle. Inasmuch as physical objects stand to the receptacle as the rapidly changing shapes stand to the gold, Plato's argument suggests that, if someone points to a physical object and asks "What is it?" the safest answer is "the receptacle." "The receptacle" identifies what the object is. If this is Plato's thesis, then the only proper answer to the "What is it?" question, asked of any physical object at all, is "the receptacle." The receptacle is the first subject: it is that of which other things are predicated but is not itself predicated of anything else. Strip off its properties, and the receptacle is all that is left. Plato's receptacle thus seems a likely target of Aristotle's discussion in Z.3. Indeed, he seems to have prepared for precisely this target when, in characterizing Plato's account of substance in Z.2, he adds to the Forms and the mathematicals "the substance of perceptible bodies" as a "third" (1028^{b}20–21).

Part (B) of the passage in Z.3, the part in which Aristotle states what he means by matter, clarifies the argument in part (A). I cannot agree with those who take part (A) to be directed against other people but part (B) to express Aristotle's own position.[30] Remember that part (C) begins by repeating that it follows "for those who employ these considerations" that matter is substance and that Aristotle finds the conclusion impossible. "These considerations" must surely refer to the considerations about matter just spelled out in part (B), and they probably include the considerations raised in part (A) as well. One need not suppose that, since Aristotle says, "I mean by matter . . . ," he offers his own definition of matter. He frequently uses the phrase λέγω δέ x in the sense "Here I mean by x,"[31] and when he uses the phrase in this way, he does not offer a definition but spells out how the concept is limited for the purpose at hand.[32] One need only compare Aristotle's specification of matter earlier in the chapter ("By matter, I mean, for example, the bronze" [1029^{a}3–4]) with that given in part (B) to recognize that, when he says "I mean by x," he can mean different things by x in different places. If in part (B) Aristotle specifies the notion of matter for the purpose at hand, then he specifies what matter is for those who accept the stripping analysis just preceding. And if the preceding argument states what Aristotle regards as Plato's

[30] Schofield 1972; and Frede and Patzig 1988, 2:42–51.

[31] See Balme 1987b, 305. Although Balme's defense concerns Aristotle's claims about form, the same point should hold for his claims about matter. Charlton (1970, 137) takes the phrase at 1029^{a}20 as I do. For an objection to such a reading of part (B), see Frede and Patzig 1988, 2:47.

[32] Balme 1987b, 305.

position, then the characterization of matter that he gives in part (B) should apply to the receptacle or to any ultimate subject that is entirely bare. The receptacle, as Aristotle conceives it, is something that is nothing in its own right; it is the ultimate subject to which all properties, whether positive or negative, belong accidentally; this alone is what the Platonist would have to say is the proper answer to the "What is it?" question asked of physical objects. So it follows for those who employ the considerations spelled out in (A) and (B) that matter alone is substance. And this conclusion Aristotle finds impossible.

The argument against the conclusion is contained in part (B), a passage that makes two major claims. First, matter in itself is neither something nor so much nor called anything else by which being is defined; second, the being for matter ($\tilde{\omega}$ τὸ εἶναι) is different from that for each of the predicates. What is the being for matter if it is different from all ways of being? This is the critical question. If matter *is* something, there must be something for it to be; but if the being for matter is different from all ways of being, there is no being for it to be: matter is something that is nothing. This concept of matter is self-contradictory. So there can be no subject that has no being of its own. Aristotle does not strip off layers of metaphorical clothes to expose the metaphorical dancer, for the dancer is something in his own right as distinct from his clothes. Instead, Aristotle peels off layers of a metaphorical onion to reveal nothing at all at the core. He has not clarified his own notion of matter by demonstrating its absurdity. On the contrary, he has shown that, given the assumed adequacy of the original subject criterion, the result is incoherence: a something that is in itself nothing. And this, as he says, is impossible.

To avoid the unacceptable outcome of the argument, certain constraints must be placed on the subject criterion, and Aristotle states these constraints in part (C): a legitimate subject must be separate and τόδε τι. My proposal that separation and thisness are refinements on the subject criterion gains plausibility if one looks ahead to *Metaphysics* H.1, where Aristotle explicitly returns to the subject criterion and again lists three ways to be substance as subject. Again he mentions the matter, the form, and the composite, but this time he explains the subjecthood of each of the three in terms of separation and thisness. "The subject is substance, in one way the matter (by matter I mean that which, though not a this [τόδε τι] in actuality, is a this [τόδε τι] in potentiality); and in another way the formula and the form, which being a this (τόδε τι) is separate in account (τῷ λόγῳ χωριστόν); and the third is that from these, of which alone there is generation and destruction, which is also simply separate (χωριστὸν ἁπλῶς)" (1042ᵃ26–31). All three sorts of subject satisfy the separation and thisness conditions in some way or other. Even matter is claimed to be potentially, if not actually, a this. *Metaphysics* H.1 relies on the conclusion of Z.3, and the task of Z.3 is to sharpen the notion of subjecthood.

SUBJECTHOOD

To understand how Aristotle clarifies the subject criterion, it is important to determine what he means by "separation" and "thisness." I shall argue that separation and thisness each have two proper interpretations, of which one is proper to forms, the other to concrete composites. So both forms and particular composites should succeed as substances according to the revised subject criterion, but they will succeed in different ways because they are separate and τόδε τι in different ways. I begin the analysis with τόδε τι, thisness.

Thisness

The expression τόδε τι consists of the demonstrative pronoun τόδε and indefinite pronoun τι. There are two general ways to regard the morphology of the expression.[33] On one interpretation τόδε τι is modeled on such phrases as ἄνθρωπός τις ("a certain man"), with the τόδε corresponding to ἄνθρωπος, the τι to τις. On the other interpretation τόδε is demonstrative, and τι indicates what the subject is. Although scholars sometimes take the phrase itself to mean "particular," this meaning is not required by either interpretation of the morphology.[34] Since the expression that indicates the kind, whichever of the two it is, can specify a kind at various levels of generality, the other expression can indicate either a particular that falls under the kind or a division of that wider kind. Thus "a certain animal" and "this animal" can pick out a specific type of animal as well as a particular token. Hence the meaning of τόδε τι does not turn on the assumed morphology. I will understand the phrase literally to mean "this something," taking the τόδε as demonstrative and the τι as indicating a kind. I shall argue that the phrase sometimes specifies a particular falling under a kind and sometimes a division of a wider kind. Consider some contexts in which the phrase appears.

Aristotle frequently mentions particulars as examples of thises. In the *Categories* he claims that a primary substance, such as a particular man, is τόδε τι, whereas its species and genus are not (5, 3ᵇ10–18). In the *Meta-*

[33] On this topic, see Frede and Patzig 1988, 2:15. An earlier discussion occurs in Smith 1921, 19.
[34] This point is stressed by Lear (1987, 151) in his discussion of one interpretation.

physics he sometimes calls concrete composites τόδε τι.[35] For example, in *Metaphysics* Θ.7 he identifies both a definite matter and a composite as τόδε τι, saying of wood that "this is potentially a box, and this is [the] matter of a box—[wood] in general of [box] in general, and *this* wood (τοδὶ τὸ ξύλον) of *this* [box] (τουδί)" (1049ᵃ23–24). The use of the strengthened demonstrative τοδί instead of the weaker τόδε strongly suggests that he is speaking of a particular instance of wood and a particular box.[36] This wood present before us is the matter out of which a particular box will be made; this wood (now present before us) and this box (which will exist if all goes as planned) are presumably tokens of types.

Furthermore, in a much-discussed passage at the end of *Metaphysics* M.10, he uses τόδε τι apparently for particulars belonging to categories other than substance. In this passage both actual knowledge—the activity of theorizing in which a person possessed of knowledge sometimes engages—and the object actively thought on that occasion are called τόδε τι. For example, the grammarian actively contemplates this A: both the grammarian's episodic act and the object actively thought are τόδε τι (1087ᵃ15–21). And the object actively thought, namely this A, is an A (τόδε τὸ ἄλφα ἄλφα) (1087ᵃ20–21). This A, which the grammarian actively contemplates on a given occasion, belongs to a determinate type (because this A is an A, and A is a fully determinate letter), but it is also an instance of that determinate type: this A is presumably a token of A.[37]

In these passages, then, Aristotle uses τόδε τι to indicate a particular instance falling under a kind. Elsewhere, however, the function of τόδε in the phrase τόδε τι seems better interpreted as specifying a definite division of some wider kind indicated by τι. Aristotle often speaks of substantial forms as τόδε τι, and although these designations are sometimes regarded as evidence of his commitment to particular forms[38]—forms proper to a single composite alone—it is doubtful whether τόδε τι, when applied to forms, has this implication. Many passages indicate that forms can be shared by a number of individuals, and sometimes the shared form is evidently the form of the species. In fact, one important text claims both that the form is shared and that it is undivided (ἄτομον).[39] At the

[35] Although some instances of τόδε τι are ambiguous between the composite and the form (e.g., Z.1, 1028ᵃ12; Z.12, 1037ᵇ27), the following instances fairly clearly refer to the composite: Z.8, 1033ᵃ31; 1033ᵇ19–26; Z.11, 1037ᵃ1–2; and Z.13, 1038ᵇ5–6.

[36] As Cooper (1975, 28–29) points out, however, even τοδί sometimes specifies, not a particular, but a specific type (see, e.g., *Met.* Z.7, 1032ᵇ6–9; 1032ᵇ18–21); an alternative interpretation thus cannot be excluded.

[37] On this point I agree with A. C. Lloyd (1981, 24); cf. Annas 1976, 190–91. For a different view, see Lear 1987, 171–72.

[38] See, e.g., Sellars [1957] 1967 (for reservations, Albritton 1957); A. C. Lloyd, 1981, 38–40; and Whiting, forthcoming.

[39] This translation of ἄτομον, instead of the more usual "indivisible," was suggested to me by James Lennox (cf. Lennox 1985, 86–87), who has convinced me more generally that

end of *Metaphysics* Z.8 Aristotle says that a generated composite consisting of such and such form in these fleshes and bones is Callias or Socrates, and that Callias and Socrates differ because of their matter, since their matter is different, but are the same in form because the form is undivided (1034ᵃ5–8). If the undivided form that Socrates and Callias share is τόδε τι, then the form merits the title not on grounds of its particularity but on grounds of its determinateness; and in this case the determinateness attaches to the form of the species, not to an individual form proper to each man.

Elsewhere Aristotle evidently envisages forms below the species level. Recent work on his embryology in *Generation of Animals* convincingly shows that, to account for the transmission of parental characteristics in reproduction, he differentiates the species form into individual forms.[40] Even so, this step does not commit him to *particular* forms, that is, to forms that cannot be replicated.[41] Indeed, Aristotle's theory of inheritance suggests that, if reproduction were absolutely successful, the male parent would produce his exact duplicate, an offspring displaying the same individual form. Those who attribute particular forms to Aristotle must explain why he claims that the object of a definition is a form and a universal.[42] How can forms be particular and yet also be the proper objects of definition? In *Metaphysics* Z.15 Aristotle's answer seems clear: particulars cannot be defined as particular. He mentions the sun, which is one of a kind. One can try to define the sun as particular, but if another object should appear that has all the properties of the sun, the object will be a sun. So the account is general, even if only one object satisfies the account (1040ᵃ33–ᵇ1). Thus a form, however specific—indeed even if so specific that one object alone displays it—is not particular, because it is repeatable, even if not repeated.

Some writers have argued that, in calling a form τόδε τι, Aristotle has in mind a particular form whose differentiation from others of the same type is determined by the matter in which it is realized. Thus, when he claims in *Metaphysics* Λ.5 that the matter and form and moving cause of two individuals are different (1071ᵃ27–29), the claim has been taken to mean that the two forms—which are intrinsically the same—differ from one another because they belong to distinct individuals (the distinctness of the individuals having been determined by the constituent matter).[43] This suggestion seems rather like saying that Socrates and Callias inhabit

---

Aristotle can regard an entity as determinate in one context that he divides further in another.

[40] See *G.A.* IV.3; Balme [1980] 1987; and Cooper 1988.

[41] On the distinction between individuals and particulars, see Code 1986, 412–14 and n. 5.

[42] *Met.* Z.10, 1035ᵇ33–1036ᵃ1; Z.11, 1036ᵃ28–29.

[43] See Lesher 1971, 174–75; and Hartman 1977, 63–64.

different cities because Socrates' city is his and Callias' city is his.[44] It is surely more likely that in *Metaphysics* Λ Aristotle contemplates the differentiation of forms below the species level. Forms are τόδε τι because they are determinate kinds, but the degree of determinateness may be differently envisaged in different contexts.[45]

I have considered two distinct, though equally legitimate, uses to which Aristotle puts the expression τόδε τι—one to indicate a particular of some kind, the other to indicate a determinate kind. He should not be confined to one privileged use. This would not be the only occasion that he applies the same phrase both to a particular and to a fully determinate sort; the same ambiguity occurs in his use of τὸ καθ' ἕκαστον ("particular").[46] In any case, even if one grants that τόδε τι has two distinct applications, there is still an important connection between them: Aristotle regularly contrasts what is τόδε τι with what is strictly universal or generic—that is, predicated in common of a number of things that are specifically different.[47] And, in fact, there are two relevant contrasts with the universal to be drawn, a contrast between token and type and a contrast between determinate and determinable. So it not surprising that τόδε τι does double service and specifies the definite item in either context.

One interpretation of τόδε τι, which takes the τόδε to indicate a definite division of a wider kind specified by τι, is appropriate for a form and picks out a determinate kind. The other interpretation, which takes the τόδε to indicate an instance falling under a kind specified by τι, is appropriate for a particular composite.

Separation

The adverb χωρίς ("separately") is sometimes used spatially: two entities exist separately if they occupy different places, together if they occupy one place.[48] But the cognate adjective χωριστός, a term that Aris-

---

[44] I owe this analogy to Paul Coppock.

[45] On this topic, see Pellegrin 1982 (summarized in Pellegrin 1987); Balme 1987a, 71–73; Lennox 1985, 79–82; 1987a; 1987b; and Gotthelf 1985.

[46] See Cooper 1975, 28–29.

[47] *De Int.* 7, 17ª38–ᵇ1, contrasts universals, like man, with particulars, like Callias, and specifies a universal as "what is naturally predicated of a number of things." It seems necessary to distinguish a strict notion of universal, proper to genera, with a wider notion that includes fully determinate kinds, which, though repeatable and definable, are individual and τόδε τι. A substantial form is individual because it is fully determinate but universal because it is repeatable and definable. For a different interpretation of the two sorts of universals, see Modrak 1979. Texts contrasting τόδε τι and universal include *Cat.* 5, 3ᵇ10–18; *Met.* B.6, 1003ª8–12; Z.8, 1033ᵇ19–26; Z.13, 1038ᵇ34–1039ª2; and M.10, 1087ª15–25. I discuss below a distinction in Θ.7, 1049ª18–ᵇ2, which is important for Aristotle's theory of matter (see pp. 149–61).

[48] E.g., *Phys.* v.3, 226ᵇ21–23; and *Met.* K.12, 1068ᵇ26–27.

totle may have introduced himself,[49] has two main technical uses in the central books of the *Metaphysics*: to denote separation in being or account, and to denote simple separation or separation in existence. A recent computer survey of the uses of χωριστός in Aristotle indicates that the word should regularly be translated "separate."[50] (Translators have always recognized "separate" as the correct translation of χωριστός in many contexts, but they have consistently preferred "separable" in some.) I will translate χωριστός as "separate" throughout. The question is, How are entities separate in account or being, and how are entities separate in existence?

In the passage cited earlier from *Metaphysics* H.1, Aristotle states that form is separate in account (τῷ λόγῳ) and that the composite is simply separate (χωριστὸν ἁπλῶς) (1042ᵃ28–31). He adds that some forms are simply separate and some are not (1042ᵃ31). Most Aristotelian forms cannot exist separately from matter, although they can be defined without reference to it; thus, for example, the human soul can exist only if it is enmattered, but it can be defined without mentioning the sort of matter in which it is realized.[51] But Aristotle's theory also includes a special group of forms that can exist without matter, of which the Prime Mover is an instance, and these forms are separate not only in account but also in existence. He suggests that, in respect of their separate existence, such immaterial forms resemble ordinary material composites. I shall treat the two notions of separation in turn, beginning with separation in account or being.

In *Metaphysics* Z.5 Aristotle indicates that an entity B is not separate in account (being) from an entity A if A is the subject of B and if the name (or account) of A must be mentioned in the account of what B is (1030ᵇ23–25). In general, failure of separation occurs if an item depends on a distinct subject for its existence and cannot itself be clarified without reference to that subject. There is failure of separation if a predicate belongs to a subject καθ᾽ αὑτό in the second way that I considered earlier. Thus, snubness is not separate in account from the nose; male and female are not separate in account from animal; and whiteness is not separate in account from surface. In each of these cases, there is a distinct subject with-

---

[49] Donald Morrison (1985a, 92) offers this hypothesis on the basis of a computer survey of Greek authors prior to and contemporaneous with Aristotle. He finds no evidence of the adjective χωριστός prior to Aristotle.

[50] See Morrison 1985a.

[51] Aristotle's claim about forms in H.1 might seem problematic because *De An.* II.1 gives a series of definitions of soul, all of which mention the matter in which the soul is realized (see, e.g., Leszl 1970, 502–7, 513–16). But in fact the claim in H.1 is based on an argument in Z.10 and 11 showing that the account of the form need not refer to matter. I consider this topic in chapter 4 below, pp. 131–33.

out which the property cannot exist and that must be mentioned in the account of what the property is. In Z.1 Aristotle suggests that all entities housed in nonsubstance categories depend for their being on substances (1028ᵃ20–29); apparently there is always something in the category of substance on which the existence of the property depends and with reference to which it is defined—health with reference to living thing, snubness with reference to nose, and so forth.[52]

Forms, Aristotle says in H.1, are separate in account. So forms should be definable without reference to a distinct subject in which the form is realized. Although the account of a form will need to mention various items (which in Z.10 and 11 Aristotle calls parts of the form), such parts belong to the form καθ' αὑτό in its first sense, as distinguished earlier. Thus man is defined with reference to animal, triangle with reference to lines, a syllable with reference to letters.[53] Forms are separate in account because there is no distinct subject to which the form itself belongs that must be mentioned in its defining account. Thus, unlike snubness, whose account specifies one thing belonging to another, either the account of the form does not display this composite structure, or if it does, the two items mentioned in its account are not distinct from each other.[54] To recall the scheme mentioned in the Introduction, snubness is defined as concavity in the nose—a c defined as a b in an a, where a, b, and c are all distinct. By contrast, a form c, which is separate in account, is defined either as a b (where c and b have the same nature) or as a b in an a, where all three items a, b, and c share a single nature. Separation in account apparently concerns an entity's conceptual independence from other more basic entities with reference to which it is defined.

The other notion of separation is simple separation or separation in existence. The past few years have witnessed a lively debate on this topic,[55] but I need not enter into that controversy. Chapter 7 will argue that Aristotle refines his notion of simple separation in such a way that only a select group of entities succeeds as simply separate, and therefore as ontologically primary. The unrefined notion of simple separation, however, seems fairly straightforward.

In the *Physics* Aristotle states that entities predicated of a subject are not separate: "For none of the other things [e.g., quality or quantity] is separate except substance; for all of them are predicated of the substance as a

---

[52] On this topic, see Frede [1978] 1987.

[53] See *Met.* Z.10, 1034ᵇ25–26; 1035ᵃ10; Z.11, 1036ᵇ7–20; and Z.12 and H.6 on the definition of man as "biped animal"; cf. Δ.25, 1023ᵇ22–24; and *Po. An.* 1.4, 73ᵃ34–37.

[54] See *Met.* Z.11, 1037ᵃ33–ᵇ4. Aristotle's treatment of forms will be discussed in more detail in chapter 4.

[55] See Fine 1984, 1985; Morrison 1985a, 1985b, 1985c. Cf. the earlier treatment in Mabbott 1926.

subject" (1.2, 185ᵃ31–32). This statement suggests that to be simply separate an entity must be such that it is not predicated of a subject; thus the
proposal recalls the doctrine of the *Categories*. In that work Aristotle insists that everything other than primary substances depends for its existence on a primary substance (5, 2ᵇ3–6). If the quality whiteness exists, it
exists because there is a particular substance, such as a horse, that is white;
if the species man exists, it exists because there is a particular substance,
an individual man, that is man. A passage in *Metaphysics* Z.1 seems to
express the view of the *Categories*, but Aristotle now states the thesis in
terms of separation: "For none of the other predicated things is separate,
but only this [substance]" (1028ᵃ33–34).[56]

Simple separation belongs to those entities that ground the existence of
other things. The things that fail to be simply separate depend for their
existence on some underlying subject that provides their support. In the
Categories that grounding role is played by the primary substances, by
entities like a particular man and a particular horse. In *Metaphysics* Z Aristotle still claims that substance grounds the existence of other things,
and H.1 suggests that he still believes that the particulars of the *Categories*,
now viewed as composites, are the entities that succeed as simply separate. Immanent forms are not separate in this way because, although they
do not depend on anything else for what they are, they do depend for
their existence on an underlying subject.

If simple separation concerns the grounding role that an entity plays,
someone might ask why the matter described in Z.3 is not simply separate, since it is treated as the ultimate subject to which all properties belong accidentally; Aristotle even says that substance is predicated of it
(1029ᵃ23–24).[57] This subject might seem to inherit the role played in the
Categories by the primary substances, the particular man and the particular horse, because, like them, it is the subject on which things that are
predicated depend. But there is an important difference between the primary substances of the *Categories* and this contemplated subject. While
they possess some definite identity, this subject has none; in fact, it fails
to be a subject at all for that very reason. The matter described in Z.3 is
neither separate nor τόδε τι, and it fails on both counts because there is
nothing that it is in its own right (καθ' αὑτό). Since there is nothing that

---

[56] Although the statement seems to express the same view as the *Categories*, it remains
unclear how the statement relates to the concept it seems meant to explain in Z.1, namely,
priority in time. On this topic, see Frede and Patzig 1988, 2:19–20.

[57] This claim has been much discussed, and the crux has been whether the item predicated
of the matter is the form or the composite. See Owens 1963, 82–85; Leszl 1970, 503; Happ
1971, 662–67; Kung 1978, 155; Brunschwig 1979, 132; Loux 1979, 10–11. Since the claim
occurs in the midst of an argument that, on my view, is directed against an opponent, I have
no stake in this debate.

it is in its own right, it is nothing at all. Obviously, an object must exist if there is to be any question of separate existence.

Metaphysics Z.3 gives no clue to the interpretation of separation and thisness, and Aristotle leaves the concepts vague for a reason. Had he decided on a particular interpretation, he would also have had to decide in favor of either the form or the composite. But he does not choose one over the other. Instead he suggests that, in virtue of their separation and thisness, both the form and the composite have better credentials than matter to be substance as subjects. I have argued that each notion has two chief interpretations, one appropriate to the form, the other to the individual composite. If I am right, the form and the composite succeed as subjects in different ways. The form satisfies the revised subject condition because it is a determinate kind (i.e., it is τόδε τι) and because it can be defined without reference to a distinct subject (i.e., it is separate in account). The concrete composite satisfies the revised subject condition because it is a particular of some kind (i.e., it is τόδε τι) and because it grounds the existence of other things but does not itself depend in this way on anything else (i.e., it is simply separate).

But there is a snag in the whole scheme: what is the status of Aristotle's own concept of matter, which he still refers to as substance at the end of Z.3?

THE PROBLEM OF MATTER

The end of Z.3 still lists matter as one of the three sorts of substance (1029ᵃ30–33), and Aristotle sets it aside, together with the composite, to investigate that very perplexing notion, form. Matter, he says, "is in a sense clear" (1029ᵃ32). Now, the matter that is in a sense clear is plainly not the matter that he has just shown to be utterly obscure.[58] The matter to which he refers is presumably matter of the sort that he illustrated at the outset, matter like bronze. People grasp, or think they grasp, what matter like bronze is. But Aristotle expresses his own reservations by saying that matter is only in a sense (πως) clear. And his qualms go deeper than this statement suggests: he is less decisive in awarding priority to the form and the composite than one might expect. Notice how he hedges his claim: "Therefore the form and the composite would seem (δόξειεν ἄν) to be more substance than the matter is" (1029ᵃ29–30). Why the potential optative? Why does Aristotle hedge?

Perhaps Aristotle recognizes the exclusion of an unspecifiable subject as a mixed blessing because, with that specter eliminated, the alternative is a matter with some definite identity as matter. But if matter, as matter,

[58] This point was called to my attention by G.E.R. Lloyd.

can have its own proper identity, this conception endangers the entire scheme because, if bronze as bronze is a proper example of matter, the particular bronze out of which a statue is made appears to satisfy the revised subject condition and, indeed, to do so at the expense of both the form and the composite. The bronze seems to be τόδε τι in the way that a statue is τόδε τι, since it is a particular of some kind. Furthermore, the bronze seems to be simply separate, since it can exist apart from a statue and possess its own properties.

If matter is a proper subject in virtue of its own nature, then the form of a composite fails to be a proper subject. Although the form is τόδε τι and separate in account, a subject is supposed to be that of which other things are predicated but which is not itself predicated of anything else. But the form is predicated of the matter, and the matter is distinct from it. The form of a statue depends upon bronze (or some similar stuff) for its existence, while the bronze has no comparable need for the form of the statue; the bronze can exist on its own before it acquires the form and can continue in existence after the form has been removed. To be sure, the matter depends for its identity and existence on its own form (the form in virtue of which the bronze is bronze), but the bronze does seem to enjoy an independence from the form of a statue; that form, and indeed any shape, belongs to it accidentally. Since the form is predicated of the matter, the matter apparently undermines the claim of the form to be a substance as subject.

The matter deprives the composite of vertical unity. For if the composite consists of a determinate form that belongs to a distinct and determinate matter, then the nature of the composite is twofold: part of its nature is determined by the form, and part by the matter in which the form is realized. Thus, the statue consists of two natures—the shape that accounts for its being a statue, and the bronze that serves as subject for the shape.

The problems posed by matter at the level of the statue repeat themselves at lower levels. The bronze itself can be subjected to hylomorphic analysis—bronze, which serves as matter for a higher composite, is itself a composite of a simpler matter and form. Bronze is an alloy of copper and tin (its matter), which have been combined in some definite ratio (its form). Do these simpler materials have a better claim to be subjects than the form of the bronze, and do they deprive the composite bronze of vertical unity? What lies at the bottom of Aristotle's system? What does hylomorphic analysis yield when applied to the copper and then to the matter of copper? Z.3 teaches one main lesson. If one strips off layers of forms, each belonging accidentally to the matter below, the analysis does not finally yield something that is in itself nothing. Either the stripping continues indefinitely, uncovering at each stage a subject that is something in its own right but composed of an intrinsic form that belongs accidentally to the matter below, or the stripping finally exposes a subject that, although something in its own right, is not composed of a form realized in a distinct matter—in other words, a subject that is not a composite.

Aristotle adopts the second alternative. There is an ultimate matter, and the matter is something in its own right. So the pressing question is the credentials this entity has for being a subject. Does hylomorphic analysis finally disclose a subject that has less claim to be separate and a this than the composite it constitutes? And if so, is the priority of the composite and its form preserved all the way up? As chapter 2 will indicate, the possibility that prime matter is the ultimate subject has not yet been ruled out. Or does hylomorphic analysis yield an ultimate subject with strong credentials for subjecthood? And is this subject a source of difficulty for Aristotle's preferred candidates?

Chapter 2 will argue that the four elements—earth, water, air, and fire—are the ultimate subjects in Aristotle's system of the sublunary world. The elements are simple bodies, which are not composites, but they are nonetheless genuine subjects. This conception of ultimate matter, together with a view about material persistence that Aristotle adopts in *Metaphysics* Z, has troubling consequences for the unity of material composites and calls into question the subjecthood and even the unity of substantial form. These puzzles will be addressed in chapter 4—but first to the roots of his system: the four elements.

CHAPTER TWO

THE ELEMENTS

How much has the analysis of *Metaphysics* Z.3 established about Aristotle's concept of matter? If that analysis is correct, it establishes one main point: Aristotle rules out a subject that is nothing in its own right (καθ' αὑτό). His argument shows that, for something to be a subject at all, it must be specifiable as something in itself. So a legitimate subject must have certain essential properties that are mentioned in its defining account, because no subject can be the bearer of accidental properties alone. On turning to the bottom of Aristotle's physical system, then, and asking what sort of ultimate matter there is, one can be sure that Aristotle's ultimate matter, if it counts as a subject, will have some essential features.

But upon reflection, the demand that any subject, including an ultimate subject, have certain essential properties is not telling for the debate about Aristotle's doctrine of ultimate matter. Some commentators who locate an account of prime matter in Z.3 have claimed that Aristotle's ultimate matter is unspecifiable, but they often overstate their own view; for, in construing the argument of Z.3 in which Aristotle strips the subject of its properties, they assume that he leaves the potentialities intact.[1] Therefore, they do not regard Aristotle's ultimate matter as entirely bare after all. The matter is bare in the sense that no actual categorial properties belong to it in its own right, since all such determinate properties belong to it accidentally; nonetheless, the matter is essentially characterized by its potential to possess those actual determinate features. So the subject has some being in its own right, because it is in itself potentially something, so much, and so on.

I argued in chapter 1 that Aristotle explicitly removes the potentialities from the subject whose existence he there entertains and that they should not be reimported into the later description of matter in Z.3. But if my analysis of Z.3 has succeeded, one still need only concede that neither Aristotle's own general concept of matter nor his concept of ultimate matter is to be traced to the central argument of that chapter. And this concession need carry no large implications for the standard conception of Aristotelian matter as the subject of potentialities. One must simply recognize, as most interpreters implicitly do, that at least the potentialities must belong to the subject essentially. This understanding of Aris-

[1] See, e.g., Owens 1963, esp. 79 and 92; and Robinson 1974, esp. 183–87.

totle's ultimate matter is not affected by anything I have said about *Metaphysics* Z.3.

This chapter will examine Aristotle's theory of ultimate matter. The main question is what sort of matter he envisages at the foundation of his system. The tradition holds that prime matter, a subject whose being is exhausted by its potentialities, lies at the foundation. I shall challenge this view and argue that Aristotle's system is grounded instead in the four simple bodies—earth, water, air, and fire—which are the ultimate objects that satisfy the revised subject condition of *Metaphysics* Z.3. I shall begin by highlighting some points relevant to the recent debate about prime matter, then argue that two texts crucial to the debate, *On Generation and Corruption* I.4, on the distinction between generation and alteration, and *On Generation and Corruption* II.4, on elemental transformation, do not employ the doctrine; I shall then discuss the nature of the elements in light of Aristotle's account of elemental transformation.

The Appendix contains interpretations of three passages—the first from *On Generation and Corruption* II.1, the second from II.5, and the third from I.3—that are all customarily cited as evidence for Aristotle's commitment to prime matter. The first two, which introduce and conclude Aristotle's account of elemental change, might fairly be cited against my account of the elements, which is largely based on the theory sandwiched between them. The third, which directly precedes the chapter distinguishing alteration and generation, might be cited against my interpretation of that distinction. But these passages can be accommodated on the account that I propose.

PRIME MATTER

Since antiquity prime matter has enjoyed a hallowed place in the Aristotelian system. That system displays an awesome completeness, with God (pure form and actuality) at the top and prime matter (pure matter and potentiality) at the bottom. And between these two poles matter and form combine to yield physical objects of lesser or greater perfection. At the bottom of the scale are the four elements, which are mainly material; then come simple uniform stuffs, like the metals; further up the scale are plants, the simplest living things; then appear the various animals, crowned by man; higher still are the heavenly bodies, whose potentiality is so weakened as to humble them only to local circular movement without risk of destruction. At the very top is the Prime Mover, God, who is wholly immune to the commotion of the physical bodies below.

Aristotle offers an account of God as pure actuality in *Metaphysics* Λ, and he argues for a Prime Mover in *Physics* VIII. But his failure to provide anything approaching a comparable account of prime matter, a pure potentiality, is now well known.[2] He does not use the expression πρώτη ὕλη ("first matter") in this connection. Although he occasionally uses the phrase for an ultimate determinate matter, as in *Metaphysics* Θ.7, where he entertains the possibility that fire is πρώτη ὕλη (1049ª24–27), he typically uses the expression for the first matter relative to some composite—for example, the bronze relative to works made out of bronze. In *Metaphysics* Δ.4 he notes the ambiguity of the expression. "[In one way] nature is the first matter (πρώτη ὕλη) (and this in two ways, either the first relative to the thing itself or the first in general. For example, in the case of works made out of bronze, the bronze is first relative to these, but in general, perhaps water [is first], if all meltable things are water)" (1015ª7–10). But here, as in *Metaphysics* Θ.7, the ultimate first matter is not what the tradition calls "prime matter."

On one occasion Aristotle does discuss a pure potentiality, but he does so unsympathetically. In *On Generation and Corruption* 1.3 he questions whether there can be unqualified or substantial coming-to-be, if such coming-to-be involves the generation of a substance from what is potentially but not actually a substance.

> For if something comes to be, it is clear that there will be some substance in potentiality, but not in actuality, from which the generation will arise and into which the thing being destroyed must change. So (1) will something, among the things in actuality, belong to this? I mean, for example, will that which is only a this (τόδε) and being in potentiality, but which is simply not a this and not being, be quantified or qualified or somewhere? For if it is nothing (μηδέν) but everything in potentiality (πάντα δυνάμει), it follows that what is not in this way is separate (χωριστόν), and furthermore—what the first philosophers continued to fear most of all—that coming-to-be [takes place] from nothing (ἐκ μηδενός) preexisting. But (2) if, though not characterized as being a this (τόδε τι) or substance (οὐσία), it will be any of the other things we mentioned [namely, quantified, qualified, or somewhere], the affections (πάθη) will, as we said, be separate (χωριστά) from substances. (317ᵇ23–33)

Aristotle solves the difficulty by insisting that the generation of one substance is the destruction of another, and the destruction of one substance the generation of another.[3] So generation does not proceed from a pure

---

[2] The traditional view that Aristotle believed in prime matter has been challenged by King 1956; Charlton 1970, Appendix, and 1983; and Furth 1988, 221–27; cf. Jones, 1974. Some who defend the traditional view concede that Aristotle is less forthcoming on the topic than was earlier thought; see Lacey 1965, esp. 461–68; cf. Solmsen 1958, 243.

[3] *G.C.* 1.3, 318ª23–35; 318ᵇ33–35; 319ª17–22.

potentiality but from something that, though potential, is actually something else.

Those who believe that Aristotle is committed to a pure potentiality will stress that the pure potentiality here described is not his own prime matter, because prime matter does not exist separately and is never the preexisting entity from which a generation proceeds.[4] Prime matter is supposed to persist through generations whose terminus a quo and terminus ad quem are determinate entities. Water comes to be from air; prime matter is merely the continuant through the transformation.

Let us for the moment agree that prime matter is neither that from which something is generated nor that into which something is destroyed but merely what persists when one determinate entity, such as water, comes to be from another determinate entity, such as air. If we reflect on the criticisms that Aristotle levels against the separate pure potentiality, it is questionable how viable a continuant he would find a pure potentiality to be. He says of the pure potentiality that it is "nothing," "simply not a this," and "not being." It is actually nothing and potentially everything. How can something that is actually nothing guarantee that a transformation of air into water is a generation of water from air rather than a destruction of air into nothing and an emergence of water out of nothing—the scenario that the first philosophers continued to fear most of all? Furthermore, on the traditional scheme, the elements are composites consisting of pairs of qualities and prime matter. In *On Generation and Corruption* II.3 Aristotle says that fire is hot and dry, air hot and wet, water cold and wet, and earth cold and dry (330^b3-5). The pair of qualities hot and wet are the form of air, and its matter is prime matter. But surely the composite just described succumbs to Aristotle's second objection because prime matter, being a pure potentiality, is not a this or substance but is qualified as hot and wet. It would certainly appear that the affections are separate from substance because the substratum they inform is actually nothing. And it is hard to believe that, having leveled such objections, Aristotle would be content to posit such an entity at the foundation of his own system.[5]

Still, there is a genuine problem for which prime matter is supposed to be the solution. What persists through elemental transformation? Aristotle thinks that elemental transformation is empirically evident, since

---

[4] See Robinson 1974, 177–78. But Robinson ignores Aristotle's final objection that, if a pure potentiality is characterized by properties (πάθη), the properties will be separate from substance. This objection should be telling against prime matter as Robinson conceives it.

[5] Even so, Graham (1987), having explicitly ignored Aristotle's objection to properties belonging to a pure potentiality (477), attributes to Aristotle the doctrine to which he objects (e.g., 478) and then argues that Aristotle's theory is incoherent precisely because it relies on that doctrine (483–84).

water can be seen evaporating into steam, and clouds condensing into rain.[6] But the transformation of air into water is not merely a replacement of entities: the water has come to be *from the air*. To account for the connection between the element destroyed and the element generated, it seems that some part of the first should survive in the second, as in other typical changes. Indeed, Aristotle's general treatment of change in *Physics* I.7 apparently demands that every change, including substantial generation, involves a continuant (190^a13-21; 190^b9-17).[7] Although *Physics* I.7 does not mention the elements explicitly, there is no reason why they should escape the requirement; there is, however, a good reason why they should not escape, since something must guarantee that a change of air into water is a genuine conversion of the one element into the other, and not an arbitrary replacement of entities. Without a continuant, the sheer replacement risks the destruction of the air into nothing and the emergence of the water out of nothing, a situation that both Aristotle and his predecessors agree is impossible.[8] So all changes, including elemental ones, require horizontal continuity between the preexisting entity and the result. The tradition claims that prime matter guarantees such continuity in the elemental context.

I have pointed out, however, that there is reason to question whether Aristotle would regard prime matter, a pure potentiality, as an adequate continuant, given his objections in the passage quoted from *On Generation and Corruption* I.3.[9] But I will not press that question. Instead I shall assume that he might have held such a doctrine and shall ask whether in fact he did. I now turn to *On Generation and Corruption* I.4, an important text for the friends of prime matter because here he distinguishes generation from alteration and does so, it is claimed, on the basis of the sort of continuant involved in the two situations. In contexts of alteration the continuant is perceptible; in contexts of generation the continuant is imperceptible prime matter. Again, there is reason to ask why Aristotle

---

[6] See *De Cae.* III.6, 304^b25-27; *G.C.* II.4, 331^a7-9.

[7] This claim would be disputed by Charlton (1970, 77, 139–41). I discuss *Phys.* I.7 below (see pp. 98–108).

[8] See, e.g., *Phys.* I.8, 191^b13-17; *G.C.* I.3, 317^b11-18; cf. *Met.* B.4, 999^b8.

[9] Sheldon Cohen (1984) offers a proposal concerning Aristotle's ultimate matter that does not face the same difficulties as the standard view. According to Cohen, Aristotle's ultimate substratum has quite definite potentialities and at least one actual essential feature—spatial extension. Although Cohen's proposal provides Aristotle with a viable continuant for elemental change, it faces a different problem. In *G.C.* I.1 Aristotle objects that the early materialists, who posited a single ultimate substratum, reduced generation to the alteration of that permanent substratum (314^a8-11; cf. II.5, 332^a6-9). If Aristotle holds the view that Cohen attributes to him, then his own theory invites the same objection. Since Aristotle carefully distinguishes elemental transformation from alteration (see pp. 46–67), an interpretation should preferably not commit him to their identification.

would regard an epistemological criterion like perceptibility as an adequate basis on which to ground a metaphysical distinction between alteration and generation, but I will not press that question either. Instead I shall show that the standard reading of this text does not withstand a careful examination. Contrary to traditional opinion, the text provides no evidence for Aristotle's commitment to prime matter. Properly understood, however, the text does shed valuable light on his theory of matter and substantial generation.

ALTERATION AND GENERATION

Aristotle opens his treatise *On Generation and Corruption* by asking whether generation and alteration are the same or, as their names suggest, different (1.1, 314ᵃ4–6), and he devotes the first several chapters to deciding the question. In 1.4 he presents his own account of the difference between the two sorts of processes. I translate the chapter in full but divide it into eight parts for later reference. (The text in part [E] may have suffered some corruption and may have a line transposed; I follow the order in the manuscripts rather than that printed in Joachim's edition.)

(A) Let us specify the difference between alteration and generation—for we say that these changes differ from each other. Since, then, the subject (τὸ ὑποκείμενον) is one thing and the property that is naturally predicated of the subject (τὸ πάθος ὃ κατὰ τοῦ ὑποκειμένου λέγεσθαι πέφυκεν) is another thing, and there is a change of each of these (ἑκατέρου τούτων), (319ᵇ6–10)

(B) there is alteration when the persisting subject (ὑπομένοντος τοῦ ὑποκειμένου), which is perceptible (αἰσθητοῦ ὄντος), changes in its own properties (ἐν τοῖς ἑαυτοῦ πάθεσιν), which are either contraries or intermediates (e.g., the body, remaining the same [body], is healthy and again sick, and the bronze, being the same [bronze], is round and at another time angular); (319ᵇ10–14)

(C) but when a whole changes, if something perceptible does not remain as the same subject (ὅταν δ' ὅλον μεταβάλλῃ μὴ ὑπομένοντος αἰσθητοῦ τινος ὡς ὑποκειμένου τοῦ αὐτοῦ), but as blood [comes to be] from the semen as a whole or air from water or water from air as a whole, such [a process] is then a generation, and a destruction of the other thing, and especially if the change happens from something imperceptible to something perceptible either to touch or to all the senses—e.g., when water comes to be [from] or perishes into air, for air is pretty nearly imperceptible. (319ᵇ14–21)

(D) In these cases [e.g., changes from air into water], if some property of a contrariety remains the same in the thing that came to be and in the thing that passed away (ἄν τι ὑπομένῃ πάθος τὸ αὐτὸ ἐναντιώσεως ἐν τῷ γενομένῳ καὶ τῷ φθαρέντι) (e.g., when water comes to be from air, if both are transparent or cold), the other [resulting item] to which it changes must not be a property of this [persisting property] (οὐ δεῖ τούτου θάτερον πάθος εἶναι εἰς ὃ μεταβάλλει). Otherwise [the change] will be an alteration. (319ᵇ21-24)

(E) For example, [suppose that] the musical man perished, and the unmusical man came to be, and the man remains the same. If, therefore, the musicality and the unmusicality were not [each] in itself (καθ᾿ αὑτό) a property (πάθος) of this [man], there would be a generation of the one [the unmusical] and a destruction of the other [the musical]. So these [unmusicality and musicality] are properties (πάθη) of man, though [we can of course speak of] a generation and destruction of the musical man and unmusical man. But[10] now [even if we speak in this way] this [unmusicality, musicality] is a property (πάθος) of what remains [man]. So such [changes] are alteration. (319ᵇ25-31)

(F) When, therefore, the change of a pair of contraries concerns the quantity, there is growth and diminution; when it concerns place, locomotion; when it concerns the property and the quality, alteration; but when nothing remains of which the other [resulting item] is a property or generally accidental (ὅταν δὲ μηδὲν ὑπομένῃ οὗ θάτερον πάθος ἢ συμβεβηκὸς ὅλως), there is generation, and the [opposite change] is destruction. (319ᵇ31-320ᵃ2)

(G) Matter in the strictest sense (μάλιστα κυρίως) is the subject (τὸ ὑποκείμενον) receptive of generation and destruction, but in a certain way it is also the [subject] for other changes, because all the subjects (τὰ ὑποκείμενα) are receptive of certain contrarieties. (320ᵃ2-5)

(H) In this way, then, let us define generation—whether it exists or not, and how it exists—and alteration. (320ᵃ5-7)

This chapter is often interpreted as distinguishing alteration from generation by the sort of subject (ὑποκείμενον) that survives an exchange of properties (πάθη). In a nonsubstantial change the subject is a perceptible substance, and the properties replaced are nonsubstantial; in a substantial change the subject is the imperceptible material part of a perceptible whole, and the properties replaced are formal. Thus Aristotle uses the word ὑποκείμενον for two sorts of subjects—for a perceptible whole in nonsubstantial changes, for the imperceptible part of a perceptible whole

---

[10] Joachim (1922), following Philoponus (*In G.C.* 68.30–69.3), transposes this clause to 319ᵇ28 after τοῦ δὲ φθορά ("a destruction of the other [the musical]"). Williams in his Clarendon translation (1982) follows the original manuscript order.

in substantial changes—but the role of the subject as a continuant is the same in both contexts. The details of this view and my criticisms will be spelled out in the following subsection. My own view agrees with the standard assessment of alteration (and nonsubstantial change generally) but differs in the assessment of substantial change. I shall argue that the word ὑποκείμενον is used consistently to specify a perceptible whole but that the role of the subject differs in nonsubstantial and substantial changes. This view will be defended in my reconstruction below of *On Generation and Corruption* 1.4.

Conditions for Alteration and Generation

According to the standard reading of *On Generation and Corruption* 1.4, Aristotle offers two criteria for a change to count as an alteration, both given in part (B).[11] A change is an alteration (1) if the subject that undergoes an exchange of its properties (πάθη) is perceptible and persists unaltered through the change, and (2) if the properties exchanged are directly or naturally predicated of the persisting perceptible subject as its own. The second provision is supposed to be contained in the clause μεταβάλλῃ ἐν τοῖς ἑαυτοῦ πάθεσιν ("[it] changes in its *own* properties") (319ᵇ11–12). Both provisions are crucial.

In a generation the subject, which undergoes a replacement of properties, persists through the change but is imperceptible. Imperceptibility is the chief feature of a subject that persists through generation. But there is a difficulty about generation that explains why the second condition for alteration is also needed. In part (D) Aristotle describes a situation in which a perceptible property, for example, transparency or coldness, survives a substantial generation, such as a change of air into water. The situation, which he regards as a generation, apparently involves a persisting perceptible subject, since prime matter, although in itself imperceptible, is rendered perceptible by the surviving transparency or coldness. He therefore needs a provision that allows for the persistence of a perceptible subject even in contexts of substantial generation but that differentiates such cases from alterations. As scholars have typically construed the chapter, Aristotle distinguishes substantial generations involving a perceptible subject from alterations by insisting on a difference in the way the property replaced belongs to the perceptible subject in the two situations.

Aristotle is taken to claim in part (B) that, in contexts of alteration, the property replaced must belong to the persisting perceptible subject *as its*

---

[11] See Joachim 1922, 107; Williams 1982, 99. Joachim credits Zabarella for recognizing the second criterion.

own. In part (D) he is supposed to deny that, in cases of generation, the property replaced belongs to the persisting perceptible subject in this way. On this interpretation the property lost or acquired does belong to the persisting perceptible subject in a way (namely indirectly or unnaturally) but does not belong to it as the subject's own (directly or naturally).

What is the doctrine of natural and unnatural predication on which Aristotle's account in *On Generation and Corruption* 1.4 is supposed to rely? The *Analytics* discusses the doctrine.[12] If a white man becomes musical, whiteness and musicality are each naturally predicated of the man because the man is the subject for both properties. But since the man remains white when he comes to be musical, one can also say, "the white (thing) comes to be musical," and once the change has been completed, one can say, "the white (thing) is musical"; so there is a sense in which musicality can be predicated of the white or, more precisely, of a subject identified by whiteness. But musicality is unnaturally predicated of the white. It is only because both musicality and whiteness are naturally predicated of the same subject, the man, that it is permissible to predicate one property (musicality) of a subject identified by the other property (the white). But the predication is unnatural.

On the proposed interpretation of *On Generation and Corruption* 1.4, if a white man comes to be musical, the change is an alteration because the subject of which the musicality is naturally predicated is perceptible, since the man is perceptible. But in a generation the situation is different because, if a perceptible property persists—if, for example, in a transformation of air into water something transparent persists—the properties exchanged are unnaturally predicated of the persisting perceptible subject, and the subject of which they are naturally predicated, namely, prime matter, is imperceptible. So the change still counts as a generation, even though something perceptible persists.

I find neither of the proposed conditions in the text of *On Generation and Corruption* 1.4. It is a curious fact that the authors who adopt this position locate both conditions in Aristotle's specification of alteration in part (B) but have trouble with his account of generation in part (C). Aristotle does not obviously state the conditions that he is supposed to endorse for generation. On the traditional view, one expects Aristotle to make the following claims in part (C): There is generation (1) if the subject that undergoes an exchange of its properties (πάθη) is imperceptible, and (2), if it should happen that something perceptible remains, the properties exchanged are not (naturally) predicated of that persisting perceptible subject as its own. Yet part (C) fails to mention the πάθη that are

---

[12] See *Po. An.* 1.4, 73ᵇ5–10, and the discussion in Barnes 1975, 115–18. Cf. *Po. An.* 1.22, 83ᵃ1–23; *Pr. An.* 1.27, 43ᵃ34–36; *Met.* Δ.7, 1017ᵃ7–22.

49

supposed to be exchanged; it fails to mention an imperceptible persisting subject; and it says nothing that sounds remotely like the doctrine of natural and unnatural predication. Instead the text contains an apparently difficult claim. Aristotle says, "When a whole changes. . . ." He should not have said this because, on the traditional view, the whole thing does not change, since prime matter, the imperceptible material part of both the composite destroyed and composite generated, remains. Commentators focus most of their attention on making sense of this clause.

But the serious problem seems to go unnoticed. Aristotle does not say that, in a generation, "something imperceptible" remains; nor, in fact, does he say that "nothing perceptible" remains. He says, rather, "When a whole changes, if something perceptible does not remain as the same subject . . . such [a process] is then a generation, and a destruction of the other thing" (319^{b}14–18).[13] Why should one take this sentence to imply that, in a generation, something *imperceptible* remains? The question becomes all the more urgent if the passage is compared with Aristotle's summary of generation in part (F), a passage that, not surprisingly, defenders of the traditional view regularly pass over in silence:[14] "But when *nothing* (μηδέν) remains of which the other [resulting item] is a property or generally accidental, there is generation, and the [opposite change] is destruction" (319^{b}33–320^{a}2). "Nothing" does not mean "nothing perceptible."

Now, it is just possible that the word for "perceptible"—αἰσθητόν— has dropped out of the manuscripts in part (F) at 320^{a}1. Philoponus reads the word in his sixth-century commentary on the treatise, so perhaps αἰσθητόν was present in the text that Philoponus used.[15] But given the absence of the word from all the manuscripts and the fact that Philoponus paraphrases rather than quotes the rest of the sentence, it seems more likely that he took Aristotle's theory of generation to require an imperceptible substratum, and so he introduced the word into the text. Even modern editors and translators who agree with Philoponus about the need for an imperceptible substratum have resisted the temptation to adopt his text.[16] Without the word, however, Aristotle sums up his ac-

[13] The sentence is rightly construed by Jones (1974, 499 and n. 21), who takes "something perceptible" to refer to a substantial individual, such as water or air.

[14] Joachim (1922) ignores the lines in his commentary; Robinson (1974, 170–71), though claiming to have shown, against Charlton, that the chapter concerns prime matter, apparently overlooked these lines. Williams (1982, 102–3 and 216–17) attempts to explain them but concludes that they should be ignored because they conflict with the conclusion in part (G)—at least as Williams interprets it (103). I shall discuss Williams's interpretation of part (G) below, pp. 61–62.

[15] Philoponus (*In G.C.* 69.15–17).

[16] Curiously, Joachim fails even to mention Philoponus's reading in his critical apparatus, and neither he nor Williams discusses the textual issue.

count of generation by saying that generation occurs when nothing persists of which the resulting item is a πάθος or in any way accidental. Yet, according to the tradition, prime matter persists, and the properties exchanged are πάθη of it. It therefore appears that changes involving prime matter are excluded from the status of generation by Aristotle's statement. But Aristotle mentions elemental transformations as examples of generations in part (C) and defends them as generations in part (D) (together with [E]), so it would be unfortunate if such transformations turned out to be alterations after all.

I have already indicated that part (C) fails to demand the persistence of an imperceptible substratum as a condition for generation, so the likely reason for its omission in part (F) is that the condition was never required in the first place. Certainly, given that imperceptibility is supposed to be the distinguishing mark of the persisting subject in contexts of generation and destruction, it is remarkable that no such demand is explicitly made—or, if it was made, that it should have been lost from all the manuscripts.

The other condition, concerning direct or natural predication, becomes less important once it is recognized that no demand is made for an imperceptible subject. Still, let me give the condition its due. Commentators have put a great deal of weight on the reflexive pronoun ἑαυτοῦ at 319^{b}10–12: "There is alteration when the persisting subject, which is perceptible, changes in its *own* properties." Suppose that the pronoun carries the force that has been claimed for it. Aristotle says that there is alteration if a perceptible subject persists and if the properties exchanged are naturally predicated of it. His statement leaves open the possibility that, in a generation, a perceptible subject persists and that the properties exchanged are πάθη of it: they simply cannot be πάθη of the persisting perceptible subject as its own or naturally. Aristotle takes up the issue for generation in part (D). Recall what he says:

> (D) In these cases [e.g., changes from air into water], if some property (πάθος) of a contrariety remains the same in the thing that came to be and in the thing that passed away (e.g., when water comes to be from air, if both are transparent or cold), the other [resulting item] to which it changes must not be a property (πάθος) of this [persisting property] (οὐ δεῖ τούτου θάτερον πάθος εἶναι εἰς ὃ μεταβάλλει). Otherwise [the change] will be an alteration. (319^{b}21–24)

My rendering of the line quoted in Greek is not the most obvious one. A more obvious translation is "the other πάθος to which it changes must not belong to this [persisting πάθος]." But those who believe that Aristotle here employs the doctrine of natural and unnatural predication seem to

51

prefer my translation,[17] and presumably they prefer it because Aristotle ought not to prohibit simple belonging, since the resulting item does belong to the persisting perceptible item. The resulting item simply does not belong directly, naturally, or to the subject as its own. So they adopt my translation (and it is probably correct because section [F] again juxtaposes θάτερον and πάθος, and there θάτερον is evidently to be construed as subject and πάθος as predicate). On the preferred translation Aristotle claims that the resulting item must not be a πάθος of the persisting perceptible item; if it is, the change is an alteration.

On reflection, however, the preferred translation does not help very much, because, on the traditional view, the resulting item is supposed to be a πάθος of the persisting item. The resulting item simply cannot be a πάθος of the persisting item as its own or naturally. Since Aristotle adds no saving qualifier, he seems to exclude from the status of generation precisely those changes that he wants to preserve. Suppose that something transparent persists through a transformation of air into water. According to the traditional view, the properties exchanged in this transformation belong to the persisting transparent in the way that the musical belongs to the white (if a white man is musical); the resulting item is a πάθος of the persisting transparent because it belongs to the persisting transparent unnaturally. But since Aristotle says that, if the resulting item is a πάθος of the persisting item, the change is an alteration, the transformation of air into water is an alteration. This is not the wanted result.

One might solve the problem by urging that Aristotle reserves the word πάθος for properties that belong to a subject naturally and would avoid the term in specifying a property that belongs to a subject unnaturally. If one adopts this assumption, then part (D) can be understood, on the favored translation, to insist that the resulting item not be a πάθος, or naturally predicated, of the persisting perceptible item. Thus the claim will not rule out belonging in general, but only natural belonging. In fact, this restriction on the use of πάθος to situations of natural predication has some warrant. Notice that Aristotle opens the chapter with this distinction between a subject (ὑποκείμενον) and a property (πάθος): "Since the ὑποκείμενον is one thing and the πάθος that is naturally predicated of the subject (ὃ κατὰ τοῦ ὑποκειμένου λέγεσθαι πέφυκεν) is another thing . . . " (319ᵇ8–9). The specification of a πάθος as something "naturally" predicated of a subject may indicate that Aristotle would restrict use of the word πάθος to contexts of natural predication.

But if πάθος is an appropriate word only in situations in which one item is naturally predicated of another, then Aristotle nowhere introduces the proposed criterion about natural or direct predication. That criterion, it

---

[17] See Joachim 1922, 108; Williams 1982, 14, 100; cf. White 1972–1973, 73–76.

will be recalled, was supposed to be introduced by the word ἑαυτοῦ in the phrase ἐν τοῖς ἑαυτοῦ πάθεσιν (319ᵇ11–12). If πάθος is used only for a property that belongs to a subject naturally, then ἑαυτοῦ adds nothing special about direct or natural belonging that is not already implicit in the word πάθος. Either ἑαυτοῦ has no special force, or if it does, it may simply exclude from the status of genuine alteration so-called Cambridge changes (changes a subject can suffer, not by undergoing a real change itself, but by becoming differently related to something else that undergoes a real change).[18] Either way, there is no sign of a doctrine of natural and unnatural predication, and so there is no reason to think that Aristotle relies on such a doctrine in part (D). The alternative, if one supposes that ἑαυτοῦ does have the force that has been proposed for it, is the consequence that I mentioned earlier, namely, that Aristotle excludes from the status of generation the very changes that he had meant to defend.

So neither condition stands the test. *On Generation and Corruption* 1.4 does not advocate a role for prime matter in generation. Let me now explain what Aristotle does say about alteration and generation in this important text.

On Generation and Corruption 1.4: A Reconstruction

In the opening chapters of *On Generation and Corruption*, Aristotle criticizes both those materialists who supposed that all things are generated out of a single ultimate stuff and those who supposed that all things are generated out of a plurality of ultimate materials. He faults the first group for reducing generation to alteration, and he faults the second group for treating generation and destruction as a mere aggregation and separation of the ultimate persisting ingredients. Aristotle first introduces his own distinction between alteration and generation in 1.2 in response to the pluralists. This passage holds several keys to the interpretation of 1.4.

But simple and complete generation is not defined by aggregation and separation, as some say, with alteration as change in something continuous. In fact, this is where all the mistakes are made. For simple generation and destruction are not brought about by aggregation and separation, but when a whole (ὅλον) changes from this to this (ἐκ τοῦδε εἰς τόδε). Although these people think that all such change is alteration, there is a difference. For within the subject (ἐν τῷ ὑποκειμένῳ) there is a factor corresponding to the formula (κατὰ τὸν λόγον) and a factor corresponding to the matter (κατὰ τὴν ὕλην). When, therefore, the change occurs in these, there will be generation

---

[18] I owe this suggestion to Tim Maudlin. On Cambridge changes, see Geach 1969, 71–72; cf. McDowell 1973, 136–37.

or destruction. But when the change occurs in the properties (ἐν τοῖς πάθεσι) and is accidental (κατὰ συμβεβηκός), there is alteration. (317ᵃ17–27)

Generation is not due to aggregation and separation, as some people think, but takes place when a whole changes from this to this. Some people regard all such changes as alteration, but they are mistaken.[19] Why are they mistaken? Aristotle suggests that there are two ways to change from this to this. People must recognize that, within the subject (τὸ ὑποκείμενον), there are two factors, a factor corresponding to the formula and a factor corresponding to the matter; when the change occurs in these intrinsic features, features that contribute to what the subject is, there is generation and destruction; but when the change occurs in the πάθη, features accidental to the subject, the change is an alteration.

Aristotle's distinction between generation and alteration seems to rely on his distinction between two sorts of properties—those that contribute to the nature of the subject and those that are accidental to it. If an entity loses some property accidental to what it is, then it continues in existence but is altered. For example, if a man loses his musicality, he persists as a man because musicality is accidental to what man is; the change is thus an alteration. If, on the other hand, a man loses his soul or body, features that make him a man, the man himself is destroyed because he cannot survive the loss of features on which his very nature depends.

Keep in mind the way Aristotle uses ὑποκείμενον and πάθος in this passage. The ὑποκείμενον is a whole that possesses two intrinsic features— one corresponding to the formula, and one to the matter. The πάθη are not intrinsic features but properties that the ὑποκείμενον can lose without going out of existence. With this observation, I return to 1.4.

Parts (A) to (C) spell out the doctrine of 1.2. Aristotle begins by distinguishing the ὑποκείμενον as one thing and the πάθος, which is naturally predicated of the ὑποκείμενον, as something else, and he claims that each of these can change. He thus indicates that one sort of change will concern the πάθη, the other the ὑποκείμενον. There is alteration when the persist-

---

[19] Aristotle may also have in mind his own account in the *Physics*. According to the criteria stated in *Phys.* v.1, changes between a pair of positive termini (described in *G.C.* as ἐκ τοῦδε εἰς τόδε) are not generations or destructions but nonsubstantial changes between contrary termini. Substantial generations and destructions do not occur between contrary termini because substance has no contrary (*Cat.* 5, 3ᵇ24–27; *Phys.* 1.6, 189ᵃ32–33; v.2, 225ᵇ10–11). He identifies the termini of substantial changes as contradictories and describes such processes as occurring from negative to positive (generation) or from positive to negative (destruction). Aristotle's standard account of generation will be discussed in chapter 3. His challenge in *G.C.* is to show that elemental transformations are generations, despite the fact that the termini of the changes are contraries (e.g., hot-cold), and despite the fact that the elements themselves are contrary to one another (*G.C.* ii.3, 331ᵃ1–3; ii.8, 335ᵃ3–6).

ing ὑποκείμενον, which is perceptible, changes in its πάθη, which are either contraries or intermediates—for example, there is alteration when the body, remaining the same body, is healthy and at another time sick; or when the bronze, remaining the same bronze, is round and at another time angular (319ᵇ10–14). In these situations the ὑποκείμενον is unaffected by the change: the body remains the same body, and the bronze remains the same bronze. The intrinsic features of the body and the bronze—those features that correspond to the account and the matter—are unassailed. Only the πάθη, those features accidental to the subject, are affected. So the change is an alteration, not a generation.

In a generation the ὑποκείμενον itself is assailed. Aristotle comments that there is generation when a whole (ὅλον) changes, if something perceptible does not remain as the same ὑποκείμενον (319ᵇ14–16). For example, when blood comes to be from the semen as a whole, or air from water, or water from air as a whole, there is a generation of one thing and a destruction of the other (319ᵇ16–18). In such cases the intrinsic features of the ὑποκείμενον, those features corresponding to its formula or its matter, are assaulted; and so the ὑποκείμενον, unable to remain the same perceptible whole without those determining features, is itself driven out of existence. *Generation of Animals* explains that, in sexual reproduction, the body of the semen dissolves and evaporates in performing its task;[20] with the loss of its body, the semen cannot remain the same perceptible ὑποκείμενον but gives way to the blood in the body of the female. Similarly, when air comes to be from water, or water from air, some intrinsic feature of the preexisting element is lost, and consequently the original element is destroyed and a different element emerges. The preexisting whole cannot survive as the same ὑποκείμενον when it loses an intrinsic feature. Heat and wetness are intrinsic features of air, and coldness and wetness of water; these features are not mere πάθη, mere accidental properties, whose loss an element can withstand and remain what it is. So, if the heat of the air is lost, the air itself is destroyed into something else.[21]

On this interpretation of parts (A) to (C), the term ὑποκείμενον applies to the same type of entity throughout, namely, a perceptible whole, but the role of that entity differs in alteration and generation. In an alteration the entity survives the change when its πάθη are replaced; but in a generation it is the preexisting entity from which a new ὑποκείμενον is generated or the resulting entity into which something else is destroyed. Thus the ὑποκείμενον for generation is not a continuant. By contrast, on the traditional view the role of the ὑποκείμενον is the same in alteration and generation, since it is a continuant in both contexts, but the term ὑποκεί-

[20] *G.A.* II.3, 737ᵃ11–12.
[21] On the mechanics of such transformations, see below, pp. 68–75.

μενον applies to two types of entity—in alteration to a perceptible whole, in generation to the (imperceptible) material part of such a whole. Thus, although the two interpretations correspond in their assessment of alteration, the dispute concerns the sort of item that Aristotle calls a ὑποκείμενον in contexts of generation and the role that he takes that entity to play.

Metaphysics Z.3 and H.1 indicate that the matter, the form, and the composite can each be called a ὑποκείμενον, so Aristotle certainly could, as the commentators suppose, apply the term in On Generation and Corruption 1.4 to the composite that underlies an alteration and to the material component that underlies a generation. Moreover, the end of On Generation and Corruption 1.3 indicates that he is prepared to call the material part of the simplest bodies a ὑποκείμενον, for he speaks of "what underlies (ὃ . . . ὑπόκειται) [the elements]" (319^{b}3–4).[22] So there is some reason to expect him to appeal to this notion in 1.4. Furthermore, the conclusion in part (G), which contains the first explicit mention of matter in 1.4, might seem to confirm that the chapter employs two sorts of ὑποκείμενα—one for alteration, another for generation. Here Aristotle contrasts matter in the strictest sense, which he identifies as the ὑποκείμενον receptive of generation and destruction, with matter in a derivative sense, which he identifies as the ὑποκείμενον for other sorts of changes.

But if the commentators are right in tracing Aristotle's distinction between alteration and generation to a difference between the ὑποκείμενα in the two situations, then he has set up the distinction in part (A) incorrectly. After contrasting the ὑποκείμενον and the πάθος, he should have said that, depending on the type of ὑποκείμενον, there will be alteration or generation. This is not what he says. Having contrasted the ὑποκείμενον and the πάθος, he says that there can be a change of each of these (ἑκατέρου τούτων, 319^{b}10). This claim is nonsense on the standard interpretation because that view entails that both alteration and generation concern a change of the same items—the πάθη—and differ in respect of the type of ὑποκείμενον in which the πάθη are realized. Since Aristotle does not mention two types of ὑποκείμενον in part (A), there is no reason to expect his characterization of alteration in part (B) and of generation in part (C) to turn on a difference between the ὑποκείμενα in the two situations. On the contrary, given the opening claim in part (A), one expects the subsequent distinction spelled out in parts (B) and (C) to concern a change in the πάθη in alteration, and a change in the ὑποκείμενον in generation. And the promise of part (A) is fulfilled in (B) and (C) only if Aristotle applies the word ὑποκείμενον to a single type of entity, a perceptible whole, and if the subject plays different roles in the two sorts of

[22] See my analysis of this passage in the Appendix.

processes. In alteration it survives an exchange of accidental properties; in generation it is itself destroyed and replaced by a different subject.

Part (C) does not mention an imperceptible continuant for substantial change; in fact, it refers to no continuant at all. Part (C) does mention something imperceptible, but the imperceptible item is a preexisting subject, which is destroyed, or a resulting subject, which is generated. Aristotle says, "And [there is generation and destruction] especially if the change happens from something imperceptible to something perceptible either to touch or to all the senses—e.g., when water comes to be [from] or perishes into air, for air is pretty nearly imperceptible" ($319^{b}18$–21). The imperceptible air is not a surviving material component but a ὑπο-κείμενον that comes to be or is destroyed. This example is probably a concession to ordinary experience. In the previous chapter Aristotle points out that many people associate generation with the emergence of something perceptible from something imperceptible, and he declares the view to lead to mistakes (1.3, $318^{b}18$–33). On his own view all four elements are differentiated by tangible differentiae—the hot, the cold, the wet, and the dry. Although air is "pretty nearly" (ἐπιεικῶς) imperceptible because it is the hardest of the four elements to detect, it too is perceptible.

To sum up: In part (C) the word ὑποκείμενον applies to perceptible bodies, such as the elements, which come to be and are destroyed. Aristotle does not mention another sort of ὑποκείμενον—the material part of a perceptible whole—that persists and is imperceptible. It is therefore not surprising that he should omit the word αἰσθητόν with μηδέν (to yield "nothing perceptible") in his final characterization of generation in part (F). In contrast to alteration, which occurs when a ὑποκείμενον survives an exchange of πάθη, generation occurs when nothing remains of which the resulting item is a πάθος or any sort of accident. Since the preexisting ὑποκείμενον is destroyed by the loss of some intrinsic feature, the ὑπο-κείμενον does not survive as a subject of which the resulting item is a πάθος. Instead, a new ὑποκείμενον, characterized by its own distinctive features, emerges; the first ὑποκείμενον (e.g., air) is replaced by a different ὑποκείμενον (e.g., water). And evidently, if anything does persist through this transformation, what results will not be a πάθος of it—if it were, the change would be an alteration. The summary in part (F) thus accords with the account of generation in part (C).

Aristotle takes up the problem of persistence in parts (D) and (E). He wants to guard the possibility of some sort of continuity in contexts of substantial generation, and the task is to demonstrate that such continuity is possible without reducing generation to alteration. He therefore treats two sorts of examples that display structural similarities and shows that one change is a generation (D), the other an alteration (E). In section (D) he entertains the possibility that, in a transformation of air into water, some πάθος of air survives in the water. For example, both the original air and the resulting water might be transparent or cold, and if so, the transparency or coldness survives the substantial change.

Some scholars are troubled by Aristotle's mention of coldness as a persisting πάθος and recommend a textual emendation.[23] Their concern is that, according to Aristotle's official doctrine in Book II, the property that air and water share is wetness, not coldness. Since air is hot and wet and water cold and wet, coldness is the property acquired in a transformation of air into water, while wetness is the surviving common property. But those puzzled have missed the meaning of πάθος in this chapter: a πάθος is an accidental property of a ὑποκείμενον, not an intrinsic feature of it. Aristotle chooses transparency and coldness judiciously in order to exploit the structural parallel between a substantial generation, which involves a persisting πάθος and ὑποκείμενα that are replaced, and an alteration, which involves a persisting ὑποκείμενον and πάθη that are replaced. He chooses coldness as an example of a persisting πάθος because, if common to air and water, it is a shared accident, not a shared intrinsic feature. Ordinary experience attests that, just as air and water can both be transparent or murky, so they can both be cold or hot. There is, then, no call to alter the text.

In part (D) Aristotle claims that, in contexts of generation, if a πάθος persists, the resulting item must not be a πάθος of the persisting πάθος. For example, if the transparent persists in a transformation of air into water, then the resulting item must not be a πάθος of the transparent. The text does not make clear whether the resulting item is the resulting ὑποκείμενον (water) or the intrinsic feature (coldness), which by replacing air's heat accounts for the resulting water. Some commentators take the phrase one way, some the other.[24] For Aristotle's main point it makes no difference which choice one makes, since the final summary in part (F) stipulates that a generation occurs when nothing persists of which the resulting item is a πάθος; if either the resulting coldness or the resulting water were a πάθος of the surviving transparent, the change would reduce to alteration.

Although Aristotle's point must hold whichever decision one makes, it seems preferable to take the resulting item to be the resulting water, the new ὑποκείμενον. In the first place, Aristotle has just mentioned air and water as the items that come to be and pass away, and he says nothing

---

[23] See Williams 1972, 301–3.

[24] Williams (1972, 302–3; 1982, 14, 100, and 102) takes the resulting item to be the intrinsic feature, such as coldness; Joachim (1922, 108), although not explicit, probably concurs. Charlton (1970, 75), White (1972–1973, 73–75), Robinson (1974, 170), and Miller (1978, 116 n. 29) take the resulting item to be the resulting ὑποκείμενον, such as water.

about those intrinsic features whose replacement accounts for the generation and destruction. Second, if he did have in mind the resulting intrinsic feature, then the example itself would be unduly confusing, since coldness is the resulting intrinsic feature in a transformation of air into water, as well as one of the items mentioned as a persisting πάθος. And finally, Aristotle seems to be playing with the notions of πάθος and ὑποκείμενον in both parts (D) and (E), and the structural parallel between the two paradigms is captured if the resulting item is the resulting ὑποκείμενον, water. He is interested in the fact that generations might involve a persisting πάθος when one ὑποκείμενον is replaced by another. Since alterations too involve the persistence of something and the replacement of something else, the question is, How do the two sorts of changes differ despite the similarity?

Now consider part (E). Aristotle discusses an alteration, a change—unlike the one just discussed—in which the resulting item is a πάθος of what persists. He then considers what the change would have to be like for it to count as a generation. Although this section of Aristotle's argument is obscure in some of its details (possibly due to corruption), the overall thrust of the passage seems clear enough. Recall the argument:

(E) For example, [suppose that] the musical man perished, and the unmusical man came to be, and the man remains the same. If, therefore, the musicality and the unmusicality were not [each] in itself (καθ' αὐτό) a πάθος of this [man], there would be a generation of the one [the unmusical] and a destruction of the other [the musical]. So these [unmusicality and musicality] are πάθη of man, though [we can of course speak of] a generation and destruction of the musical man and unmusical man. But now [even if we speak in this way] this [unmusicality, musicality] is a πάθος of what remains [man]. So such [changes] are alteration. (319ᵇ25–31)

I have stressed the importance of Aristotle's distinction between a ὑποκείμενον, which has intrinsic features, and a πάθος, which belongs to a ὑποκείμενον accidentally and whose loss the subject can withstand. He now considers what would happen if musicality and unmusicality were not in themselves πάθη of man but were proper ὑποκείμενα in their own right.[25] If musicality and unmusicality were not dependent, as in fact they

---

[25] Several writers take καθ' αὐτό ("in itself") together with πάθος ("property") to indicate, not that musicality is a πάθος because of what it is (a quality), but that it is a special kind of πάθος of man, namely, a καθ' αὐτὸ πάθος ("essential accident") (Joachim 1922, 109–10; Williams 1982, 100). But, as these authors recognize, musicality is an accident of man, not an essential property. So they find the doctrine of natural predication lurking in the phrase and argue that the absence of καθ' αὐτό with πάθος in part (D) indicates that, in part (D), the resulting item (the emergent property, such as coldness; cf. above n. 24) belongs to the

are, on an underlying subject, then there would be a generation of unmusicality (as an independent ὑποκείμενον) and a destruction of musicality (as an independent ὑποκείμενον). And of course this is absurd because musicality and unmusicality are qualities. Unlike the water and air of the preceding example, entities that can exist on their own without the persisting transparent, musicality and unmusicality depend for their existence on an underlying subject. So musicality and unmusicality are πάθη of man. Aristotle's conclusion is clear: such changes, processes involving the replacement of πάθη in a surviving subject, are alterations (319ᵇ30–31).

The two clauses (319ᵇ29–30) immediately following the argument and immediately preceding the conclusion are, however, somewhat puzzling.[26] My translation interprets them as a response to an implicit objection concerning common Greek idiom, to which Aristotle responds: Although one can speak of the "generation" and "destruction" of the musical man and unmusical man—as he does himself in the opening lines of part (E) (319ᵇ25–26)—this fact about language does not alter the metaphysical fact that musicality and unmusicality are πάθη of man. Whether a man's becoming musical is described as an alteration of the man or as a generation of the musical man, the change is still an alteration.

In parts (D) and (E) Aristotle has shown that, even if generations and alterations are structurally similar in respect of replacement and persistence, generation is still importantly different from alteration. Alteration involves a resulting item that is a πάθος of the persisting item: a ὑποκείμενον survives, and πάθη are replaced. By contrast, if a generation involves a persisting item, the resulting item is never a πάθος of the continuant: instead, a πάθος survives and ὑποκείμενα are replaced. He sums up the account in part (F), where he also mentions growth and locomotion to complete the survey of the four sorts of changes. The three sorts of nonsubstantial changes differ markedly from substantial generation and destruction in respect of the role of the ὑποκείμενον. In nonsubstantial changes the ὑποκείμενον remains the same when its accidental properties (quantities, locations, qualities) are replaced, but in substantial generation and destruction the ὑποκείμενον itself is destroyed and a new ὑποκείμενον emerges because factors intrinsic to the ὑποκείμενον are lost.

---

surviving perceptible item (e.g., the transparent) unnaturally. This interpretation of καθ' αὑτό in part (E) does not answer the objection I raised earlier in the text. If Aristotle introduces the criterion about natural predication in part (B), then he rejects the transformation as a generation in part (D); if he does not introduce the criterion in part (B), then there is no reason to suppose that the criterion is an issue in the chapter at all.

[26] One of these lines Joachim transposes; the other line Williams (1982, 100–101) suggests would be better excised.

Part (G) focuses on the ὑποκείμενον, and for the first time in the chapter, Aristotle mentions matter explicitly.

(G) Matter in the strictest sense (μάλιστα κυρίως) is the ὑποκείμενον receptive of generation and destruction, but in a certain way it is also the [ὑποκείμενον] for other changes, because all the ὑποκείμενα are receptive of certain contrarieties. (320ª2–5)

This passage has important implications for Aristotle's theory of matter. He states what he means by "matter in the strictest sense" and says that it is the subject receptive of generation and destruction. The subjects for other sorts of changes can also be called "matter," but in a derivative sense.

Commentators, having found prime matter earlier in the chapter, find it here as well. But if prime matter, or indeed any material component, is the item described in part (G), the description itself is misleading. Aristotle's description of matter as "the ὑποκείμενον receptive of generation and destruction" seems, on its face, to characterize a subject that can come to be and pass away, and therefore a subject that is perishable.[27] Prime matter, as traditionally conceived, is indestructible;[28] more generally, the material component in a substantial change is supposed to be the persisting item rather than the item that comes to be and perishes. Scholars will admit that Aristotle phrases the description misleadingly and will argue that he does not mean that the subject itself comes to be and is destroyed but only that something comes to be and is destroyed when the subject, which is receptive of contrary properties, actually receives them.[29] The justification for this proposal is taken to lie in Aristotle's subsequent comparison between matter in the strict sense and the subjects for other changes. These other subjects can be called matter in a derivative sense, he says, "because all the ὑποκείμενα are receptive of contrariety." Thus, in saying that matter in the strict sense is receptive of generation and destruction, Aristotle is supposed to mean that matter persists when contrary properties are replaced.

Consider the implications of this proposal. A subject is receptive of contrariety if it can survive an exchange of contrary properties; and if it survives such an exchange, the contrary properties belong to the subject accidentally. Thus a man is the subject of the contrariety musicality and nonmusicality because he can have either property without ceasing to be the subject that he is: a man. Matter is supposed to be receptive of generation and destruction because it too can receive contrary properties;

---

[27] Cf. Charlton 1983, 200.
[28] See, e.g., Zeller 1897, 1:345; Joachim 1922, 97.
[29] See Williams 1982, 103, 212–13.

when one contrary replaces the other, something (e.g., air) perishes, and something else (e.g., water) comes to be. Yet, if this is Aristotle's view, then the production of water from air is not after all a generation but a mere alteration, because the transformation involves a replacement of properties accidental to the underlying material. Such changes are excluded as generations in the preceding part (F), which claims that generation occurs when nothing remains of which the resulting item is a πάθος or in any way accidental. It is implausible that the transformation of air into water should now reduce to alteration, since the chapter has forcefully argued that it is a generation. The alternative is to suppose that part (G) contradicts the conclusion in part (F).[30] Neither alternative will do, and since the problem arises in the first place from an unlikely interpretation of "receptive of generation and destruction," the received reading of part (G) should be rejected.

If part (G) is consistent with the rest of the chapter, the subject receptive of generation and destruction, which Aristotle identifies as matter in the strictest sense, should be the whole perceptible subject described in part (C), which comes to be and passes away. The subject does not survive a substantial generation, because, with the loss of some intrinsic feature, it ceases to exist—for example, with the loss of its intrinsic heat, air is destroyed and water is generated. Water and air are presumably examples of matter in the strictest sense, and in the preceding argument of 1.4, they are treated, not as continuants, but as subjects that come to be and perish. As subjects, they can also be classed among the items receptive of contrariety, and when they are so classed, they are continuants that undergo nonsubstantial changes—changes of quality, quantity, or place. Thus water is not only something that comes to be and passes away (and therefore matter in the strictest sense) but also something that can be moved from one location to another, be increased or reduced in amount, and alter from transparent to murky. The items that count as matter in the strictest sense can be the subjects for nonsubstantial changes, as can all perceptible bodies, and when serving as matter in the derivative sense, the elements are continuants.

If "matter in the strictest sense" applies to subjects that come to be and pass away, Aristotle might seem to cast his net too widely, since all perceptible bodies in the sublunary realm are perishable, and at least some of these bodies are presumably not matter "in the strictest sense." Indeed, organisms, although perishable, are elsewhere said to be substances in the strictest sense (μάλιστα οὐσίας).[31] Moreover, in *Metaphysics* H.5 Aristotle explicitly denies that complex bodies are the matter for their own de-

---

[30] This is apparently Williams's view (1982, 102–3).
[31] *Met.* Z.7, 1032ª18–19.

struction—an animal, for example, is not the matter of a corpse, nor potentially a corpse, although it is destroyed into one; and wine is not the matter of vinegar, nor potentially vinegar, although it is destroyed into vinegar.[32] Clearly, then, not every subject that comes to be and passes away counts strictly as matter.

Aristotle often describes matter as "that from which (ἐξ οὗ) a product is generated that is present in (ἐνυπάρχοντος) [the product], as the bronze of a statue and the silver of a bowl."[33] This description suggests that something designated as matter initially exists separately as that from which a composite is generated and later is an ingredient of the generated object. According to this description, Aristotle calls "matter" something that (1) can exist apart from a higher complex, such that the product is generated from that material (hereafter the "preexisting" matter), and that (2) can serve as an ingredient in that higher whole, such that the material is somehow present in that whole (hereafter the "constituent" matter). Whatever satisfies this description should be an instance of matter— bronze for a statue, copper and tin for bronze, and earth and water for copper. These examples indicate that an entity that serves as the matter for some greater complex is typically itself a composite consisting of a form that organizes simpler ingredients. Given Aristotle's usual description of matter, an entity that is itself generated is a proper instance of matter if it can serve as an ingredient of something else. *Metaphysics* H.5 clarifies his view. Aristotle denies that wine is the matter of vinegar, although it can be destroyed into vinegar, and claims instead that water is the matter of both wine and vinegar (1045ᵃ1–2). Water is not only an ingredient of both liquids, it is also the simple stuff into which vinegar is destroyed and the preexisting stuff from which wine is generated (1045ᵃ3–6). Thus water is the separate preexisting matter from which wine is generated, and once the wine has been generated, the water is a constituent present in the wine. Water, in its relation to wine, satisfies Aristotle's standard description of matter.

But if Aristotle's strict notion of matter in *On Generation and Corruption* I.4 applies to entities as ingredients of a higher complex, then the conclusion in part (G) relies on considerations that have not been stated in the preceding argument, and the description itself is inappropriate. The chapter has ignored the typical contexts of generation and destruction in which a simpler matter, such as water, is worked up into a composite whole, such as wine, or in which a generated whole degenerates into something simpler. And the description of matter as the subject "recep-

[32] *Met.* H.5, 1044ᵇ34–1045ᵃ2.

[33] *Phys.* II.3, 194ᵇ23–26; cf. *Phys.* I.9, 192ᵃ31–32; *G.A.* I.18, 724ᵃ23–26; *Met.* Δ.4, 1014ᵇ17–18; 1014ᵇ26–35. Cf. *Met.* A.3, 983ᵇ6–10.

tive of generation and destruction" is unsuitable for the materials involved in such constructions because such materials are, in respect of
those constructions, not themselves generated or destroyed but are the
continuants when other things come to be or pass away. In the example
of the generation of wine from water, the water, which is the matter of
wine, is not itself receptive of generation and destruction, since it survives
the generation of wine and is an ingredient of that higher construct. *On
Generation and Corruption* 1.4 has focused on a special type of generation
and destruction in which the preexisting subject is itself destroyed and
replaced by a different subject, as air is destroyed into water; and the only
continuants mentioned in connection with these transformations are two
accidental properties of the subjects that undergo the replacement: transparency and coldness. These properties are not ingredients of the elements, because they cannot exist on their own; transparency and coldness
are treated as qualities ($\pi\acute{\alpha}\theta\eta$), and as such, they are not the sorts of entities
that Aristotle would regard as proper instances of matter. The description
in part (G) of matter in the strict sense does not specify a continuant and
so presumably does not apply to entities serving that standard material
role.

Given the general argument of 1.4, Aristotle's strict notion of matter
should apply to those entities alone on whose generation and destruction
the chapter has focused: the four elements. Someone might object that
the description cannot be confined to the four elements because Aristotle
mentions one other example of generation and destruction, the produc-
tion of blood from the productive seed ($\gamma o \nu \acute{\eta}$) (319[b]16). This example is
peculiar, as commentators have noticed.[34] Aristotle usually talks about
concocting semen out of simple blood in the body of the male parent—a
generation that conforms with other typical generations in which the
product is worked up out of simpler matter that remains within the product as an ingredient. Having reversed the order of the generation, Aristotle seems to describe a different situation, namely, the conversion of the
semen into the special blood of the female in the act of reproduction.
Neither the semen nor the inseminated blood that results from the conversion is elsewhere identified as matter; the semen is an efficient cause of
generation, and the inseminated blood is a product that results when the
untreated female material ($\kappa\alpha\tau\alpha\mu\acute{\eta}\nu\iota\alpha$) acquires the soul principle by the
action of the seed. Since neither item in this conversion is a proper in-
stance of matter, the example simply illustrates a particular type of generation proper to the elements but otherwise unusual: a generation in
which the preexisting and resulting entities share the same degree of
complexity.

[34] See Joachim 1922, 108.

Elemental transformations differ strikingly from typical constructive generations of the sort I described earlier. Whereas most generations yield a product that is more complex than the material from which it was generated, the elements come to be from one another, and hence from nothing simpler than themselves. In this respect elemental transformations resemble nonsubstantial changes rather than other substantial generations because nonsubstantial changes, too, involve opposed terms (contrary qualities, quantities, or places) that share the same complexity. This similarity may in fact explain why Aristotle dwells on the distinction between alteration and generation in the opening chapters of *On Generation and Corruption*. And the analogy between elemental transformation and alteration is crucial in 1.4 itself. Parts (D) and (E) exploit the similarity between the generation of water from air and the alteration of a man from musical to unmusical, and the point of the exercise is to show that, despite the parallel structure, the two sorts of processes are crucially different. Part (G) should be consistent with the rest of the chapter, and if it is, Aristotle's description of the strict notion of matter specifies those entities whose transformations have been shown to be generations and destructions. And since Aristotle's single nonelemental example (the conversion of the productive seed into the inseminated blood), although matching the structure of elemental change, concerns entities that Aristotle does not regard as matter, the elements alone should be examples of matter in the strictest sense. Remarkably, the description does not even specify the elements in their usual role as ingredients of higher constructs, since, in those typical contexts, the elements are continuants rather than entities "receptive of generation and destruction." Apparently, the elements are matter in the strictest sense because they are the ultimate stuffs that come to be and pass away.

Aristotle may have a special reason to speak of the elements as matter in the strictest (μάλιστα κυρίως) sense. Although the reason is not given in 1.4, I shall argue that the elements are, in the cosmic scheme of things, the ultimate matter in the sublunary realm. Let me contrast my view with one current among some interpreters of Aristotle. There is a widespread conviction that matter is a purely analytical notion, that an entity counts as matter simply in virtue of its role in a particular context.[35] For exam-

[35] See, e.g., Wieland 1970, 209; Leszl 1970, 517–18; and Jones 1974, 494–97. The prevalence of this view was called to my attention by G.E.R. Lloyd and James Lennox. Defenders of the interpretation rely on Aristotle's claim in *Phys.* II.2 that matter is a relative term (πρός τι): "And furthermore, matter is one of the relative terms, because for a different form there is a different matter" (194b8–9). The claim need not imply, however, that matter is a purely analytical notion. Aristotle may simply be saying that different materials are appropriate for different products (cf. Charlton 1970, 97). In the preceding discussion in *Phys.* II.2, Aristotle points out that an artisan makes or prepares his material with a view to the function that it

ple, the analysis of a statue yields bronze as its matter and the shape as its form. If the bronze in its turn is analyzed, the bronze now counts, not as matter, but as a "quasi-substance" whose matter is tin and copper and whose form is some ratio of those ingredients. If the analysis is applied to the elements, something counts as matter and something as form, and scholars disagree about what this ultimate analysis yields. On this view, a particular entity, such as bronze, counts as matter in some contexts but not in others.

Although I agree that Aristotle uses matter and form as analytical tools, I do not agree that matter is merely an analytical notion. To understand some of the central puzzles in Aristotle's metaphysics, it is important to recognize that matter is an *ontological* notion. Many materials can be subjected to hylomorphic analysis, but the composite material does not gain a different ontological status simply because it consists of a simpler matter. Bronze is matter because various artifacts can be made out of it—and it is matter whether or not one of these productions is presently in question, and whether or not its own production and its own matter are presently being discussed. Aristotle sometimes says that an artisan makes the matter that he will use in a higher construction.[36] If the product of a generation can be called "matter," then something called "matter" can be a composite of a simpler matter and form; the generated matter is still matter, even though it is itself a composite. The status of an entity as matter or form is not one that is legislated simply by the context. Just as certain entities are qualities or quantities, so certain entities are matter or form. Matter, form, and nonsubstantial properties differ from one another ontologically because each bears a distinctive relation to the object whose matter, form, or nonsubstantial properties they are. While a nonsubstantial property modifies a substance accidentally because the substance can survive its loss without ceasing to exist, a substantial form determines the essential nature of the entity whose form it is, and its loss entails the destruction of the entity itself.

The important and vexed question that Aristotle addresses in the *Metaphysics* is how matter is related to the entity whose matter it is, and how matter is related to the form of that object. Sometimes he regards the relation between the matter and the composite as comparable to that between a nose and snubness, but sometimes as comparable to that between a nonsubstantial property and the composite it modifies; sometimes he

---

will serve; e.g., the craftsman chooses a particular kind of wood and prepares it for the production of a helm. There is no suggestion that the wood is matter only relative to the helm or that the wood would be a different matter were it used instead for a box. In *Met.* H.4 Aristotle points out that the same materials can often be used for various products, e.g., wood for both a box and a bed (1044ª25–27).

[36] *Phys.* II.2, 194ª33–34; 194ᵇ7–8.

regards the relation between matter and form as comparable to that between a typical substance and a nonsubstance, but sometimes as comparable to that between a genus and a differentia. To appreciate the force of the question and Aristotle's various attempts to answer it, one must be prepared to view matter as more than an analytical notion. It will turn out that entities that count as matter in an ontological sense are uniquely related to the composite whose matter they are and to the form of that object.

Defenders of prime matter will doubtless agree with me that Aristotelian matter is an ontological notion. The great chain of being extends from pure form at the top of the scale to pure matter at the bottom. Prime matter, which lies at the foundation, must be an ontological notion because it accounts for continuity through substantial change. My view is, in a way, remarkably traditional, since I, too, envisage a cosmic scale, at one end of which is pure form and at the other pure matter. But contrary to the traditional conception, the cosmic scheme is grounded not in an indeterminate prime matter but instead in a set of simple and identifiable elements. I shall argue that, unlike other higher materials, which are composites of a simpler matter and form, the elements, though they can be analyzed into matter and form, are, ontologically speaking, *pure matter*: they are not composites of simpler ingredients organized by form. I suggest that in part (G) Aristotle calls the elements matter in the "strictest" sense because they are the ultimate matter in the sublunary sphere.

ELEMENTAL TRANSFORMATION

The Aristotelian cosmos is divided into two parts, one realm extending from the sphere of the moon outward to the sphere of the fixed stars, the other extending downward from the sphere of the moon to the center of the earth. The four elements—earth, water, air, and fire—are confined to the lower region. The heavenly spheres and the celestial bodies within them are constituted out of a fifth element known as aether. Aether and the four sublunary elements obey different physical laws. Aether moves naturally in a circle and, unlike its lower counterparts, is not a source of perishability. The four sublunary elements move naturally in straight lines—fire toward the periphery of the sublunary sphere, earth toward the center, and air upward and water downward to the intermediate regions. The cosmos is a plenum. In the realm above, the heavenly bodies observe their orderly, if complex, march. Below, there is feverish activity.

Presumably, if the affairs of the lower cosmos were unaffected by those of the heavens, the elements would long since have sorted themselves out into layers: all the earth would be settled in a ball at the center and surrounded by all the water, then by all the air, and finally by all the fire.

Even as it is, a large quantity of each element occupies its appropriate region. But the elements can never sort themselves out because the sun's twofold motion—its daily westward rotation with the sphere of the fixed stars and yearly eastward motion along the ecliptic, resulting in longer and shorter days—translates itself down to the sublunary sphere in the elemental change witnessed in seasonal variation.[37] So there is abundant activity. Not only do dislocated elements move toward their proper places, but in the course of their motion they often interact. And their interaction sometimes results in the transformation of one element into another and sometimes in the combining of elements into composite bodies. Such random combinations will not account for the generation of complex bodies of the sort that Aristotle finds most interesting—living organisms—but elemental interaction alone does seem adequate to account for the generation of some composite materials, such as minerals and natural metals, stuffs whose constitution and behavior he studies in his chemical treatise, the *Meteorology*.

On Generation and Corruption treats both the transformation of the elements into one another and their combination into composite uniform materials. Since my present aim is to explain the nature of the elements themselves, I shall focus on elemental transformation. How is such transformation possible? Must the elements themselves be composites of matter and form in order to undergo such transformations? Can Aristotle avoid the difficulty that the first philosophers feared most of all, that the generation will involve the emergence of something out of nothing? Must he, after all, posit a single ultimate substratum to guarantee that the transformation of one element into another is a genuine conversion of the first into the second and not a sheer replacement involving the destruction of the first into nothing and the emergence of the second out of nothing?

Elemental transformation is the one context in which prime matter might be seriously needed, yet Aristotle gives a highly detailed account of the various mechanisms for such transformations and is silent about the role that prime matter is supposed to play. All the work seems to be done by the four contraries.

The Four Mechanisms for Transformation

Each of the four elements has two defining features: earth is cold and dry, water cold and wet, air hot and wet, and fire hot and dry (*G.C.* II.3 330^{b}3–5). Although Aristotle specifies the hot, the cold, the wet, and the dry in various ways, he most frequently calls them "contraries" (ἐναν-τία) and "differentiae" (διαφοραί). He also specifies the features that cor-

---

[37] See *G.C.* II.10, esp. 336^{a}31–^{b}24.

respond in two elements, for example, the wetness of air and water, as "corresponding factors," or "tallies" (σύμβολα).[38] In addition, he calls the contraries "forms" (εἴδη) and "principles" (ἀρχαί) of the elements (II.2, 329^{b}7–10);[39] and in *Parts of Animals* II.1 he calls them "potentialities" (δυνάμεις) and "matter" (ὕλη).[40] Although on one occasion he says that the elements are constituted out of contrary παθήματα ("affections") (*G.C.* II.3, 331^{a}1–3), it may be significant in view of *On Generation and Corruption* I.4 that, in discussing elemental transformation, he avoids calling the contraries πάθη.[41] The contraries are not merely accidental properties of the elements but their differentiating features. Aristotle says that six "yokings" (συζεύξεις), or combinations of contraries, are conceivable but excludes two of the six as impossible: a contrary cannot be yoked with its own contrary, for instance, hot with cold or dry with wet. The four yokes, then, are cold-dry, cold-wet, hot-wet, and hot-dry, and each of the yokes differentiates one sort of element (II.3, 330^{a}30–^{b}7).

In II.4 Aristotle describes four mechanisms for elemental transformation. All four mechanisms are explained with reference to the contraries, but one of the mechanisms is ruled out because it yields an impossible yoke—either contraries contrary to each other, such as hot-cold, or contraries of the same sort, such as hot-hot. Aristotle's rejection of the combination hot-hot, which amounts to a simple hot, suggests that he excludes the possibility that a single contrary on its own could differentiate a body. This exclusion is significant: for some reason he thinks that the contraries must occur in the appropriate combinations and that these combinations must consist of one member of the pair hot/cold and one member of the pair dry/wet. I shall return to this point.

Aristotle concludes II.4 with a summary of what he takes himself to have shown. "So it is at the same time clear that some [elements], changing from one into one, come to be when one item perishes; and that some [elements], changing from two into one, come to be when more items perish. It has been stated, then, that all [the elements] come to be from every [other], and in what way [their] change into one another occurs" (331^{b}35–332^{a}2). There are two fundamental sorts of elemental change, the first a transformation of one element into one other, which occurs when

[38] In common usage σύμβολον refers to each half or corresponding piece of a bone or other object that two individuals who draw up a contract break between them (Liddell, Scott, and Jones 1968, 1676). Each individual keeps his part so that either contractor may on a later occasion have proof of the identity of the person presenting the corresponding piece.

[39] Cf. *P.A.* II.2, 648^{b}2–10.

[40] *P.A.* II.1, 646^{a}15–17; cf. *Meteor.* IV.11, 389^{a}29–31.

[41] When Aristotle regards the hot, the cold, the wet, and the dry as accidental properties of the elements or higher bodies, he frequently calls them πάθη; see, e.g., the treatment of coldness at *G.C.* I.4, 319^{b}21–24, discussed above, p. 58.

one item perishes, the other a transformation of two elements into a third, which occurs when more than one item perishes. Of Aristotle's four mechanisms presented in the body of the chapter, the first two mechanisms describe the transformation of one element into one other, and the last two mechanisms (of which one is impossible) describe the transformation of two elements into a third. To understand Aristotle's theory of the elements, take special note of his claim that, in some elemental changes, one item "perishes" and that in others more than one item "perishes." He will say what items perish, and his answer is revealing.

Aristotle gives a detailed account of the four mechanisms. He characterizes the first mechanism as quick and easy. One element is transformed into another adjacent to it with which it shares a corresponding factor (σύμβολον).

A. QUICK REVERSIBLE CHANGE

For example, air will result from fire when one factor changes (for the one [fire] was hot and dry, and the other [air] is hot and wet, so that air will result when the dry is overpowered [κρατηθῇ] by the wet). Again water will result from air, if the hot is overpowered by the cold (for the one [air] was hot and wet, and the other [water] is cold and wet, so that water will result when the hot changes). And in the same way earth will result from water and fire from earth. For both elements have corresponding factors (σύμβολα) relative to both; for water is wet and cold, and earth is cold and dry, so that earth will result when the wet is overpowered. And again, since fire is dry and hot, and earth is cold and dry, if the cold is overpowered, fire will result from earth. So it is clear that generation for the simple bodies will be in a circle, and that this mode of change is very easy because corresponding factors (σύμβολα) are present in adjacent elements. (331ᵃ26–ᵇ4)

By contrast, the second mechanism is slow and difficult. By this mechanism an element is transformed into another nonadjacent to it (with which it shares no σύμβολον).

B. SLOW REVERSIBLE CHANGE

It is possible for water to come to be from fire and earth from air, and again air and fire from water and earth,[42] but [such transformations] are more difficult because there is a change of more [factors]. For it is necessary, if fire is to result from water, that both the cold

---

[42] This line (331ᵇ5) should be understood chiastically: by the slow mechanism air comes from earth, and fire from water. Cf. Joachim 1922, 221.

and the wet perish, and again, if air is to result from earth, that both the cold and the dry perish; and the situation is similar if water and earth are to result from fire and air, for it is necessary that both [factors] change. This generation is therefore more time-consuming. (331^b4–11)

The third mechanism is easier ($\dot{\rho}\acute{\alpha}\omega\nu$) than the second but not reversible ($o\dot{v}\kappa$ $\epsilon\dot{\iota}\varsigma$ $\check{\alpha}\lambda\lambda\eta\lambda\alpha$).[43] By this mechanism two elements nonadjacent to each other can be transformed into a third.

C. QUICK IRREVERSIBLE CHANGE

But if one [factor] of each [of two elements] perishes, the change is easier ($\dot{\rho}\acute{\alpha}\omega\nu$) but not reversible ($o\dot{v}\kappa$ $\epsilon\dot{\iota}\varsigma$ $\check{\alpha}\lambda\lambda\eta\lambda\alpha$), but from fire and water will result earth or air ($\dot{\epsilon}\kappa$ $\pi\nu\rho\dot{o}\varsigma$ $\mu\dot{\epsilon}\nu$ $\kappa\alpha\dot{\iota}$ $\ddot{\upsilon}\delta\alpha\tau o\varsigma$ $\ddot{\epsilon}\sigma\tau\alpha\iota$ $\gamma\hat{\eta}$ $\kappa\alpha\dot{\iota}$ $\dot{\alpha}\acute{\eta}\rho$),[44] and from air and earth [will result] fire or water. For when the cold of water and the dry of fire perish, there will be air

[43] Translators typically render the phrases $\epsilon\dot{\iota}\varsigma$ $\check{\alpha}\lambda\lambda\eta\lambda\alpha$ (lit., "into one another") and $o\dot{v}\kappa$ $\epsilon\dot{\iota}\varsigma$ $\check{\alpha}\lambda\lambda\eta\lambda\alpha$ ("not into one another") as "reciprocal" and "not reciprocal"; e.g., Joachim (in Barnes 1984) and Forster (1955); Williams (1982) translates "mutual" and "not mutual." It is unclear what these authors intend by their translations. Since the third mechanism differs from the previous two in failing to be $\epsilon\dot{\iota}\varsigma$ $\check{\alpha}\lambda\lambda\eta\lambda\alpha$, the phrase should indicate some significant divergence from the other cases. All three mechanisms involve an element that causes the transformation, and that element presumably suffers a reciprocal reaction. If fire becomes slightly cooler in generating fire from earth, then fire also becomes cooler (and presumably wetter) in generating fire from earth and air (on this reciprocality, see *G.C.* 1.7, 324^a30–$^b13$; cf. *G.A.* IV.3, 768^b15–25). So such reciprocality cannot be the issue. There is, however, a sense in which the first two mechanisms permit the elements to change "into one another" and the third not. If fire acts on air to produce fire, by an analogous process (a quick change) air can act on the newly generated fire to reproduce air. And similarly, if fire acts on water to produce fire, by an analogous process (a slow change) water can act on the fire to reproduce water. In both cases an element of the original sort can be reproduced by a mechanism analogous to that of its own production. But if fire acts on air and earth to generate fire (a case dealt with by the third mechanism), two elements of the original sort cannot be reproduced from the fire by the original process that produced the fire. Although one or the other of the original elements can be reproduced by the first mechanism—air acting on the fire to reproduce air, or earth acting on the fire to reproduce earth—the pair of elements cannot be generated from fire in a single step either by the action of a single element or by the joint action of air and earth. Suppose that air destroys the dryness of fire and the earth its heat; in this case neither feature of the fire is left. Aristotle seems to rule out such simultaneous double destruction in treating the second mechanism (see below). But even if he allowed it, the product would be water, not air and earth. So the difference between the third mechanism and first two turns on the reversibility of the process. I therefore translate $o\dot{v}\kappa$ $\epsilon\dot{\iota}\varsigma$ $\check{\alpha}\lambda\lambda\eta\lambda\alpha$ as "not reversible."

[44] At 331^b13–14 I follow Joachim and Williams in translating the first $\kappa\alpha\dot{\iota}$ as "and" and the second as "or." Cf. Forster 1955, 283. The phrasing is somewhat perplexing because Aristotle uses the same idiom with a different sense to describe the second mechanism (see above, n. 42).

(for the hot of the one [fire] and the wet of the other [water] are left); but when the hot of the fire and the wet of the water [perish], there will be earth because the dry of the one [fire] and the cold of the other [water] are left. And similarly from air and earth [will result] fire or water. For when the hot of the air and the dry of the earth perish, there will be water (for the wet of the one [air] and the cold of the other [earth] are left); but when the wet of the air and the cold of the earth [perish], there will be fire because the hot of the one [air] and the dry of the other [earth]—the features belonging to fire—are left. And the generation of fire is confirmed by sense perception; for flame is most evidently fire, and flame is burning smoke, and smoke is from air and earth. ($331^b12–26$)

Finally, Aristotle mentions a fourth mechanism, the transformation of two adjacent elements into a third. This mechanism he excludes because the outcome would feature either a pair of contraries contrary to each other (an impossible yoke) or two contraries identical with each other.

D. IMPOSSIBLE MECHANISM

In the case of adjacent elements there cannot be a change into any of the bodies, if one [factor] in each of the elements perishes, because either the same or contrary [factors] are left in both; from neither of the alternatives is it possible for a body to come to be. [Thus no body would result] if, for example, the dry of the fire should perish and the wet of the air (for the hot in both is left). But if, on the other hand, the hot of each [should perish], the contraries, dry and wet, are left. And similarly also in the other cases, for the same [factor] and the contrary [factor] are present in all the adjacent elements. ($331^b26–34$)

Aristotle has described four scenarios, the last of which he excludes. First suppose that some displaced air is traveling toward its proper place, the region above water, and en route encounters a large quantity of water. The air is unlikely to reach its destination because it must interact with the water obstructing its passage. Because of the water's greater abundance, the air is apt to be transformed by the water into more water. The obstructing water and the displaced air have one feature in common, wetness (the σύμβολον), and one feature opposed, since the air is hot, the water cold. The air will be unaffected by the water in respect of its wetness, since that is their common feature. But the heat of the air is likely to be "overpowered" by the coldness of the more abundant element, and if this occurs, the air itself will be destroyed. In place of the air there will be something cold and wet: more water.

Aristotle suggests that each element can be transformed into the one adjacent to it by this first easy mechanism: air results from fire, water from air, earth from water, and fire from earth. The transformation is cyclical. Although he describes the cycle as occurring in a single direction, he later indicates that the cycle can also occur in the other direction, for he mentions the emergence of air from water and of fire from air.[45] And it seems reasonable that, just as air obstructed by a larger quantity of water is apt to be transformed into water, so water obstructed by a larger quantity of air is apt to be transformed into air. Apparently, then, by the first mechanism each element can be transformed into either element adjacent to it—fire into air or earth, air into fire or water, and so on—since adjacent elements have one feature in common and one opposed.

Now suppose that some fire traveling upward to its proper place at the periphery encounters a large quantity of water. Fire and water are non-adjacent elements and thus have no features in common, fire being hot and dry, and water cold and wet. The fire is likely to be transformed into water by the larger quantity of water. Aristotle's treatment of this sort of case is especially interesting because a transformation involving elements that share no common features might seem, in particular, to require prime matter to serve as the continuant. But he simply says that this transformation is "more difficult" and "more time-consuming" than the first because there must be a change of more factors. If the fire is to be transformed into water, both the heat and the dryness of the fire must be overpowered and perish, and apparently an attack on both of its features takes longer than an attack on only one. Why should this be so? It is understandable that the overpowering of two features is more difficult than the overpowering of one, but why should Aristotle insist that the overpowering takes *longer*? Why not say that the water destroys both features of the fire at once? Then fire could be transformed into water as quickly as it can be transformed into air. The mechanism would still differ from the first in demanding a double attack, but it would not differ in speed. Did Aristotle think that a double attack was bound to be harder and more time-consuming than a single attack? A comparison with the third mechanism indicates that this factor is not the source of the difficulty.

Suppose that some air and earth coincide on their respective journeys toward their proper places and that their passage is jointly obstructed by a large body of water. This is the sort of situation handled by the third mechanism. The air and earth are likely both to be changed into water. Aristotle describes this situation: "For when the hot of the air and the dry of the earth perish, there will be water (for the wet of the one [air] and

[45] G.C. II. 10, 337ᵃ4–6.

the cold of the other [earth] are left)" (331^{b}19–21). In this situation, as in the previous one, two features are attacked, yet Aristotle describes this mechanism as *easier* (ῥᾷων) than the second case (331^{b}12). The issue of ease or difficulty thus does not turn on the number of features attacked. The distinctive mark of the third situation is that two different elements are attacked in respect of one feature each, while the other feature of each element "is left." The heat of the air and the dryness of the earth perish, but the wetness of the air and the coldness of the earth are left to yield a single new element: water.

The problem in the second situation is that two features of the *same* element must be overpowered, so the mechanism is "more difficult" and the change is "more time-consuming." Now if prime matter is a silent partner in the business of elemental change, as many commentators would like to think, they need to explain why a change of fire into water takes longer than a change of fire into air, and why it takes longer than a change of fire and water together into air. The role of prime matter, after all, is to guarantee that something persists through elemental change. Therefore, if prime matter is doing its job, an element should require no longer to be transformed into an element nonadjacent to it than it requires to be transformed into an element adjacent to it. Just as an apple need take no longer to turn red from green and sweet from sour than to undergo one of those changes alone, so prime matter should need no longer to change from hot and dry to cold and wet than to undergo one of those changes alone.

Aristotle does not mention prime matter. Instead he says that the transformation of one element into another nonadjacent to it is "more difficult" and "more time-consuming" because more factors change. If water is to result from fire, both the heat and dryness of fire must perish. Aristotle is evidently preoccupied with continuity, and the worry is that, if both features of the fire were destroyed simultaneously, nothing would persist. To avoid this consequence he suggests that the change takes more time: first one feature is overpowered, and then the other. If the change occurs in two stages, continuity is preserved because a different factor can "be left" at each stage. For example, the dryness of fire can first be overpowered to yield an interim air, and then the heat can be overpowered finally to yield water; alternatively, the heat of fire can first be overpowered to yield an interim earth, and then the dryness be overpowered to yield water. By either two-stage route water finally emerges from fire, but continuity is preserved because some factor is preserved at each stage. Thus a transformation of fire into water is not a sheer replacement of entities but displays the continuity that all changes must display.

Someone might ask why, if this is Aristotle's theory, he distinguishes the second mechanism from the first, since transformations proper to the second scheme apparently take place by means of two quick changes, one after the other. The answer is that Aristotle has set out to show that each element can come to be from every other.[46] If he used only the first mechanism to explain the transformation of one element into another, he could explain how water comes to be from air or earth, the elements adjacent to it, but not how it comes to be from fire, the element nonadjacent to it. The transformation between nonadjacent elements is not simply two quick changes, because two quick changes would be caused by two distinct elements operating one after the other. Instead, a slow change is caused by a single element that operates first in respect of one of its features and then in respect of the other. For example, by two quick changes water could emerge from fire. First, some air acting in respect of its wetness must transform the fire into air; second, some water acting in respect of its coldness must transform the newly generated air into water. By a slow change, on the other hand, an agent water can act directly on the original fire to generate more water by acting first in respect of its wetness (to produce an interim air) and then in respect of its coldness to yield water as the final product.

The earlier analysis of *On Generation and Corruption* 1.4 gave no reason to expect Aristotle to appeal to prime matter in his account of elemental change. He said there that a generation takes place when a whole changes, when something perceptible does not remain as the same ὑποκείμενον. And his account of the actual mechanics of elemental change bears out the original promise. One ὑποκείμενον, such as air, is transformed into a different ὑποκείμενον, such as water, the first ὑποκείμενον giving way to the second. The later discussion characterizes the transformations in greater detail by explaining that each of the ὑποκείμενα consists of two intrinsic features and that every kind of elemental change demands the persistence of one of those features. Even the problematic transformation of one element into another nonadjacent to it meets the requirement. Aristotle insists that this change requires more time to allow one feature to be destroyed and then the other and to ensure that some feature survives through each stage.

The Status of the Contraries

What is the status of the contraries in *On Generation and Corruption* II.4? Has Aristotle reified the contraries by allowing them, as one scholar colorfully puts it, "to fall upon one another in the good old hostile Presocratic way"?[47] If he ignores prime matter, is he guilty of such reifi-

[46] See G.C. II.4, 331ᵃ11–23; cf. 331ᵇ36–332ᵃ2.
[47] Solmsen 1958, 252.

cation?[48] Certainly Aristotle uses vivid language suited to the description of a battlefield when he says that one contrary "is overpowered" ($\kappa\rho\alpha\tau\eta\theta\tilde{\eta}$) by another and "perishes" ($\phi\theta\alpha\rho\tilde{\eta}$), while another contrary "is left standing" ($\lambda\varepsilon\acute{\iota}\pi\varepsilon\tau\alpha\iota$). His suggestion that the contraries perish is surprising. At the outset of his discussion in II.1, he plainly states that the elements change into one another ($\tau\alpha\tilde{\upsilon}\tau\alpha$ $\mu\grave{\varepsilon}\nu$ $\gamma\grave{\alpha}\rho$ $\mu\varepsilon\tau\alpha\beta\acute{\alpha}\lambda\lambda\varepsilon\iota$ $\varepsilon\acute{\iota}\varsigma$ $\check{\alpha}\lambda\lambda\eta\lambda\alpha$) but the contraries do not ($\alpha\acute{\iota}$ δ' $\grave{\varepsilon}\nu\alpha\nu\tau\iota\acute{\omega}\sigma\varepsilon\iota\varsigma$ $o\grave{\upsilon}$ $\mu\varepsilon\tau\alpha\beta\acute{\alpha}\lambda\lambda o\upsilon\sigma\iota\nu$) (329^{a}35–^{b}3). If the contraries do not change into one another but nevertheless perish, has Aristotle finally fallen prey to the very consequence that he has tried so hard to avoid, the destruction of something into nothing? Surely this is exactly the outcome if he has reified the contraries.

Stranger still, Aristotle had a perfectly viable alternative of which he was surely aware. *On Generation and Corruption* II.4 echoes an earlier discussion. Aristotle's topic and even his metaphors call to mind the battle of opposites in Plato's *Phaedo*, and Aristotle's metaphors in fact suggest that his own theory is cast in the light of Plato's discussion. Aristotle can scarcely have forgotten that Plato offered two alternatives to account for what happens when an opposite is attacked by its own opposite: if heat advances on a body's coldness, either the coldness is destroyed or it "retreats" and "gets out of the way."[49] Aristotle could certainly have adopted the second alternative. He could have claimed that, when water emerges from air, the heat, whose loss accounts for the destruction of air, itself "retreats" and enters into a new combination—for instance, with the dry. Thus every elemental change effected would entail a second simultaneous and subsidiary change. The elements themselves would keep changing, and there might sometimes be more of one, sometimes more of another, but the elemental contraries themselves would persist intact and keep recombining.[50]

Aristotle could have told such a story, but he does not. He adopts Plato's other alternative. The contraries do not retreat but perish when attacked by their opposite. So either Aristotle has made an unfortunate and quite unnecessary mistake, or he does not hypostasize the contraries. It should be evident which interpretation to prefer. When he says that the heat of air perishes, he means that something ceases to be hot. In fact, since heat is a defining feature of the air, the ceasing of air to be hot is a destruction of air. Air cannot withstand the loss of an intrinsic feature, so the loss of such a feature entails the destruction of the entity itself; the air is destroyed and in its place is something else, namely, water, which is

[48] Some writers have supposed that Aristotle reifies the contraries. See King 1956, 378; and Furth 1988, 221–27. For objections, see Robinson 1974, 183; and Scaltsas 1985, 217–18, 235 n. 14.

[49] *Phaedo* 102a10–107b10.

[50] For a view along these lines, see Furth 1988, 221–27.

wet as the air was but also cold. At any point during the process there is some subject to which the wetness belongs—first to the air and then to the water.

This is precisely the idea that the friends of prime matter find unacceptable. Is the proposal that the elements are made out of properties? Must there not be some stuff for those properties to inform in order to yield the elemental bodies? Such questions, however, rest on a misconception.

The Nature of the Elements

The questions are misconceived because Aristotle treats the elements as the ultimate ingredients out of which all bodies of greater complexity in the sublunary realm are composed. We are not entitled to ask out of what further ingredients the elements themselves are composed because there are no simpler ingredients. Unlike higher material bodies, which are composed out of the elements and so can be analyzed into the elements as their matter, the elements themselves are not composed out of any simpler stuffs and so cannot be similarly analyzed. This immunity from further division is the reason why Aristotle claims that the elements are generated from one another.[51] The elements must come to be from one another because, unlike all other generated things, there is nothing simpler from which they can be produced. Although the elements are not composed out of simpler matter, they can nonetheless be analyzed to determine what survives an elemental transformation and what is replaced. So one can specify a factor corresponding to the form and a factor corresponding to the matter of an element. But elemental matter is not an ingredient, and elemental form is not an arrangement or structure imposed on an ingredient. In fact, as we shall see, the decision about what counts as the form and the matter of an element is flexible and depends entirely upon the particular elemental transformation that is being described.

The fundamental mistake is to suppose that Aristotle must construct the elements out of more basic ingredients. To be sure, the mistake has some rationale because he does construct higher bodies out of the elements by means of such processes as combination ($\mu\iota\xi\iota\varsigma$). But he is firm in his insistence that the elements are not constructed, that they come to be from one another and not from a simpler body. He demonstrates the existence of elements by arguing that there must be ultimate ingredients out of which the higher bodies are composed. He argues *down* to the sim-

[51] With G.C. I.3 (references cited above, n. 3), cf. De Cae. III.6, 305ᵃ14–32.

ple bodies. He does not start at the bottom, armed with a metaphysical stuff and a set of Presocratic powers, and try to construct them.

I am therefore not proposing that Aristotle constructs the elements out of properties. That would be peculiar—though no more peculiar, perhaps, than what the tradition itself proposes. The elements are not constructed out of simpler ingredients. Instead, Aristotle takes for granted that there are physical objects and undertakes to explain their behavior. Since part of that explanation demands that there be ultimate ingredients, he argues that there are elements from which higher bodies are constructed. Let us now consider his argument for the existence of elements and what he means when he speaks of their matter and form.

The Simple Bodies

Aristotle defines a bodily element in *De Caelo* III.3. An element is that into which other things can be divided by some physical process but which cannot itself be further divided by an analogous process. For example, some physical operation can be performed on wood to extract its elemental ingredients; if burned, wood will yield ash (a form of earth) and burning smoke (a combination of fire and air).[52] Thus the elemental constituents of wood—earth and air—can be extracted from the wood by a physical process. The elements are simple bodies because no physical procedure will extract simpler ingredients from them. Aristotle offers this account of a bodily element:

> Let an element of bodies be that into which the other bodies are divided (διαιρεῖται), which is present in (ἐνυπάρχον) [the other bodies] either potentially or actually (for in which way this occurs is still disputable), and which is itself indivisible (ἀδιαίρετον) into [bodies] different in form (τῷ εἴδει). . . . If our statement [identifies] an element, there must be bodily elements. For in flesh and wood and each thing of this sort, fire and earth are potentially present. For if these [fire and earth] are separated out (ἐκκρινόμενα) of those [flesh and wood], they [fire and earth] are apparent. But neither flesh nor wood is present in fire, either potentially or actually; for [if it were] it could be separated out (ἐξεκρίνετο). (302ª15–25)

[52] The chemistry of smoke (καπνός) is somewhat obscure. In *G.C.* II.4 (331ᵇ25–26) Aristotle calls flame "burning smoke" and identifies it as a form of fire that results from the transformation of the two elements earth and air. But in *Meteor.* IV.9 (388ª2–3) he regards smoke as a combination of fire and air produced by reducing wood, which is a combustible compound of earth and air (*Meteor.* IV.7, 384ᵇ15–17; IV.10, 388ª32), into its elemental ingredients. Fire, as well as earth and air, results from this reduction because fire, in causing the combustion, transfers its own features to the material acted upon.

Aristotle evidently envisages a physical operation of separation. Fire and earth are potentially present in flesh and wood because they can be separated out and be made "apparent." This sort of physical process comes to a halt with earth, water, air, and fire, since no further ingredients can be extracted. The elements cannot be divided into simpler bodies because they are themselves the simplest bodies.

Aristotle distinguishes simple bodies from composites but calls all of the former and some of the latter natural bodies. In *De Caelo* I.2 he calls a body "natural" that can move locally in space in virtue of its own nature (καθ' αὑτό), and he identifies the nature of such bodies as their principle of motion (κινήσεως ἀρχὴν εἶναί φαμεν αὐτοῖς) (268ᵇ14–16).[53] He divides the class of natural bodies into two groups.

> Since among bodies some are simples (ἁπλᾶ) and some are compounds (σύνθετα) from these (by simples I mean those bodies that have a principle of motion in accordance with nature, for example, fire and earth and the forms of these[54] and the other kinds like them), so too the motions must be in some cases simple and in other cases somehow combined (μικτάς), and the motions of the simple bodies are simple and the motions of the compound bodies combined, even though [a compound] is moved according to the prevailing [elemental constituent]. (268ᵇ26–269ᵃ2)

The elements are not composites.[55] If they were, simpler bodies could be extracted from them, and they would be generated out of the simpler bodies. And if there were simpler bodies, these bodies, to be bodies at all, would have to engage in simple motions. Yet there are only three sorts of simple motions—toward the center, away from the center, and around the center. Two of the sublunary elements move toward the center, two sublunary elements away from the center, and aether around. There can be no simpler bodies because there are no simpler motions;[56] and since there are no simpler bodies, the elements are not composites. They are simple. Or, to put the point as I did earlier, they are *pure matter*.

Composite bodies consist of both matter and form, the form organizing simpler ingredients to yield a complex body whose nature differs from that of the ingredients. But at the bottom there are no simpler ingredients than the elements themselves. The elements are constituents of other things but are not themselves the products of such composition.

---

[53] Cf. *Phys.* II.1, 192ᵇ8–23.

[54] On the various forms of the elements (e.g., boiling, frozen), see *G.C.* II.3, 330ᵇ21–30.

[55] Cf. *De Cae.* I.5, 271ᵇ17–18. This point is stressed by King (1956, 373, 377) but has gained little currency, perhaps because of the harsh criticism his paper received from Solmsen (1958, see esp. 245).

[56] See *De Cae.* I.2, 268ᵇ14–26; cf. III.6, 305ᵃ22–31.

Accordingly, it is peculiar to speak of their matter and form. As I have indicated, Aristotle often specifies matter as something from which other things are generated and that survives in the product,[57] a specification that captures the elements as the preexisting matter for, and constituent matter of, complex bodies (as well as other higher materials in relation to yet higher composites) but that simply does not apply to the elements as that from which they are themselves generated. Unlike typical generations, which involve the persistence of the simpler ingredient from which the product is generated, the air from which water is generated is irrevocably lost. The air does not persist as an ingredient of the water. Although air can be regenerated from the water, such regeneration is comparable to turning a sword into a plowshare, not to reducing a sword to bronze. The important difference between the ordinary situation and the elemental is that the item preserved in the elemental context is not an ingredient but a feature that differentiates the element destroyed and the one generated.

Elemental "Matter" and "Form"

On Generation and Corruption II.2 identifies the hot, the cold, the wet, and the dry as the principles (ἀρχαί) and forms (εἴδη) of perceptible body. These properties ultimately account for a body's tangibility. Aristotle goes on to characterize the pair hot/cold as active (ποιητικά) and the pair dry/wet as passive (παθητικά) (329^b24–26). These pairs of properties explain a body's capacity to act on other things and to be affected by other things. Having stressed that the four elements must each be active and passive in order to interact (329^b22–24), Aristotle proceeds in II.2 to characterize each of the active and passive capacities and to show how various other properties, such as the fine and the coarse, derive from the basic pair of passive properties, the wet and the dry. He gives a useful summary in *Meteorology* IV.1.

> We have distinguished the four causes (αἴτια) of the elements and the four elements resulting from the yokes (συζυγίας) of these. Of these [causes] two are active, the hot and the cold, and two are passive, the dry and the wet. This is confirmed by induction. For in all cases heat and coldness appear to determine, unite, and change both things alike in kind and things unlike, and to moisten and dry and harden and soften [them]. But things that are dry and wet are determinable and suffer the other affections just enumerated, both things that are simply [dry or wet] and compound bodies consisting of both [dry and wet]. Furthermore, the fact is clear from the formulas by which we define the natures of these factors; for we specify the hot

[57] See above, p. 63, and references cited in n. 33.

and the cold as active (for to cause combination is as it were what it is to be active), and [we call] the wet and the dry passive (for in virtue of its being affected in a certain way, a thing is called "easy to determine" or "difficult to determine"). (378^{b}10–25)

Equipped with this useful distinction between hot and cold as active determinants and dry and wet as passive determinables, Aristotle goes on in *Meteorology* IV to explain the constitution and dispositional properties of various uniform stuffs, such as metals, minerals, and assorted liquids. The constitution and behavior of these materials—their solidification, breakability, combustibility, and so on—are ultimately due to the action of hot and cold and the response of wet and dry.

Each of the four elements is characterized by one active and one passive feature, and presumably because actual tangibility depends upon both sorts of factors, Aristotle rules out the fourth mechanism for elemental change that would yield something characterized as simply hot-hot. Presumably he excludes the two yokes hot-cold and dry-wet for two reasons. First, tangibility demands features of both sorts (temperature and humidity), and second, a body cannot be differentiated by incompatible essential properties.[58] He uses the vivid metaphor of a yoke, which in Greek calls to mind a pair of well-matched animals or a married couple, to indicate that two complementary factors jointly define a particular element. Since no body can be essentially characterized by features that exclude each other, only four yokes are possible, and each pair includes an active determinant (hot or cold) and a passive determinable (dry or wet). When Aristotle discusses the composition of compound bodies, he regards the two cold elements, earth and water, as basically passive, and he sometimes suggests that, in a way, coldness belongs on the passive side because it is a defining property of these two elements.[59] Since they are preeminently passive, earth and water are the main ingredients of physical bodies in the sublunary realm; and heat is the principal source of material change. Both in the *Meteorology* and in the biological works, Aristotle is quite consistent in treating heat as an active principle and dry and wet as passive principles. The cold is sometimes treated as an active principle and sometimes as the mere absence of heat.

It is striking, then, that in the account of elemental transformation, the hot, the cold, the wet, and the dry seem to disregard their standard roles. Each element can act on every other, and each can be acted upon by every other. If some fire transforms some earth into fire, the fire acts in virtue

[58] Cf. Aristotle's criticism of Anaximander at *G.C.* II.5, 332^{a}20–26, and the discussion of this passage below in the Appendix.

[59] See *Meteor.* IV.5, 382^{b}5–7; IV.11, 389^{a}29–32. Coldness can be regarded as passive when it is treated as the absence of heat; see, e.g., *Meteor.* IV.2, 380^{a}7–8.

of its heat, and the earth suffers in respect of its coldness; but if the fire transforms some air into fire, the fire acts in virtue of its dryness, and the air suffers in respect of its wetness. And if some air transforms the fire into air, the fire suffers in respect of its dryness; and if some earth transforms the fire into earth, the fire suffers in respect of its heat. Furthermore, each of the four contraries can be either the feature exchanged or the one that persists. In the elemental context, as in every other context of change, Aristotle treats certain items as active or passive, replaced or persisting. But the contraries, which observe their distinctive roles in higher contexts, are in the elemental context active or passive, replaced or persisting as the situation demands.

Aristotle can speak of items as "matter" or "form" in the elemental context to mark the role that an entity plays in a particular change. He can call the item that persists "matter," and the item that results from the replacement "form." As I have indicated, however, the treatment of one contrary as matter and another as form depends on the transformation that is being described. He avoids explicit mention of matter and form in the actual account of elemental change, but he does speak of elemental matter in the preface to that discussion in *On Generation and Corruption* II.1 and in his summary in II.5, and these passages have fueled the defense of prime matter. Yet, even if one rejects the traditional view, it comes as no surprise that Aristotle speaks of elemental matter, since he indicated early on, in the key passage quoted from *On Generation and Corruption* I.2, that subjects (ὑποκείμενα) that undergo generation and destruction have features corresponding to form and matter. Still, some defenders of the traditional position will doubtless remain unpersuaded that Aristotle can do without prime matter, and since they might appeal to these passages as the final authority for their view, I show in the Appendix how these texts can be accommodated within the present account.

The four elements—earth, water, air, and fire—are the simple bodies, and each is identified as what it is by a pair of contraries. Aristotle says that two contraries are yoked together, using this metaphor to indicate that the two contraries jointly define a particular element. Although the elements have two defining features, they are not composites, since they are not composed of simpler ingredients. They are pure matter, and as such, they can justly be called matter in the strictest (μάλιστα κυρίως) sense. The cosmic scale resembles the traditional scheme: crowned by pure form, the scale is rooted in pure matter. The pure matter, however, is the elements themselves. These simple materials come to be from, and pass away into, one another, and they also serve as the ultimate ingredients out of which composite bodies are generated.

82

CHAPTER THREE

GENERATION

Let me review the argument so far and indicate its further direction. I argued in chapter 1 that Aristotle refines the criteria for subjecthood. After opening the investigation in *Metaphysics* Z.3 with the view familiar from the *Categories*—that a subject is that of which other things are predicated but which is not itself predicated of anything else—he objects that the notion is unclear and demonstrates that, unless certain constraints are placed on the subject criterion, the doctrine leads to incoherence; for unless the condition is clarified, the subject might be nothing at all. To avoid this outcome Aristotle insists that a legitimate subject must be separate and a τόδε τι. Forms and composites satisfy the revised criterion in different ways: a form is separate in account because there is no distinct subject of which it is predicated that must be mentioned in its defining account, and it is τόδε τι because it is a determinate kind; a composite is simply separate because it grounds nonsubstantial properties but does not depend for its own existence on the entities it grounds, and it is τόδε τι because it is a particular of some definite kind. By demanding separation and thisness—provisions tailored especially to the form and the composite—Aristotle aims to show that the form and the composite have stronger credentials to be substance as subjects than matter does.

But even in Z.3 Aristotle expresses reservations about matter, and his theory of ultimate matter, which was explored in chapter 2, suggests that his qualms are well founded. The four elements are the ultimate matter in the sublunary realm because, while they can be extracted from bodies of greater complexity, no simpler body can be extracted from them. Moreover, they seem to be proper subjects. They satisfy the unrevised subject criterion because other things, including nonsubstantial properties and the species and genera that classify the elements, are predicated of them, but they are not themselves predicated of anything else. Furthermore, as we shall see in this chapter, Aristotle's theory of substantial generation suggests that, when a composite body is generated out of the elements, the form of that higher body is predicated of the simpler matter. As I indicated at the end of chapter 1, in such a view the elements pose problems both for the substantiality of forms as subjects and for the substantiality of composites as unities.

Not only do the elements satisfy the unrevised subject criterion; they seem also to satisfy the revised criterion by being separate and τόδε τι.

Since portions of the elements can exist on their own when uncombined, the elements are simply separate in this state. Since everything in the sublunary realm is made out of the elements, all material composites—and their substantial forms—apparently depend for their existence on the elements, while the elements, which can exist apart from these complex wholes, have no comparable need for the higher entities. Furthermore, each element has a definite identity determined, on the one hand, by a yoke of differentiating features and, on the other, by its special nature (φύσις), which enables it to move upward or downward to its proper place.[1]

One might question whether the elements are proper particulars deserving to be called τόδε τι, since they are masslike stuffs devoid of internal structure.[2] But Aristotle treats them as thises in his discussion of elemental generation in the opening chapters of *On Generation and Corruption*,[3] and he seems to regard the mass of a single element, which is discontinuous with others of the same type, as a particular. In *Topics* I.7, for example, he claims that two drafts of water from the same well, though strikingly similar, are the same only in species (103ª14-23).[4] The two drafts are distinct individuals because they are discontinuous with each other.[5] Each draft is itself one because of its own continuity. The mass of a single element has, in fact, a special claim to unity because, according to *Metaphysics* I.1, any naturally continuous body is one, and the unity is greater for those bodies whose motion is indivisible and simple (1052ª15–21). The mass of a single element is apparently a unity because its motion is simple and cannot be divided into simpler motions.[6]

The elements thus seem to be separate and τόδε τι, at least in their uncombined state. Aristotle also treats higher materials as τόδε τι. Although commentators suggest that a material regarded as τόδε τι is not

---

[1] See *De Cae.* I.2, 268ᵇ14–269ª2; *Phys.* II.1, 192ᵇ8–15.

[2] Some writers have attributed to Aristotle a distinction between proper individuals (composites), specified by count nouns, and stuffs (matter), specified by mass terms. Laycock (1972, 7–8) and Jones (1974, 482–83) argue that stuffs are not thises; Chappell (1973, esp. 685–96) argues that stuffs are not separable from composites. But I agree with Dancy (1978, 399–403) that Aristotle's doctrine of separation and thisness is independent of the distinction between countable individuals and measurable stuffs.

[3] See *G.C.* I.3, 318ª35–ᵇ18; and 318ᵇ33–319ª17. It makes sense that Aristotle should treat the elements as definite individuals when he discusses their own generation and destruction. Dancy (1978, 401–2) cites *Met.* B.5, 1001ᵇ31–33, which, though a dialectical passage, clearly implies that the elements are τόδε τι.

[4] On Aristotle's various notions of sameness, see White 1971.

[5] On discontinuity as a means of distinguishing individuals, see *Met.* Δ.6, 1015ᵇ36–1016ª17 and 1017ª3–4; and Charlton 1972, 240–42. Cf. *Phys.* V.4 on the individuation of changes; as I understand the argument, Aristotle distinguishes changes of the same sort experienced by the same individual by the discontinuity in time (see Gill 1984, 14–21).

[6] See *De Cae.* I.2, 268ᵇ14–269ª2.

regarded as matter, the evidence shows, on the contrary, that, even while regarding an entity as matter, Aristotle is prepared to call it τόδε τι.[7] I pointed out in chapter 1 that in *Metaphysics* Θ.7 he speaks of this wood (τοδὶ τὸ ξύλον) as the matter (ὕλη) of a particular box (1049ᵃ24). In *Metaphysics* Δ.2 he states a parallel between artifacts and matter, saying that one can speak both of this statue, of a statue, or of image generally, and of this bronze (χαλκοῦ τοῦδε), of bronze, and of matter generally (ὅλως ὕλης) (1014ᵃ11–12). He repeats the parallel in his discussion of causes in *Physics* II.3, 195ᵇ7–9. Evidently, he sees no problem in specifying a stuff both as "matter" and as a "this."

The central problem to which my argument is leading is the status of generated composites. Do they succeed as genuine definable substances or not? The answer to this question depends upon how one regards the matter that constitutes a composite. In typical generations a composite emerges from simpler matter—for example, a statue from bronze, bronze from tin and copper, and tin and copper from earth and water. These generations resemble elemental transformations to the extent that both processes yield a product from a definite and particular matter. But the generation of most composites differs from that of the elements because, unlike the elements, which are generated from one another rather than from a simpler stuff, typical composites emerge from a simpler entity that survives in the outcome. Recall Aristotle's standard description of matter as "that from which (ἐξ οὗ) a product is generated that is present in (ἐνυπάρχοντος) the product."[8] A sculptor makes a statue out of bronze, and the bronze survives in the product. The critical question, whose answer decides the status of composites, is the nature of that material presence. If the preexisting matter persists in the product as the same particular stuff, then the generated composite fails to be a definable unity because, in specifying what the composite is, two distinct items need to be mentioned—the form that identifies the composite, and the matter in which the form is realized.

This chapter continues to set the scene for the central act, whose crux—the unity of material composites—will be the topic of chapter 4. The problem of composite unity becomes clear from examining the role of matter in generation. I shall begin with a passage in *Metaphysics* H.1 in which Aristotle argues that matter is substance. As I interpret the argument, Aristotle defends the substantiality of matter by appeal to its status in substantial generation, a context in which the preexisting matter has a nature in its own right. The argument is important both in showing that Aristotle regards matter, in certain contexts at least, as an actual

---

[7] Dancy (1978, 401–3) calls attention to this point.

[8] See above, p. 63, and references in n. 33.

this and in raising the critical question about the status of the matter that survives within the generated object. For if the preexisting matter from which a product emerges is τόδε τι, and if the matter remains "present in" the product, what is the status of that constituent matter, and how does that status affect the unity of the object whose matter it is? Next I shall discuss the general account of generation to show the main respects in which typical generations diverge from nonsubstantial changes. Substantial and nonsubstantial changes differ in structure, and Aristotle uses different models to describe the processes. The model for nonsubstantial change is familiar and is commonly called the "replacement model"; the model for substantial generation and destruction, which has received less attention, I call the "construction model."

Having delineated the main differences between the two models, I shall turn to *Physics* I.7, which is the centerpiece of most treatments of Aristotle's theory of change. *Physics* I.7 is fundamental both for the theory of change and for the theory of potentiality and actuality, which will be discussed in chapter 6. Contrary to some assessments, however, the importance of *Physics* I.7 lies, not in its account of the replacement model (an assumption that has led some scholars to overlook the difference between substantial changes and other processes), but in its account of the principles required for all changes. All changes involve three principles—form, privation, and subject—but different changes are described by different models. I shall end with a discussion of material persistence. First, then, the argument that matter is substance.

MATTER AS SUBSTANCE

There is a common assumption that, for Aristotle, matter as such is merely potential, and the assumption is supposed to be justified by the various passages in which he says that matter is τόδε τι in potentiality,[9] and that the matter of a thing is its potentiality both to be and not to be.[10] The central text that supports this assumption is *Metaphysics* H.1. In this chapter Aristotle returns to the subject criterion of Z.3, again claims that the subject is substance, and again lists the three candidates that seem to be substance as subjects—the matter, the form, and the composite of both—but this time he ranks the three contenders in terms of thisness and separation. There is no question but that matter comes third. While both the form and the composite have good credentials because each in its own

[9] *Met.* H.1, 1042ᵃ27–28; *De An.* II.1, 412ᵃ6–11. If one accepts (as I do not) Jaeger's (1957, 245) conjectured δυνάμει at *Met.* Λ.3, 1070ᵃ10, this text might also be cited; read as it stands, the text refers to matter as a "τόδε τι in appearance."

[10] *Met.* Z.7, 1032ᵃ20–22; Z.15, 1039ᵇ27–31; Θ.8, 1050ᵇ8–28, G.C. II.9, 335ᵃ32–33; *De Cae.* I.12, 283ᵇ3–5.

way is a separate this,[11] matter is said to be not actually but merely potentially τόδε τι (1042ᵃ26–28). This claim has encouraged the belief that
matter as such cannot be actually τόδε τι.

For two reasons Aristotle's statement is unlikely to have the force that
has traditionally been assigned to it. First, as I pointed out earlier, various
passages indicate that he recognizes materials as both matter and τόδε τι.
Second, in *Metaphysics* H.1, the very chapter in which he denies that matter is actually τόδε τι, he goes on to argue that matter too is substance,
defending his conclusion by appeal to a context in which matter is actually τόδε τι, namely, substantial generation. If the chapter is consistent,
Aristotle must be making two kinds of claims when he first denies that
matter is actually τόδε τι and later uses its actual thisness in a particular
context as evidence for its claim to substantiality.

Aristotle's argument for the substantiality of matter has been widely
misunderstood for the simple reason that, given his earlier denial that
matter is actually τόδε τι, commentators are unwilling to admit that,
immediately afterward, he recognizes matter as actually τόδε τι. But that
is precisely what he does, arguing as follows:

> That matter too is substance is clear. For in all the opposite changes
> there is some subject (ὑποκείμενον) for the changes, for instance, in
> respect of place what is now (νῦν μέν) here and again (πάλιν δέ)
> elsewhere, and in respect of growth what is now (νῦν μέν) so big
> and again (πάλιν δέ) smaller or greater, and in respect of alteration
> what is now (νῦν μέν) healthy and again (πάλιν δέ) sick. And simi-
> larly in respect of substance what is now (νῦν μέν) in generation and
> again (πάλιν δέ) in destruction, and now (νῦν μέν) a subject as τόδε
> τι and again (πάλιν δέ) a subject as deprived (ὡς κατὰ στέρησιν).
> (1042ᵃ32–ᵇ3)

To show that matter too is substance, Aristotle presents four contrasts,
each concerning one of his four sorts of changes: locomotion, growth
and diminution, alteration, and generation and destruction. In all four
situations there is a subject that undergoes the change. He concludes the
survey with a final contrast, saying that in one situation the subject is τόδε
τι, and in another situation deprived. On my view, Aristotle claims that
the subject in generation is τόδε τι and the subject in destruction deprived, but most commentators do not agree.[12]

W. D. Ross offers an interpretation that has met with general ap-

---

[11] I take the καί ("and" or "also") in καὶ χωριστὸν ἁπλῶς ("also simply separate") at 1042ᵃ30
to indicate that, in addition to being τόδε τι (mentioned already in connection with the
matter and the form), the composite is also simply separate.

[12] Charlton (1970, 131–32) is an exception, though the details of our interpretations differ.

proval.[13] According to Ross, the final contrast refers back only to the fourth case concerning generation and destruction, and the contrast applies chiastically. Thus Ross allows the subject in destruction to be τόδε τι, while barring the title to the subject in generation. Ross explains, "What underlies or undergoes destruction is matter qualified by a positive form, i.e., a τόδε τι; what underlies generation is matter qualified by a privation."[14] Ross may have in mind the production of a statue. If a sculptor produces a statue from a lump of bronze, the lump of bronze—which is used in the generation—is a subject deprived of the shape of the statue; but if someone destroys the statue, the statue—which is destroyed—is a τόδε τι because it is identified by the shape of the statue.

This reading ignores the force of Aristotle's syntax. Aristotle lists four oppositions and then concludes with a final contrast, marking the oppositions not with the usual μέν . . . δέ construction but with a stronger and more unusual construction: νῦν μέν . . . πάλιν δέ ("and now . . . but again"). Since the final contrast employs the same syntax, the parallel construction suggests that the "subject as this" specifies either the last or all the subjects of the preceding νῦν μέν clauses, and the "subject as deprived" either the last or all the subjects of the preceding πάλιν δέ clauses. If the parallel construction is taken seriously, Aristotle claims that "what is now in generation" is a "subject as τόδε τι." Had he intended the final contrast to apply chiastically to the final case, he could certainly have varied the syntax on the fifth occasion.

Ross's reading also yields an inadequate argument for Aristotle's claim that matter is substance (1042ᵃ32), since the entity that succeeds as a this, which Ross identifies as the matter for destruction, is in fact a typical composite, such as a statue. Genuine matter, the matter for generation, is merely a subject deprived. Why should such a subject have a proper claim to be substance? The proposal is in any case excluded by a claim in *Metaphysics* H.5. Here Aristotle expressly denies that a composite destroyed is the matter for its own destruction and says that, although vinegar comes to be from wine when wine is destroyed, wine is neither the matter for vinegar nor potentially vinegar (1044ᵇ34–35). Not wine, but water, which was the matter for wine, is the matter for vinegar (1045ᵃ2). So Ross's version cannot be right.

Aristotle repeats his syntactic construction five times, saying that a subject is now here and again elsewhere, now so big and again larger or smaller, now healthy and again sick. These are the three sorts of nonsubstantial changes involving a subject that alters in its accidental properties.

---

[13] See Ross 1924, 2:227. The view is endorsed by the London Seminar (see Burnyeat et al. 1984, 2); for reservations, see Furth 1985, 126–27.

[14] Ross 1924, 2:227.

He describes the fourth case as "what is now in generation and again in destruction" and draws the conclusion, "and now a subject as τόδε τι and again a subject as deprived." The final contrast does apply only to the fourth case, as Ross claimed, but the parallel syntax five times repeated makes clear that the application is not chiastic. Matter that is turned into something else has its own proper identity; it is τόδε τι in virtue of what it actually is, apart from what it becomes. Aristotle says in H. 5 that wine comes to be from simple water (1045ᵃ6). The simple water, prior to the generation, is a separately existing stuff with its own distinctive nature. Thus, the matter from which the wine is generated is actually τόδε τι. Matter in contexts of destruction, on the other hand, is not a separate entity but a component of the composite destroyed. According to H. 5, although wine is destroyed into vinegar, it is not the matter of vinegar. Instead, the water that was the matter of wine is also the matter of vinegar. Thus, the water, which was a separately existing entity from which the wine was generated (and so was an actual τόδε τι), is merely a material component of wine when the wine is destroyed. Since the matter engaged in the destruction of wine is simply a material component, and since the destruction deprives that material component of the form responsible for the wine, the subject in contexts of destruction (the material component) is a subject deprived. Therefore, it is not the matter in contexts of destruction that legitimates the claim that matter is substance because that matter is merely a subject deprived. Aristotle's claim that matter too is substance is sustained by the matter in contexts of generation. Because matter in generation is actually τόδε τι, Aristotle says at the outset "that matter too is substance is *clear*."

When Aristotle says earlier in H. 1 that matter is not actually but merely potentially τόδε τι, he focuses on matter that can be turned into a particular product and considers it in relation to that product. Thus, the water that can be turned into wine, although actually water, is potentially but not actually wine. The passage at the end of H. 1 accords with the earlier text because the claim that matter is actually τόδε τι does not concern the relation of matter to a higher complex: the matter is *potentially this*. Instead the claim concerns what the matter is in itself, and it is *actually this*.

The crucial question, whose answer determines the status of composites, is whether the matter that has been made into the product is still actually the stuff that it was before the generation occurred. Note that this question is not affected by Aristotle's claim that the matter in destruction is a subject deprived, for destruction deprives the matter of the form of the higher composite. The question I am asking concerns what the matter is in itself. When a statue is made out of bronze, is the stuff that constitutes the statue, which before the production was actually bronze, still actually bronze? In *Metaphysics* Z and H Aristotle assumes that it is and, on that assumption, denies that composites are definable unities. In *Metaphysics* Θ, on the other hand, and in many of his works on natural philosophy, he assumes that the constituent matter is no longer actually what it was before the production occurred. On this assumption he reaches an entirely different verdict concerning the status of generated composites. The first treatment will be discussed in chapter 4, the second in chapter 5.

I now turn to the general account of generation. Although the crucial question about material continuity will be signaled, I defer discussion of Aristotle's alternative treatment until chapter 5, in order first to set out the consequences, based on the assumption that matter actually survives, that Aristotle derives in *Metaphysics* Z.

CHANGE AND GENERATION

Chapter 2 discussed Aristotle's distinction between generation and alteration in *On Generation and Corruption*. Aristotle treats this topic in detail in his work on the elements because elemental transformation differs from typical substantial generations. In fact, the transmutation of the elements is in many respects more readily compared to nonsubstantial changes than to other generations, and this anomaly accounts for the fact that *On Generation and Corruption* 1.4 first compares generation and alteration and then meticulously distinguishes the two. Ordinary substantial generation is structurally different from nonsubstantial change.

The Replacement Model and Generation

In the first book of the *Physics* Aristotle presents a general account of change, which involves three principles, or ἀρχαί: a pair of opposed terms, and a subject (ὑποκείμενον) that survives when one of the opposed pair replaces the other. He calls the opposed terms "form" and "privation" and the subject "matter." Using these three principles, he develops a matrix, commonly called the replacement model, to describe nonsubstantial changes, such as a man's becoming musical or traveling from Athens to Thebes. Several points about the model need clarification.

First, the opposed terms must be opposed in an appropriate way. Often the items opposed are designated as contraries, which have an equal ontological status under a common genus, as black and white under color. But even if the opposed terms are not specified as contraries, there must nonetheless be a path, fixed by a series of points, between the terminus a quo and the terminus ad quem. Furthermore, the intervening points should have a status comparable to that of the termini, such that the entire series constitutes a linear continuum. Thus, the locations Athens and

Thebes are properly opposed because they mark off a continuum within the category of place. White and musical, on the other hand, are not properly opposed because, although both items inhabit the category of quality, there is no path from one to the other. Aristotle says that, if a man comes to be musical from having been white, he does so accidentally because the man who was not-musical happened also to be white. Properly speaking, the musical comes to be from the not-musical.[15]

Notice that, in the example of the musical man, the opposed terms have been specified as contradictories, as "not-musical" and "musical." Even if the opposed terms are specified as contradictories, the referent of the negative expression can regularly be redescribed as a series of ontologically similar terms on a path leading to but excluding the positive term. The point to be stressed is that, however the opposition is specified, the specification indicates a linear continuum within a particular category. I will speak of changes occurring along such a series as structurally *linear*. Both circular and rectilinear motion count as structurally linear because both involve continuous paths of spatial locations. And changes in the category of quality and quantity involve comparable series in those categories.

Second, Aristotle's replacement model requires that something persist through the change, that some part of the preexisting entity survive in the product. Because the continuant guarantees that coming-to-be is not a sheer replacement of entities, it preserves change from the Parmenidean objection against absolute replacement—the objection that change simply involves the destruction of one thing into nothing and the emergence of something else out of nothing. In typical nonsubstantial changes a composite substance persists through the replacement of its nonsubstantial properties; for example, the man who travels from Athens to Thebes, or who becomes healthy from sick, survives as a man.

Third, changes that fit the replacement model are typically reversible.[16] The man can learn music, forget what he learned, and undergo the lesson again. He can travel back and forth between Athens and Thebes and can recover his health, relapse, and recover once more.

Substantial generations diverge in important respects from this standard scheme. First, in typical generations the opposed terms are not contraries. Since Aristotle frequently insists that substance has no contrary,[17] the termini of a substantial generation should be opposed in some way other than contrariety. In *Physics* v.1 he says that the termini in substantial

---

[15] See *Phys.* I.5, 188ª31–ᵇ8.

[16] Not always; the circular motion of the cosmos occurs in a single direction.

[17] See *Cat.* 5, 3ᵇ24–27; *Phys.* I.6, 189ª32–33; v.2, 225ᵇ10–11. The elements are notable exceptions to this rule; see *G.C.* II.3, 331ª1–3; II.8, 335ª3–6.

generation and destruction are contradictories.[18] In fact, a survey of examples suggests that the opposed terms display different degrees of complexity: a human being, for example, is generated from the productive blood of the female, called the καταμήνια, and is destroyed into a corpse. The human being, which emerges from the καταμήνια and is destroyed into the corpse, is more complex than either the preexisting material from which it is generated or the posthumous product into which it perishes. The human being is defined by a set of functions that constitute the soul; neither the preexisting καταμήνια nor the subsequent corpse possesses these vital functions. Since the termini on the upward path differ from each other in complexity, and those on the downward path in a similar manner, substantial generations and destructions are not structurally linear. Although the process can be continuous, the path involves a series of upward or downward *steps*.

Second, given this stepwise path, substantial changes are frequently irreversible.[19] A human being, once generated, cannot be reduced again to the female blood (καταμήνια), nor can the human being be regenerated out of a corpse.

For the present it will be assumed that generation and nonsubstantial change are comparable on the issue of the persisting subject. As I said earlier, Aristotle's view on this question has important implications for the larger question about the unity of composites. Yet even if one assumes a resemblance between the two sorts of processes on this issue, the special path of substantial generation requires that material persistence in this context be understood somewhat differently from that in nonsubstantial contexts. Given the special path of generation, the lower-level matter will, at each higher step, acquire a new layer of form. Thus, although the lowest-level matter remains a real constituent in the highest-level product, that low-level matter will not be the proximate constituent matter of the high-level complex. For example, although a statue is ultimately made out of earth and water, its proximate matter is bronze. Earth and water are its ultimate matter because bronze is made out of copper and tin, and they are made out of earth and water. Although the earth and water provide ultimate horizontal continuity through the series of productions of the metals and the statue and through their later destructions, the elements stand at some remove from the proximate matter of the statue.

[18] Phys. v.1, 225ᵃ12–20.

[19] Again, not always; in many cases it is possible to extract the original matter from the product, as bronze from a statue or bricks from a house. On the difference between irreversible and reversible processes, cf. *Met.* α.2, 994ᵃ22–ᵇ3. The reason why some generations are reversible and others not will be discussed below, in the section "Horizontal Unity," pp. 108–10.

Contraries and Contradictories

In *Physics* v. 1 Aristotle discusses the main structural difference between those processes that he regards as proper changes (κινήσεις) and those that he regards as generations or destructions. The difference turns on the nature of the opposition between the termini. He lists four possible modes of transition: one from positive to positive (e.g., from black to white), a second from positive to negative (e.g., from white to not-white), a third from negative to positive (e.g., from not-white to white), and a fourth from negative to negative (e.g., from not-white to not-musical) (225ᵃ3–7). He immediately excludes the fourth option because a transition involving two negative termini lacks an appropriate opposition between contraries or contradictories (225ᵃ10–12). There are, then, three acceptable modes of transition. He identifies processes from negative to positive and from positive to negative as transitions between contradictories and calls the one generation, the other destruction. He also claims that a generation can be simple or qualified. A generation is simple if the negative terminus a quo and positive terminus ad quem are contradictories within the category of substance, qualified if the termini are contradictories in a nonsubstantial category. Similarly, a destruction is simple or qualified depending upon whether the positive terminus a quo and negative terminus ad quem are located in the category of substance or in a nonsubstantial category. Transitions from positive to positive occur between contraries or intermediates within a particular category: both termini of the transition have a positive designation—as, for example, black and white.

Aristotle restricts change (κίνησις) proper to transitions from positive to positive (225ᵃ34–ᵇ5) but says that transitions in quality, quantity, and place all count as κινήσεις (225ᵇ5–9). Such processes involve contrary termini. A nonsubstantial change can also count as a qualified generation or destruction if one of the termini is specified as the contradictory of the other. But, as I said earlier, even if the opposed terms are specified as contradictories, the referent of the negative expression can regularly be redescribed as a linear series leading to the positive term. Thus not-white can be redescribed as a series terminating in black or gray or some other definite color and leading to white. A qualified generation or destruction can therefore be redescribed as a proper change. Such processes are structurally linear, between termini on a continuum within one of the categories of quality, quantity, or place, and this fact is not altered by the way the termini are described.

But in the case of unqualified generation and destruction, even if the negative terminus is redescribed as positive, the maneuver does not license such processes to count as proper κινήσεις because the termini, however described, are not contraries, and the path from one to the other does not constitute a linear series. Instead, the path consists of a series of upward or downward steps, which are marked by entities that differ from one another in their complexity. Substantial generations are thus constructive, destructions degenerative.

THE CONSTRUCTION MODEL

In *Metaphysics* H.5 Aristotle offers an account of generation and destruction that will be called the *construction model*.[20] He begins the discussion by considering how the matter is related to a pair of opposed terms. The first conception reflects the replacement model, the second does not.

> There is a puzzle concerning how the matter of each thing stands to the opposites. (1) For example, if the body is potentially healthy, and sickness is the opposite of health, is [the body] potentially both? And is water potentially wine and vinegar? Or (2) is it the matter of one [opposite] in virtue of a positive state (καθ' ἕξιν) and in virtue of the form (κατὰ τὸ εἶδος), and the matter of the other in virtue of a privation (κατὰ στέρησιν) and destruction contrary to nature (φθορὰν τὴν παρὰ φύσιν)? (1044ᵇ29–34)

If the relation between matter and the opposed terms is conceived in the first way (1044ᵇ30–32), each member of the pair of opposed terms is a positive goal of the subject's potentiality: as health and sickness are goals of potentialities possessed by the body, so wine and vinegar are goals of potentialities possessed by the water. Since both goals are equally positive, the transition from one to the other should count, in the terminology of *Physics* v.1, as a transition from positive to positive. Because the opposed terms have the same ontological status, the passage between them should be structurally linear and should therefore count as a proper κίνησις.

Aristotle questions whether the relation between water and wine and between water and vinegar involves a pair of opposed terms with an equally positive status. The second conception (1044ᵇ32–34) regards the opposed terms as having a different status. He suggests that water is the matter for one of the opposed states in virtue of a positive character (καθ' ἕξιν) and in virtue of the form (κατὰ τὸ εἶδος), but the matter for the other in virtue of a privation (κατὰ στέρησιν) and destruction contrary to nature (φθορὰν τὴν παρὰ φύσιν). One member of the contrasted pair

---

[20] H.5 has been largely ignored by scholars, but see the helpful discussions by Anscombe (Anscombe and Geach 1961, esp. 51–52) and Sharples (1983, esp. 102–5).

is thus regarded as positive and the other as its privation.[21] A transition between such a contrasted pair might be linear, or it might not be. If the items specified as positive and negative can be redescribed as contraries within a particular category, then the process should be linear regardless of the fact that one term is identified as positive and the other as its privation. *Physics* v.1 calls such processes qualified generations or destructions, and such processes can regularly be redescribed as proper changes (κινήσεις)—as transitions from positive to positive. Unqualified generations and destructions, on the other hand, which are transitions between contradictories that admit no such redescription, should fit only the second conception of *Metaphysics* H.5. In these cases the termini differ in complexity, and the terminus alone that is more complex will be the positive goal of a subject's potentiality. The negative terminus, although it can serve as a goal, will do so only "in virtue of a privation [of the positive goal] and a destruction contrary to nature" (1044^{b}33–34).

In the rest of *Metaphysics* H.5 Aristotle offers an account of destruction and generation based on the second conception. He envisages an entire cycle of generation and destruction that begins and ends with some simple stuff.

> There is a certain difficulty also why the wine is not matter of vinegar nor potentially vinegar (even though vinegar comes to be from it) and why the animal is not potentially a corpse. In fact they are not, but the destructions are accidental, and the matter itself of the animal is in virtue of destruction (κατὰ φθοράν) a potentiality and matter of the corpse, and the water of vinegar. For they [the corpse, vinegar] come to be from these [the animal, wine] as night from day. And as many things as change into one another in this way [i.e., as night from day] must return to the matter, e.g., if an animal comes to be from a corpse, there must first be a return to the matter, and then in this way an animal comes to be; and vinegar must first return into water, and then in this way wine comes to be. (1044^{b}34–1045^{a}6)

The thesis of this passage, to which I have called attention before, is that an object destroyed, for instance, wine, is not the matter of that into which it is destroyed. Thus wine is not the matter of vinegar. Instead, some ingredient of the higher composite—in this case water—remains the matter of the resulting simpler object. Moreover, vinegar comes to be from wine, but wine cannot come to be directly from vinegar. If the change were structurally linear—if wine and vinegar were equally positive goals of the water's potentiality—wine should be avail-

---

[21] On Aristotle's general preference for treating one member of a pair of opposites as positive and another as negative, see G.E.R. Lloyd 1962 and [1964] 1970.

able from vinegar, just as vinegar is available from wine. As I indicated earlier, linear changes are typically reversible: a person can be now in Athens, later in Thebes, and then in Athens again. But the changes that Aristotle here envisages are not reversible: the vinegar must first perish into simple water before wine can be reproduced. The important point is that the positive goal is more complex than the outcome of its destruction; wine is more complex than vinegar, and a living organism than a corpse. In the cases that Aristotle describes, destruction must terminate in some simple material before another high-level complex can come to be.

The upward and downward path thus consists of an ordered series of entities, with one definite item marking the apex of the pyramid and another securing the foundation. According to Aristotle's account in H. 5, it appears that the lowest-level item, which exists simply at the end of an old cycle and start of a new, is potentially the highest in virtue of a positive state (καθ' ἕξιν) and potentially those in the downward series in virtue of a privation of that positive state (κατὰ στέρησιν). In the example of water, wine, and vinegar, the water—whether in its simple initial state or once it constitutes the wine—is potentially wine καθ' ἕξιν but potentially vinegar κατὰ στέρησιν.

Two strands of this analysis should be distinguished. According to the construction model, wine is "from" (ἐκ) water in two ways. First, wine comes to be from water because water is an earlier stage in the production of wine. The separately existing water—an actual τόδε τι—from which the production of wine begins, ceases to exist on its own once the wine has been produced. Second, wine is from water because if wine is analyzed by the sorts of procedures that Aristotle describes in *Meteorology* IV, water will appear as a major component.[22] Water, which is for a time an ingredient of wine, survives the whole cycle and finally exists simply.

A passage in *Generation of Animals* 1.18 helps to clarify the two ways in which wine is from water.[23] In this passage Aristotle distinguishes four ways in which one entity comes to be "from" (ἐκ) another. The first two instances illustrate the distinction of H. 5, and Aristotle contrasts these with a third involving a pair of opposed terms that, however described,

---

[22] *Meteor.* IV.1–11 gives a rich account of the elemental constitution and dispositional properties of a wide variety of uniform stuffs; on this topic see Furley 1983 and Lennox forthcoming. Stuffs are classified as primarily earthen or watery, or as combinations, depending on the way they respond to such procedures as heating and cooling. For instance, materials that solidify when cooled and become liquid when heated have a watery nature (IV.6, 383ᵃ8–13), while those that are solidified by both heat and cold are compounds of earth and water (383ᵃ14–26). On the nature of wine, see IV.5, 382ᵇ13; IV.7, 384ᵃ3–6; 384ᵃ12–14; IV.10, 388ᵃ30–ᵇ9; 389ᵃ7–11; IV.11, 389ᵃ25–27.

[23] Cf. *Met.* H.4, 1044ᵃ23–25.

can be treated as positive contraries. The third case belongs to the replacement model, the first two to the construction model.

> But there are many ways in which one thing comes to be from another (ἄλλο ἐξ ἄλλου)—for [something comes to be from another] in one way (1) as we say that night comes to be from day and a man from a boy, because the one comes after the other; in another way (2) as a statue comes to be from bronze and a bed from wood; and for as many other things as we say are generated things that come to be from matter, the whole is from something that is present in it and altered in form (ἔκ τινος ἐνυπάρχοντος καὶ σχηματισθέντος τὸ ὅλον ἐστίν). And in another way (3) as the unmusical (man) is from the musical and as the sick (man) is from the healthy and generally as the contrary is from the contrary. And in addition to these, as Epicharmus piles up the expressions, (4) the abuse is from slander, and the fight from abuse; all of the latter are from something [that is] a principle of motion. (724ᵃ20–30)

The present discussion can ignore the fourth case, which concerns efficient causes. The relevant examples are the first two. The first way in which one thing comes to be from another is that in which night comes from day or a man from a boy: the one comes after the other. In this way wine comes from water, vinegar from wine, and water from vinegar. Such processes are irreversible because the stages of production and degeneration are ordered. Hence they differ from cases of linear replacement, such as a person's becoming unmusical from musical or sick from healthy, as described in (3). The first example captures one aspect of Aristotle's construction model of *Metaphysics* H.5. Wine perishes into vinegar, vinegar into simple water, and only by following this pattern can wine be reproduced. If one thinks of the ordered production of entities, the simple water, which exists on its own at the end and start of a cycle, goes out of existence as that separate entity when the wine comes to be.

But in another way the water is not lost because wine is from water in the second way as well, as a statue is from bronze or a bed from wood. An analysis of wine will reveal water as a major component; water is an ingredient of wine that is "present in" (ἐνυπάρχον) the wine but "altered in form" (σχηματισθέν). According to the interpretation suggested earlier, the water survives in the wine and so is "present in" the higher-level complex, but because it has acquired an additional layer (or layers) of form in the upward steps of generation, the water is "altered in form." During degeneration the water loses layers of form until it finally exists simply. Thus, according to the construction model, the water from which wine is generated is both the preexisting entity from which the wine is generated and an ingredient present in the higher-level complex.

CHAPTER THREE

THE PRINCIPLES OF CHANGE

Physics I.7 argues that all processes involve three principles. I have delayed discussing this important chapter because, without a prior grasp of the construction model, one might think that Aristotle here presents a model for all changes. He does not do that. Different sorts of processes are described by different models—a fact that is clearly presupposed by the various examples discussed. The chapter simply considers the number of principles required for processes in general and argues that there must be three: a pair of opposed terms and a persisting subject. The application of the three principles within the replacement model is well understood,[24] but their application within the construction model has been largely overlooked.

In the opening chapters of *Physics* I, Aristotle surveys the views of his philosophical predecessors on the question of principles and gets them all to agree that there are two—a pair of opposed terms. Thus the musical comes to be from the not-musical, the white from the black, and so on: the termini must be properly opposed. Once he has shown in I.5 that every coming-to-be and perishing must involve an appropriate opposition, he argues in I.6 that the items opposed do not act on each other but on a subject (ὑποκείμενον); and he suggests that this item is a third principle in addition to the pair of opposed terms. But *Physics* I.6 states that the question whether there are two principles or three must still be decided, and that decision is reached in *Physics* I.7. *Physics* I.7 demonstrates that all processes involve three principles.

Aristotle opens *Physics* I.7 by discussing the alteration of a man who becomes musical. He evidently intends to generalize certain features of this discussion to all processes because he prefaces his account by saying that he will initially treat all becoming because the proper method is first to consider what is common and only then to consider what is peculiar to particular cases (189^{b}30–32). It is important to decide how much of his treatment of the musical man he regards as common to all changes. In his discussion of this paradigm, Aristotle surveys the ways in which Greek speakers ordinarily describe a man's becoming musical. Since he thinks that the structures of language often reflect the underlying real structure of the entities described, he may envisage an analysis of change based on the linguistic evidence;[25] but if so, he presumably does not extend that analysis because, as scholars have noticed, he later points out that Greek speakers describe other changes in other ways.[26] The importance of Ar-

---

[24] See esp. Waterlow 1982, 1–45.

[25] On this topic, see Owen [1961] 1975; Wieland 1970, 110–40; Jones 1974, 476–78; Waterlow 1982, 1–45; and Bostock 1982, 179–96.

[26] See Wieland 1970, 110–40; and Jones 1974. For an attempt to reconcile Aristotle's linguistic claims, see Code 1976.

istotle's reflections on language has, however, sometimes been overemphasized. In *Physics* I.7 he invokes ordinary usage for one main reason, to demonstrate that all processes, however described, involve a third principle—a ὑποκείμενον that survives the process. Since the three principles are crucial for Aristotle's theory of change and for his theory of potentiality and actuality, and since Aristotle's treatment of the ὑποκείμενον bears on the issue of definable unity treated in *Metaphysics* Z, I shall consider the chapter in detail.[27]

The Musical Man

Aristotle begins his treatment of change as follows:

[When] we say that one thing comes to be from another and that something comes to be from something different, we speak either of simples or compounds. What I mean is this: it is possible [to say] (1) "a man comes to be musical," or (2) "the not-musical comes to be musical," or (3) "the not-musical man [comes to be] a musical man." By a simple thing that comes-to-be, I mean the man and the not-musical, and by a simple thing that it comes to be, [I mean] the musical. When we say "the not-musical man comes to be a musical man," both what it becomes [musical man] and what becomes [not-musical man] are compound. (189^{b}32–190^{a}5)

Aristotle calls "simples" those items that are designated with reference to a single category. Thus man is simple because man is specified with reference to the category of substance, and the not-musical and the musical are both simples because they are specified with reference to the category of quality. Musical man and unmusical man, on the other hand, are "compounds" because their designation mentions items from more than one category.

Aristotle now points out certain peculiarities in the way that people talk about coming-to-be.

In some of these cases we say not only that "this comes to be" but also "[comes to be] from this," for example, (2') "from [the] not-musical [comes to be] [the] musical," but not in all cases; for it is not the case that [we say] (1') "[the] musical came to be from man," but (1) "a man came to be musical." Of the things that come-to-be that we call simple things that come to be, one item remains when it comes to be and the other does not remain. For the man remains and is a man when he comes to be musical, but the not-musical and the unmusical remain neither simply nor when they have been compounded. (190^{a}5–13)

---

[27] My treatment of *Phys.* I.7 has benefited from suggestions by Sarah Broadie.

The claim that some of the original three statements about coming-to-be ordinarily admit reformulation and some not is a point to which Aristotle will return, so it will help to schematize his claims. Let x stand for the item that remains and *not-ϕ* and ϕ stand for the pair of opposed terms, one of which replaces the other. The first passage offers the following ways to describe a change:

(1) [the] x comes to be ϕ.
(2) [the] not-ϕ comes to be ϕ.
(3) [the] not-ϕx comes to be ϕx.

The second passage says that (1) is not reformulated as:

(1′) [the] ϕ comes to be from x.

But (2) can be reformulated as:

(2′) [the] ϕ comes to be from [the] not-ϕ.

He later says (190ᵃ29–31) that (3) can be reformulated as:

(3′) [the] ϕx comes to be from [the] not-ϕx.

Aristotle next draws some general conclusions, and this passage indicates how much of the discussion about the musical man he means to generalize to all processes.

> These things having been distinguished, if one looks closely in the way I suggest, one can grasp this point from all generated things (ἐξ ἁπάντων τῶν γιγνομένων), namely, that something—the thing that comes-to-be—must (δεῖ) always (ἀεί) underlie (ὑποκεῖσθαι), and this [the underlying thing], even if it is one in number, is not one in form. By [one] "in form" I mean the same in account; for the being of a man and of the unmusical are not the same. And the one remains, but the other does not remain. That which is not opposed remains (for the man remains), but the not-musical and the unmusical do not remain, nor does that compounded from both, for example, the unmusical man. (190ᵃ13–21)

This passage makes clear how much of the preceding discussion pertains to all changes. Aristotle does not generalize an analysis based on the numbered statements, but he does indicate that, in all changes, there must always be something that underlies, namely, a preexisting subject that comes to be, and that, even if this subject is one in number, it is not one in form. In Aristotle's paradigm, the man and the not-musical are one in number: both "man" and "not-musical" pick out the same individual, a man who lacks knowledge of music. But the expressions specify that individual in different ways, and hence the subject that undergoes the change, though one in number, is not one in form; the account of what it is for the subject to be a man differs from the account of what it is for the subject to be not-musical. One expression picks out the entity as a substance of a particular sort; the other picks it out as qualified in a particular way. Specified in one way, namely, as "man," the entity remains; but specified in the other way, namely, as "not-musical," it does not remain. Aristotle has claimed that all changes resemble the paradigm to this extent: the preexisting subject, though one in number, is not one in form—regarded in one way, the subject survives the change, but regarded in another way the subject does not survive but is replaced.

The Statue

Aristotle now returns to the survey of linguistic forms introduced earlier and points out that such usage is not standard in all cases.

The [formulation] "from something comes to be something," and not "this comes to be something," is used more in the case of things that do not remain, for example, (2') "from [the] unmusical comes to be [the] musical," but not (1') "from man." Yet that very formulation is sometimes used of the things that remain; for we say (4') "a statue comes to be from bronze," and not (4) "bronze comes to be a statue." But the [change] from that which is opposed and does not remain is described in both ways, both "from this [comes to be] this," and "this [comes to be] this." For both (2') "from [the] unmusical" and (2) "the unmusical" "comes to be musical." And so likewise in the case of the compound. For we say both (3') "from [an] unmusical man" and (3) "the unmusical man" "comes to be [a] musical [man]." (190ª21–31)

Aristotle here amplifies his earlier discussion of the ways in which speakers describe a man's becoming musical. In speaking of simples, people do not use (1'), but they use (2'), and in fact prefer it to (2). But although they prefer (2'), they use (2) as well. And they use both formulations (3) and (3') in talking about the compound. But these ways of speaking do not apply in all cases, for people sometimes say "this comes to be from this," when "from this" specifies what remains. Whereas speakers do not use (1'), "the musical comes to be from man" (where man is what remains), they do use (4'), "the statue comes to be from bronze" (where bronze is what remains). Moreover, in their talk about the statue, people do not use (4), "bronze comes to be a statue," although this construction parallels (1), "a man comes to be musical," which they do use.

Why should the conventional ways of describing the coming-to-be of a statue differ from those describing the coming-to-be of something musical? This question has exercised scholars,[28] but the text does not demand an answer to this question. Aristotle does not say how one ought to speak in light of his own theory but simply says that this is how Greek speakers do sometimes (ἐνίοτε) speak (190ª24–25); and he does not here applaud or fault such ordinary practice. He is concerned, as he is throughout the chapter, with the number of principles, and by invoking common usage here, as he did earlier, he shows that the standard ways of describing change imply an underlying subject (ὑποκείμενον). Even though the description of the production of a statue differs from the description of the coming-to-be of a musical man, the ὑποκείμενον is still specified in the description, since people say "a statue comes to be *from bronze*," even though they do not say "bronze comes to be a statue." Aristotle can in fact explain why ordinary usage differs in cases of this sort, and an observation in *Physics* I.5, that in some instances the opposed term is nameless (188ᵇ10–11), suggests that he knows the reason in I.7. People say that a statue comes to be "from bronze" rather than "from the unstatued" because Greek (like English) lacks names for the relevant privations. He explains the linguistic practice elsewhere but ignores the explanation here because the reason for the practice is not his present concern.[29]

The Seed

Once it is clear that Aristotle's project in *Physics* I.7 is merely to show that all processes require a ὑποκείμενον, his next example, concerning the generation of plants and animals from seed, is not the dramatic problem that it has sometimes been taken to be.[30] To continue the translation:

But coming-to-be is said in many ways. And in some cases there is no [unqualified] coming-to-be but [merely] a this coming to be something, while only in the case of substances is there unqualified coming-to-be (ἁπλῶς γίγνεσθαι). In the other cases it is clear that something—the thing that comes-to-be—must underlie (for quantity and quality and relative[31] and where come to be *of* some subject [ὑποκειμένου τινός] because substance alone is predicated of no other subject [μηθενὸς κατ᾽ ἄλλου λέγεσθαι ὑποκειμένου], but all the rest [are predicated] of substance). But that even substances, and whatever things simply are, come to be *from* some subject (ἐξ ὑπο-

---

[28] See Jones 1974, esp. 483–88; and Code 1976.

[29] *Met.* Z.7, 1033ª5–23; Θ.7, 1049ª18–ᵇ2. For a discussion of these texts, see below, pp. 122–25, 151–60.

[30] Charlton (1970, 76–77), for example, finds a "serious gap" in Aristotle's argument concerning this example.

[31] Following Ross (1936, 492), I excise καὶ ποτέ ("and when") at 190ª35.

κειμένου τινός), would become clear to one looking closely. For always (ἀεί) there is something that underlies (ἔστι ὃ ὑπόκειται) from which (ἐξ οὗ) the thing generated comes to be, for example, plants and animals from seed. (190ᵃ31–ᵇ5)

Although this passage has troubled commentators because the seed does not survive the generation of a plant or animal, as a man survives an alteration to musicality or bronze the production of a statue, the passage presents no serious difficulty. Aristotle contrasts substances, which he says are not predicated of a subject, with nonsubstantial properties, which are so predicated. This is simply the doctrine of the *Categories*, which he maintains in a revised form in the *Metaphysics*, as we saw in chapter 1. His point is that, even though substances are not predicated *of* any other subject, they nonetheless come to be *from* a subject. Thus, the subject to which he refers is the preexisting subject from which the substance is generated.[32] Even in the earlier passages Aristotle refers to the preexisting compound as the ὑποκείμενον and claims that, although it is one in number, it is not one in form. Described in one way the ὑποκείμενον survives, and described in another way it does not survive but is replaced. In the case of the musical man, the compound unmusical man is the ὑποκείμενον from which the musical man emerges. Described as "man," the ὑποκείμενον survives the change; described as "unmusical," however, the ὑποκείμενον does not survive. The difference between the example of the seed and the earlier example of the musical man is simply that, whereas Aristotle explicitly says that part of the preexisting ὑποκείμενον survives the generation of the musical man, he does not say that part of the preexisting ὑποκείμενον survives the generation of a plant or an animal from seed. But this omission need not indicate that nothing survives.

Aristotle next describes various sorts of substantial generation and argues that, in these cases too, there is a third principle, a component subject that underlies both the preexisting compound and the resulting product.

Things that are generated in the unqualified way are generated, some by a change of form, for example, a statue; some by addition, for example, things that grow; some by subtraction, for example, the Hermes from the stone; some by composition, for example, a house; and some by alteration, for example, the things that are turned in respect of their matter. And it is clear that all the things generated in this way come to be from subjects (ἐξ ὑποκειμένων). So it is clear

---

[32] Cf. Charlton 1970, 77 and 135–36; Jones 1974, esp. 498–99; and Bostock 1982, 187–89; for a related but different view, see Code 1976, 358–59.

from what has been said that every (ἄπαν) generated [product] is always (ἀεί) compound (συνθετόν); and there is something generated [a product], and there is something [a preexisting subject] which comes to be that, and this [the preexisting subject] is twofold (διττόν); for it is either the ὑποκείμενον or what is opposed (τὸ ἀντικείμενον). And by "to be opposed" I mean the unmusical, and by "to underlie" I mean the man; and the shapelessness and formlessness and disorder are what is opposed, and the bronze or the stone or the gold is the ὑποκείμενον. (190ᵇ5–17)

Aristotle's survey of ways in which simple generation occurs—by change of form, addition, subtraction, and so on—are all, he says, plainly examples of generation from a preexisting ὑποκείμενον; but the survey is also supposed to show that, in all such cases, the thing generated is compound (συνθετόν) and that the preexisting subject from which the product is generated is similarly twofold (διττόν). There is the ὑποκείμενον proper, and there is the item opposed. He lists examples, deploying the distinction first for the original case of qualified generation (the unmusical is the item opposed, the man is the ὑποκείμενον) and then for some of the cases of simple generation just surveyed (shapelessness, formlessness, or disorder is the item opposed, and the bronze, the stone, or the gold is the ὑποκείμενον).

Aristotle does not explicitly spell out his view about the seed, but his view seems plain enough. Since the seed is a ὑποκείμενον from which a plant or animal emerges, the seed must be compound, for he claims to have shown that all preexisting subjects are compound. So one part of the seed is the item opposed and the other is strictly the ὑποκείμενον. He does not expressly mention plants and animals in his survey of simple generations (190ᵇ5–9). Perhaps he groups them with the things that come to be "by addition," since he mentions things that grow (τὰ αὐξανόμενα); but the present survey need not be complete. The mode of generation of a plant or animal from seed, which he treats at length in *Generation of Animals*, is not a topic that requires explanation in *Physics* I.7. Aristotle's task in this chapter is simply to show that, for all changes, whether qualified or unqualified, the entity from which the product comes to be is compound, one part being the item opposed and the other the ὑποκείμενον. And that he has adequately shown.

In this section Aristotle has argued that, in simple generations, if one admits that a product comes to be from a ὑποκείμενον, one must also admit that both the product and the preexisting ὑποκείμενον are compound, and that one part of the preexisting compound is strictly the ὑποκείμενον and the other part opposed. Aristotle does not modify his earlier claim, imported from the *Categories*, that substances are not predicated of a distinct subject, but his argument suggests that within the compound subject—whether the preexisting or resulting compound—the opposed term is predicated of the ὑποκείμενον proper.

The Product

The next part of *Physics* 1.7 focuses on the resulting compound.

Plainly, then, if there are causes and principles of things that exist by nature, from which first [causes and principles] they [the natural products] are and come to be nonaccidentally but each according to its substance, everything (πᾶν) comes to be both from the subject (ἐκ τοῦ ὑποκειμένου) and the form (τῆς μορφῆς). For the musical man is composed in a certain way from man and musical; for you will analyze the accounts[33] [of such compounds] into the accounts of those [the ὑποκείμενον and the form]. It is clear therefore that generated [products] come to be from these [the ὑποκείμενον and the form]. And although the [resulting] ὑποκείμενον is one in number, it is two in form. On the one hand, there is the man and the gold and generally the countable matter (ἡ ὕλη ἀριθμητή) (for it [the matter] is more a this [τόδε τι]; and the generated [product] comes to be from it nonaccidentally, while the privation or contrariety is accidental). On the other hand, the form is one, for example, the arrangement or the musicality or any of the other things predicated (κατηγορουμένων) in this way. (190ᵇ17–29)

This passage contains a number of crucial statements. The product is a compound consisting of two distinct features—the form and the matter[34]—and the account of the product is analyzed into the accounts of these two features. The product, though one in number, is two in form, since its nature includes both form and matter. Moreover, this twofold nature seems to be structured: the form is predicated of the underlying matter. Thus Aristotle's theory seems to be that the product is generated from a (compound) ὑποκείμενον, of which part is the ὑποκείμενον proper; the ὑποκείμενον proper survives in the resulting (compound) ὑποκείμενον, and within the resulting compound the form is predicated of the ὑποκείμενον proper, which is identified as the "countable" matter. It is significant, in view of Aristotle's discussion of definable unity in *Metaphysics* Z, as we shall see in chapter 4, that he claims in *Physics* 1.7 that

---

[33] I retain τοὺς λόγους ("the accounts") at 190ᵇ22; the use of the plural is unproblematic because Aristotle is talking about products generally. Reasons for excising the words are given by Ross (1936, 493).

[34] On the distinctness of the ὑποκείμενον and items predicated, see 190ᵇ33–35; 191ᵃ1–3.

the account of the generated compound is analyzed into the accounts of its two components. Apparently, the definition of a composite reflects its complex structure.

The ὑποκείμενον

In *Physics* I.7 Aristotle uses the word ὑποκείμενον both to specify the preexisting and resulting compounds and to specify that part of the compound that survives the change, and he argues that all changes involve, not only a pair of opposed terms, but also a surviving ὑποκείμενον. Toward the end of the chapter he describes the third principle.

> The underlying nature (ἡ ὑποκειμένη φύσις) is understood by analogy. For as bronze stands to a statue or wood to a bed or the matter and what is shapeless before it has acquired the shape to any of the other things having shape, so this [the underlying nature] stands to substance and the τόδε τι and what is (τὸ ὄν). (191ᵃ7–12)

This passage is often cited in discussions of prime matter. It is claimed that Aristotle uses analogy to specify his ultimate substratum because, being nothing actual in its own right, prime matter can be characterized in no other way.[35] But *Physics* I.7 has scarcely been preparing for an ultimate substratum in need of characterization, and nothing in the chapter suggests that the ὑποκείμενον lacks a proper identity. Indeed, Aristotle has insisted that its nature is distinct from that of the form (190ᵇ33–191ᵃ3). He has argued that all changes involve a third principle—a ὑποκείμενον—and so he now describes that principle. He uses analogy to show that, as the ὑποκείμενον stands to the product in particular cases, such as bronze to a statue or wood to a bed, so the ὑποκείμενον—whatever underlies—stands to the product.[36]

This passage bears a striking resemblance to the one quoted earlier from *Generation of Animals* I.18. Recall Aristotle's second example of the way in which one thing comes to be from (ἐκ) another. "In another way [one thing comes to be from another], as a statue comes to be from bronze and a bed from wood; and for as many other things as we say are generated things that come to be from matter, the whole is from some-

---

[35] See, e.g., Zeller 1897, 1:350 and n. 2; A. Mansion 1946, 72; Solmsen 1960, 86; and Owens 1963, 91–92. The interpretation already occurs in Simplicius (*In Phys.* 225.26–233.10), who regards analogy as Aristotle's version of the "bastard reasoning" by which, in the *Timaeus*, Plato says that one grasps the receptacle. On the way in which Aristotelian matter became conflated with a widely accepted interpretation of Platonic matter, see Charlton 1970, 141–45.
[36] On Aristotle's use of analogy in this passage, see Jones 1974, 494–97; cf. Owen 1978–1979, 6.

thing that is present in it and altered in form" (724ᵃ23–26). Although this passage describes how a compound comes to be from matter, and the one in *Physics* I.7 characterizes the relation between the ὑποκείμενον and the compound, both passages display the same overall structure. Both begin with two concrete examples that exhibit the appropriate relation, then generalize to all cases that exhibit the relation, and conclude with a theoretical claim about the relation between the ὑποκείμενον/matter and the compound. Aristotle even uses the same concrete examples (bronze and statue, wood and bed) in both texts. The two passages might seem to differ only in the final theoretical claim. In *Physics* I.7 Aristotle says, "[As the aforementioned instances of matter stand to the compound], so this [the underlying nature] stands to substance and the τόδε τι and what is (τὸ ὄν)." In *Generation of Animals* he says, "[For the aforementioned compounds] the whole is from something that is present within it and altered in form." But the two texts could certainly express the same doctrine, since the *Physics* leaves vague precisely what the relation between the ὑποκείμενον and compound is. If *Physics* I.7 does reflect the same view as *Generation of Animals*, then the ὑποκείμενον stands to the product as that "from which" the product is generated and as something "present in" the product but "altered in form." As I have interpreted the doctrine, the ὑποκείμενον remains present in the product but acquires an additional form.

The seed does not properly fit this scheme because the seed is a stage in the generation of a plant or animal and thus fits, not the second, but the first scheme described in *Generation of Animals* (I.18, 724ᵃ21–23).[37] In the case of the seed, there is some component, the ὑποκείμενον proper, from which the seed (and ultimately the plant or animal) is generated, and it is this more ultimate item that is "present in" the organism but "altered in form." *Metaphysics* H.5, which I discussed earlier, does not say what this ultimate matter is but mentions only that there is a "first matter" into which the organism must be finally destroyed before an organism can be regenerated. There are several reasons for thinking that earth, or some assortment of elements, is the first matter. In the *Meteorology* Aristotle identifies earth as the ultimate outcome of organic destruction;[38] in *Meta-*

---

[37] Even so, *G.A.* I.21, 729ᵇ12–18, suggests that an organism comes to be from the preexisting matter in the way that a bed comes to be from wood. The organic and artificial examples seem dissimilar because, in the case of the seed, since the privation is part of what the seed is, the seed goes out of existence when the organism emerges; while, in the case of wood, since the privation is merely accidental to what the wood is, the wood can survive as wood. The two examples are in fact comparable because in both instances the preexisting entity survives in the outcome as the ὑποκείμενον proper but not as the privation.

[38] *Meteor.* IV.1, 379ᵃ16–26.

physics Θ.7 he considers whether earth is potentially a human being;[39] and in *Metaphysics* H.4 he mentions earth together with fire as material causes of a human being but denies that they are proximate material causes.[40] These passages strongly suggest that he regards earth, or a combination of elements, as the ultimate outcome of organic destruction and the starting point of organic generation.

Aristotle says more about the ὑποκείμενον and the nature of its persistence in *Physics* I.9, and I shall return to that discussion in chapter 5. For now it is enough to recognize that the account in *Physics* I.7 concerns the number of principles required for all changes, nonsubstantial and substantial. Aristotle does not present the replacement model as the scheme for all changes, but he does argue that there are three fundamental principles proper to all processes. These principles will be involved whatever the model used to describe a particular change. All changes, then, require a surviving ὑποκείμενον, which accounts for horizontal unity.

HORIZONTAL UNITY

Aristotle's construction model might be visualized as a sort of step pyramid whose topmost platform is the highest-level composite and whose base is the ultimate matter. A complete cycle of generation begins from the foundation, advances upward by steps to reach the height of the edifice, and then proceeds downward by steps on the further side to complete the cycle at the foundation. Many generations and destructions can occur without traversing the entire pyramid. For example, the bronze from which a statue is made and into which the statue is destroyed can be reused in the production of another artifact without first being destroyed into its own ultimate materials. The whole circuit seems to be needed only in those situations in which the steps on the upward path do not match those on the downward, as in Aristotle's simple example of wine in *Metaphysics* H.5. Wine must first be destroyed into water before it can be reproduced because vinegar, which marks a step on the downward path of wine destruction, cannot serve as a step on the upward path of wine production. Similarly, organisms must perish into some ultimate material because the steps in their generation differ from those in their destruction. But in other situations in which destruction yields a material from which another complex product can be reproduced directly, the generation can recur either at the highest step or at intermediate steps of the pyramid.

The construction model accommodates substantial change against the

---

[39] *Met.* Θ.7, 1049ᵃ1.
[40] *Met.* H.4, 1044ᵇ2–3; cf. Λ.5, 1071ᵃ13–14.

Parmenidean objection that generation is sheer replacement. Generation is not total replacement because, at some level of the hierarchy, material continuity, or "horizontal" unity, is preserved: the matter from which a composite is generated remains "present in" the composite. In the case of artifacts the immediate matter from which the product is generated is typically present in the product—as, for example, the bronze in a statue and the bricks and stones in a house. In the case of living things the situation is more complicated because the matter from which the organism immediately emerges is not the matter into which it is destroyed. For instance, the female blood (καταμήνια) from which blooded animals are generated is a stage proper to the generative path alone. In these cases some more ultimate matter must account for the horizontal unity.

The central question is how one should regard the entity that accounts for horizontal unity. I have argued that, in *Metaphysics* H.1, Aristotle justifies his claim that matter is substance by pointing out that matter in generation is an actual τόδε τι. For example, a statue is produced from bronze that, though merely potentially a statue, is actually bronze. When the statue has been generated, is the constituent bronze still actually bronze? Quite evidently it is—indeed, the statue seems simply to be bronze shaped in a particular way. Aristotle's discussion of form and matter in *Physics* I.7 plainly expresses this conception. He speaks of the countable matter, instanced by gold, and claims that the form is predicated of it. And the same view seems to be presupposed in *Metaphysics* Z.3: Aristotle mentions three candidates for subject—the matter, the form, and "that from these" (τὸ ἐκ τούτων)—and lists the bronze as matter, the "shape of the visible appearance" as form, and the statue as that from both. The statue is simply the compound of the definite shape and the definite material.

But if Aristotle accounts for horizontal continuity by supposing that a distinct matter survives and, at each step of production, acquires a new layer of form, then he faces the two problems that I mentioned earlier—one concerning the subjecthood of the form, and one concerning the unity of the composite. The form apparently fails to satisfy the subject criterion of the *Categories* and *Metaphysics* Z.3 because the form is predicated of a distinct subject. So although the form may satisfy the thisness and separation conditions, the fact that it is predicated of something else suggests that it fails to be a substance as subject. The composite apparently fails to be substance because it lacks "vertical" unity. Since the ultimate matter survives the transition of levels intact (and, in the case of products yielded by partial cycles, some higher-level matter survives as well), the surviving matter makes a distinct contribution to what the composite is. The contribution of the matter is distinct from that of the form because the matter can exist before it acquires the form and can survive its loss. So the composite lacks vertical unity because it consists of two distinct natures—a form that determines its proper identity, and a matter in which the form is temporarily realized.

In *Metaphysics* Z Aristotle addresses the question of unity, and he defends the form as a definable unity but rejects the composite. I now turn to that argument.

CHAPTER FOUR

MATTER AND DEFINITION

Metaphysics Z.4–12 treats essence as substance, the second of the four conceptions of substance that Aristotle lists at the beginning of Z.3, the first of which—subjecthood—was the topic of chapter 1. The essence (τὸ τί ἦν εἶναι) of an entity is that set of features specified in its definition (Z.5, 1031ᵃ12). Contrary to what one might expect, Aristotle does not take the essence of an entity to be whatever is mentioned in answer to the question "What is it?" (τί ἐστι). Instead of designating as the essence whatever turns up in the account of an object, he restricts the notion of essence to features of a certain sort and then argues that only those entities are definable whose nature is exhausted by features of that sort. An account can be given of other things, but because the account mentions features that are not included in the essence, the account is not a proper definition.[1]

Aristotle argues in *Metaphysics* Z that the form of a perishable object is strictly definable. The composite itself is not. Part of his argument on behalf of the form and against the composite occurs in *Metaphysics* Z.7–9, which treats substantial generation at length. Although many commentators have claimed that these chapters intrude in the midst of the main argument of the book,[2] they are vital to the conclusion for which Aristotle prepares in Z.4–6 and that he completes in Z.10–11. The account of generation in Z.7–9 agrees in a number of respects with the treatment of change in *Physics* I.7, as discussed in chapter 3. According to Z.7–9, whatever is generated is generated from matter; and the matter, which persists as an identifiable subject within the product, must be mentioned in the account of the generated object. Aristotle argues that forms are not generated; since forms are ungenerated, they do not contain matter, and so their account need not refer to a material constituent. Composites, on the other hand, are generated, and so their specifying account must mention their matter. The composite fails to have a single unified and definable nature because its matter makes an independent contribution to what it is; the being of a composite is determined in two ways, as *this* form *in this* matter (τόδε ἐν τῷδε). Because the nature of a composite is determined in two ways—by the features that make it the

---

[1] See *Met.* Z.4, 1030ᵃ2–17.

[2] For this view, see, e.g., Ross 1924, 2:181; Furth 1985, 114–15; and Frede and Patzig 1988, 1:21–26, 31–33. For a defense of the relevance of Z.7–9 to other parts of Z, see S. Mansion [1971] 1979; cf. Balme 1987b, 303.

sort of thing that it is, and by the distinct subject in which those features are realized—the composite resembles snubness, a quality whose account must specify not only a determining feature (concavity) in the category of quality but also a distinct and perceptible subject (nose) in which that determining feature is realized. *Metaphysics* Z repeatedly invokes the analogy with snubness and with entities like snubness to clarify the nature of material composites.

The argument on behalf of form is not yet complete once Aristotle has shown that forms do not contain matter, for even the immanent form of a perishable object might be compared to snubness. Unlike the composite snub nose, which contains matter, the quality snubness does not contain matter but is nonetheless defined with reference to it. An immanent form, though claimed to be separate in account, cannot exist apart from matter. Must the account of the form then specify the definite matter in which the form is realized? For example, must the account of human soul mention the flesh and bones, or some other definite stuff, in which the soul always appears? In *De Anima* II.1 Aristotle gives a series of definitions of soul, all of which refer to matter. To quote only one of those definitions, soul is defined as "the first actuality of a natural instrumental body" (ἐντελέχεια ἡ πρώτη σώματος φυσικοῦ ὀργανικοῦ) (412ᵇ4–6). Does the form itself lack definable unity because its account displays the structure "this in this," in the way that snubness does? In Z.10 and 11 Aristotle addresses this question and argues that the snubness analogy does not apply to forms. Although the analogy with snubness holds for generated composites and for their species and genera, the form of a generated object is strictly definable.

The conclusion in Z concerning material composites is not the end of the story, which ultimately reaches a quite different verdict about their status. There is reason to expect the thesis in Z to be superseded. After spelling out in Z.12 why forms are definable unities, and after treating the universal as substance in Z.13–15, in Z.16 Aristotle reassesses the original list from Z.2 of candidates that seem to be substances, and he makes a remarkable claim. Recall that among the original examples were animals and plants, their parts, and the elements. The argument in Z, which has determined what "substance" does and does not mean, should now provide an adequate basis on which to decide which of the initial examples are genuine substances and which not.

Aristotle rejects both the elements and the parts of animals but leaves room for whole plants and animals. He excludes the elements, saying, "None of these [earth, water, air, and fire] is one, but like a heap, until it is worked up (πεφθῇ) [lit. "concocted"] and some unity comes to be from them" (1040ᵇ8–10). This statement indicates both that the elements fail to be substances because they are more like heaps than real unities and that certain entities generated out of the elements are unities and therefore substances. In the same passage he excludes the parts of animals and gives as his reason that, if they are removed from the whole animal, they lose their ability to function as the parts that they were.[3] Since he says nothing against whole plants and animals, these composites apparently escape the purge to take their place among (and perhaps preeminently among) the entities regarded as "unities" that come to be from the elements.

The sort of unity that Aristotle denies to the elements and grants to some of their products seems to be the unity of structure. The elements lack such unity because, as pure matter, they are heaps rather than complex wholes.[4] By contrast, at least some things produced from the elements display a degree of complexity and coherence of structure that enables them to count as unities. This seems straightforward enough. The trouble is that the claim is not justified by the preceding chapters of Z. Aristotle says a great deal in *Metaphysics* Z about unity and about which things are unities, but the unity discussed is not the unity of structure but definable unity—the unity that an entity can have only if its account need not specify one thing in another—the unity that I have characterized as "vertical." Aristotle's claim in Z.16 seems curiously at odds with the earlier argument in Z, and the statement is all the more curious because, according to the requirement for definable unity, the elements seem to have a better claim to be substances than the structurally unified composites that they compose. Because the elements are pure matter and not composite wholes, they seem comparable, in respect of definable unity, to substantial forms. Since the elements are not composed of simpler matter, their account should not display the structure "this in this." The elements thus seem to be vertical unities.[5]

The negative conclusion about composites in the earlier chapters of Z is not final. The claim in Z.16 suggests that Aristotle's argument in *Metaphysics* Z does not match his intuition about the relative status of the elements and generated composites. This discrepancy might also explain why in Z.17 he begins the whole inquiry over again and suggests a new meaning for "substance" that does not appear on the original list in Z.3: substance as unifying cause. Although Z.17 and most of H still reflect the central vision of Z, which bars composites from strict definable unity, the final chapter of H takes up the problem of definition again. And this time Aristotle does not restrict definable unity to forms but claims that the

---

[3] *Met.* Z.16, 1040ᵇ5–8 and 1040ᵇ10–16.

[4] I am grateful to G.E.R. Lloyd, whose suggestions about the treatment of unity in Z.16 helped me to clarify my account of unity in the earlier part of *Met.* Z.

[5] In fact, the elements are not vertical unities, but their failure is somewhat different from that of composites in *Met.* Z; on this topic see below, pp. 235–40. For one indication of Aristotle's view about the elements, see *De An.* III.4, 429ᵇ10–11.

unity of matter and form can be solved by the same solution. Thus H.6 seems to reject the earlier conclusion about composites and to offer a different answer. The argument in Z leads to an interim conclusion, which Aristotle will later deny. The end of this chapter will take a first look at the alternative answer in H.6.

COMPOSITES AND SNUBNESS

The account of snubness displays the structure "this in this"—"one thing in another"—and so is not properly unified. To understand the nature of snubness, recall Aristotle's two types of καθ' αὑτό predication described in *Posterior Analytics* 1.4 and in *Metaphysics* Δ.18.[6] According to the first type, a predicate B belongs to a subject A καθ' αὑτό if B (the predicate) is mentioned in the account of what A (the subject) is. Thus, for example, animal belongs to man καθ' αὑτό because animal, which is predicated of man, is mentioned in the account of what man is; and line belongs to triangle καθ' αὑτό because line, which is predicated of triangle, is mentioned in the account of what triangle is. According to the second type, a predicate B belongs to a subject A καθ' αὑτό, if A is the proper subject of B and is mentioned in the account of what B (the predicate) is. Thus, for example, snubness belongs to the nose καθ' αὑτό because, as the immediate subject for snubness, the nose is mentioned in the account of what snubness is.

In discussing snubness, and entities like it, it is useful to distinguish the *nature* of the entity from its *essence*. The answer to the question "What is snubness?" spells out what the entity is, including, first, the determining feature that distinguishes snubness from other properties and, second, the definite subject that, in virtue of what it is, is the proper subject of snubness. Part of the nature of snubness is determined by concavity, which differentiates this state of the nose from others, and which belongs to snubness καθ' αὑτό in the first way; but, in addition, part of the nature of snubness is determined by the nose, which is the proper subject of snubness and to which snubness belongs καθ' αὑτό in the second way. So the nature of snubness is determined in two ways—by concavity, which differentiates snubness from other nose shapes, and by nose, in which snubness is primarily realized. If essence and nature are distinguished, one can say that concavity, which belongs to snubness καθ' αὑτό in the first way, is the essence of snubness. But the nature of snubness is everything that must be mentioned in answering the question "What is snubness?" The answer to this question is concavity (a quality) in the nose (a substance). Thus the nature of snubness is concavity in a nose, but the essence of

---

[6] See above, pp. 24–25.

snubness is simply concavity, the property that explains why this state of the nose is snubness rather than, for instance, aquilinity. Although in some cases the nature and essence coincide, in most cases they do not. When the nature of an entity does not coincide with the essence and includes more than the essence, Aristotle says that the account is "from addition."

Aristotle begins *Metaphysics* Z.5 with the following puzzle:

> There is a puzzle, if someone denies that a definition is an account "from addition," namely: Of which things that are not simple but have been coupled will there be a definition? For one must clarify them from addition. I mean, for example, there is nose and concavity, and snubness is something called from both: "this in this" ($τόδε$ $ἐν$ $τῷδε$); and it is not indeed accidentally ($κατὰ$ $συμβεβηκός$) that either concavity or snubness is a property of the nose, but in virtue of what nose is ($καθ᾽$ $αὐτήν$). (1030^b14–20)

Aristotle goes on to explain that an account of a property like snubness must mention either the account or the name of the subject in which the property is realized, since the property cannot be clarified apart from that subject (1030^b23–26), and he concludes that such entities are not strictly definable (1030^b26–28).[7]

In *Metaphysics* E.1 Aristotle claims that living things and their parts resemble snubness, and he contrasts them with other entities that resemble concavity.

> We must not fail to notice the type of essence and account, because without such awareness the inquiry is idle. Of things defined and of their what it is ($τί$ $ἐστι$), some are like snub and some like concave. And these differ because the snub is taken together with the matter (for the snub is a concave nose), but the concave is without perceptible matter. If indeed all natural things are analogous to snub, e.g., nose, eye, face, flesh, bone, and animal as a whole, and leaf, root, bark, and plant as a whole (for the account of none of them is without [reference to] change, but always includes matter), [then] it is clear how one must seek and define the what it is ($τὸ$ $τί$ $ἐστι$) for natural things, and why, too, it belongs to the natural philosopher to study those aspects of the soul that are not without matter. (1025^b28–1026^a6)

Notice that Aristotle not only compares composites and their parts to snubness, but that at the end of the passage he suggests that some parts

---

[7] Two helpful discussions of the snub analogy are given by S. Mansion (1969) and Balme (1984).

of the form of a living organism are not without matter and that these aspects are studied by the natural philosopher. *De Anima* indicates that all soul functions, with the exception of intellect (νοῦς), are realized in some material part;[8] and the definition of soul in *De Anima* II.1, which I cited earlier, suggests that matter is mentioned in its definition. This point will be addressed in *Metaphysics* Z.10 and 11. Aristotle thinks that he must show that the forms of perishable objects are vertical unities, even though they depend for their existence on matter of a very definite sort. But for the moment the central concern is the analogy between composites and snubness. If coupled entities like snubness are not definable, as suggested in Z.5, and if living things such as men and horses resemble snubness, as suggested in E.1,[9] then composites are not definable. Although an account of them can be given, which specifies what they are, the account will not be a strict definition because it specifies "this in this," where the two items are distinct. But if composites are not definable, then they are not conceptually primary things but must be defined through other things that are conceptually prior to them. And so they will not be primary substances according to the criterion of conceptual priority defended in the *Metaphysics*.

Why should one think that the essence of a composite is merely part of what it is? One might argue that composites resemble snubness in consisting of coupled constituents, yet differ from snubness in that both constituents—the matter and the form—are part of their essence. If this were the case, then an account specifying both the form and the matter would mention nothing "in addition" to the essence because the essence itself would be compounded from both.[10] But there are objections to this proposal. In an important passage at the start of his treatment of essence, Aristotle limits the notion of essence to the form of a composite.

ESSENCE

Aristotle begins his treatment of essence in Z.4 with a statement whose sense remains controversial. But despite its difficulty, the passage can be understood as distinguishing the essence of a composite from the entity that, by receiving the essence, is the immediate subject for the composite. Thus the passage can be understood as barring the matter of a composite from the essence. Aristotle excludes various items from the essence. Using the example of an individual man, he first eliminates those features that belong to the man accidentally. He then turns to the example of a

---

[8] See *De An.* II.1, 413ᵃ3–7; on separate intellect, see II.2, 413ᵇ24–27; III.4, 429ᵃ24–27; 429ᵇ4–5; III.5, 430ᵃ17–18; cf. *G.A.* II.3, 736ᵇ27–29.

[9] Cf. *Met.* K.7, 1064ᵃ23–26.

[10] For an interpretation along these lines, see Balme 1984, 5; and 1987b, 304–5.

white surface, and he eliminates surface from the essence of white. Like snubness, which stands in a καθ' αὑτό relation to the nose, so whiteness stands in a καθ' αὑτό relation to surface. Surface must be mentioned in the account of whiteness because surface is the proper subject in which whiteness is realized.[11] So the relation between whiteness and surface exemplifies the second καθ' αὑτό relation: the subject turns up in the account of what the predicate is. Aristotle compares man and whiteness (not, as some scholars think, man and surface),[12] and the point of the analogy is to exclude the matter of a composite from its essence and thereby to restrict the essence to the determining feature that belongs to the composite καθ' αὑτό in the first way.

Although Aristotle discusses the relation between whiteness and surface rather than that between a man and his matter, there is reason to think that the passage concerns the matter of a substantial composite because the passage directly following says, "Since there are also composites (σύνθετα) in the other categories (for there is some subject [ὑποκείμενον] for each, for example, for quality and quantity and when and where and motion), we must consider whether there is an account of the essence of each of these" (1029ᵇ22–26). This statement suggests that Aristotle takes himself to have just dealt with composites in the first category, the category of substance. Although his example—whiteness—is in fact an item from the category of quality, he uses the example to clarify substantial composites. There is some proper subject with reference to which man is defined in the way that whiteness is defined with reference to surface, but this item is not part of man's essence, although it contributes to man's nature. Aristotle uses whiteness to illustrate his point about material composites, but entities like whiteness are among the things that he promises to go on to discuss.

I translate the text as follows:

> The essence (τὸ τί ἦν εἶναι) for each thing is what the thing is called in virtue of itself (καθ' αὑτό). For the being for musical is not the being for you; for you are not musical in virtue of yourself. So what you are in virtue of yourself [is your essence]. But this [essence] is not indeed everything [that contributes to what you are]; for [your essence is] not [what you are] καθ' αὑτό in the way that white is to surface, because the being for surface is not [the same as] the being for white. But neither is [the essence] that from both, the being for

---

[11] Cf. *Met.* Δ.18, 1022ᵃ29–31.

[12] Among those who take surface to be the focus, see Ross (1924, 2:167, 168) and the London Seminar (Burnyeat et al. 1979, 17–20). I agree with Furth (1985, 105–7) and Frede and Patzig (1988, 2:59–61) that the topic is whiteness. For a third view, that the argument concerns white surface, see Woods 1974–1975.

white surface, because it [surface] is added (πρόσεστιν). Therefore [the account] in which it [surface] will not be present in the account specifying it [white]¹³ is the account of the essence for each thing, so that if the being for a white surface is the being for a smooth surface, the being for white and the being for smooth are one and the same. (1029ᵇ13–22)

Several points seem clear. First, having said that the essence for each thing is what the thing is καθ᾽ αὐτό, Aristotle focuses directly on a typical composite substance, a man ("you"), to determine the essence. He excludes from the essence those properties that belong to the man accidentally ("for the being for musical is not the being for you; for you are not musical in virtue of yourself"). He then repeats, "What you are in virtue of yourself [is your essence]." Next he restricts the notion of essence: "But this is not indeed everything." From this point on, the meaning of the text is disputed.

Interpreters find the last two clauses particularly puzzling, and for those who take the preceding discussion to concern surface rather than whiteness, it is not surprising that the final statement seems to reflect a new departure and not to fit the earlier argument.¹⁴ But the end of the passage gives a fairly clear indication of the item on which the preceding argument focused. Aristotle concludes, "So that if the being for a white surface is the being for a smooth surface, the being for white and the being for smooth are one and the same." The proposed identification of white and smooth is purely hypothetical, based on the theory of Democritus,¹⁵ but the point is that, if what it is to be a white surface is the same as what it is to be a smooth surface, then the essence of white is identical to the essence of smooth, and so the essence of white can be specified in terms of smoothness. If the passage is coherent, then the preceding argument should concern the essence of white rather than the essence of surface.¹⁶

The important point on my reading is that Aristotle excludes from the essence what turns up in the account of man in the way that surface turns up in the account of white. White is defined with reference to surface, but

---

¹³ Most commentators understand this line to rule out circular definitions and so take the two mentions of αὐτό to refer to the same entity, either surface or white, depending on which is regarded as the one being defined. But the argument gains an overall coherence if the line concerns "addition," to which Aristotle has just objected. The ἄρα at 1029ᵇ19, which is obscure on the standard reading, then introduces a consequence. (In this passage, as often in his discussion of definition, Aristotle confuses use and mention.)

¹⁴ See Ross 1924, 2:168; and the London Seminar (Burnyeat et al. 1979), 17–20.

¹⁵ See De Sens. 4, 442ᵇ11–14; cf. Ross 1924, 2:168.

¹⁶ A disadvantage of Woods's view (1974–1975) (see above, n. 12) is that the final lines must be expanded to include a reference to the being for white surface.

since the being of surface is different from the being of white, surface is not the essence of white, even though it is mentioned in the account that specifies what white is. Similarly, man is defined with reference to some sort of matter, but since the being for man's matter is different from the being for man (just as the being for surface is different from the being for white), it follows that man's matter is not man's essence. Nor is the account of man's essence the account that specifies both man's formal and material parts because such an account is "from addition." The account of white that specifies the being for white surface is not an account of the *essence* of white (though it is a full account of what white is) because a reference to surface is added (πρόσεστιν). The account of the essence of white is the account in which surface is not mentioned but that specifies white. Thus, if one supposes that what it is to be a white surface is the same as what it is to be a smooth surface, then the essence of white can be specified as smooth because the being for white and the being for smooth are (on Aristotle's hypothesis) one and the same.

This conclusion indicates the sort of thing that will count as the essence of man. Even though man's matter contributes to the nature of man (as part of the answer to the question "what is man?"), as surface contributes to the nature of white (as part of the answer to the question "what is white?"), the essence of man does not include the matter, just as the essence of white does not include surface. The essence of man should be something comparable to smooth in Aristotle's analogy. For example, suppose that man is defined as biped animal. Both man, the species, and biped animal, the differentiated genus—entities that classify individual human composites—are treated later in Z as universal composites, as composites of form (human soul) plus matter (human matter) taken universally.[17] This treatment is entirely appropriate, since species and genera classify individual composites as wholes. Conceived as universal composites that include matter, man is comparable to white surface, biped animal to smooth surface. The essence of man should be the part of biped animal that specifies man without addition. Therefore the essence of man should be the form of biped animal (minus the generalized matter), or simply human soul.

Aristotle frequently identifies essence and form,[18] so the outcome of my analysis is not remarkable, even if some would dispute my reading of

[17] See Z.8, 1033^{b}24–26; Z.10, 1035^{b}27–30; Z.11, 1037^{a}5–7. Aristotle uses the word εἶδος for both the species (a universal composite) and the form, and this ambiguity has led some scholars mistakenly to identify the two. The distinction is pointed out by Ackrill ([1972–1973] 1979, 67), Loux (1979, 3), and Balme ([1980] 1987, 296–98), and the whole issue is clarified by Driscoll (1981, esp. 141–48).

[18] See, e.g., *Met.* Z.7, 1032^{b}1–2; 1032^{b}13–14; Z.10, 1035^{b}14–16; 1035^{b}32; and H.4, 1044^{a}36. Cf. Bonitz 1870, 219^{a}47–49.

the text in Z.4. The crucial point on my reading is this: If Aristotle restricts the essence of a composite to its form but thinks that the nature of a composite is determined by more than its form, then material composites are not definable unities. And if they are not definable unities, then they are not conceptually primary things because they must be explained through other things (namely, their form and matter), which are conceptually prior to them.

In *Metaphysics* Z.6 Aristotle argues that there are some things whose nature is exhausted by their essence, and he calls such entities "primary" things (1031^b11–14; 1032^a4–6). These entities are primary because they are not defined through anything else; they are strictly definable. But the class of primary things must still be decided. In Z.7–9 he turns to the question of substantial generation, and this discussion, far from being intrusive, shows that the account of anything generated must refer to some distinct matter. He argues that forms are not generated, and so are not defined with reference to matter that they contain, but that composites, which are generated, must include a reference to matter in their account.

GENERATION AND DEFINITION

A change can occur in three ways: by nature, by art, or by spontaneity (Z.7, 1032^a12–13). Aristotle focuses in Z.7–8 on artificial production and extends his conclusions to natural production at the end of Z.8. I ignore the account of spontaneity in Z.9. He claims that everything generated is produced by something (ὑπό τινος) and from something (ἔκ τινος) and becomes something (τί) (1032^a13–14). The "something" that comes to be is a composite product specified according to (κατά) one of the four categories in which change can occur: substance, quantity, quality, or place (1032^a14–15).[19] For example, a man and a plant are products in the category of substance, and something musical is a product in the category of

---

[19] I endorse the traditional interpretation of τί given by Ross (1924, 2:180). Various scholars take the "something" to specify the form rather than the resulting composite; see Owen 1978–1979, 16–21; the London Seminar (Burnyeat et. al. 1979, 53, 55); and (with reservations) Frede and Patzig 1988, 2:105–6. The London Seminar and Frede and Patzig cite *Met.* Λ.3, 1069^b36–1070^a2 for a similar distinction: there is "something" (τί) that comes to be (the matter), a "by something" (ὑπό τινος, the first mover), and a "to something" (εἴς τι, the form). It seems doubtful, however, that the form referred to as εἴς τι in *Met.* Λ is the referent of τί of Z.7 because in Z.7 Aristotle illustrates the "something" with a man and a plant (1032^a18–19) and goes on to say (apparently in reference to the examples just mentioned) that all generated things have matter (1032^a20). Frede and Patzig agree that the examples are ordinary composites (2:108–9). Owen and the London Seminar seem to reach their assessment by assimilating the universal composite (species) with the form; cf. n. 17 above. For objections to such an assimilation, see Driscoll 1981, esp. 141–48.

quality. The "by which" in natural production is the form of the generator (1032ᵃ24–25), in artificial production a form in the soul of the craftsman (1032ᵃ32–ᵇ2). The "from which" is the matter (1032ᵃ17). Thus the
three items involved in generation—the from which, the by which, and
the resulting something—are simply the matter, the form, and a composite whose determining feature belongs to one of the four categories of
change: substance, quantity, quality, or place.

Aristotle specifies the matter of a composite as its potentiality to be and
not to be: "each of them [natural and artificial products] is able both to be
and not to be, and this is the matter in each" (δυνατὸν γὰρ καὶ εἶναι καὶ
μὴ εἶναι ἕκαστον αὐτῶν, τοῦτο δ᾽ ἐστὶν ἡ ἐν ἑκάστῳ ὕλη) (1032ᵃ20–22).
Although matter is potential, it also has some distinctive nature in its own
right—for instance, the bronze, which is potentially a statue, is itself actually bronze. Aristotle points out that, in general, the "from which" (ἐξ
οὗ) is nature (φύσις) as well as the "in virtue of which" (καθ᾽ ὅ) (1032ᵃ22–
23)—both the matter and the form are natures.[20] This point is important
because, if the composite is generated from a definite matter and in virtue
of a definite form, Aristotle is likely to regard the generated product as
determined by two distinct natures—the matter and the form. Recall that
Physics I.7 claims that every generated product comes to be from a subject
(ὑποκείμενον) and a form—for instance, the musical man from man and
musical—and that the account of the product is analyzed into the accounts
of these components (190ᵇ19–23). The same view is evident in Z.8: Aristotle claims that the craftsman produces neither the form nor the matter
but something else, namely, "this form in something else" (τὸ εἶδος
τοῦτο ἐν ἄλλῳ) (1033ᵃ32–34).[21] The artisan does not make the bronze or
the spherical shape but makes "the bronze spherical" or, as Aristotle more
often puts it, "the bronzen sphere."[22] The craftsman makes the bronzen
sphere in the sense that "from this (ἐκ τουδί), which is bronze, he makes
this (τοδί), which is [a] sphere" (1033ᵇ1–3). The bronzen sphere is compounded from bronze (the matter) and from sphere (the form) (1033ᵇ8–
9). The proposal corresponds to that in *Physics* I.7.[23]

Aristotle argues that the form is not generated because all generated
products are made from something. If forms were generated, they would

[20] On matter as nature, see *Met.* Δ.4, 1014ᵇ16–18; 1014ᵇ26–35; and *Phys.* II.1, 193ᵃ9–30.
Cf. Bonitz 1870, 839ᵃ1–11.

[21] See the helpful discussion of this topic in Frede and Patzig 1988, esp. 2:129–30; the
product is not identical with the matter or the form separately but with their combination.

[22] I have adopted James Lennox's suggestion of using "bronzen" as the adjective for
"bronze."

[23] The text at 1033ᵇ9 has sometimes been questioned, since the ἐκ ("from") is not repeated
with the genitive σφαίρας ("sphere"). But since the same construction occurs twice in *Phys.*
I.7, 190ᵇ20–22, it seems certain that the ἐκ governs both χαλκοῦ and σφαίρας.

have to be made in the same way that composites are made (1033ᵇ3–4). Thus, one would have to make the form by imposing a further form on a further matter.²⁴ But then that further form would have to be made by imposing a further form on a still further matter, and so on indefinitely (1033ᵇ3–8; 1033ᵇ11–17). Accordingly, forms are not generated, and since they are ungenerated, they do not contain matter. Composites, on the other hand, since they are generated from form and matter, contain matter: composites are this (the form) and this (the matter) (τὸ μὲν τόδε τὸ δὲ τόδε) (1033ᵇ17–19).

Since the composite consists of a definite form realized in a definite matter, the account of the composite must mention the matter. Again this proposal accords with that in *Physics* 1.7 (190ᵇ22–23). In Z.7 Aristotle says, "Is it [the matter] one of the things [mentioned] in the account? We specify what bronzen spheres are (τί εἰσι) in both ways, mentioning both the matter, that it is bronze, and the form, that it is such and such shape, and this [shape] is the genus into which [the bronzen sphere] is first placed. Of course the bronzen sphere includes the matter in its account" (1033ᵃ1–5). And in Z.8 he extends this conclusion from artificial cases to natural. "The whole this (τὸ ἅπαν τόδε), Callias or Socrates, is like this bronzen sphere, and man and animal are like bronzen sphere generally" (1033ᵇ24–26).

Given the parallel between natural things and artifacts, the account of natural things must mention the constituent matter. And the reference to matter is required not only in the account of the concrete composite, which is generated and destroyed, but also in the account of the species and genera that classify the various particulars. This view is expressed in Z.10. "Man and horse and the entities related thus to the particulars, but universally, are not substance but a certain composite (σύνολον) from this formula (ἐκ τουδὶ τοῦ λόγου) and this matter (τησδὶ τῆς ὕλης) taken universally" (1035ᵇ27–30). And again in Z.11: "It is clear too that the soul is the primary substance, and the body is matter, and man or animal is that from both taken universally" (1037ᵃ5–7). Thus the account of a generated composite, whether artificial or natural, and the account of its species and genera must refer to the matter as well as the form.

There is, however, a puzzle concerning the claim in Z.7 that the account of an artifact must mention the matter. Why, if this is so, does ordinary Greek idiom not reflect the important metaphysical fact that a composite consists of a form realized in a distinct subject? Why do Greek speakers speak of a "bronzen" statue instead of a "bronze" statue? The

²⁴ Although Aristotle explicitly says that, if the form were generated, it would have to be generated "from something," which might suggest that only a further matter is needed, his claim that the production of the form would match that of the composite indicates that the generation would require a further form as well as a further matter. Cf. 1033ᵇ11–19.

preference for an adjective instead of a noun in specifying an object's constituent matter suggests an analogy between matter and nonsubstantial
properties: just as Greek speakers call a man "healthy" rather than
"health," so they call a statue "bronzen" rather than "bronze." But nonsubstantial properties need not be mentioned in the account of a substance
because they modify the substance accidentally. Why then, if people specify the matter in the way that they specify the nonsubstantial properties,
should a reference to the matter be included in the account? The common
idiom might suggest that matter is merely a property of the higher-level
object rather than a metaphysical subject to which the form belongs.

Aristotle's response to this objection is revealing. He explains why the
practice arose but then suggests that language is misleading because it fails
to reflect accurately the true nature of change. His conclusion thus supports his earlier claim that the account of a composite must mention the
matter. But the passage is more deeply revealing if it is compared with a
similar passage in *Metaphysics* Θ.7. In Θ.7 Aristotle returns to the question
about linguistic usage, but instead of faulting ordinary practice, he defends it. I have suggested that *Metaphysics* Z–H offer one verdict, and
Metaphysics H.6 and Θ another, concerning the status of material composites, and the difference between this passage and the one in Θ.7 provides
crucial evidence for that claim. The passage in Θ.7 will be discussed in
chapter 5. Aristotle first treats the topic as follows:

> Concerning that from which (ἐξ οὗ) as matter things come to be,
> some things, when they have come to be, are called not "that"
> (ἐκεῖνο) but "that-en" (ἐκείνινον), for example, the statue [is called]
> not "wood" but "wooden," and the healthy man is not called that
> from which [he came to be]. The reason is that [a resulting thing]
> comes to be from the privation (ἐκ τῆς στερήσεως) and from the sub-
> ject (τοῦ ὑποκειμένου), which we call the matter (for example, both
> the man and the sick [one] come to be healthy), yet [the resulting
> thing] is preferably said to come to be from the privation, for ex-
> ample, from the sick [one] comes to be [someone] healthy rather
> than from man. And so the healthy [one] is not called "sick" but
> "man," and indeed "the healthy man." But in the case of those things
> whose privation is unclear and nameless, for example, in [the case
> of] bronze [the privation] of whatever shape or in [the case of] bricks
> and beams [the privation] of a house, [the product] seems to come
> to be from these [materials] as in the former case [the healthy thing
> comes to be] from a sick [thing]. Hence, just as in that situation the
> resulting thing is not "that" from which [it came to be], so neither
> in this situation is the statue "wood," but takes on a derivative name
> "wooden" (not "wood"), and "bronzen" (but not "bronze"), and

"stonen" (but not "stone"), and a house is "bricken" (but not "bricks"); although, if someone looked closely, he would not simply say that a statue comes to be "from wood" or a house "from bricks," because it is necessary that that from which [the product] is generated changes and does not persist. This is the reason, then, for the linguistic practice. (1033ª5–23)

In this passage Aristotle attributes the practice of calling a composite "that-en" (ἐκείνινον) with reference to its matter to the fact that the language lacks names for the appropriate privations. Greek (like English) is weak on names for nonstatues and nonhouses, and Aristotle suggests that, because of this linguistic inadequacy, people are accustomed to say that "a statue comes to be from bronze" rather than that "a statue comes to be from the unstatued." Speakers prefer the latter formulation if there is a name for the privation, as there typically is in nonsubstantial changes. In the typical cases the customary formulation is "the healthy [thing] comes to be from the sick [thing]" rather than "the healthy [thing] comes to be from the man." This description of ordinary usage reflects Aristotle's survey in *Physics* I.7.[25] In Z.7 Aristotle justifies the use of "that-en" expressions for an object's constituent matter by suggesting that it emerged by analogical reasoning. Just as speakers do not call the resulting healthy thing by the name of that from which it came to be (they do not call the healthy thing "sick"), so they do not call the statue by the name of that from which it came to be (they do not call the statue "bronze"). In the case of the healthy thing, they call it "man," and in the case of the statue, they modify the name of bronze and call the statue "bronzen." Thus Aristotle explains the linguistic practice as arising in the first place from a shortcoming of language and in the second place from a valiant, though misguided, attempt on the part of speakers to preserve some sort of consistency with the standard cases.

The end of the passage indicates that Aristotle takes the linguistic consistency gained to obscure the actual facts about change. He concludes by saying that, if a person looked closely, he would not simply say that a statue comes to be "from wood" or a house "from bricks" because "that from which [the product] is generated changes and does not persist." Since the wood persists, it is not entirely accurate to say that a statue comes to be "from wood." It would be better instead to say that the statue comes to be from the privation (the unstatued), as in the standard examples, because the privation is the item that changes and does not persist. The final claim evidently concerns the privation because Aristotle begins Z.8 by mentioning the "by something" and the "from something" and stipulates that, despite the preceding discussion, the "from something"

25 Cf. *Phys.* I.7, 190ª5–8; 190ª23. See above, pp. 99–101.

124

will now be understood as "not the privation but the matter" (1033ª25–
26).[26] Thus Aristotle's point in the passage at the end of Z.7 is that the
convention of describing the generation of an artifact as "from the matter" is misleading because it suggests that the matter does not survive and
hence that the product should not be called by the name of that surviving
stuff. Since the convention is in fact misleading, there should be no objection to calling the statue "wood," just as one calls the healthy thing
"man,"[27] because wood is the surviving subject in the substantial change,
as the man is the surviving subject in the nonsubstantial change. This
conclusion is precisely the one he needs in order to support his earlier
claim that the bronzen sphere (despite its name) has matter in its account.

Metaphysics Z.7–9 shows that the account of any generated object must
mention the matter because the matter makes a distinct contribution to
what the object is. But the contribution of matter to the concrete composite is even more problematic than one might expect because Aristotle
claims at the end of Z.8 that two composites that share the same form
differ in their matter (1034ª5–8). Although these particular differences are
lost in the account of the universal composite, which specifies the matter
"universally," these particular differences must be enumerated in the account of the individual. Such a list will include an indefinite number of
properties that characterize the matter, many of which the composite can
lose and still survive.[28] Thus, if the account of the composite must mention the matter at all, the formula will be highly unwieldy, and furthermore, any change in matter is apt to affect the account of the composite
object.[29] As Aristotle says in Z.15, the account of an individual is easily

---

[26] On this claim and the connection between Z.8 and the end of Z.7, see the London
Seminar (Burnyeat et al. 1979, 62–63) and Frede and Patzig 1988, 2:131.

[27] Cf. Code 1976, esp. 360–63. The members of the London Seminar (Burnyeat et al.
1979, 61–62) notice that Aristotle's claim at the end of the passage undermines his defense
of the use of "that-en" expressions for an entity's constituent matter, but they seem not to
notice that Aristotle's aim is precisely to undermine that defense in order to show that the
account of a composite must mention the matter. Scholars seem to overlook the connection
between 1033ª5–23 and the passage that directly precedes, 1033ª1–5; Ross (1924, 2:186) even
suggests that the final passage is irrelevant.

[28] Cf. *Met.* Z.15, 1040ª27–33. On the indefiniteness of matter, see *G.A.* IV.10, 778ª4–9
(cited in Balme 1984, 1).

[29] See Z.15, 1039ᵇ27–1040ª7. On Balme's view, Aristotle solves the problem of unity in
Met. H.6 by regarding all the material properties as part of the individual essence. Balme
deals with the problem of material changeability by suggesting that the definition of an
individual includes all the matter at a given moment ([1980] 1987, 295; 1984, 5; 1987b, 304–
5). Thus, an individual is definable, but a different definition applies at different times.
Although I am persuaded that, in his treatment of inheritance in *G.A.* IV.3, Aristotle builds
all material accidents (such as eye color) into the individual essence of the male parent to
explain their replication, I am not convinced that this is his solution in H.6. See below,
chapter 5, esp. pp. 163–70.

overturned (1040ᵃ5–7). On the positive side, Z.7–9 preserves forms from this difficulty. Since forms are not generated, they do not contain matter, and so their account need not mention a constituent matter. Still, this is not yet enough to show that forms are definable without reference to matter because, even if the form of a perishable object is itself immaterial, it cannot exist without matter. So it might be necessary to mention the sort of subject in which the form is always realized. Thus forms might themselves be like nonsubstantial properties whose account must specify the immediate subject. This is the central topic of Z.10–11.

THE ACCOUNT OF THE FORM AND THE COMPOSITE

What sorts of items must be mentioned in the account of the form, and what sorts must be mentioned in the account of the composite?[30] Aristotle points out in Z.10 that a definition is an account, that every account has parts, and that the parts of the account should correspond to the parts of the thing (1034ᵇ20–22). Since an account will specify in language the real nature of the object, it is important to determine which parts of the object need to be mentioned.

In Z.10 Aristotle distinguishes two sorts of parts, some of which must be mentioned in the account of the whole, and some not. For example, the definition of a circle need not mention the segments, nor that of a right angle the acute, nor that of a man the finger. On the other hand, the definition of a syllable must mention the letters (1034ᵇ24–32). In Z.11 Aristotle criticizes certain Platonists who think that a circle or triangle can be defined without reference to lines and continuity (1036ᵇ7–20), and the criticism suggests that he takes these parts to stand to the mathematical shapes as the letters to the syllable. Recall Aristotle's two types of καθ᾽ αὑτό predication: lines belong to a triangle καθ᾽ αὑτό in the first way because lines, which are predicated of triangle, must be mentioned in its defining account.[31] Such parts, which belong to the subject καθ᾽ αὑτό in the first way, must be mentioned in the account of the whole, and so are designated as *prior* to the whole. But the other parts mentioned are *posterior* because they are defined as what they are with reference to the whole rather than the whole with reference to them. For example, an acute angle is defined with reference to the right, as "less than a right angle" (1034ᵇ28–32; 1035ᵇ6–8); similarly a segment of a circle is defined with reference to the whole circle, and a finger with reference to the whole human being (1035ᵇ9–11). Clearly, if parts are themselves defined as what

---

[30] My treatment of *Met.* Z.10–11 has benefited from Sarah Broadie's criticisms.
[31] See *Po. An.* I.4, 73ᵃ34–37.

they are with reference to the whole, a mention of them adds nothing to the account of the whole.

After drawing his initial distinction between the parts prior to a whole and those posterior, Aristotle turns explicitly to the parts of substance (1034^{b}34), stating once again that there are three types of substance: the matter, the form, and that from these (1035^{a}1–2). The matter, he points out, is in one way called a part of something and in another way not (1035^{a}2–3). The matter is not a part of the form (1035^{a}3–^{b}3), and although the matter is part of the composite, it is in a sense prior and in a sense posterior (1035^{b}14–31). Aristotle's general proposal seems to be the following: (1) the form can be defined without reference to matter, and (2) the composite is defined with reference to some but not all of its material parts.

There are two major questions: first, why is the form definable without reference to matter if there is a matter in which it is always realized? And second, what sort of matter must be mentioned in the account of the composite, and what sort need not be mentioned? The answers to these two questions are interrelated. Aristotle's account in Z.10–11 suggests that the proximate subject for the substantial form is defined with reference to the form: this matter is determined by a set of functions that constitute the form. An animal's functional matter is its organic body. This organic body can be specified in two ways, either functionally with reference to the form or simply as the stuff in which those functions are realized. The matter, specified functionally, is posterior to the form and need not be mentioned in the account of the form. And since the functional matter is posterior to the form, it is posterior to the composite as well; a mention of the functional matter adds no information that is not already available from an account of the form.

But the composite is generated out of simpler matter and is destroyed into simpler matter, and the simpler matter, which underlies the functions and which survives their removal, must be mentioned in the account of the composite. In *Metaphysics* Z Aristotle speaks of the flesh and bones as the matter into which an animal is destroyed (1035^{a}18–19; 1035^{a}31–^{b}1). Since the flesh and bones can persist after the functions have been removed, the nature of flesh and bones is independent of the animal's form. Aristotle worries about whether this matter must also be mentioned in an account of the form, if the form is always realized in it (Z.11, 1036^{a}26–^{b}7). Although he has already shown in Z.8, and recalls in Z.10, that a form does not contain matter, since it is ungenerated (1035^{a}28–31), a form could still resemble snubness in requiring a reference to the distinct subject in which it is always realized. Aristotle argues that the relation between the form and the distinct matter in which it recurs is not like that between snubness and nose, for the stuff in which the form is realized is not in fact the proximate subject for the form, since the form could be realized in other comparable materials; on the other hand, the matter that is the proximate subject for the form is itself defined with reference to the form. The matter, then, that is posterior to both the form and the composite is the *functional* matter in which the form is realized (for instance, the organism's living body specified functionally); while the matter that is irrelevant to the form but prior to the composite is the *lower* constituent matter in which those functions are realized and that survives the composite's destruction (in the case of animals, the flesh and bones).[32]

This account can be motivated by appeal to the theory of living organisms on which Aristotle relies in Z.10 and 11.

Functional Matter

Recall that *Metaphysics* H.5 claims that an animal is ultimately generated from and destroyed into some simple material. In *Generation of Animals* Aristotle describes the reproduction of a new animal as starting with the copulation of male and female parents, with the male contributing form and the female material.[33] But the account can be pushed further back to show that an animal ultimately derives from a simple material. The male and female residues employed in reproduction, the semen and κατα-μήνια, are both products of worked-up (concocted) blood,[34] the female blood being less worked up than semen.[35] Blood, from which the semen and καταμήνια are both generated, is itself identified as food in its final form[36]—the product of food concocted first in the stomach and then in the heart. And the food from which the blood is generated is another living organism, either plant or animal. But whether an animal feeds on

---

[32] Other interpreters (see the London Seminar [Burnyeat et al. 1979, 82–85]; cf. Ross 1924, 2:198–99; Frede and Patzig 1988, 2:187–88) think that Aristotle takes the same material parts (the functional parts, such as hands and fingers) to be in a sense prior and in a sense posterior to the composite. The London Seminar suggests that the parts are posterior in definition and prior in some other sense. But since the whole discussion concerns definition, it seems more probable that the priority at issue is definitional. Furthermore, although scholars mention the central organ (heart or brain), which Aristotle says is simultaneous with the whole animal (1035^{b}25–27), they make no provision for the flesh and bones, which are treated in Z.10, not as functional matter, but as the matter into which the composite is destroyed. This matter, unlike the functional parts, should be prior in definition to the whole animal, since it can exist apart from the whole. The flesh and bones stand to a human being as the letters to a syllable; the syllable is divided into the letters, and they are prior to it (1034^{b}24–28; 1035^{a}9–12). Cf. the analogy between the syllable (and its letters) and flesh (and its elemental ingredients earth and fire) at Z.17, 1041^{b}11–33.

[33] *G.A.* I.20, 729^{a}9–11.

[34] See *G.A.* I.19, 726^{b}5–11 and 726^{b}30–727^{a}2.

[35] See *G.A.* I.20, 728^{a}26–27; cf. II.3, 737^{a}27–30.

[36] *P.A.* II.3, 650^{a}34–^{b}3; II.4, 651^{a}14–15.

other animals or directly on plants, the food for all animals ultimately derives from plants. Plants themselves acquire their nourishment from water and earth.[37] So, if the thread of organic generation is followed back to its ultimate source, it leads to earth and water: these are the simple sources from which organic generation begins. Since earth is the final outcome of organic destruction,[38] the generation of organisms presumably begins and ends with earth.

Chapter 7 will consider the generation of organisms in more detail, but for now it is enough to recognize that there are definite steps in the upward path of generation and downward path of destruction and that there are different materials at different levels. The various materials share a common substratum—the simple matter that begins and ends the generative process—but they differ in form. *Metaphysics* Z.10–11 adopts the view that the highest-level matter, the body of the organism, survives only as long as the composite itself survives. The nonuniform (ἀνομοιο-μερῆ) parts of an organism—parts that are indivisible into parts like the whole, such as arms, legs, and face—cannot be separated from the whole animal and survive as the parts that they were. A finger, for example, if separated from the animal, is merely "homonymous"—a finger in name only (1035ᵇ24–25), and no better than one made out of wood or painted in a picture.[39] Since Aristotle frequently relies on the homonymy principle in discussing material parts, let me briefly explain it.[40]

In the opening chapter of the *Categories*, Aristotle contrasts homonymy with synonymy. Two entities are *homonymous* if they share the same name but the name applies to the two objects for different reasons (1ᵃ1–6). For example, a man and a picture of a man are both called "animal," but not for the same reason.[41] Suppose that the genus animal is defined as "living thing that moves itself." This definition marks off animal from plant, both of which are classified as living things. When the name "animal" is used for a particular man or the species man, the name applies because man is something that satisfies the definition of animal: man is a living thing that moves itself. If the name "animal" is used for the picture of a man, the name applies, not for that reason, but because a pictured man is a two-dimensional representation of something that moves itself. Thus

[37] G.C. II.8, 335ᵃ10–14; cf. P.A. II.3, 650ᵃ21–23; II.10, 655ᵇ33–37.

[38] *Meteor.* IV.1, 379ᵃ16–26; cf. IV.12, 390ᵃ22–24.

[39] Such claims about the organic parts are very frequent; see, e.g., G.A. I.19, 726ᵇ22–24, II.1, 734ᵇ24–27; *De An.* II.1, 412ᵇ18–22; *Meteor.* IV.12, 389ᵇ32–390ᵃ2; 390ᵃ10–13.

[40] On this topic, see Ackrill [1972–1973] 1979, 70–73.

[41] Ackrill (1963, 71) points out that the word ζῷον, which originally meant "animal," came to be used for pictures and other representations, whether they represented animals or not. In what follows I assume that Aristotle is using the word in its original sense. If he is using it in the extended sense, then his example of homonymy is comparable to the example of "bank" mentioned below.

the reason why a pictured man is called "animal," though related to the reason why a genuine man is so called, is not the same. And presumably the explanations could be entirely different. English uses the name "bank" both for the earth that bounds a river and for an establishment for depositing money. Although the reasons for calling the two entities by the same name are unrelated, the entities satisfy Aristotle's criteria for being homonymous. By contrast, two entities are *synonymous* if they share the same name and for the same reason (1^a6–12). Thus both a man and an ox are called "animal" because both are living things that move themselves; hence the name applies to both for the same reason. The two entities are synonymous with respect to the name "animal."

In saying that a dead finger is merely homonymous and no better than one made out of wood or painted in a picture, Aristotle straightforwardly applies the homonymy principle from the *Categories*. Although a dead finger can be called a "finger," the explanation for the application, although related to the explanation for the proper application, is not the same. The living finger merits its name because it is able to perform certain functions that contribute to the life of the whole animal. The dead finger shares the same appearance, and may for some time retain the structure and texture that it previously had, but because it can no longer operate in the way that it earlier did, it is no longer a genuine finger but equivalent to the representation of one. The nonuniform parts of an organism depend for their identity on the soul of the creature, which determines their functions, and for this reason their existence coincides with that of the creature whose parts they are. In Z.11 Aristotle explains, "For it is not a hand in every state that is part of a man, but one able to perform its function, so that it is ensouled; and if it is not ensouled, it is not a part" (1036^b30–32). Thus the hand depends for its own identity on the soul of the human being. And although a dead hand may look like a hand, it has ceased to be genuine because it can no longer perform the operations proper to hands—the grasping, holding, and so on—that determine an object as a hand.[42] The whole complex array of nonuniform parts makes up the body of the organism and serves as its functional matter. And the whole body, like each of its nonuniform parts, depends for what it is on the soul of the creature.[43] Thus, at the moment when a human being dies, the functional body too is destroyed. Although the dead body may preserve the appearance that it had when living, it is quite different because, with the loss of soul, it can no longer operate as it previously did. Specified functionally, the organism's living body is posterior to the form because it claims its own identity from the form.

[42] On hands, see *P.A.* II.1, 646^b23–25; cf. IV.10, 690^a31–$^b3$.
[43] See *De An.* II.1, 412^b22–26; *Meteor.* IV.12, 389^b31–32.

Matter and the Account of the Form

The form of a perishable object is described in *Metaphysics* H.1 as "separate in account" (1042ª28–29). But the form of a sensible substance is not simply separate because it must be realized in some particular matter. The form of a human being, for example, is always found in flesh and bones.[44] Recall that *Metaphysics* E.1 mentions that part of the job of the natural philosopher is to study those aspects of soul that are not without matter. The question is why, if the form must be realized in some definite matter, the account of the form need not refer to the matter. Why should substantial form not resemble snubness, since it too is regularly realized in some definite matter? Aristotle considers this question in Z.11.

> Someone might also reasonably ask which parts belong to the form and which not, but to the composite. And indeed, if this is not clear it is not possible for each thing to be defined; for the definition is of the universal and the form; so, if it is not clear which of the parts are material and which not, neither will the account of the thing be evident. In the case of those things, then, that occur in [materials] different in form, for example, a circle in bronze and stone and wood, it seems clear in these cases that neither bronze nor stone belongs at all to the substance of circle because [a circle] occurs apart from them; but in the case of things that are not seen to exist apart, nothing prevents the situation from being the same for them, just as if all the circles ever seen were bronzen; for nonetheless the bronze would be no part of the form, although it would be hard to make the separation in thought. For example, the form of man always appears in fleshes and bones and in such parts; are these then parts of the form and account? Or not, but matter, but because [the form of man] does not occur in other [materials], we cannot make the separation? (1036ª26–ᵇ7)

The form of man resembles snubness because it always appears in the same materials. Like snubness, which always occurs in the nose, the form of man always occurs in flesh and bones. Nevertheless, Aristotle suggests, the form of man is more like a circle, which can be realized in various materials and so need not be defined with reference to any particular one. Any particular sort of matter is accidental to the circle because it can occur in others; since people have seen circles made out of various stuffs, they have no trouble making the separation. They do have difficulty, however, in the case of a form that always appears in the same ma-

---

[44] *Met.* Z.11, 1036ᵇ3–4 (quoted below). In Z.10 and 11 Aristotle speaks of the matter as something "upon which" (ἐφ' ἧς) the form comes to be (ἐπιγίγνεται). See Z.10, 1035ª4–5; 1035ª12 (which should probably read ἐφ' οἷς); Z.11, 1036ª31–32; 1036ᵇ6.

terial, for instance, the form of man in flesh and bones. In this case it might seem that the matter contributes to the form in the way that the nose contributes to snubness. But the situation is not the same. Aristotle says that cases in which a form is realized in a single material could resemble those in which a form is realized in various materials. Suppose that every circle were made of the same stuff. Even if this were so, the stuff would still not contribute to the nature of the circle, though the separation would be hard to make. He suggests that the form of man is like the hypothetical circle. Although the human soul always occurs in flesh and bones, these materials are accidental to the soul in much the same way that bronze is accidental to a circle.

Why should this be so? If the form of man could be realized in materials other than flesh and bones, as Aristotle suggests, then the relation between the human soul and the flesh and bones is not like that between snubness and nose, because the human soul could exist without these materials in a way that snubness cannot exist without the nose.[45] Snubness depends on the nose for what it is because, if concavity is realized in another material, the property itself is different. Recall that concavity realized in the legs is not snubness but bowleggedness.[46] The identity of the form does not depend on flesh and bones; it can be independent because, according to *Metaphysics* Z, flesh and bones are not the proximate subject in which the human soul is realized: the immediate subject for the form is the functional matter. Although Aristotle elsewhere includes flesh and bones among the functional parts,[47] in *Metaphysics* Z he cites these materials as the matter into which the composite human being is destroyed.[48] If the composite is destroyed into flesh and bones, they survive the death of the creature. Accordingly, the corpse still consists of these actual materials, even if they constitute merely homonymous hands and fingers.

Aristotle can argue that the form of a perishable object is separate in account because the proximate subject for the form is the functional matter, not the matter into which the composite is destroyed. Although the realization of the specific array of functions may require that there be stuff of a quite definite sort,[49] even perhaps that the stuff be flesh and bones, the particular stuff does not contribute to the nature of the form. On the contrary, the natural philosopher can presumably derive the properties

---

[45] Cf. Balme [1980] 1987, 294; Nussbaum and Putnam forthcoming, 7–17.

[46] *S.E.* I.31, 181^{b}35–182^{a}3.

[47] *G.A.* II.1, 734^{b}24–31; cf. *Meteor.* IV.12, 390^{a}14–15.

[48] *Met.* Z.10, 1035^{a}18–19; 1035^{a}31–^{b}1.

[49] Elsewhere Aristotle says that certain materials are "hypothetically necessary" if a particular end is to be realized; e.g., if there is to be a functional saw, it must be made out of iron (or at least some hard resistant stuff); see *Phys.* II.9, 199^{b}34–200^{a}15; 200^{a}30–^{b}8; *P.A.* I.1, 639^{b}24–27; 642^{a}9–13. This topic has been widely discussed recently; see Balme 1972, 76–84; Sorabji 1980, 143–54; and Cooper 1985.

that the stuff must have if he knows the functions that the matter is called to perform.[50] If the functions of a human being are to be realized, there must be matter that is sufficiently rigid, flexible, and so on; there must be some appropriate stuff that accommodates the relevant functions. But the nature of that material stuff contributes nothing to the form. The form requires that there be something that has the relevant functions, but the matter, functionally characterized, is wholly determined by the form. So the form predicated of the functional matter is not an instance of one thing predicated of another (ἄλλο κατ' ἄλλου λέγεσθαι) because the nature of the form and the functional matter is one and the same. Forms can therefore count as conceptually primary things because they are not defined through something else.[51]

Forms are vertical unities. The definition of soul in De Anima II.1 as "the first actuality of a natural instrumental body (σώματος φυσικοῦ ὀρ-γανικοῦ)" (412^{b}4–6) does not mention matter with an independent nature, for the body itself is specified as an instrument. Like other typical instruments, the body is defined by its function. Thus the nature of the organic body as such derives from the soul. Aristotle's definition of soul may be faulted for not conveying adequate information about the soul, but the conclusion should not be that the soul is defined with reference to some distinct matter. Aristotle can and does give a more informative account of soul in terms of functions alone.[52]

Having shown that form is a vertical unity, Aristotle can also argue that, in its relation to the functional matter, form is a subject. Remember that a subject is that of which other things are predicated but which is not itself predicated of something else (Met. Z.3, 1028^{b}36–37). Predicating the form of the functionally specified matter is not an instance of predicating one thing of another. Even so, this defense of the form as subject remains unsatisfactory because there is still a problem about the form and the lower matter of which it is predicated. As long as the lower matter is conceived as a distinct subject to which the form belongs, the form itself cannot satisfy the subject criterion because it is predicated of something else. The solution to this problem cannot emerge from Aristotle's treatment in Metaphysics Z but requires the modified account in H.6 and Θ.

Matter and the Account of the Composite

Individual composites actually contain matter because they come to be and pass away, and their constituent matter is in one way contemporane-

---

[50] Cf. Frede and Patzig 1988, 2:213; and Frede forthcoming, 12–14.

[51] See Met. Z.4, 1030^{a}7–14; Z.11, 1037^{a}33–^{b}4; cf. Z.6, 1031^{b}11–14. On this topic, see Frede forthcoming, esp. 16–27.

[52] De An. II.3, 414^{b}20–415^{a}13.

ous with them and in another way not. Their constituent matter, although functionally specified with reference to the substantial form, is also some definite stuff. And that definite stuff both receives the functional organization and survives the destruction of the individual when those functions have been removed. As Aristotle repeats in Z.10, a human being is destroyed into flesh and bones. The proximate matter of a living human is the flesh and bones functionally organized into a human body. Insofar as the proximate matter possesses a functional organization, it is defined with reference to the form and so is posterior in account to both the form and the composite. But insofar as the proximate matter is flesh and bones, which can survive the loss of the soul, the matter is distinct from the form and can exist without it. The flesh and bones, as we have seen, do not deprive the form of definitional unity because the form could be realized in other appropriate materials, even if in fact it always appears in these. But the flesh and bones do deprive the individual composite of definitional unity because the composite actually contains these materials as the substratum in which the functions are realized. Hence the account of the composite must specify both the form and the stuff in which the form is realized.

In Z.11 Aristotle criticizes Socrates the Younger, who apparently compared composites to circles and thought that a composite could, like a circle, be adequately defined without a reference to matter.[53] According to Aristotle, this proposal is unsound and leads away from the truth;[54] composites should be defined as "this in this." The passage begins with a reference to a view criticized just earlier (1036b7–20). Certain Platonists regard even formal parts as material parts and so eliminate them, with the result that they cannot differentiate entities that are evidently different.[55] Aristotle proceeds as follows:

[53] Although this passage resembles the one I discussed earlier, in which Aristotle compares the form of man to a circle (1036a26–b7), the thesis of Socrates the Younger concerns the *composite* man, whereas the earlier passage concerns the *form* of man. Notice that the first passage explicitly mentions "the form of man" (τὸ τοῦ ἀνθρώπου εἶδος) (1036b3), whereas this one speaks of "the man" (τὸν ἄνθρωπον) (1036b27) and "the animal" (τὸ ζῷον) and describes the latter as "something perceptible" (αἰσθητόν τι) (1036b28–29).

[54] On my view, in saying that the proposal is unsound and leads away from the truth (1036b24–26), Aristotle indicates that he rejects it. Other scholars urge that he simply means that the proposal (which, on their view, he basically accepts) is misleading because it might give the wrong impression. See Frede and Patzig 1988, 2:209–10; Frede forthcoming, 12; cf. Nussbaum and Putnam forthcoming, 17.

[55] According to Aristotle, in defining a triangle, the Platonists assume that lines and continuity are material parts and, eliminating them, define triangle as a number. He then objects that, on this view, the triangle and the number are indistinguishable. On his own view, lines are formal parts of a triangle, which must be mentioned in the account of the triangle (cf. *Po. An.* 1.4, 73a34–37). I thank Sarah Broadie for her insight concerning this argument.

We have pointed out, then, that there is a difficulty in the business of definition and why; so the reduction of all things in the way just described [by certain Platonists] and the elimination of matter is useless labor; for some things are presumably this [form] in this [matter] (τόδ᾽ ἐν τῷδε) or these things in such and such a state (ὡδὶ ταδὶ ἔχοντα). And the comparison about animal, which Socrates the Younger used to make, is not sound; for it leads away from the truth, and makes one suppose that it is possible for man to be without his parts, just as the circle [can be] without the bronze. But the situation is not similar; for an animal is something perceptible,[56] and it cannot be defined without [reference to] motion, and so not without its parts' being in some state. For it is not a hand in every state that is part of a man, but one able to perform its function, so that it is ensouled; and if it is not ensouled, it is not a part. (1036ᵇ21–32)

The definition of the animal must refer to the parts that are functionally organized. It is not enough to specify the functions alone (such an account would be an account of the form); the materials to which those functions belong must also be mentioned, in the case of an animal, the flesh and bones. These are the parts that are in the relevant state (ὡδὶ ταδὶ ἔχοντα), and because the parts that receive the functions can themselves be identified apart from those functions (since they can survive after the functions have been removed), the functions belong to the materials as "this in this," the two items being distinct. Since the functions belong to the underlying material as "one thing said of another," the definition of the composite is not a unity and therefore not strictly a definition.

Furthermore, the failure of unity within the individual composite results in a failure of unity within the universal composite, such as the species man and the species horse and the genus animal. Although the universal composite contains no actual matter, since it is ungenerated, its account must nonetheless refer to matter. The account of the species and genus must specify the matter because the universals classify concrete composites as wholes and not merely their formal part. So, if the lower constituent matter contributes to the nature of the individual, such matter, taken universally, must also be mentioned in the account of the species to which the individual belongs. I have called attention to several texts in which Aristotle claims that the universal composite consists of the form and the matter taken universally.[57] Like the account of snubness, the account of the universal composite displays the structure "this in this," or "one thing in another." Although the account of the universal

---

[56] I read αἰσθητόν, which occurs in the manuscripts, rather than αἰσθητικόν ("perceptive"), conjectured by Frede and Patzig (1988, 2:210–11); cf. Frede forthcoming, 8.

[57] See above, p. 122.

composite need not mention the particular material differences between the individuals it classifies, it must mention the common nature of that material. This is what it means to say that the universal composite is from matter "taken universally." Since the account of the universal composite must mention the matter, it now turns out that, while such composites resemble snubness, the individual is really comparable to a snub nose. A snub nose, as Aristotle evidently enjoys explaining, is concavity-in-a-nose in a nose.[58] The concrete composite is specified with reference to matter and also contains matter. The matter turns up twice over in its account, both as the universal sort proper to its kind and as the particularized stuff proper to itself.

At the end of Z.11 Aristotle sums up the main points about essence and definition that have been established in Z.4–11.[59] According to my reconstruction of the earlier argument, he should conclude that forms alone are strictly definable because they alone are unities. Some account of the generated composite can be given, but because it must mention the particular and changeable matter in which the functions are realized, the account is not a definition. Indeed, the specification will need revision whenever the composite changes. The final summary accords with this interpretation, with one crucial difference: Aristotle now suggests that composites are definable in terms of their form alone (1037^{a}26–29).[60] Even so, he does not say that an account of the form is an adequate account of the composite; and since he immediately reinvokes the analogy between a particular man and a snub nose, he presumably intends no modification of the

[58] See *Met.* Z.5, 1030^{b}28–1031^{a}1; cf. Z.11, 1037^{a}30–32. On this topic see Balme 1984, esp. 2–4.

[59] Many scholars describe the connection between the summary and earlier passages in Z.4–6 and 10–11 and point out that no reference is made to Z.7–9. They regard this as confirming evidence that Z.7–9 is a later addition and not part of the main project of Z.4–6 and Z.10–11; see Ross 1924, 2:204; Furth 1985, 121; Frede and Patzig 1988, 2:217–18. But if I am right that (1) the defense of forms and rejection of composites as definable unities depends upon whether or not matter must be mentioned in the account, (2) things that contain matter must be defined with reference to matter, and (3) whether something contains matter depends upon whether or not it is generated, then the summary in Z.11, which mentions that composites do but forms do not contain matter (1037^{a}25–26), is an implicit reference to Z.7–9.

[60] I agree with those who take this claim to conflict with Aristotle's general view in Z.10–11; see Ross 1924, 2:205; the London Seminar (Burnyeat et al. 1979, 97–98); and Balme 1987b, 302. Frede (forthcoming) argues that the claim conflicts only with the passage criticizing Socrates the Younger and proposes that that is the passage to be reinterpreted. But even if one restricts the context to Z.10–11, there are a number of passages besides the one about Socrates the Younger that apparently conflict—in particular, those comparing composites to snubness or snub noses (1035^{a}17–27; 1037^{a}29–^{b}5 [part of the final summary]) and those specifying universal composites as having both formal and material features (1035^{b}27–31; 1037^{a}5–10). It therefore seems more likely that the final passage presents the new departure.

earlier theory. That theory has led relentlessly to the conclusion that composites are not definable. Still, the claim may foretell the final conclusion of H.6 and Θ, since the ultimate task will be to show that composites can be defined with reference to their form alone, and that such an account is an adequate definition. But Aristotle has given no argument yet for the adequacy of such an account.

So what the essence is and in what sense it is in virtue of itself (αὐτὸ καθ᾽ αὑτό) has been stated generally for every case, and why in some cases the account of the essence contains the parts of the thing defined, and in some cases not. And [we have stated] that in the account of substance the material parts will not be present, for they are not parts of that substance [the form] but of the composite substance. And of the latter [the composite] there is in a sense an account and in a sense not. For there is no account of it with its matter (for it is indefinite),[61] but there is [an account of it] in respect of the primary substance—for example, of man, the account of the soul. For the form within is the substance, and the thing composed out of the form and the matter is called the composite substance. For example, concavity [is the form within] (for from this and the nose there are snub nose and snubness, since the nose will be doubly present in these). But in the composite substance, for instance, in snub nose or Callias, the matter too is present. And [we have stated] that the essence and each thing are in some cases the same, as in the case of primary substances, for example, curvature and the being for curvature, if this is primary.[62] I mean by primary [substance] what is not specified by being one thing in another (ἄλλο ἐν ἄλλῳ), that is, in a subject as matter (ὑποκειμένῳ ὡς ὕλη). But things that are matter or compounded with matter are not the same [as their essence]; nor are things that are one accidentally, for instance, Socrates and musical, for these are the same accidentally. (1037ᵃ21–ᵇ7)

---

[61] Ross (1924, 2:205) and others regard the "indefinite" matter as prime matter, but other commentators do not agree; for one view, see Frede and Patzig 1988, 2:218. I agree with David Balme (1984, 1, 4–5) that the indefiniteness of the matter concerns the variability of its properties (see above, p. 125 and n. 28), and I owe the idea of interpreting the indefiniteness in this way in *Met.* Z to Tim Maudlin. In *Met.* Θ.7 Aristotle again speaks of matter as "indefinite" (1049ᵃ36–ᵇ2) but for a different reason; see below, pp. 151–55.

[62] I retain the example about curvature, although Jaeger (1957) and Frede and Patzig (1988, 2:219) regard it as a gloss. Even though curvature is in fact a quality and not a primary substance, Aristotle has relied extensively on analogies between properties like concavity and substantial forms, whose accounts need not refer to matter, and between properties like snubness and composites, whose accounts require the reference. Since he has just reinvoked the analogy with snubness in discussing composites, it is appropriate for him also to reinvoke the analogy between curvature and forms; cf. Z.10, 1036ᵃ1–2.

According to this passage, form is strictly definable because its account need not refer to matter. Since forms are ungenerated, they do not contain matter; and although forms cannot exist without matter, the matter required for their realization is fully determined by the form. Therefore substantial form succeeds as a primary thing because it is not specified as "one thing in another," that is, as something in "a subject as matter." Although the form can be defined as "this in this," as in the definitions of soul in *De Anima* II.1, the two items specified are not distinct from each other. Hence a definition of soul that mentions the functional body is not a definition through something else that claims conceptual priority. On the other hand, the composite, which is generated, contains matter; and since the constituent matter possesses an indefinite assortment of features that distinguish the composite from others of the same sort, the composite as such is not definable. Its nature must be spelled out as "one thing in another"—a form in a distinct material subject. To the extent that the composite is definable at all, it is definable with reference to its form alone. This claim, which seems entirely unsupported by the earlier argument, may be a present concession to the entities that will ultimately be shown to be definable unities.

If this were the end of the story, Aristotle's verdict about composites would seem to be fatal. But the story continues. At the end of Z Aristotle treats substance as the cause of unity for generated composites, expands this account in H, and in H.6 returns once more to the topic of definitional unity and this time argues that composites as well as their forms are definable unities.

Vertical Unity

Aristotle opens the discussion in H.6 by recalling a puzzle about definition that had been raised earlier,[63] and he asks, "What is the cause of the unity [of definition]?" (1045^{a}8). Given the discussion of definition in Z, one might expect H.6 to confine its own discussion to the unity of form. But formal unity is not the the only topic of H.6. Aristotle presents two sorts of examples and claims that both admit the same solution. The first example concerns the unity of form and recalls a previous discussion in Z.12; the second concerns the unity of the material composite.

Aristotle first asks why man is one thing and not many. Since the name "man" can apply to either the composite or the form,[64] one might initially question whether his treatment concerns man as species (a universal composite) or man as form. But that question is unimportant because, even if

---

[63] See *Met.* H.3, 1044^{a}2–6.
[64] *Met.* Z.10, 1035^{b}1–3; Z.11, 1037^{a}7–10; H.3, 1043^{a}29–^{b}4.

he treats the species, which is defined with reference to matter, his topic is not the unity of matter and form but the unity of genus and differentia, and such unity is problematic for both the form and the species.[65] I assume that the discussion concerns the account of the form. Aristotle states the problem as one that a Platonist faces, and he objects that the difficulty cannot be solved by those who approach definition as the Platonists do. Aristotle states his own solution in his response to them.

The Unity of Genus and Differentia

Aristotle asks, Why is man one thing and not many, if man partakes of more than one thing, for instance, animal and biped?

> So what is it that makes man one, and why is man one and not many, for instance, animal and biped, especially if, as some say, there is animal itself and biped itself? For why is not man those things themselves, and so men will exist by participation not in man nor in one thing but two, animal and biped, and so generally man would be not one but more than one—animal and biped? Evidently, then, for those who proceed thus in their customary way of defining and speaking, it is not possible to explain and solve the difficulty. (1045ᵃ14–22)

In response to this difficulty, Aristotle offers the following proposal: "But if, as we say, there is on the one hand matter (τὸ μὲν ὕλη) and on the other hand form (τὸ δὲ μορφή), and the one in potentiality (τὸ μὲν δυνάμει), the other in actuality (τὸ δὲ ἐνεργείᾳ), the thing being sought would no longer seem to be a difficulty" (1045ᵃ23–25). Aristotle charges that the Platonist cannot overcome the problem of unity. If man partakes of two separate Platonic Forms, Animal and Biped, then man is not one thing because man partakes of two distinct natures, animal and biped. Aristotle proposes that animal and biped—here treated as the genus and the differentiating feature of man—should be viewed, the one as matter or potentiality, the other as form or actuality; and he claims that, if the issue is handled in this way, the problem about unity ceases to be a difficulty.

The unity of genus and differentia is in fact a much simpler problem than the unity of matter and form, but the puzzle about genus and differentia is evidently supposed to bear on the deeper puzzle because the passage that follows next (1045ᵃ25–33) tackles that very topic and asks, What is the cause of the unity of bronze and sphere? And Aristotle claims that

---

[65] Just as the composite man is defined with reference to the genus animal and differentia biped, so human soul can be defined with reference to the genus soul and those differentiating features that mark off the human soul from others; cf. De An. II.3, 414ᵇ32–415ᵃ12.

the difficulty is the same as the earlier one and that the solution is to view one part as matter and potentiality, the other part as form and actuality. So he apparently thinks that his account of the unity of genus and differentia will help to solve a comparable problem about the unity of matter and form. Let us, then, consider why he takes his proposal, that matter is potentiality and form actuality, to solve the problem of the unity of genus and differentia.

Aristotle's puzzle in H.6 recalls an earlier discussion in Z.12.[66] There he poses the question as follows: "Why is something, whose account we call a definition, one—for example, man [whose account is] 'biped animal'? For let this be the account of man" (1037^b11–13). In Z.12 Aristotle asks, Why are animal and biped one and not many? Why is the combination biped animal different from an accidental unity like white man? He claims that, in the case of white man, there is a plurality when one term does not belong to the other but a unity when it does; when the subject possesses the attribute, the white man is one thing (1037^b13–18). But the unity is accidental. In the case of animal and biped, he insists that the first does not partake of the second; the genus does not partake of its differentiae, as a man partakes of whiteness.

This observation is significant. Aristotle denies that a genus partakes of its differentiae because the items that differentiate a genus are contraries and hence, if the genus did partake of them, it would simultaneously partake of contraries (1037^b18–21). Of course, an object can partake of contraries simultaneously, if the opposed properties belong to it accidentally and if they characterize the subject in different respects. As Plato wrote in the *Phaedo*, Simmias can be at once large and small—large in comparison with Socrates, and small in comparison with Phaedo.[67] But the differentiae are evidently not accidental properties of the genus, since it is the determinable kind that the differentiae determine. Nor can the genus partake of the differentiae as essential properties because, if it did, it would partake of mutually exclusive essential features. Animal, for example, would be both footed and footless, winged and wingless, and so on, and this is impossible.[68]

Since the genus does not partake of its differentiae, its relation to the differentiae is not that of a subject to its accidental or essential properties. Instead, the genus is that common character shared by its various differentiated species. The genus locates an object within a general group consisting of entities with common properties; and if someone undertakes to define an entity, this classification is a useful starting point from which to begin the differentiation. But once the specific features have been singled

---

[66] On the unity of definition in Z.12, see Frede forthcoming, 22–26.

[67] *Phaedo* 102a10–103c9.

[68] Cf. Aristotle's objections to Anaximander's ἄπειρον ("boundless") in *G.C.* II.5, 332^a20–26, discussed below in the Appendix.

out that distinguish one object from others within the larger group, no information is added by mentioning the genus.[69] If, for example, to be an animal is to be a living thing that moves itself, and if one knows that a human being is something that moves itself in a two-footed fashion, no information is added by mentioning the general features of which man's capacities are specific differentiations. Aristotle says in Z.12 that, if someone performs the division correctly, taking a differentia of a differentia (e.g., two-footed as a differentia of footed), he can define the species with reference to the last differentia alone. The last differentia is the form and substance of the thing defined (1038^a25-26). In fact, the situation is more complicated than portrayed in Z.12 because an entity is differentiated in a variety of ways (by style of motion, perception, feeding, reproduction, and so forth);[70] but, even so, the simplified point of Z.12 should hold: if the division has been properly performed, the definition can be stated, without reference to the genus, in terms of the final differentia (or set of differentiae) alone. Thus, a definition of man as "biped animal" does not specify two things, animal and biped, but one thing in two ways. And since the genus is not something over and above its differentiae, it is not some distinct entity that needs to be tied together with them. In Z.12 Aristotle suggests that the genus either does not exist at all apart from its species, or if it does, it exists merely "as matter" (1038^a5-9). In H.6 he calls the genus matter and potential because the genus is something indefinite that can be divided into definite species, and he calls the differentia form and actuality because the differentia marks off some definite species from among the possible differentiations.

The unity of genus and differentia is unproblematic because the genus is indefinite and general but not distinct in nature from its differentiated species. Once Aristotle recalls in H.6 how the genus and differentia are unified and points out that the one (genus) is matter and potentiality, and the other (differentia) form and actuality, he turns to the recalcitrant problem about the unity of matter and form.

The Unity of Matter and Form

Aristotle considers a bronze sphere and claims that the difficulty in this case is the same as the one about biped animal. He says that there is no longer any difficulty if one thinks of the bronze as matter and potentiality, and the sphere as form and actuality.

---

[69] Cf. *Cat.* 5, 2^b7-22.

[70] In *P.A.* 1.2–3 Aristotle argues that proper definition in biology requires that one divide by many differentiae at once, and he objects to the view, which *Met.* Z.12 might be taken to hold, that a species can be marked off by a single differentiating feature. The account in Z.12 may be simplified merely for the sake of clarity. On definition in the biology, see Balme 1972, 101–19; 1987a; Gotthelf 1985; Lennox 1987a; 1987b; and Bolton 1987.

This difficulty would be the same too if [we supposed that] the definition of cloak were "the spherical bronze." For this name ["cloak"] would be a sign of the account. Therefore, the question is, What is the cause of the unity of the spherical and the bronze? Indeed the difficulty disappears because the one is matter (τὸ μὲν ὕλη), the other form (τὸ δὲ μορφή). So what is the cause of this, of something in potentiality (τὸ δυνάμει ὄν) to be in actuality (ἐνεργείᾳ εἶναι), except the maker, in the case of things [for which] there is generation? For there is no other cause of the sphere in potentiality being a sphere in actuality, but this was the essence for each. (1045ᵃ25–33)

This passage is extremely puzzling, given the treatment of composites in *Metaphysics* Z. How can Aristotle think that the problem of the bronze sphere admits the same solution as that for biped animal? According to the account of composites in Z, matter like bronze is a distinct subject to which the spherical shape belongs. Thus, the shape is in the bronze, as *this* form *in this* matter. The relation of subject to predicate can be spelled out in various ways—for example, one might say that the bronze partakes of the shape, as a man who is white partakes of whiteness.[71] The problem of unity for material composites results from the fact that, although the bronze is potentially spherical, it is also actually bronze. Thus, in spelling out what the composite is, one must specify two distinct things—the matter and the form. Both the matter and form are conceptually prior to the composite itself because it is defined with reference to them.

Later in the chapter Aristotle seems to reject the conception of matter and form that he has exploited up until now. He criticizes various ways of treating the relation between matter and form.

On account of this difficulty [about unity] some people speak of participation (μέθεξιν), and they puzzle about what the cause of participation is and what participation is; and some [speak of] communion (συνουσίαν),[72] as Lycophon says that knowledge [is a communion] of knowing and soul; and some [speak of] living as a combination (σύνθεσιν) or binding together (σύνδεσμον) of soul and body. And yet the same account applies to all cases; for being healthy too will be either a communion or binding together or composition of soul and health, and the bronze being a triangle will be a combination of bronze and triangle, and being white a combination of surface and whiteness. The reason is that they seek a unifying (ἑνοποιόν) formula and a difference (διαφοράν) between potentiality and actuality. (1045ᵇ7–17)

---

[71] Cf. Z.12, 1037ᵇ14–18.
[72] I exclude ψυχῆς at 1045ᵇ10, following Ross (1924) and Jaeger (1957).

Aristotle concludes by recalling his earlier discussion about the bronze sphere.

> But, as we have said, the proximate matter and the form are the same and one, the one in potentiality (⟨τὸ μὲν⟩ δυνάμει), the other in actuality (τὸ δὲ ἐνεργείᾳ), so that it is like seeking what the cause is of unity and being one; for each thing is some one thing, and what is in potentiality (τὸ δυνάμει) and what is in actuality (τὸ ἐνεργείᾳ) are somehow one, so that there is no other cause [of the unity] unless there is something that produced the movement from potentiality to actuality. (1045ᵇ17–22)

The conception to which Aristotle objects, according to which matter and form are viewed as distinct and then combined to yield a unified whole, is precisely the one that he himself used in his treatment of composites in *Metaphysics* Z. Composites were compared to snubness and snub noses; such entities are what they are because a distinct and definite subject (such as a nose) possesses a property (such as concavity). And that possession can be described in various ways, such as participation, communion, or whatever. In Z.7 Aristotle says that the account of a bronze sphere mentions the matter because the object is specified in both ways, as "bronze" and as "sphere" (1033ᵃ1–5). Since the matter and form are distinct, one seeks a unifying relation. Thus, one might say that the bronze "partakes" of sphericality or that the shape "belongs to," or "is in," the bronze. The bronze sphere, as conceived in Z, displays the structure *this in this*, or *one thing in another*. Aristotle's present proposal, which he states in his conclusion, and which apparently restates the earlier suggestion concerning the bronze sphere, is that the proximate matter and form are *one and the same*—the one in potentiality, the other in actuality. Apparently, then, the earlier passage does concern a conception other than the one that I traced through the middle chapters of Z.

What is Aristotle's proposal? Since, on the one hand, he rejects the idea that matter and form are distinct and must be tied together by some unifying relation and claims, on the other, that the unity of the bronze sphere is to be understood in the same way as that for biped animal, it seems possible that he thinks that matter and form really are comparable to genus and differentia. Recall that, in his treatment of genus and differentia in Z.12, he considered and rejected the idea that the genus partakes of the differentia (1037ᵇ18–22). In H.6 he also denies that matter partakes of form. If the matter is a sort of genus and the form a differentiating feature, then the generic bronze should not partake of the spherical shape any more than animal partakes of biped.

Such an interpretation, however, in no way guarantees that the same solution will work for the bronze sphere that works for biped animal be-

143

cause, even if matter is a genus, the bronze, which the spherical differentiates, is a different sort of genus from animal, which biped differentiates. Generic bronze is not the characteristic genus of sphericality. On the contrary, shape is the genus that sphericality differentiates in the way that biped differentiates animal. And although the mention of an ordinary genus, like shape, adds no information once sphericality has been mentioned, this does not seem to be true of bronze in relation to sphericality. The nature of bronze cannot be determined simply by inspecting sphericality, since the concept of bronze is not included in the concept of the spherical, as that of shape is. Therefore, if the bronze must be mentioned in an account of the bronze sphere, information is still added because bronze is identified by distinct properties that sphericality does not entail. Thus, even if Aristotle regards bronze as a genus and the shape as a differentiating feature, there remains a puzzle about how the unity can be achieved.

Before the puzzle in H.6 can be properly understood, to say nothing of its solution, Aristotle's theory of generation needs to be reexamined. In his treatment of generation Aristotle suggests a crucial modification of the construction model that leaves room for the positive assessment in H.6 that composites are vertical unities.

CHAPTER FIVE

THE UNITY OF COMPOSITE
SUBSTANCES

Consider again the paradox of unity. Vertical unity, as I have characterized it, is definable unity. An entity is a vertical unity only if its nature can
be specified without mentioning one thing in another, where the two
items mentioned are distinct from each other.[1] If an entity C is defined as
a B in an A, where all three items are distinct, then A and B are conceptually
prior to C.[2] Vertical unity guarantees an entity conceptual priority because
a vertical unity is not defined through something else that is prior to it.
Aristotle argues forcefully in *Metaphysics* Z that substantial forms are vertical unities: since forms are ungenerated, they do not contain matter; and
although the form of a perishable object cannot exist without matter, the
form is conceptually independent of the persisting matter in which it is
realized. And if, in some cases, a form is defined with reference to functional matter (as is the soul in *De Anima* II.1), the matter, functionally
characterized, does not deprive the form of vertical unity because the nature of the functional matter is not distinct from the form itself. So the
form can be defined as "this in this" without loss of vertical unity; there
is no loss of vertical unity if a C is defined as a B in an A, where A, B, and
C have the same nature.

If composites are to succeed as genuine or primary substances, they
must be vertical unities. Yet, since they are generated and since generation
demands horizontal unity, how can they be vertical unities? In order to
avoid the Parmenidean objection against change, Aristotle insists that
there is a continuant which guarantees that the generation of something
new is not a sheer emergence of something out of nothing. A generated
product comes to be from something else, and the matter of the preexisting entity survives in the product. Since the entity that accounts for horizontal continuity can exist before it constitutes the composite and can
continue in existence after the composite has been destroyed, the continuant has a nature distinct from the form that makes the composite the
sort of thing that it is. But if the continuant is a distinct subject within the
composite, the composite itself is not a vertical unity because its nature is
specified as one thing in another, as "this in this," where the two items—

---

[1] *Met.* Z.4, 1030ᵃ2–17; Z.11, 1037ᵃ33–ᵇ7.
[2] Cf. Introduction, pp. 3–5.

the form and the matter—are distinct from each other. Thus the demand for horizontal unity conflicts with the demand for vertical unity.

Is there a solution to the paradox of unity for material composites? In *Metaphysics* H.6 Aristotle seems to think that there is, for he claims that the proximate matter and form are one and the same—the one in potentiality, the other in actuality (1045^b17–19). According to my analysis of *Metaphysics* Z, the matter of an organism, functionally characterized, is posterior to both the form and the composite because the functions are determined by the form of the organism. The problem for composites arises because their proximate matter is not exhausted by the functional characterization but is, in addition, some distinct stuff that has those functions. And that identifiable stuff survives when the composite is destroyed. Hence that distinct stuff is the source of the failure of unity for composite bodies.

If Aristotle could account for horizontal unity without requiring the persistence of a distinct subject that temporarily receives the form, he might be able to demonstrate that composites are vertical unities after all. If he could show that there is a continuant that preserves substantial change from the Parmenidean objection, yet one that contributes nothing to the nature of the composite, then perhaps he could offer a defense of composites, which contain matter, analogous to the defense of immanent forms, which cannot exist without it.

This is precisely what his construction model,[3] properly interpreted, enables him to do. Recall that generation, on the construction model, crosses levels and that the generated product is more complex than the stuff out of which it is generated. The matter from which the composite is generated survives, but at the lower level. This point is crucial. As I have interpreted the model so far, and as Aristotle interprets it in *Metaphysics* Z, the lower-level matter survives as an actual subject within the product and acquires a new form. Thus, at the highest step of the generative cycle, the ultimate simple matter is still an actual constituent but is covered with layers of form. This conception of material persistence leads to a failure of vertical unity for generated composites. But Aristotle has another way to interpret the model, and by giving a different interpretation of the way in which the matter survives at the lower level, he can resolve the paradox of unity for composites.

POTENTIAL CONTINUANTS

In chapter 2 I quoted a passage from *De Caelo* III.3 that illuminates the present topic.

---

[3] On Aristotle's construction model, see above, pp. 94–97.

Let an element of bodies be that into which the other bodies are divided (διαιρεῖται), which is present in (ἐνυπάρχον) [the other bodies] either potentially or actually (for in which way this occurs is still disputable), and which is itself indivisible (ἀδιαίρετον) into [bodies] different in form (τῷ εἴδει). . . . If our statement [identifies] an element, there must be bodily elements. For in flesh and wood and each thing of this sort, fire and earth are potentially present. For if these [fire and earth] are separated out (ἐκκρινόμενα) of those [flesh and wood], they [fire and earth] are apparent. But neither flesh nor wood is present in fire, either potentially or actually; for [if it were] it could be separated out (ἐξεκρίνετο). (302ᵃ15–25)

Aristotle suggests that there are two ways in which the matter could be "present in" the higher-level complex and says that the way in which the simpler stuff is present remains disputable. The matter might be actually present or it might be merely potentially present, but in either case it should be possible to extract the matter by some physical process. The uniform stuffs, flesh and wood, are not present in fire either potentially or actually because fire cannot be dissolved into those stuffs. On the other hand, the simple stuffs, fire and earth, are present in the higher materials because flesh and wood are constructed out of the elements and can by some procedure be dissolved into them again. Aristotle suggests that the elements are merely potentially present in the complex stuffs.

In *Generation and Corruption* I.10 Aristotle discusses two sorts of combination: σύνθεσις, which preserves the ingredients intact and which we might call a "mixture," and μίξις, which preserves the ingredients merely potentially and which we might call a "compound" or "chemical combination."[4] The famous barley drink consisting of barley, cheese, and wine, which Heraclitus said must be kept stirred, is a σύνθεσις;[5] if the drink is allowed to stand, the ingredients immediately separate because the components are actually present in the combination. But uniform bodies (ὁμοιομερῆ)—stuffs that can be divided into parts like the whole, such as the flesh and wood mentioned in *De Caelo*—do not break down into their ingredients in this straightforward manner because in a genuine μίξις the ingredients are not actually present. Even so, a chemical combination is produced from ingredients that were originally separate, and those ingredients can be separated out again. Aristotle gives this account of chemical combination:

---

[4] For helpful discussions of the difference between σύνθεσις and μίξις, see Bogaard 1979, esp. 11, 18–19; and Waterlow 1982, 83–87.
[5] Heraclitus DK B125.

Not everything can be chemically combined (μικτόν) with every-thing, but each of the items combined must exist separately (χωρισ-τόν), and none of the properties (πάθη) is separate [hence properties are not entities that enter into a combination]. But since some entities exist in potentiality, some in actuality, it is possible for items com-bined somehow to exist and not to exist, for when something that is other in actuality has been generated from them, still [the ingredi-ents] are each in potentiality what they were before they were com-bined, and not destroyed—for this was the difficulty that emerged earlier. And it is clear that the items combined both come together from having been separate earlier (πρότερον ἐκ κεχωρισμένων) and are able to be separate again (δυνάμενα χωρίζεσθαι πάλιν). So nei-ther do they remain in actuality, like body and white, nor are they destroyed (either one of them or both), for their potentiality is pre-served (σώζεται γὰρ ἡ δύναμις αὐτῶν). (327ᵇ20–31)

The ingredients of a compound exist separately as those ingredients be-fore they enter into the combination and will exist separately again once the combination has been dissolved. While the compound exists, the in-gredients, although not destroyed, are not actually present either—their potentiality alone is somehow preserved.[6]

In *Physics* I.9 Aristotle offers a general account of the role of matter in substantial generation and again insists that the preexisting matter is ac-tually destroyed but preserved in potentiality. "In a sense it [the matter] comes to be and is destroyed, but in a sense not. For as that in which (τὸ ἐν ᾧ), in itself (καθ' αὑτό) it is destroyed (for the thing destroyed, the privation, is in this); but as potential (κατὰ δύναμιν), in itself (καθ' αὑτό) it is not [destroyed], but on the contrary, it must be undestroyed and ungenerated" (192ᵃ25–29).[7] This passage claims that, in one sense, the matter is in itself (καθ' αὑτό) destroyed and in another sense it is in itself (καθ' αὑτό) preserved. As the subject in which (τὸ ἐν ᾧ) the privation is located, the matter is in itself destroyed; but as potential, it is in itself preserved. Aristotle is not merely claiming that the matter is accidentally

---

[6] For two interpretations of Aristotle's theory that differ from each other and from my own, see Joachim 1922, 179–81, and Bogaard 1979, 19–21. According to Joachim, the in-gredients of a μίξις are preserved at a "lower grade of being"; according to Bogaard, when a new level of actuality is achieved, the ingredients are "screened from our view," not be-cause their powers are lowered, but because they are modified by the new powers gained. I disagree with the latter proposal because it suggests that the ingredients are actually pre-served (even though modified) within the generated compound.

[7] This passage is frequently cited as evidence for Aristotle's commitment to prime matter. See, e.g., Zeller 1897, 1:345 nn. 1, 3; A. Mansion 1945, 74–75; and Robinson 1974, 173–75. By contrast, Happ (1971, 35, 296–97) takes the "first" subject to be the proximate matter for generation (e.g., καταμήνια or bronze); cf. Charlton 1970, 83.

destroyed when the privation in it is destroyed because he says that the matter as "that in which" the privation is located is in itself destroyed when the privation in it is destroyed.[8] Water and earth, once they have been worked up into a compound, such as copper, have ceased to be separate subjects in which the "uncoppered" privation is located; they have been actually and in themselves destroyed as the subjects that they originally were and so cannot be reidentified within the copper as those stuffs. Still, in another way, the water and earth are not in themselves destroyed because they survive as potential, being in this sense "undestroyed and ungenerated." According to this passage, as in the passage on μίξις, the preexisting matter is actually destroyed but survives in the product potentially.

What is the meaning of Aristotle's claim that the preexisting matter survives in the product potentially but is actually destroyed? *Metaphysics* Θ.7 provides a valuable guide.

GENERIC MATTER

In *Metaphysics* Θ.7 Aristotle undertakes to explain when the preexisting matter from which a product is generated can properly be said to be potentially that product. Thus the immediate topic of Θ.7 is the preexisting material, not the material continuant, and Aristotle's question is, Which of the various materials in the upward steps of generation is the one to which the potentiality belongs to be the highest-level product? Is the lowest-level matter potentially the highest-level product, or not? According to the construction model in H.5, a human being perishes into a corpse and a corpse into some simple matter. Only then can a human being be generated again. Is the ultimate simple matter potentially a complex physical object such as a human being? Is earth, for example, potentially a man? Aristotle asks this question at the beginning of Θ.7 and answers in the negative (1049^a1). The ultimate matter must first be worked up into something else, and that matter may have to be worked up further. *Metaphysics* Θ.7 asks the question for both artifacts and living things. The present discussion will be restricted to artifacts.[9]

Is earth potentially a statue? It is not, Aristotle says. Earth must first be worked up into bronze, and only then is there matter that is potentially a statue ($1049^a16–18$). He offers a criterion by which to decide when the preexisting matter deserves to be called potential: the matter is potential if it does not itself impede the generation by needing something added,

---

[8] The point is mistaken by Robinson (1974, 173–75); cf. Ross 1936, 498.

[9] The treatment of organisms will be discussed in chapter 7, in the section "The Life Cycle."

subtracted, or changed ($1049^{a}8–11$). Thus earth is not potentially a statue because it is too crumbly and dry; earth is difficult if not impossible to mold, and if it can be molded it is apt to lose its shape. Earth must first be worked up into a material, such as bronze, that has the right dispositional properties for the production of a statue.[10] Only if the materials for construction are suitably prepared are they strictly potentially the product. Earth is potentially tin and copper, but it must first be chemically combined with water and transformed into these metals, and these metals must themselves be chemically combined before there is a material that has an adequate set of dispositional properties for the construction of a statue. Only once bronze has been generated is there something that is potentially a statue in the sense that the matter itself needs nothing added, subtracted, or changed. Aristotle's proposal seems to be that a subject has a potentiality for a particular goal only if its own nature is suitable for the realization of that goal. I will call Aristotle's criterion the *suitable-kind* condition. A material belongs to a suitable kind if it possesses the dispositional properties required for the production of a particular product. This condition is fundamental for Aristotle's theory of potentiality, which will be discussed in more detail in chapter 6.

Since different physical objects have different functions to perform, different materials are suitable for different productions.[11] Wood, for example, is not a viable material for ovenware because wood is combustible when subjected to heat;[12] but clay, which is solidified by heat and cannot be softened, is ideal for such products.[13] Earth is an ingredient of both wood and clay but does not itself possess the dispositional properties proper to either.[14] However, if combined in a proper ratio with water (in the case of clay) or with air (in the case of wood),[15] the resulting combination is clay or wood; so earth is potentially clay and potentially wood, and once properly combined with water to yield clay, there is matter of a suitable kind for some higher-level product, such as an ovenware pot.

Aristotle has claimed that, if the matter is suitable for a particular out-

---

[10] Various scholars emphasize the role of dispositional properties in Aristotle's account of potentiality; see, e.g., Dancy 1978, 404–6; Freeland 1987, 396–98; and Lennox forthcoming.

[11] Cf. *Met.* H.4, $1044^{a}27–29$, which insists on such suitability, saying that a saw cannot be made out of wood or wool.

[12] See *Meteor.* IV.9, $387^{b}14–388^{a}9$.

[13] Aristotle discusses several dispositional properties of clay: mode of solidification (*Meteor.* IV.6, $383^{a}14–26$; cf. IV.3, $380^{b}8–11$); unsoftenability (IV.7, $384^{b}1–23$), inflexibility (IV.9, $385^{b}27–29$), and breakability (IV.9, $386^{a}9–12$).

[14] See, e.g., *Meteor.* IV.7, $384^{b}15–16$ (on wood), and IV.6, $383^{a}14–26$ (on clay).

[15] The view expressed in *Meteorology* IV, that wood is a compound of earth and air, might seem to conflict with that cited above from *De Caelo* III.3, according to which wood is a compound of earth and fire; but in fact every composite body contains all four elements (see *G.C.* II.8).

come, it must be such that no further additions to, subtractions from, or changes in it are needed before it is brought into service. This is not to say, however, that proper preparation is sufficient for the actual survival of the preexisting matter when production takes place. The potter's clay must still be molded and fired, and only then does something exist that is an ovenware pot. Eggs, flour, water, butter, and sugar must be mixed and baked, and only then is there something that is cake. And although both products share many features in common with the original ingredients, one need not suppose that those original stuffs actually persist in the product. In *Metaphysics* Θ.7 Aristotle attributes a potentiality to the preexisting material that is properly prepared, but he apparently envisages a further transformation of the matter when it becomes the final product. This point emerges from the second half of the chapter.

In the second half of *Metaphysics* Θ.7 Aristotle reconsiders a question that he had discussed in Z.7: Why do Greek speakers specify the matter of a complex product with an adjective instead of a noun?[16] In Z he wanted to show that a reference to the matter is required in the account of a composite because the constituent matter contributes to the identity of the generated whole, whose nature displays the structure this (form) in this (matter), where the matter and the form have distinct natures. Since Aristotle generally prefers a metaphysical theory that accords with common intuitions, he frequently relies on facts about language to guide his metaphysical claims.[17] But his proposal about composites in Z.7 did not find support in ordinary Greek idiom. His claim suggested that people should speak of statues as "bronze," but in fact they normally speak of them as "bronzen." So he needed to explain why the linguistic convention arose and to show that the normal way of describing a product with reference to its constituent matter does not reflect the metaphysics of change.

In *Metaphysics* Θ.7 his attitude is quite different, and instead of disparaging the practice, he defends it as the proper way to specify the constituent matter. The entire discussion helps to clarify his view of the material continuant.

This and That-en

It seems that, when we call something not "this" (τόδε) but "that-en" (ἐκείνινον)—for example, the box not "wood" but "wooden," and the wood not "earth" but "earthen," and similarly with earth, if it is not in this way some other thing (ἄλλο) but that-en—that

---

[16] See above, pp. 122–25.
[17] Cf. pp. 98–102 above.

(ἐκεῖνο) [with reference to which we call something "that-en"] is always, in the unqualified sense, potentially the next item up in the series.[18] For example, the box is not earthen or earth, but wooden. For this (τοῦτο) [wood] is potentially a box, and this is the matter of a box—wood in general of box in general, and this wood (τοδὶ τὸ ξύλον) of this box. (1049ᵃ18–24)

I have called attention to this passage before because it indicates that the preexisting matter, which is potentially some product, is actually something in its own right; the particular wood, for example, is both potentially a box and actually wood. But Aristotle's main point is that one does not call the product "this" (τόδε) with reference to the matter out of which it is made, but "that-en" (ἐκείνινον). Although the wood that is potentially a box is called "wood," the box is called not "wood" but "wooden."

Now, if the preexisting matter survives as an actual subject within the generated product, there should be no objection to calling the box "wood." This seemed to be Aristotle's conclusion when he considered the same linguistic point in Z.7. But in this passage he says nothing about the actual survival of the preexisting material. In fact, he goes on to compare the way people specify an object with reference to its constituent matter to the way they specify an object with reference to its nonsubstantial properties and concludes that such conventions are entirely proper in both cases because both the matter and the nonsubstantial properties are indefinite (1049ᵃ36–ᵇ2). Apparently the production starts with wood, which is a definite subject, but once the production is finished, that definite subject has given way to a another: the box. And the original wood, although it survives as a constituent, has become indefinite. The wood with which the craftsman started no longer actually exists but has been transformed into an entity higher up the scale. And even though the preexisting matter is "present in" this higher construct, its presence is not of the sort that would legitimate calling the higher product by the name of that material. Because the constituent matter is indefinite, one does not call the box "wood," but "wooden." This account accords with that given in the various texts concerning the potential continuant: the preexisting matter is in a sense destroyed because it actually ceases to be that definite subject, but it is also in a sense preserved because it is "present in" the

---

[18] As Ross (1924, 2:256) points out, Aristotle's parenthetical remark breaks his grammatical construction, so that the subject of the sentence (ἐκεῖνο ["that"], 1049ᵃ21) does not share the same reference as the relative pronoun (ὃ) in the opening clause (1049ᵃ18). Aristotle starts by talking about the product that is called "that-en" with reference to its matter and concludes by talking about the matter with reference to which the product is called "that-en."

higher product as something potential or indefinite. Since the preexisting matter has been actually destroyed, the product should not be called "this" with reference to it, but since the matter survives potentially, it is acceptable to call the product "that-en" with reference to it.

The wood that the carpenter uses to construct a box is potentially a box because, in virtue of its dispositional properties, it is a suitable material for box construction. The wood is hard, fissile, and inflexible. It possesses certain features in common with wood in general, certain features special to its variety (maple, oak, pine), and it has many peculiar features that differentiate it from other woods of the same sort, such as grain, distribution of knots, and so forth. The wood in the carpenter's shop also has a particular shape and size. Although some scholars think that the shape provides the wood with whatever claims it has to thisness,[19] the shape and size of the wood are nonsubstantial, and therefore accidental, properties of it; the wood's claim to thisness derives from its being a definite subject that can possess such nonsubstantial properties.[20] Since wood is a suitable material for a wide variety of products, the particular wood in the carpenter's shop has potentialities for a variety of goals, only one of which is realized when the carpenter produces a box. And once the wood has been made into a box, that material is part of a larger complex that constitutes the box. And this new item, the box, has a distinct set of properties lacked by the materials that were used in its construction. The box is not the original wood but wood that has been arranged, joined, and finished in such a way that certain functional capacities—those capacities that make the object *a box*—can be realized. Since the new object can realize these new capacities, the box is not the wood with which the carpenter started but something else, namely, the entire assemblage of parts that exists only once the product is finished.

One might reasonably object that the box is simply the original materials with a new set of properties that they originally lacked. It seems fair to say that the collection of beams and joints in the carpenter's shop, which was then "boxless" (a nameless privation), is now structured in such a way that the same collection can be called a "box." And presumably this is exactly what Aristotle would have said in discussing the question in *Metaphysics* Z.[21] But if he were now to say this, he should con-

---

[19] See, e.g., Jones 1974, 482–83. This view is rejected by Dancy (1978, 402–3).

[20] Cf. above, pp. 83–85. I disagree with the London Seminar (Burnyeat et al. 1984, 131–32) that the thisness of materials, such as the one designated as τόδε τὸ ξύλον ("this wood"), derives from the composite at the next level up.

[21] This also appears to be Aristotle's view in *Met.* H.2–3. At 1043ᵃ14–28 he says that a house can be defined in three ways—as matter, as form, or as a composite of both. The material definition is a list of the materials (stones, bricks, beams); the formal definition is

clude, as he did then, that there is nothing wrong with calling a box "wood," since that definite material continues to be the subject to which the structure belongs. But he does not conclude that the box should be called "wood." Instead, he says that speakers are entirely correct to call the box "wooden" because the matter is "indefinite" (1049ª36–ᵇ2).

In *Metaphysics* Z, too, Aristotle describes the matter as indefinite, saying that the composite cannot be defined as composite because the matter is ἀόριστον (1037ª27).[22] But the indefiniteness of the matter there envisaged is not the same as that envisaged here. According to the account in Z, the flesh and bones in which the organic functions are realized and that survive the death of the animal are definite stuffs whose nature is independent of the form of the creature. These are the materials that must be mentioned in the account of a universal composite, such as the species man. The flesh and bones, which are mentioned in the account of the species, are matter "taken universally"; the description "flesh and bones" specifies the matter common to all human beings. The flesh and bones of each human being have their own idiosyncratic character, and according to Z.8, differences in flesh and bones differentiate two men who share the same form. "And when the whole [exists], such and such form (τὸ τοιόνδε εἶδος) in these fleshes and bones (ταῖσδε ταῖς σαρξὶ καὶ ὀστοῖς), [there is] Callias and Socrates; and they differ on account of their matter (for it is different), but they are the same in form (for the form is undivided [ἄτομον])" (1034ª5–8). In *Metaphysics* Z, the indefiniteness of the matter concerns the various and changeable properties of the matter rather than the material stuff itself; the so-called fleshes and bones are quite definite stuffs. Two individuals differ in their matter because their flesh and bones have distinct properties. And the matter of a single individual is indefinite because the properties of one's flesh and bones alter over time. This indefiniteness explains the claim in Z.15 that any account of an individual is easily overturned; the matter of an individual is subject to change.[23]

In *Metaphysics* Θ.7 Aristotle calls the matter indefinite for a quite different reason, for he compares the matter itself to nonsubstantial properties. Thus the matter is indefinite, not because it possesses an indeterminate set of properties, but because it is itself a sort of property that, like nonsubstantial properties, depends for its definiteness on some actual subject to which it belongs.

The construction model involves a shift of levels, and Aristotle now denies that the simpler persisting matter is a definite subject present in the

---

a specification of the function; and the compound definition is a combination of both, later specified as "a shelter from bricks and stones lying thus" (1043ª31–32).

[22] See above, p. 137.

[23] See *Met.* Z.15, 1039ᵇ27–1040ª7.

higher construct. Of course, many features of the original matter survive to characterize the higher object, including those that make a stuff wood, those that make a stuff a particular variety of wood, and even many of those that were peculiar to the particular wood in the carpenter's shop. The craftsman works with the special features of his materials to achieve a successful outcome, and many of the idiosyncrasies of his raw material are preserved in the product.[24] Aristotle endorses the practice of calling a box "wooden" because the adjective marks the connection between the properties of the box and those of the preexisting material. One calls a box "*wooden*" because the properties of the unfinished wood survive to characterize the box. The original wood and the box share a generic connection because they have many of the same features. But it would be improper to call a box "wood" because the original materials do not survive as the actual subject to which the structure of the box belongs. Those materials have been transformed into the box, and only the properties of the original materials survive to characterize the higher object. Thus one properly calls a box "wood*en*" to indicate that the properties rather than the definite material survive in the higher product.

Subject and Universal

In the next part of Θ.7 Aristotle claims that the relation that holds between wood and a box and between earth and wood holds between a simpler matter and a higher construct all the way down to the ultimate matter. In this passage Aristotle proposes a hierarchy among the elements, each element specified as "that-en" with reference to the one below. This is not a hierarchy that he endorses. According to his elemental theory, the four elements are all simple bodies that stand at the same ultimate level. But here he suggests a hierarchy to illustrate the relation that holds generally between a composite and the matter at the next level down. The important point is not what entity here counts as the ultimate matter but its status relative to the item at the next level up. He says:

> If there is something primary, which is no longer called "that-en" with reference to something else, this is prime matter ($\pi\rho\omega\tau\eta$ $\ddot{\nu}\lambda\eta$); for example, if earth is air-en, and the air is not fire but fire-n, fire is prime matter, which is not a $\tau\delta\delta\varepsilon$ $\tau\iota$.[25] For the universal ($\tau\delta$ $\kappa\alpha\theta\delta$-

[24] On this topic, and its connection with Aristotle's embryology, I have profited from reading Cooper 1988.

[25] Modern editors reject an alternative manuscript tradition that, omitting the negation at 1049ᵃ27, gives, "which is a $\tau\delta\delta\varepsilon$ $\tau\iota$." I agree with Ross (1924, 2:256–57) that the later argument requires the negation.

λου)²⁶ and the subject (τὸ ὑποκείμενον) differ in this respect: in being a τόδε τι or not. (1049ᵃ24–29)

According to this account, at each level an entity is called "that-en" with reference to the item at the next level down. Just as a box is called "wooden" with reference to wood, and wood called "earthen" with reference to earth, so, if there is an ordered hierarchy of earth, air, and fire, earth is called "air-en" with reference to air, and air is called "fire-n" with reference to fire. If there is nothing further with reference to which fire is called "that-en," then fire, which is the first matter at the bottom of the whole series, is not a τόδε τι.

I have argued that the preexisting matter for generation is a τόδε τι. Each item, which is potentially the next item up in the series, is an actual this. The particular wood, which is potentially a box, is actually wood; the particular earth, which is potentially wood, is actually earth. And if there is a hierarchy of elements of the sort that Aristotle describes, the particular air, which is potentially earth, is actually air. Why does Aristotle claim that thisness fails at the bottom? Why should fire, which is potentially air, not be actually fire—actually τόδε τι?

There is no reason why fire should not be actually τόδε τι, if the matter at issue is the preexisting matter out of which the air is made.²⁷ But Aristotle is talking about fire, not as a preexisting material, but as the constituent matter of the entity at the next level up. And if one speaks of the constituent matter, thisness fails at each step of the vertical series. Just as fire as a constituent of air is not τόδε τι, so neither is air as a constituent of earth τόδε τι. This is why speakers call the higher entity "that-en" and not "this" with reference to its lower neighbor. At each stage the matter below contributes certain properties to the entity above it, but that higher entity is identified by other properties that make it the definite entity that it is. The fire that has been made into air is not itself a definite stuff that has acquired a new set of properties. Instead, the name "fire" when applied to the constituent matter of air specifies only a set of properties that modify the air. The particular air is called "fire-n" because the air possesses the properties of fire, yet the identity of air is determined by other properties that make the air to be air. So the name "fire" merely identifies the material genus to which the air belongs. Thus fire as a constituent of air, which contributes certain properties to the air, is a *universal* and not a this. The relation between the constituent fire and the air that it consti-

²⁶ At 1049ᵃ28 I adopt the manuscript reading in preference to the conjectured καθ᾿ οὖ ("of which"), which is printed in modern editions. See below for my reasons.

²⁷ Perhaps this fact accounts for the manuscript discrepancy concerning the negation at 1049ᵃ27 (see above, n. 25).

tutes is repeated all the way up the series. As a constituent, the lower-level matter is a universal and not a τόδε τι.

The preexisting matter is preserved in the product in the sense that many of the properties that identified the preexisting material as a definite stuff survive in the product. But those properties characterize the product merely generically by connecting the product with other objects that share the same features. In part because the preexisting matter survives as a set of properties that modify the higher object, Aristotle says that the preexisting matter survives in the product potentially. But more important, he says that the preexisting matter survives potentially because those same properties, which merely modify the higher complex, are sufficient to identify a simpler stuff. Thus, when the higher object is destroyed, the simpler stuff will be recreated as a separately existing entity, identified by those properties. Because the simpler stuff can be separated out, it is present in the higher complex potentially. Recall that Aristotle frequently specifies matter as something that is "able both to be and not to be." This description, although sometimes ascribed to a definite matter, can also be ascribed to the indefinite matter. The potential survival of the lower materials is the potentiality *not to be* (the higher construct): the goal of this potentiality is a lower entity. One should recognize, too, that, just as a potentiality to be the higher entity can be attributed to the preexisting material out of which the product is made, so the same potentiality *to be* the higher construct can also be attributed to the indefinite continuant. Thus, the continuant has both the potentiality to be and not to be the high-level entity. I shall return to this point.[28]

Commentators have mistaken the force of this passage because they expect prime matter, the ultimate subject to which properties belong, to preside at the bottom. And modern editors have somewhat obscured Aristotle's meaning by following Apelt in altering the word καθόλου ("universal") at 1049ª28 to καθ᾽ οὗ (lit. "of which" and usually translated "subject"). This expression recalls the predicative relation between form and matter adopted in *Metaphysics* Z. Although, given what Aristotle goes on to say, the passage can be understood even with Apelt's conjecture, the point emerges more plainly if the original manuscript reading is kept. The relation between form and matter is fundamentally different from that between a nonsubstantial property and the subject it modifies. The critical difference is that, in the case of form and matter, the form predicated is the definite τόδε τι and the subject of which it is predicated is indefinite and universal, while in ordinary predicative contexts, the property predicated is indefinite and universal and the subject of which it is predicated is a definite τόδε τι.

---

[28] See below, the section "The Revised Construction Model," and chapter 7.

Matter and Accidents

The final part of *Metaphysics* Θ.7 distinguishes a universal from a definite subject by calling attention to the fact that people use the same locution (an adjective instead of a noun) in specifying an object both with
reference to its nonsubstantial properties and with reference to its constituent matter. Just as speakers call a box "wooden," not "wood," so they
call a man "musical," not "musicality," and "white," not "whiteness."
Aristotle concludes that the use of adjectives in preference to nouns in
both situations is justified because both the matter and the accidents
(πάθη) are indefinite.

> For example, a man—both body[29] and soul—is the subject (ὑποκεί-
> μενον) for properties (πάθεσι), and the musical or the white is a
> property. And when the musicality becomes present in it, that [the
> subject] is called not "musicality" but "musical," and the man is
> called not "whiteness" but "white," and not "a walk" or "a motion"
> but "walking" or "moving," as something that-en (ἐκείνινον). So
> in cases of this sort, the final thing is substance; but in cases that are
> not of this sort, but [cases in which] what is predicated is a certain
> form (εἶδός τι) and a this (τόδε τι), the final thing is matter and
> substance in the material sense (οὐσία ὑλική). And it follows quite
> correctly that something is called "that-en" with reference to the
> matter and the πάθη; for both are indefinite (ἀόριστα). (1049ᵃ29–ᵇ2)

Aristotle calls attention to the fact that Greek speakers specify the nonsubstantial properties and the constituent matter of a concrete object in
the same way, for they say both "the man is musical" and "the box is
wooden." This analogy suggests that composites are definite subjects to
which both the nonsubstantial properties and the matter belong. But at
1049ᵃ34–36 he draws a different analogy by contrasting two sorts of "final" things. In one case, when the item predicated is a nonsubstantial
property, the final thing is substance; but in the other case, when the item
predicated is a certain form and τόδε τι, the final thing is matter and
substance in the material sense.

On the traditional reading of this passage, Aristotle's mention of two
sorts of final things is a mention of two sorts of subjects, both of which
can possess properties. First, the composite is a subject of which nonsubstantial properties are predicated; second, matter is a subject of which
form is predicated.[30] And since the matter is the subject to which the form
belongs, Aristotle's linguistic parallel between matter and accidents does

---

[29] Notice Aristotle's mention of "body" at 1049ᵃ30; the body is the functional matter,
which is a proper subject for accidents.

[30] See Ross 1924, 2:256–58; Leszl 1970, 503; and Kung 1978, esp. 143, 155–56.

not reflect the significant metaphysical parallel. For the metaphysical analogy relates matter to substance, as subjects, and form to accidents, as predicates. So there is a curious crisscross between the linguistic analogy, on the one hand (according to which matter is analogous to the accidents), and the metaphysical analogy, on the other (according to which matter is analogous to the composite substance).[31] In fact, on the standard view, the linguistic analogy between matter and accidents is entirely misleading.

This unsatisfactory outcome reflects the fact that commentators expect the relation between matter and form to match that between a composite and its nonsubstantial properties, and it is presumably the same expectation that has prompted them to accept Apelt's conjecture at 1049ª28: the reading of καθ᾽ οὗ ("of which") instead of καθόλου ("universal"). Aristotle has, of course, encouraged this expectation by his treatment of form and matter in *Metaphysics* Z. But that very treatment led to the conclusion that composites lack vertical unity, and H.6 suggests that that conclusion can be avoided. So there is reason now to expect a difference between the two sorts of relations. And in Θ.7 Aristotle indicates that the relations are different because, if he regarded them as comparable, he should defend the use of the noun instead of the adjective in specifying the matter of a composite. If a box is a box because the form of a box belongs to the wood, then it should be entirely proper to call the box "wood." But Aristotle now objects to that locution on the ground that the matter is indefinite.

If my assessment of the earlier argument is correct, the linguistic analogy illuminates the metaphysical analogy by showing that, although substance is the subject for nonsubstantial properties and matter for form, the relation between subject and predicate in the two situations differs in important respects. Since matter is a universal, like the accidents, and not a definite subject, what it means to say that form is predicated of matter is not that the form belongs to the matter or that the matter partakes of the form (in the way that whiteness belongs to a man or a man partakes of whiteness). Instead, to say that form is predicated of matter is to say that the form *determines* or *differentiates* the matter as a material *genus*.[32] Aristotle's account in Θ.7 spells out the proposal in H.6: the relation between matter and form resembles that between an ordinary genus and differentia. Although there are significant differences between ordinary and material genera, they are similar to at least the extent that the relation

---

[31] This point is stated in Brunschwig 1979, 145–52.

[32] Brunschwig (1979, 153–58) also regards the matter-form relation as one between a genus and differentia; our views differ because he takes the linguistic specification to be a definition, and I do not. On my view, a material genus differs from an ordinary genus because the concept of the material genus, unlike that of an ordinary genus, is not included in the concept of the differentiating form.

between them and the differentiating form is not such that the genus partakes of the differentiating feature—or is tied to it by some other similar relation. If the constituent matter is a sort of genus, or potentiality, the definiteness of the composite depends upon the specific differentiation of that material kind.

But now, if the constituent matter is merely potential, and if potential existence means that the preexisting matter contributes certain properties to the higher level object and that those properties can identify a simpler matter once the composite has been destroyed, it is no longer clear that such matter has a detrimental impact on the vertical unity of the higher complex. The trouble concerning composites stemmed from the thesis that the constituent matter is a definite subject to which the formal properties belong, and hence that the nature of the composite is determined in part by that constituent subject. In *Metaphysics* Z the composite was viewed as a compound consisting of a definite matter of which the form is straightforwardly predicated. Now the constituent matter is conceived, not as a definite subject to which formal properties belong, but as itself a set of properties that modify the higher-level object. And although such properties will doubtless account for certain aspects of the object's behavior, there is no need to suppose that they contribute to its identity. Human beings are ultimately made out of earth, and because they are made out of earth, they sometimes display behavior proper to that material. For example, human beings fall downward if not supported, and they have this tendency because they are made of a stuff whose nature it is to move toward the center. But it is not the nature of human beings qua human to move toward the center if unimpeded. If this is correct, then the generic material, which the form differentiates, though required for that differentiation to occur,[33] does not constitute part of the καθ' αὐτό being of the higher object. And if so, the generic matter should stand in an *accidental* relation to the object it modifies, since it need not be mentioned in the account of that object.[34] There is, then, a motivation for comparing the material properties with nonsubstantial properties, as Aristotle does in Θ.7, since both sorts of properties modify the object accidentally.

A puzzle remains, however, about the claimed indefiniteness of the con-

[33] There must be some appropriate matter to be differentiated, but one should bear in mind that generic materials can be differentiated in a variety of ways and that the ultimate generic materials—the four elements—can be differentiated into all composite bodies in the sublunary realm.

[34] For the material genus to be accidental to the product in Aristotle's sense, it must be the case both that the higher object is not defined with reference to it and that it is not defined with reference to the higher object (see above, p. 24). Although one might think that the material genus acquires its identity from the higher object, I shall argue that this is not so; see the section "The Revised Construction Model" below. Cf. *Met.* I.9 for Aristotle's view that material differences are accidental to the nature of a composite.

stituent matter, for simple observation would suggest that many composites, including living organisms, consist of a quite definite matter. The vertical unity of the object thus comes again into question.

A Puzzle about Organisms

One should have qualms about the treatment of artifacts in *Metaphysics* Θ.7. Although Aristotle's view that the preexisting matter survives in the product potentially is plausible for contexts of chemical combination, it seems fairly implausible for many contexts of artificial production. Indeed, in these cases the view of *Metaphysics* Z, that the matter actually survives, accords much better with the perceptual evidence. The wood in the carpenter's shop quite obviously survives in the product as more than a set of properties that modify the object, for one can still designate the pieces of wood that make up the box and straightforwardly extract them by taking the box apart. Unless the examples are forced to fit the theory, they seem better interpreted in the previous way. If these examples are regarded as they were in Z, then the collection of preexisting materials remains actually present in the higher construct and acquires a new structure.

Aristotle might not try to defend artifacts from this objection because he denies in any case that they are substances. For example, in *Metaphysics* H.2, even while using artificial products to clarify natural composites, he points out that his examples are not substances but merely analogous to them ($1043^{a}4$–5).[35] So if someone were to insist that the nature of an artifact is twofold—properly specified as a form realized in a distinct and definite material—Aristotle might simply agree. After all, they served as convincing paradigms by which to clarify that very relation. Aristotle extends the account in *Metaphysics* Θ.7 from simple chemical compounds all the way up to artifacts, not for the sake of the artifacts themselves, but for the sake of living organisms, which seem in so many respects analogous to artifacts. But now the objection leveled against artifacts acquires some urgency when turned against their analogues. Do living organisms fail to be vertical unities for the same reason?

In *Metaphysics* Z Aristotle claims that human beings are destroyed into flesh and bones. And these materials, like the wood in a box and the bricks and stones in a house, can be observed to be actually present in a living human. Why, then, should they not undermine the vertical unity of the organism in the way that the material constituents, such as wood and bricks, undermine the vertical unity of an artificial product? In *Metaphysics* Z Aristotle seems unperplexed about the status of these ma-

---

[35] On the analogy and difference between artifacts and organisms, see Kosman 1987.

terials. Since the flesh and bones can survive the destruction of the animal, they have a distinct nature, independent of the organic functions that they temporarily possess. In *Meteorology* IV. 12, although hesitating about their status and suggesting that flesh is defined by its function (390ᵃ10–15), Aristotle indicates that flesh, bone, hair, and sinew, like copper and silver, might simply be generated by heat and cold (390ᵇ2–10).[36]

But flesh and bones play a critically different role in the generation, career, and destruction of an organism from that played by the matter of artifacts, and Aristotle cannot have overlooked the difference. For although these materials seem to survive the destruction of an organism, they are not the preexisting matter out of which the organism is made. The preexisting matter for a blooded creature is the καταμήνια,[37] which simply is concocted blood that the female organism contributes in generation. Since the καταμήνια does not contain flesh and bones, these uniform materials, which compose the nonuniform parts, are generated together with the creature. Thus the flesh and bones, although perhaps accounting for horizontal continuity when the animal dies, do not account for horizontal continuity when it comes to be. Horizontal unity in the upward steps of organic generation is guaranteed by the ultimate matter from which the καταμήνια itself derives, and this ultimate matter is earth or some combination of elements. The ultimate matter alone gives horizontal unity to the entire cycle of organic generation and destruction.

Perhaps Aristotle's reflection on this peculiarity explains the revision in his treatment of flesh and bone and the other organic tissues. In *Generation of Animals* II.1 he talks about flesh in the way that he often talks about the organic nonuniform parts. He says that, although a dead face or flesh can be called "face" or "flesh," the names are merely homonymous. Speakers use the names for the dead organic parts in the way that they might use the names for a face or flesh made out of stone or wood (734ᵇ24–27). Just as the nonuniform parts have functions to perform within the complex organic system and lose their identity if they lose their ability to operate, so flesh, too, has a function to perform and is no longer flesh if removed from the whole (734ᵇ30–31). On this view the soul of the animal determines the nature of the uniform parts as well as that of the nonuniform parts.[38]

This conception has two important consequences. First, the uniform parts, flesh and bone, do not after all account for horizontal continuity when the animal dies. Although the corpse may appear to consist of flesh and bone, these materials in fact perished when the animal died, and what

[36] On this topic, see Furley 1983, 76–77, 92; and Lennox forthcoming.

[37] *G.A.* I.19, 727ᵇ31–33; I.20, 729ᵃ9–11; *Met.* H.4, 1044ᵃ34–35.

[38] On this topic, see Ackrill [1972–1973] 1979, 72–73.

is left is called "flesh" and "bone" merely homonymously. So horizontal unity in destruction, as well as generation, is provided by more ultimate constituents. Second, flesh and bone can be actually present in the animal, just as the nonuniform parts are actually present, without themselves depriving the organism of vertical unity. Flesh and bone now belong, together with the nonuniform parts, to the functional matter of the animal, and the functionally specified matter is "posterior" to the whole (to recall the discussion of prior and posterior parts in Z. 10–11)[39] because its nature is determined by the form of the creature. Matter, functionally characterized, need not be mentioned in the account of the whole because such a mention adds no information that is not already available from an account of the form. The whole question of horizontal unity is pressed to a lower level, and the question is whether there is some further actual constituent to which the organic functions finally belong and whether this entity deprives the organic composite of vertical unity.

Once the problem is pressed to the deeper level, however, Aristotle's doctrine of potential survival provides a plausible solution. Living organisms are ultimately generated out of the elements, yet they do not actually contain these ingredients. Aristotle can say, as he does in the passage cited earlier from *De Caelo* III.3, that flesh is composed out of earth and fire, which are potentially present in the organic material and which can be extracted from it by some physical process. Since the material continuant survives only potentially, Aristotle can now argue that living organisms are vertical unities that are definable with reference to their form alone.

THE REVISED CONSTRUCTION MODEL

In discussing Aristotle's theory of generation, I have focused on three notions of matter—the preexisting matter from which a product is generated, and two sorts of constituent matter: the functional matter, which is determined by the form of the generated object and which survives only as long as the object survives, and the generic matter, which provides horizontal unity. Both the preexisting and functional matters are definite subjects—the preexisting matter is identified by its own nature, the functional matter by the form of the composite whose functional matter it is.[40] The generic matter, on the other hand, although it is a set of definite properties, is an indefinite subject relative to some higher definite form.

According to the construction model, complex bodies are worked up

---

[39] See above, pp. 126–38.

[40] Recall that the body, as well as the soul, is mentioned as the subject for nonsubstantial properties at *Met.* Θ.7, 1049^{a}30.

from simpler materials, and at each stage of construction the entity at the lower level is the preexisting matter for, and is actually transformed into, the entity at the next higher level. Earlier I compared the construction to scaling the face of a step pyramid—for example, blood is transformed into καταμήνια, and καταμήνια into a new organism. To use Aristotle's analogy from *Generation of Animals*, the product comes to be from the preexisting matter as "night from day" (I. 18, 724ᵃ21–23); there is a proper order to the series, one step coming after the other, and often (though not invariably) the cycle is irreversible.

As the construction model was initially interpreted, the ultimate simple matter is actually present throughout the cycle, acquiring additional form in the upward progression of substantial generation, and losing form in the downward sequence of substantial destruction. In this way I interpreted Aristotle's claim in *Generation of Animals* I.18 that "the whole is from something that remains within [the whole] but altered in form" (ἔκ τινος ἐνυπάρχοντος καὶ σχηματισθέντος τὸ ὅλον ἐστίν) (724ᵃ25–26). This may remain the correct interpretation for the relation between the constituent matter and certain artifacts (e.g., between bricks and a house), but Aristotle evidently rejects this interpretation for contexts in which the matter survives only potentially. In these cases the preexisting matter, though at the outset a separate identifiable stuff, survives at the lower level but only as a set of properties that modify the higher construct. And although the same properties are sufficient to determine a simpler body again, once the high-level complex has been destroyed, they do not contribute to the nature of the higher object but merely account for certain aspects of its behavior. The surviving matter has been called "generic" because, when Aristotle says that the form is "predicated" of it, the predication resembles that between a differentia and a typical genus. The genus as subject does not partake of the differentia that is predicated of it, as an ordinary subject partakes of properties, but is differentiated into some definite object. The interpretation of horizontal unity as the survival of something potential (generic or indefinite) enables him to accommodate continuity through change, but without prejudice to the vertical unity of the generated whole.

It is now worth noticing that there is, after all, a close analogy between typical substantial generations, which fit the construction model, and elemental transformations, which are structurally linear. In both cases horizontal unity is preserved, not by an underlying subject to which properties belong, but by one or more properties that belong to the higher object. The difference between the two sorts of generation is simply that, because elemental transformations are structurally linear, the surviving property contributes part of the identity of the two elements whose transformation it underlies, whereas in typical generations, which cross levels, the continuant does not play that identifying role. But the crucial similarity between elemental transformation and constructive generations on the question of horizontal unity makes them both distinctive generations and marks them off from nonsubstantial changes.[41]

In all generations some preexisting matter is actually τόδε τι. Although any preexisting matter possesses a potentiality that makes possible its transformation into a higher-level product, it typically also has a distinct identity in its own right, independent of the higher object. For example, the bronze, which can be made into a statue, is actually bronze. Although many scholars think that Aristotelian matter is identified derivatively with reference to the goal of its potentiality, this seems to be so in a very limited number of cases—indeed, only for those preexisting materials that serve a single natural outcome. In these cases the potentiality for a particular result determines the identity of the preexisting material. For example, the nature of καταμήνια is determined by the organism that it can become. In this case one might deny that the preexisting matter is a separate τόδε τι, since its nature derives from the form of the product. The καταμήνια is, however, an intermediate step in the generation of a living organism and is not the ultimate preexisting matter from which the creature derives.

In other cases materials found at intermediate steps can be fully identified without reference to the things that they can become. In the case of bronze and other materials that can serve various goals, it seems that the potentialities for higher construction follow from their natures rather than being constitutive of them. Thus, bronze can be made into a statue, a sword, a plowshare, and various other artifacts because it possesses the sorts of dispositional properties that make it a suitable matter for these products. The potentialities for higher construction are thus accidental to what the materials are in themselves. And if these potentialities are accidental to the preexisting materials, then the same potentialities will presumably still be accidental to the constituent generic material.[42] The surviving material genus has the potentiality to be the higher construct because it can be (and, in fact, has been) differentiated into that higher

---

[41] Other transformations may also be structurally linear and yet count as substantial generations because, like constructive generations, the continuant survives as a set of properties. As Donald Morrison (1988, 208–9, in response to Gill 1988) has pointed out, the production of a particular metal alloy out of two or more distinct metals is not a transformation across levels. Even so, the transformation is a generation because the ingredient metals do not actually survive within the generated alloy. On the other hand, it is questionable whether an artificial production involving a material that actually survives should count as a generation at all, even though it apparently crosses levels. Such changes seem instead to be mere alterations of the underlying matter (cf. *Phys.* II.1, 192^{b}16–23 and 193^{a}9–17).

[42] On pp. 178–80 I defend the claim that a potentiality for a particular goal survives when the goal is realized.

object. But the potentiality to be the higher object does not determine the nature of the residual material properties. And presumably because the potentialities for higher construction typically belong to the matter accidentally, Aristotle removes them along with the other accidents in his discussion of subjecthood in *Metaphysics* Z.3 (1029ᵃ11–13)—to recall a point that was stressed in chapter 1.[43]

The four elements, which are the preexisting matter for all composite bodies in the sublunary realm, can be compared to bronze. Like bronze, the identity of the simple bodies is not determined by the various goals that they can serve. To repeat another previous point, each of the elements is fully identified by its differentiating features (a yoke of cold-dry, cold-wet, hot-wet, or hot-dry) and by its intrinsic φύσις to move in a particular way.[44] This fact must be appreciated in order to understand the problem of unity for composite substances that Aristotle addresses in *Metaphysics* H.6. If the potentiality to be some higher construct is accidental to what the elements are, then they do not achieve their fullest being when combined into higher constructs. When the elements have been worked up into a higher object and survive as a material genus, the potentiality *to be* the higher object, though now realized, still determines the matter accidentally. On the other hand, the potentiality *not to be* that higher construct but to be some simpler stuff instead is a potentiality that determines the very nature of the material genus, because the properties that constitute the genus can specify the nature of a simpler body. The elements thus achieve their fullest being when they are separate in a state of uncombined simplicity. To put the point metaphorically, the elements do not "strive" upward toward complexity but downward toward simplicity.[45]

This point is crucial for Aristotle's account of deterioration and perishing. If composites are vertical unities, their perishability cannot be due to their nature. It cannot be the nature of a man qua human to cease to be human because the potentiality not to be human could never be realized by him. Therefore, on the revised construction model, the potentiality not to be human belongs to the man in virtue of his generic matter, and this generic matter can deprive the human being of his existence. Recognition that the actual properties that make up the generic matter tend to revert to the elements is also fundamental for understanding the problem of unity for composite bodies that Aristotle addresses in *Metaphysics* H.6. Simply put, the problem is that, although the vertical unity of a high-

[43] See pp. 23–25, above.

[44] See above, p. 84.

[45] The metaphor of upward striving derives from *Phys.* 1.9, 192ᵃ16–25, where Aristotle contrasts his own view with that of the Platonists, but the "inner necessity" of the striving seems to derive from the commentators. See, e.g., Zeller 1897, 1:179.

level object can be achieved, the unity is fragile and is easily destroyed. Thus, what needs to be explained is why the unity lasts, given the fact that the lower materials tend to disperse.

In addition to the preexisting matter and the surviving generic matter, some composites also have a functional matter whose identity is determined by the form of the composite. Aristotle talked about the functional matter in *Metaphysics* Z, but the notion as there interpreted, while enabling him to argue that forms are vertical unities, did not permit him to extend the argument to include composites. For although, in the case of forms, the functional matter was exhausted by its functional characterization, in the case of composites, which contain matter, the functional matter was a set of functions realized in some definite stuff. And the nature of that stuff was independent of the functional specification. Recall that he viewed the body of a human being as a set of functions realized in flesh and bones. The situation is critically altered, however, once he includes the uniform parts, like flesh and bone, among the functional parts and reinterprets the construction model to require only the potential and not the actual survival of the preexisting matter. Once the notion of horizontal unity is reinterpreted so that the lower matter is not a definite subject to which the functions belong but instead a set of properties accidental to the higher object, the nature of the functional matter, even for the composite, is fully determined by its functional characterization.

Even though composites contain matter and, if they possess functional matter, can still be defined as "this (form) in this (matter)," the functional matter that underlies the form is not distinct in nature from the form itself. Therefore, the form, though predicated of the functional matter in the normal way, is not thereby predicated of something else, as one thing of another. Hence composites that possess functional matter and whose generic matter accounts for horizontal unity can be vertical unities. Whether or not the functional matter is explictly mentioned, the definition of a composite simply is an account of its form, and thus a specification of what the composite essentially is. Moreover, such an account, although it cannot specify the composite as a particular, can—as we saw in chapter 1—be so specific as in fact to apply to a single individual alone.[46] On this theory, a definable composite is a conceptually primary entity because its nature is exhausted by its form.

There is a further corollary: a substantial form can now count as a proper subject, since the generic matter of which the form is predicated is in fact a property of the form rather than the form's being a property of it. Substantial form properly satisfies the subject criterion of the *Categories* and *Metaphysics* Z.3 because, being separate and τόδε τι, the form

---

[46] See above, pp. 32–34.

is that of which other things are predicated but is not itself predicated (in the normal way) of anything else.

The Cause of Unity

In *Metaphysics* H.6 Aristotle compares the relation between matter and form to that between genus and differentia, and he argues that neither the matter nor the genus partakes of the form.[47] He defends the analogy by reinterpreting the construction model to show that the material continuant survives, not as an actual subject to which the form belongs, but as a material genus that the form differentiates. But despite the analogy, there remains an important difference between the two sorts of genera. Although both are indefinite subjects, their indefiniteness is not of the same sort. An ordinary genus is indefinite because it is simply a more general version of its differentiated species, and for this reason the content of the genus is included in the concept of the differentiating form. The content of a material genus, on the other hand, cannot be determined simply by analyzing the form. Instead, the indefiniteness of the material genus is comparable to that of nonsubstantial properties. Like such properties, which can belong to a variety of objects and so can be identified apart from any particular one, so the material properties are independent of any particular construct. The indefiniteness is simply that, as properties, the generic matter and the accidents depend for their existence on some definite object to which they belong.

Notwithstanding the parallel between the material genus and the nonsubstantial properties, there is in this case too an important difference. Whereas nonsubstantial properties do not determine the essential nature of the bodies they modify, material properties, although they merely modify a higher-level object, can determine the nature of a simpler body. For this reason Aristotle claims the potential survival of the lower matter within the higher complex; namely, the simpler matter will again exist once the higher object has been destroyed. And this peculiar fact, which distinguishes an object's material properties from all its other properties, has vital implications for the unity of the object to which the material properties belong.

In *Metaphysics* H.6 Aristotle recognizes the difference between the material genus and the various items to which he compares it. Even as he indicates that matter and form are comparable to genus and differentia, he emphasizes the difference between the two paradigms. The major claim of H.6 is that one must seek the cause of the unity of matter and form. The unity of an ordinary genus and differentia is automatic because

[47] *Met.* Z.12, 1037^{b}18–22; H.6, 1045^{b}7–17.

the genus is simply more general and the species marked off by the differentia more specific. He says of these cases: "In the case of those things that do not have matter, either intelligible or perceptible, each is straightaway (εὐθύς) just some one thing, even as it is also just some being . . . and the essence is straightaway (εὐθύς) some one thing even as it is also some being—and for this reason there is no other cause (οὐκ ἔστιν ἕτερόν τι αἴτιον) of the unity for any of these nor of the particular being" (1045ᵃ36–ᵇ5).

The need to locate a cause arises in precisely those cases in which the generic item is not included in the concept of the differentiating form.[48] In the two passages in which Aristotle discusses the unity of matter and form, he appeals to a cause. I requote: "So what is the cause of this, of something in potentiality to be in actuality, except the maker (τὸ ποιῆ-σαν), in the case of things [for which] there is generation? For there is no other cause of the sphere in potentiality being a sphere in actuality, but this was the essence for each" (1045ᵃ30–33). And again in the final passage, he says: "But, as we have said, the proximate matter and the form are the same and one, the one in potentiality, the other in actuality, so that it is like seeking what the cause is of unity and being one; for each thing is some one thing, and what is in potentiality and what is in actuality are somehow one, so that there is no other cause [of the unity] unless there is something that produced the movement (ὡς κινῆσαν) from potentiality to actuality" (1045ᵇ17–22). In both of these passages Aristotle speaks of an efficient cause (a "maker" or "mover") as the item responsible for the unity of matter and form, and in the first passage he appears to associate the cause with the essence.

Why does Aristotle appeal to an efficient cause in discussing the unity of matter and form? Since a cause is needed in those cases in which the genus is material, he may think that the cause counteracts a certain resistance on the part of the generic material properties. I have argued that these lower material properties do not contribute to the nature of the higher construct, although they account for certain aspects of its behavior; it might therefore seem that the problem of unity for composites has been adequately solved. But, in fact, this solution only shows that composites can be unities but does not explain the unity. There remains a difficulty to which I have called attention. The material properties are sufficient to determine the nature of a simpler body—this is what it means to say that the simpler matter is potentially present in the higher object.

[48] I thus disagree with the London Seminar (Burnyeat et al. 1984, 43) that Aristotle finds no explanation necessary for the unity of potentiality and actuality. Although he finds no explanation necessary if the potential entity is an ordinary genus and the actual entity a differentia, he stresses the need for a cause if the potential entity is matter and the actual entity form.

If it were the case that the simpler matter achieved its fullest being within the composite, the fact of its separability would be unproblematic. But the potentiality to be the higher construct is merely accidental to the generic matter, while the potentiality to be the simpler matter is essential to it. The simpler matter is a source of difficulty because the elements are most themselves, not in combination, but in simple separation—because they tend to be recreated and thereby to destroy the higher object that they compose. The elements must therefore be controlled and coordinated when the object is generated and must still be controlled while the construct lasts. A controlling cause is required precisely because the unity of a composite substance is so easily destroyed. Given the recalcitrance of the lower material properties, composite bodies must be preserved as unities or they will simply degenerate into something simpler. Aristotle appeals to the cause in H.6 to explain why composites *come to be* unities and why they *remain* the unities that they have become.

Chapters 6 and 7 will consider the vital role of the cause in the generation and persistence of unified composites. This is the topic of *Metaphysics* Θ, though I shall also refer to other works for details of the theory.

CHAPTER SIX

THE CAUSE OF BECOMING

Aristotle's account of material continuity, which requires the potential, but not the actual, survival of the preexisting material, allows some material composites to be vertical—definable—unities. If the persisting material, which guarantees horizontal unity in substantial generation, contributes nothing to the nature of the generated object (as in the case of living organisms), such matter need not be mentioned in the definition of the construct. The composite can be defined with reference to its form alone. Still, a difficulty remains for the unity of composites, which results from the need to control the simpler matter and to maintain it within the higher construct. Because the lower material properties tend to revert to simpler stuffs and thus to destroy the higher object, a cause is required to offset this tendency and to preserve the unity that has been achieved.

In *Metaphysics* H.6 Aristotle appeals to the doctrine of potentiality and actuality to explain the unity of material composites, and he emphasizes the role of an efficient cause. In the next book, *Metaphysics* Θ, he turns directly to the doctrine of potentiality and actuality and mentions two spheres to which the doctrine applies: change, and some other context. He also points out that, although potentiality applies most strictly (μά-λιστα κυρίως) to change, that potentiality is not the one most useful for the present undertaking ($1045^b35-1046^a2$). The current investigation thus concerns, not change, but the other context to which he refers. *Metaphysics* Θ continues the investigation that has claimed Aristotle's attention since the beginning of *Metaphysics* Z and to which he alludes in the opening lines of Book Θ. The project, since the outset, has been to determine what entities are conceptually primary, and this has been the study of being in its primary sense, which is the study of substance (1045^b27-32).[1] Although Z and most of H regard forms alone as primary substances because they alone are definable unities, H.6 suggests that the solution for forms can be extended to material composites if their matter is viewed as potential and their form as actual. The problem in such cases is to determine the cause of unity. *Metaphysics* Θ takes up the topic of potentiality and actuality, giving special attention to the role of potentiality as active cause, in order to explain the being and persistence of perishable substances.

Aristotle turns to the second context in Θ.6, having devoted the first

[1] Cf. *Met.* Z.1, 1028^b2-7, and see above, pp. 13–15.

half of the book to the theory of change. The opening chapters of *Meta-physics* Θ focus on change for two main reasons. First, the question of how unified objects emerge, although not the primary question, is one worth answering. Second, and more important, when Aristotle turns to the second context in Θ.6, he suggests that he has discussed potentiality in connection with change to promote understanding of the potentiality proper to the second sphere (1048ᵃ25–30).[2] I shall argue that Aristotle's two potentiality-actuality models—the one concerned with becoming, the other with being and persistence—although different, are structurally parallel. Both involve a pair of potentialities, one active, and one passive, and both concern two actualities, a motion, and a product. Moreover, both appeal to an active potentiality to explain the *continuity* of motion. The difference between the two models turns on the relation between the active cause and its passive object. In contexts of change the cause and its object act and suffer in respect of distinct—indeed opposed—properties; in contexts of persistence they act and suffer in respect of the same properties. The first scheme explains how the passive object comes to have the property possessed by its cause, the second how the passive object preserves that property. The second scheme is more important because this system accounts for the survival of vertical unities in the realm of becoming. Still, it is worth examining the first model as a preliminary to the second because the second model is grounded in the first. Since both models appeal to the active cause to explain the continuity of motion, the first model can help to clarify the second. This chapter, then, will focus on the model for change, and the central aim will be to establish the framework that Aristotle extends and modifies to explain the persistence of generated unities. The second model will be the topic of chapter 7.

THE FIRST POTENTIALITY-ACTUALITY MODEL

In *Metaphysics* Θ.1 Aristotle speaks of a potentiality that is "most strictly" (μάλιστα κυρίως) called δύναμις, and he associates it with change.[3] Both in Θ.1 and in his discussion of potentiality in Δ.12, he treats a potentiality that he calls the "primary" notion—the one with reference to which other notions of potentiality can be understood.

As in his treatment of many other concepts, Aristotle uses a device that has come to be known as "focal meaning."[4] If several items are called by

---

[2] On Aristotle's two potentiality-actuality models, see Kosman 1984. I have learned a great deal from Kosman's work on this topic and follow him on a number of points, though not in the overall interpretation of the two models.

[3] For an interpretation of Aristotle's first potentiality-actuality model different from my own, see Charlton 1987.

[4] On focal meaning, see esp. Owen [1960] 1979.

the same name or by related names (as "medicine" and "medical"),[5] he looks for the central application and explains the others with reference to that one (πρὸς ἕν).[6] Thus, for example, a doctor, a patient, a procedure, an instruction, and a branch of knowledge are all called "medical." If one knows what it means to call a branch of knowledge "medical" or "medicine," the application of the name "medical" to other objects can be explained by expanding the central account of medical knowledge to specify the relation in which each of the other objects stands to medical knowledge. Thus, medicine is the art of producing health—the doctor has this art, a patient is a recipient of it, a procedure is an application of it, and so on.[7] The investigator generally explains the derivative meanings either by expanding or narrowing or otherwise altering the conditions laid down in the central context.[8]

The focal meaning of potentiality is characterized in Θ.1 as "the principle of change in another thing or qua other" (ἡ ἀρχὴ μεταβολῆς ἐν ἄλλῳ ἢ ᾗ ἄλλο) (1046ᵃ10–11). In Δ.12 Aristotle specifies the central meaning more precisely as an *active* principle of change (ἀρχὴ μεταβλητική) in another thing or in the thing itself qua other (1019ᵇ35–1020ᵃ6).[9] The central notion of δύναμις, then, is an active source of change located in an entity other than the object moved or, if the object moved is moved by itself, in the object moved considered as other. In addition to the active potentiality, Θ.1 and Δ.12 specify a passive potentiality by modifying the central account. A *passive* potentiality is a principle of being changed (ἀρχὴ μεταβολῆς παθητικῆς) by another thing or by the thing itself qua other.[10] All natural and artificial changes involve a pair of principles—one active and one passive. I will call a subject that possesses an active principle an "agent," and a subject that possesses a passive principle a "patient."

When Aristotle uses the word δύναμις in the active sense, we might prefer the translation "power," "ability," or "capacity" to "potentiality," but however the term is translated, it is important to recognize that he uses the same word to indicate both active power and passive responsive-

---

[5] According to the *Categories*, if one entity is called after another with a difference in ending, as "medical" from "medicine," it is *paronymous* (1, 1ᵃ12–15). The primary item is specified by a noun, the derivative item often by an adjective derived from the noun. Although there can be a focal relation among items that are called by the same name, the priority of the central item is more obvious if it is designated by a noun and if the entities focally related to it are specified paronymously.

[6] See *Met.* Γ.2, 1003ᵃ33–34; Z.4, 1030ᵃ32–ᵇ3; cf. H.3, 1043ᵃ29–37.

[7] See *Met.* Γ.2, 1003ᵃ34–ᵇ19.

[8] For example, the subsection "Contact" below (pp. 195–98) will describe the way in which Aristotle explains various derivative notions of contact by weakening the conditions laid down for contact in the strict sense.

[9] Cf. *Met.* Δ.12, 1019ᵃ15–20.

[10] *Met.* Θ.1, 1046ᵃ11–26; Δ.12, 1019ᵃ20–23.

ness. The builder (agent) has a δύναμις to build a house; the bricks and stones (patient) have a δύναμις to be a house. Potentialities, whether active or passive, are always directed to an end or goal—an actuality; and the potentiality is identified as the potentiality that it is with reference to the actuality. So, for example, a person's passive potentiality for health is identified as that potentiality with reference to health; the doctor's active potentiality for health is also, though in a different way, identified with reference to health. Active and passive potentiality pairs correspond because they are related to the same end or actuality.[11] Furthermore, although the active member of a corresponding pair has explanatory priority over the passive, both potentialities depend on each other for their realization. Thus a builder cannot realize his potentiality to make a house unless he has appropriate materials at his disposal, nor can bricks and stones realize their potentiality to be a house unless an appropriate agent builds them into a house.

According to Aristotle's first potentiality-actuality model, the agent and the patient are typically distinct subjects, or if the active and passive potentialities coincide in the same subject, the subject acts on itself qua other. A doctor can apply his medical art to himself but, if he does, he acts on himself qua other. As agent, the individual uses his medical art to bring about health in someone sick; as patient, he is cured of his ailment by someone who possesses the medical art. If the δύναμις to cause health and the δύναμις to become healthy coincide in the same individual, the individual acts qua doctor and is cured qua sick. The person acts and suffers in virtue of distinct properties: he acts on himself qua other. To use Aristotle's terminology, the properties in virtue of which an agent acts and a patient suffers are *contrary* or *unlike*.[12] Thus, in the medical example, the doctor acts in virtue of his active δύναμις for health on something sick. The doctor's action on the invalid results in the replacement of the privation by the positive form—the patient acquires health. The gradual replacement of the opposed properties in the patient constitutes a change; having been *unlike* the agent, the patient becomes *like* the agent.[13]

---

[11] In *Phys.* III.3 Aristotle speaks of the goal of the agent as a "deed" (ποίημα) and the goal of the patient as an "affection" (πάθος) (202ᵃ22–24), but he evidently identifies the deed and the affection, since he later objects to the idea that the doing and the suffering are two distinct motions that occur in the patient because there would then be two alterations of one thing to one form (εἰς ἓν εἶδος) (202ᵃ31–36). Apparently, then, a single form is the goal of both the agent's active potentiality and the patient's passive potentiality.

[12] According to *G.C.* I.7, agent and patient are the same and like in kind but opposed and unlike in form. An agent, in virtue of some property that it possesses (typically its own form, or a form in its soul), imposes that property on a patient that is suited to have, but actually lacks, the property. See *G.C.* I.7, 323ᵇ29–324ᵃ5; cf. *Phys.* VIII.5, 257ᵇ6–10; *Met.* Θ.1, 1046ᵃ19–29. Cf. below, p. 198.

[13] See *G.C.* I.7, 324ᵃ5–14.

This replacement of the privation by the positive form (or vice versa) in a persisting subject (ὑποκείμενον) can be described using the three principles of change for which Aristotle argues in the first book of the *Physics*—a pair of opposed principles and a surviving ὑποκείμενον. The account of change in terms of potentiality and actuality builds upon the standard scheme of *Physics* I, but with the vital addition of the active cause. By means of the three principles of change, Aristotle can characterize the replacement of properties in a surviving subject, but he cannot show that the replacement is a single continuous and dynamic event. Using the first potentiality-actuality model, he can both analyze the change in the patient and show that change is a connected progression toward a goal. The change takes place in the patient because an agent, in virtue of an active potentiality for a particular property, replaces the patient's lack with that property and thus assimilates the patient to itself. Because the first potentiality-actuality model treats this dynamic replacement, the first model is concerned with change.

It will be helpful, before examining the first model in its application to change, to look at Aristotle's distinction between potentiality and actuality in *De Anima* II.5.[14] This text describes three subjects—two identified as "potential" knowers, and a third knower as being "in actuality." Discussion of the third subject will be mainly deferred until chapter 7, since the actual knower and his activity are the focus of Aristotle's second potentiality-actuality model. Aristotle's theory of change primarily concerns a subject that is potential in the way that the first subject described in *De Anima* is. Such a subject survives a nonsubstantial change or, in a substantial change, is actually transformed but preserved in potentiality. The first subject is thus the ὑποκείμενον that accounts for horizontal unity in contexts of change. Aristotle focuses in II.5 on a nonsubstantial change, the acquisition of knowledge, and he calls "potential" both the preexisting subject who is ignorant and the resulting subject who knows.

Passive Potentialities

We must make some distinctions concerning potentiality and actuality; for just now we were talking about them in an unqualified manner. For something is "a knower" in one sense (1), as we might say that a man is a knower because man is among the things that know and have knowledge; but in another sense (2), as we at once call a knower the man who possesses grammatical knowledge. And each of these is potential [but] not in the same way (ἑκάτερος δὲ τούτων οὐ τὸν αὐτὸν τρόπον δυνατός ἐστιν), the one (1) because

---

[14] Cf. *Phys.* VIII.4, 255ᵃ30–ᵇ5. On this passage, see below, pp. 236–38.

his genus is such and his matter, the other (2) because when he wishes he is able to theorize, if nothing external interferes. But (3) there is he who is already theorizing, who is in actuality and in the strict sense knows this particular A. Now both of the first are potential knowers,[15] but the one (1), having been altered through learning and often changed from an opposite state [is a potential knower in one way], the other (2) from having arithmetical or grammatical knowledge but not exercising it to the exercise [is a potential knower] in another way (ἄλλον τρόπον).[16] (417ᵃ21–ᵇ2)

Scholars construe Aristotle's distinction between the two potential knowers in various ways. It has been suggested that the distinction concerns two kinds of potentiality, one possessed by the first subject for *becoming* a knower, the other possessed by the second subject for *being* a knower.[17] On this reading the two potentialities differ in kind because they are related to two sorts of ends, the first potentiality for change to an end state, the second for being in an end state. But the text does not indicate this kind of difference between the goals of the two potentialities. Aristotle does not speak of the first subject as a "potential learner" and the second as a "potential knower" but calls both subjects "potential knowers" (κατὰ δύναμιν ἐπιστήμονες) (417ᵃ30). This common description suggests that the potentialities of both subjects relate to the same goal.

Various other suggestions have been proposed for the difference between the potentialities. It is arguable that the potentialities of both subjects are directed to the same final end, the activity of theorizing, which Aristotle attributes to the third subject, the one "who is in actuality and in the strict sense knows this particular A" (417ᵃ28–29). Alternatively one could argue that he uses ἐπιστήμων ambiguously in describing the goals

[15] I omit Ross's (1956) additional line, 417ᵃ30ᵃ: ὄντες, ἐνεργείᾳ γίνονται ἐπιστήμονες ("being [potential knowers] come to be knowers in actuality"). Cf. n. 16 below.

[16] Most commentators take ἄλλον τρόπον ("in another way") at 417ᵇ1–2 with μεταβαλών ("[having] changed") at 417ᵃ32 to refer to another sort of transition. On this construction the first potential knower is altered to an opposite state through learning, while the second potential knower passes in another way from having arithmetical or grammatical knowledge but not exercising it to the exercise. See, e.g., Rodier 1900, 2:256; Hicks 1907, 356; Hett 1936, 97–99; and Hamlyn 1968, 23; cf. Ross 1961, 236, whose addition to the text at 417ᵃ30 (see above, n. 15) facilitates this reading. Although later in II.5 Aristotle does use δύο τρόπους ("two ways") to refer to two modes of alteration, one to a privative condition, the other to a positive condition and nature (417ᵇ14–16), this later distinction is difficult for interpreters to map onto the one they find earlier. On the two transitions, see below, chapter 7, pp. 222–27 and n. 30. It is much more likely that ἄλλον τρόπον is used, not as it is in the later passage, but as οὐ τὸν αὐτὸν τρόπον ("not in the same way") was used just earlier (417ᵃ26), to specify a different way of being a potential knower; this is how I have rendered the phrase.

[17] See Charles 1984, 19–22.

of the two potentialities to indicate, in the case of the first subject, the state of knowledge and, in the case of the second subject, the activity of knowing or theorizing. A final possibility is that the goal for both subjects is the state or possession of knowledge. I shall defend the final proposal: both the first and second subjects have a potentiality for the state of knowledge, which is the goal of a change.

In principle, any one of the three interpretations is possible. In *De Anima* II.1 Aristotle explicitly says that "actuality" is ambiguous between the state, such as knowledge (ἐπιστήμη), which enables a person to theorize, and the activity, such as theorizing (τὸ θεωρεῖν), which expresses the knowledge (412ᵃ9–11). His project in II.1 is to define the soul, the form of a living organism, and he spells out the distinction between levels of actuality in order to explain that the soul is an actuality in the way that knowledge is (412ᵃ21–23). Knowledge and soul have traditionally been called *first* actualities, theorizing and living *second* actualities. Given the distinction between levels of actuality in II.1, one could argue that the first knower in II.5 has a potentiality for the first actuality and the second knower a potentiality for the second actuality, or that the potentialities of both knowers are directed to one actuality or the other.

It seems unlikely, however, that Aristotle would attribute to the first knower a potentiality for the second actuality, since the first subject must undergo a change to acquire the positive character—knowledge—that would enable him actually to theorize. Since a change is required before the subject can demonstrate his ability, the first subject seems merely to be potentially something that potentially theorizes. The problem with the suggestion is more pronounced if one considers a subject that undergoes a substantial change. Is it appropriate to say that earth is potentially a box? Recall that Aristotle considers examples of this sort in *Metaphysics* Θ.7 and denies that a subject has the potentiality for a particular goal if it must first be changed.[18] Earth is not potentially a box because it lacks the appropriate dispositional properties to be made into a box; only once it has been transformed into wood is there a suitable material for the construction of a box, and hence only once the wood has been generated is there something that has the potentiality to be a box. The earth is merely potentially something that is potentially a box, and the potentiality of the higher object (the wood) cannot be transferred to the lower (the earth).

The paradigm that Aristotle discusses in *De Anima* is a subject that undergoes a nonsubstantial change, and since the change is nonsubstantial, the subject will survive the transition. Even so, attributing to the person who is ignorant the potentiality to theorize is rather like attribut-

---

[18] *Met.* Θ.7, 1049ᵃ16–18; Aristotle's example concerns earth, bronze, and a statue. Cf. above, pp. 149–51.

ing to earth the potentiality to be a box: the ignorant person lacks the crucial character—knowledge—that would enable him to theorize. Since the lack of ability is the reason why the first subject cannot theorize, the potentiality for that activity should not be ascribed to him. The best reason for rejecting the suggestion that the first knower has the potentiality for the second actuality is that Aristotle's account in *De Anima* II.5 ought to apply to the subject for any sort of change, whether nonsubstantial or substantial. Since it is clear in the case of substantial changes that the goal of the subject's potentiality is what the subject can become, given what the subject actually is, and not some goal further up the series, the same should be true in the nonsubstantial cases. The goal of the first subject's potentiality should then be the *state* of knowledge, since this is the proximate goal that can be realized by means of a change. Thus, I reject the idea that both potential knowers have a potentiality for the same goal, which is the second actuality.

The most common view of Aristotle's distinction is that the first subject has a potentiality for the first actuality (the state of knowledge) and the second knower a potentiality for the second actuality (the activity of theorizing). Clearly, Aristotle does think that the second subject has a potentiality that the first subject lacks, since the positive character acquired by means of the change—the knowledge—is itself a capacity for an activity. Thus, the second subject can theorize because this activity is made possible by the knowledge that he has acquired. The question is whether this is the distinction at issue in II.5, and there is reason to doubt that it is. *De Anima* II.1 points out that the term "actuality" (ἐντελέχεια) is ambiguous and can apply either to knowledge (the first actuality) or to theorizing (the second actuality). Aristotle does not say that "knowledge" (ἐπιστήμη) is ambiguous, yet the standard interpretation of II.5 assumes that it is. Given Aristotle's distinction in II.1, he could easily have said in II.5 that the first subject is a potential knower, the second a potential theorizer. Instead, he calls both subjects "potential knowers" (κατὰ δύναμιν ἐπιστήμονες). Since he distinguishes knowledge from theorizing in II.1, as two sorts of actualities, his language in II.5 is likely to be carefully chosen. If his language is precise, then both subjects should have a potentiality for the same goal—the state of knowledge—which is the first actuality. On this view, the potentialities are related to the same end, but the subjects have the potentiality in different ways (417ª26).

Many commentators will resist this suggestion because it entails that a subject retains its potentiality for a particular goal once the goal has been realized.[19] There is a common assumption that an Aristotelian potential-

---

[19] But cf. Freeland 1987, 396–97. My treatment of this topic has benefited from suggestions by Paul Coppock.

ity is lost when it has been realized. Thus, bricks and stones are potentially a house when they are lying in a heap, but once they have been constructed into a house, that potentiality is lost, having been replaced with a different potentiality, namely, the potentiality for not being a house; when the house is destroyed, this potentiality will be lost and once more replaced with the earlier one. Some interpreters accept the idea that capacities for second actualities are retained when the potentiality is realized,[20] finding it natural that someone who has the capacity to speak French preserves her capacity when she is actually speaking. These scholars agree that her capacity to speak French survives and is even enhanced by its use. But there is a different attitude about potentialities for first actualities.

The standard view is grounded in the idea that part of what it means to be potential is to be actually deprived. Thus, if to be potentially healthy is to be actually sick, then of course a person ceases to be potentially healthy when he is actually healthy because he has ceased to be actually sick. But once it is recognized that the traditional view builds the privative actuality into the notion of potentiality, the view itself should seem less appealing. It is much more likely that Aristotle attributes to a subject a potentiality for a particular goal because of what the *subject* is. In *De Anima* II.5 Aristotle says that the first knower is potential because man is among the things that know and have knowledge (417ᵃ22–24), and Aristotle goes on to say that the first knower is potential because his genus and matter are of the appropriate sort (417ᵃ27). A potentiality for knowledge can be attributed to someone ignorant because the subject is a human being, and human beings are entities that regularly do have knowledge. And if a potentiality for knowledge belongs to an ignorant man because his genus and matter are appropriate, then the potentiality will still belong to him once he actually knows, because his matter and genus will still be suitable. Thus, bricks and stones have a potentiality to be a house, not because they are presently lying in a heap (and so deprived of being a house), but because they have the sorts of dispositional properties, as bricks and stones, that make them suitable materials out of which to build a house. And they will still be suitable for housebuilding even when they constitute an actual house.

On the numerous occasions that Aristotle describes matter as something that is "able (δυνατόν) both to be and not to be,"[21] he says nothing to suggest that, given the actual state of the particular matter, its potentiality is for just one of the alternative states. The description suggests, on the contrary, that the matter has, at the same time, the potentiality for

---

[20] As evidence they cite *De An.* II.5, 417ᵇ3–5; see Kosman 1984, 131–32.

[21] For references, see chapter 1, n. 16.

each of the opposed states. At any particular time the matter will actually
be in one of the states for which it has the potentiality. So, bricks lying in
a heap have a potentiality to be and not to be a house, and one of those
potentialities—the potentiality not to be a house—is currently realized;
once they have been built into a house, they still have the potentiality to
be and not to be a house, but now the potentiality to be a house is the one
that is realized. On this view, all potentialities—for both first- and second-level actualities—are preserved when the goal is achieved. They are
preserved because potentialities are grounded in the nature of the subject
to which the potentiality belongs, not in the subject's actual state of
privation.

Aristotle presents two conditions for a subject to be a potential knower
in the first way. First, the subject must belong to a kind, members of
which do regularly have knowledge (417^a22–24); the subject's genus
(γένος) and matter (ὕλη) must be of the right sort (417^a27). Recall that
Metaphysics Θ.7, in determining when something has a potentiality for a
definite goal, says that it is potential if nothing in the subject itself prevents the generation, and if the subject needs nothing added, subtracted,
or changed (1049^a8–11). Like the subjects in Θ.7 that succeed as potential
because they are suitable materials for a particular production, the first
knower mentioned in *De Anima* is the right sort of subject to acquire
knowledge. The subject is a human being, and human beings are the sorts
of things that regularly do become knowers. The subject need not itself
be transformed prior to undergoing the transition to knowledge; the first
subject is potential because it belongs to a suitable kind. This criterion
alone determines a subject as potential.

The second criterion determines a subject's potentiality as first level.
The first potential knower must lack the property for which he has the
potentiality; Aristotle says that the subject is altered through learning and
is often changed from an opposite state (417^a31–32). Since the first subject
lacks the state for which he has the potentiality, the realization of the potentiality requires a change. To use a phrase that Aristotle uses elsewhere,
the first subject is incomplete (ἀτελής) with respect to what he potentially
is.[22] To correct the incompleteness, the subject's lack must be replaced by
the positive state opposed to the lack; and the replacement of properties—
the realization of the subject's potentiality—is the event that Aristotle
calls a change.

On this interpretation, then, the first subject has a potentiality because
of the sort of subject that he is. His potentiality is first level because of the
actual privative state that he is presently in. When he ceases to be deprived

---

[22] See *Phys.* III.2, 201^b31–33; cf. *De An.* III.7, 431^a6–7.

by undergoing a change, he does not lose his potentiality. Instead, he retains the same potentiality but moves up from first level to second.

The second subject also satisfies two conditions. Like the first potential knower, the second must be the right sort of thing to have the property for which he has the potentiality by belonging to a suitable kind. Because the subject belongs to a suitable kind, the potentiality can be ascribed to him. But unlike the first subject, the second is complete ($\tau\varepsilon\tau\varepsilon$-$\lambda\varepsilon\sigma\mu\acute\varepsilon\nu\sigma\varsigma$) with respect to what he potentially is.[23] Aristotle describes the second potential knower as one who possesses the relevant knowledge (417[a]24–25); the change leading to that possession has already occurred, and consequently the subject and his goal have been successfully unified. The second subject is said to be $\delta\upsilon\nu\alpha\tau\acute\sigma\varsigma$ in the sense that, when he wishes, he is able to theorize ($\delta\upsilon\nu\alpha\tau\grave\sigma\varsigma\ \theta\varepsilon\omega\rho\varepsilon\widehat\iota\nu$) if nothing external interferes (417[a]27–28). Since the property acquired by means of the change is itself a capacity for some activity, the second subject has a capacity that the first subject lacks. But the issue is not his capacity for activity but his potentiality for the capacity or state that enables the activity. This potentiality is second level rather than first because, in virtue of possessing the capacity, he can exercise it at will, if not prevented.

The distinction between the two levels of potentiality thus turns on the actual state of the subject. Whereas the first subject lacks the property for which he has the potentiality and so must be changed from an opposite state, the second subject already has the property for which he has the potentiality and, if not prevented, can express it at will in acts of theorizing. And so, whereas the first subject must undergo a change and therefore depends upon an external cause (or himself qua other) to rectify his lack, the second subject is already in the positive state and, in virtue of that state, is himself responsible for its exercise.

Aristotle's distinction between the two levels of passive potentiality can be simply analyzed in terms of the three principles of change for which he argues in *Physics* I, namely, a subject x and a pair of opposed terms *not-ϕ* and ϕ. The positive member of the opposed pair, ϕ, is the positive goal of the potentiality and is itself a capacity for some activity. A potentiality for ϕ can be attributed to a subject x if x belongs to a suitable kind. The subject x has a first-level potentiality for ϕ if its actual state is not-ϕ, and it has a second-level potentiality for ϕ if its actual state is ϕ.

Actualities

A number of items mentioned in *De Anima* II.5 count as actualities. Again the three principles of change from the *Physics*—designated as ϕ,

---

[23] Cf. *De An.* III.7, 431[a]7.

not-ϕ and x—provide a helpful, if partial, guide. First, the goal (ϕ) for which both subjects have the potentiality is the actuality of their potentiality. Both the subject who is sick and the one who is healthy are potentially healthy, and health is the actuality of the potentiality that both possess; here the positive state is the actuality. Second, the subject in the positive state, namely, the whole compound of subject and positive state (ϕx), is an actuality. This is the actuality, not of the potentiality (as in the previous case), but of both subjects, whether the subject presently stands at the first level or second with respect to the goal. Since the compound is the outcome of change, I will call this actuality the *product*. The privative state (not-ϕ) of the first subject counts as a third actuality, since it is the actual state of the preexisting subject and can serve as a negative goal.[24] A fourth actuality is the subject itself (x), for example, a man, whether lacking or possessing knowledge of grammar, is something definite in his own right—a human being. On the view that I am defending, the basis for attributing the potentiality lies in what the subject is in itself. (The situation is more complicated if the change is substantial and the product a vertical unity. In this case the preexisting subject is an actuality in the fourth sense. If the generation yields a functional matter, this subject is also an actuality but is not distinct in nature from the positive form [ϕ]—the first item listed above as an actuality. The lower constituent matter, on the other hand, which survives the generation, is not an actual subject but a material genus. The material genus is, quite simply, the suitable kind—the set of dispositional properties in virtue of which the preexisting matter itself was suited to become the higher product.) Fifth, the compound of subject and privative state (not-ϕx) is an actuality. The compound, the subject deprived, is a definite subject deprived in a certain way. The five items that I have called actualities correspond to the three principles of change from the *Physics*—form (ϕ), privation (not-ϕ), and subject (x)—and their possible combinations, namely, subject-form (ϕx) and subject-privation (not-ϕx).

This does not complete the list of items that Aristotle calls actualities, however. There remains the one actuality explicitly mentioned in *De Anima* II.5. He describes the knower who is actively theorizing as being "in actuality" (417^a28–29). By analogy with the other cases, both the activity itself—the theorizing—and the compound knower theorizing are actualities.[25] This actuality is the focus of Aristotle's second potentiality-actuality model. A corresponding actuality is the focus of the first model; the change undergone by the subject from the privative to positive state, or

[24] See *Met.* H.5, 1044^b29–1045^a2; cf. *Phys.* III.1, 201^a34–$^b3$.

[25] The activity is called an actuality at *De An.* II.1, 412^a9–11 and 412^a21–23; the compound is so called in *De An.* II.5 and at *Met.* Θ.6, 1048^a35–$^b9$.

from the positive to privative state, is described as an actuality but as "incomplete."[26]

Aristotle's first potentiality-actuality model chiefly concerns two actualities—the incomplete actuality, or change, and the complete actuality, or product, in which the change results. In analyzing Aristotle's theory of change, I shall also appeal to the other actualities. The rest of this chapter will focus on Aristotle's use of the first model in the account of change, and my project will be to clarify the role of the active cause and to lay out the general framework that he extends from contexts of becoming to contexts of persistence. This chapter will show that the motion proper to the first scheme, which is a continuous progression from one state to another, must be the joint actuality of an active cause and a passive object.

In spelling out Aristotle's theory, I shall focus on the account in *Physics* III. 1–3, beginning with the definition of change in III. 1; I shall argue that this initial definition—which specifies change as the actuality of something in potentiality—cannot capture change as a dynamic and directed entity because it ignores the active cause. Since the opening treatment disregards the cause, the definition could apply, on one interpretation, to an object at rest or, on another interpretation, to an object that, though active, fails to move in the appropriate direction. To show that change is a continuous development, Aristotle must appeal to a cause that both directs and coordinates the subject's motion. He introduces the cause of change in *Physics* III.2. In III.3 he argues that change is the joint actuality of a mover and a moved, and at the end of the chapter he revises the definition to include a reference to both. The new version of the definition specifies change as a dynamic, sustained, and directed event. The account of action in *Physics* III.3 is meant only to explain the continuity of change, not to provide a full explanation. To explain how the agent brings about a change in the patient, Aristotle must appeal to the agent's self-motion, a topic he discusses in *Physics* VIII.5. Since self-motion is described by the second potentiality-actuality model, this topic will be mainly deferred until chapter 7. I start, then, with the definition of change in *Physics* III.1 that ignores the active cause, and my aim is to show why the cause must be introduced; I next discuss Aristotle's general theory of agency, and then return to his revised definition of change in *Physics* III.3.

THE DEFINITION OF CHANGE

Physics III.1 states the following definition: "Change is the actuality of that which is in potentiality, as such (ἡ τοῦ δυνάμει ὄντος ἐντελέχεια, ᾗ

---

[26] *Phys.* III.2, 201ᵇ31–32; VIII.5, 257ᵇ8–9; cf. *Met.* Θ.6, 1048ᵇ18–22 and 1048ᵇ29–33.

τοιοῦτον, κίνησίς ἐστιν)" (201ᵃ10–11). This definition is evidently meant to cover substantial generation as well as the three sorts of nonsubstantial changes because Aristotle immediately applies it to the four cases: alteration, growth and diminution, generation and destruction, and locomotion (201ᵃ11–15). Given this extension, the definition should apply to all instances of becoming. Even so, he focuses on examples of nonsubstantial change and artificial production, both of which involve a definite continuant. Since I shall discuss the generation of organisms in chapter 7, I restrict the topic now, as he does, to the simpler context in which horizontal unity is guaranteed by a definite subject that survives the change. Since the continuant is a distinct subject that acquires a new property, the product of the change is an accidental, not a vertical, unity.

To understand Aristotle's definition, the first task is to determine how he uses "actuality" and "potentiality" to capture the concept of change. I start with ἐντελέχεια and then turn to δύναμις.

Actuality and the Definition of Change

I have indicated that "actuality" can be applied to a variety of items. In his definition Aristotle uses the term ἐντελέχεια, but later in the chapter he shifts to ἐνέργεια,²⁷ and he appears to use the two terms interchangeably in the continued treatment of change in *Physics* III.3. The doublet of *Physics* III.1–3 in *Metaphysics* K replaces ἐντελέχεια with ἐνέργεια in its statement of the definition.²⁸ So the two terms seem to be synonyms in this context. What does Aristotle mean by calling change an ἐντελέχεια or ἐνέργεια?

A potentiality is always directed toward an actuality, which is its goal; therefore the actuality of a potentiality should, in typical contexts, be the goal of the potentiality. The actuality of the potentiality to be healthy is health; and the actuality of a subject that is potentially healthy is a healthy subject. But neither of these actualities is the one in view because the definition defines the process to an end state, not the state or product in which the process results. So the question is, How can Aristotle's definition be interpreted in such a way that the actuality to which he refers is a process rather than a resulting state or product?

One standard suggestion is that ἐντελέχεια should not be translated "actuality" at all, but "actualization" or "realization."²⁹ On this translation ἐντελέχεια means the actualizing of a potentiality that results in the actuality or goal; thus, for example, becoming healthy is the actualizing

---

²⁷ *Phys.* III.1, 201ᵇ9–13; cf. III.2, 201ᵇ31–32.

²⁸ *Met.* K.9, 1065ᵇ16. K.9 switches freely between the two expressions.

²⁹ For this rendering of ἐντελέχεια, see Ross 1936, 536; Ackrill 1965, esp. 138–40; Charles 1984, 19–22; and Kostman 1987.

of a subject's potentiality for health. With the exception of those actualities known as "activities" (such as theorizing), all the actualities listed earlier are examples of states, objects, or compounds of object and state. Activity alone is a dynamic actuality. On the view now being considered, actualization too is a dynamic notion but is not to be identified with activity. An activity is not a transition to a different state but the expression of some capacity possessed by a subject, as theorizing is an expression of knowledge. "Actualization," by contrast, is a subject's transition from a state of privation to the actuality for which it has the potentiality. If ἐν-τελέχεια is translated in this way, a new meaning of the word must be added to the earlier list, a meaning that occurs only in those contexts in which Aristotle treats the definition of change.[30] Besides requiring a new meaning for ἐντελέχεια, the proposal faces an objection that has often been stated: if ἐντελέχεια means the process of becoming actual, then Aristotle's definition of change is uninformative because actualization itself is defined in terms of a prior notion of process.[31]

Since there is no independent justification for the translation of ἐντε-λέχεια as "actualization," and since the proposed translation in the account of change results in a circular definition, I endorse the translation "actuality" and shall try to make sense of the definition, using one of the standard meanings of that term. The question is, How can the definition be interpreted so that the actuality is the process rather than the product?

Potentiality and the Definition of Change

Some interpreters suggest that the answer lies in the sort of potentiality to which the definition refers. The potentiality, they suggest, is a potentiality for change; thus change is the actuality of that potentiality.[32] In the discussion of passive potentialities in *De Anima* II.5, I mentioned that Aristotle is sometimes taken to distinguish two sorts of potentialities—one for change to an end state, and another for being in an end state. Thus, given one designated final state, there are two irreducible sorts of potentiality—one for becoming, and one for being. Although *De Anima* II.5 seems not to disclose this distinction, since it designates the subject with a first-level potentiality, not as a "potential learner," but as a "potential knower," the motive for finding such a contrast in *De Anima* II.5 is the supposed need for potentialities for change in contexts like the one in *Physics* III.1. Aristotle is taken to define change as the actuality of that

[30] See the survey in Chen 1956, esp. 59–60.

[31] See Kosman 1969, esp. 40–43; Gill 1980, 130; and Waterlow 1982, 112–14. The circularity objection was also raised in the Middle Ages by Aquinas (*Phys.* III, Lec. 2).

[32] See Ross 1936, 536; Ackrill 1965, esp. 138–40; Hussey 1983, 58–60; Polansky 1983; and Charles 1984, 19–22.

potentiality whose end is change. And although the proposal is unappealing for the same reason that the translation of ἐντελέχεια as "actualization" is unappealing in rendering the definition circular,[33] the suggestion cannot be simply dismissed because it gains considerable support from the text of *Physics* III.1 itself.

Let me sketch the position.[34] Suppose that, for a particular state ϕ, an object has two sorts of potentialities in regard to ϕ—one for being ϕ, another for becoming ϕ. Being ϕ is the actuality of the subject's potentiality to be ϕ, and becoming ϕ is the actuality of its potentiality to become ϕ. Now Aristotle characterizes change as "the actuality of what is in potentiality, as such," and it is arguable that the function of the final phrase "as such" (ᾗ τοιοῦτον) is to identify which of the subject's potentialities is the relevant one. The proposal gains plausibility because later in the chapter Aristotle shifts from the vague phrase "as such" to the more explicit description "as changeable." He says, "Change is the actuality of what is in potentiality, when being in actuality (ἐντελεχείᾳ ὄν) it acts (ἐνεργῇ) not as itself (ᾗ αὐτό) but as changeable (ᾗ κινητόν)" (201ᵃ27–29). In speaking of the subject as changeable, Aristotle appears to have in mind a potentiality for change.

Aristotle explains his use of the expression "as" or "qua" (ᾗ):

> By "as" I mean the following. Bronze is potentially a statue, but all the same, change is not the actuality of bronze as bronze (ᾗ χαλκός); for the being of bronze is not the same as [the being] of something potentially [changeable],[35] since if it were the same simply and in respect of the account, change would be the actuality of the bronze as bronze. But it is not the same, as we said. And the situation is clear in regard to the contraries; for to be potentially healthy and to be potentially sick are different—[for if they were the same] to be sick and to be healthy would be the same—but the subject (ὑποκείμενον) both for the thing that is healthy and for the thing that is sick, whether moisture or blood, is one and the same. But since [the being] is not the same, just as color and the visible are not the same, it is evident that change is the actuality of the potential, as potential (ᾗ δυνατόν). (201ᵃ29–ᵇ5)

Contrary to the starting assumption, however, this passage does not distinguish a potentiality for change to an end state from a potentiality for

---

[33] For objections to the proposal, see Kosman 1969, esp. 44–45; Penner 1970, esp. 427–31; and Waterlow 1982, 114–16.

[34] My sketch is based on David Charles's proposal (1984, 19–22), though I ignore the details of his account.

[35] Ross (1936, 538) brackets κινητῷ ("changeable") at 201ᵃ32 as a gloss on δυνάμει τινί ("what is potential"). The word is omitted in the parallel passage in *Met*. K (1065ᵇ26) and by the ancient commentators.

being in an end state. Instead Aristotle speaks of a single potentiality, which appears to be a potentiality for change. He does claim that a subject can be regarded in two ways, as what it is in itself (e.g., as bronze) and as potential, and the earlier specification of the subject "as changeable," together with the doubtful κινητῷ (which Ross brackets in his edition), suggests that the only relevant potentiality is a potentiality for change. If this is correct, the point of the passage is that an item designated as potential can be conceived in two ways, as what the subject is in itself or as changeable. The phrase "as such" indicates that the subject is to be regarded as changeable rather than as what it is in itself. Regarded as bronze, the actuality is simply the bronze itself. But if the subject is viewed as changeable, change is its actuality, since change is the goal of the subject's potentiality for change.

The proposal seems to be confirmed by what Aristotle goes on to say.

It is clear then that [change] is this, and that [something] is changed just when the actuality is this,[36] and neither earlier nor later; for it is possible for each thing sometimes to be active (ἐνεργεῖν) and sometimes not, for example, the buildable, and the actuality (ἐνέργεια) of the buildable, as buildable, is building. For the actuality (ἐνέργεια) of the buildable is either the building or the house; but when the house exists, the buildable no longer exists; but the buildable is being built; so the building must be the actuality (ἐνέργειαν). And the building is a particular change. (201^{b}5–13)

Aristotle's claim that the buildable no longer exists once the house exists suggests that the relevant potentiality is lost once the product is finished. According to my analysis of potentiality in De Anima II.5, no potentiality is lost when a subject shifts from the first level to the second with respect to its goal. The subject retains the same potentiality for the same end; a subject that is potentially healthy when sick is still potentially healthy when actually healthy. The subject merely loses the privative state that it was previously in. So Aristotle's claim in Physics III.1 that, when the house exists, the buildable no longer exists suggests that the analysis of De Anima II.5 did not reveal the potentiality in play here. A plausible alternative, consistent with the interpretation of potentiality in De Anima, is that the potentiality lost once the product exists is the potentiality for becoming the product. A subject can no longer become what it has already become and now is. Thus the text strongly suggests that Aristotle defines change in terms of a potentiality for change.

This need not be the conclusion, however. The text admits another reading, and there is a good theoretical motive for adopting the alterna-

---

[36] I preserve the manuscript reading αὔτη ("this") at 201^{b}7. See Wicksteed and Cornford 1929, 1:198; cf. Hussey 1983, 3.

tive. It seems doubtful that Aristotle would find attractive a doctrine involving irreducible potentialities for becoming. Although his doctrine of categories, which includes two distinct categories of doing and suffering, might foster the idea that a subject has irreducible potentialities for doing and suffering, just as it has irreducible potentialities for being qualified, quantified, and located, there are also reasons to resist the idea. It makes sense that the *Categories* specifies doing and suffering as distinct categories. Many scholars agree that Aristotle worked out his list of categories by considering various questions that one might ask about a particular object, for example, What is it? (τί ἐστι), How big is it? (πόσον), How is it qualified? (ποῖον), and Where is it? (ποῦ), and many of the category titles are simply the indefinite adjectives, adverbs, and so on derived from the interrogatives. Among the questions that one might ask about an object are, What is it doing? and What is it suffering? Given these questions, doing and suffering are listed as categories.

But it is not at all clear that doing and suffering should be viewed as two distinct ways of being, on a par with being quantified, qualified, and located. When a subject does (ποιεῖ) something—causes a change—it promotes some result; and when a subject suffers (πάσχει) something—experiences a change—it enters a new state. The results of doing and suffering are specified not with reference to the categories of doing and suffering but with reference to one of the other categories, such as quality, quantity, or place. Even in the *Categories* Aristotle views change in terms of a subject and a pair of contraries (5, 4ᵃ10–21), and this discussion suggests that, even in the *Categories*, suffering—a passive change—is viewed as analyzable into components. A passive change consists of a subject and a pair of contraries from categories other than the category of suffering. In a nonsubstantial change, the subject is a substance, and the pair of contraries is housed in one of the categories of quantity, quality, or place. But if passive changes can be analyzed into components from other categories, suffering (πάσχειν) should be a metaphysically derivative category because it admits reduction to other more basic components. And if the category is derivative, then becoming should not be a distinct way of being, equal in status to substance, quality, quantity, and place.[37]

If this reduction is correct, then a potentiality for becoming should also be derivative. A potentiality is identified with reference to its actuality or goal. If the actuality can be analyzed in terms of other more basic entities, then the potentiality for that actuality should be explicable with reference

---

[37] Cf. *Phys.* III.1, 200ᵇ33–201ᵃ9; Aristotle lists the four categories in which change occurs and concludes that there are as many kinds of change as there are kinds of being. Although the final claim might misleadingly suggest that change can occur in all ten categories, the reference is plainly restricted to the four sorts of being earlier mentioned: substance, quality, quantity, and place. Thus, the four sorts of becoming are correlated to the four sorts of resulting categorial being.

to those same entities. Since change can be analyzed in terms of the three principles of change from *Physics* I—a pair of opposed terms and an underlying subject—the potentiality for change should admit a similar reduction. Thus, it should be possible to analyze Aristotle's definition of change in terms of the basic notions of potentiality and actuality and the three principles from *Physics* I. There should be no need to appeal to a potentiality for change.

The assumption that Aristotle defines change in terms of a potentiality for change seems to arise in part from the fact that, in speaking of particular potentialities, he typically constructs potentiality words from verbs rather than from nouns or adjectives. He speaks of the "buildable" (or more literally, the "housebuildable" [οἰκοδομητόν]), the "alterable," the "increasable," the "decreasable," and so on. Such expressions can of course specify potentialities for changes, but they need not. When Aristotle aims at precision in specifying a subject in potentiality, he speaks of, for example, "what is potentially healthy." And the subject specified as "potentially healthy" may be actually sick or actually healthy. So, in order to indicate whether the subject is actually in the privative state or actually in the positive state, he needs to describe the subject as "potentially healthy and actually sick" or as "potentially healthy and actually healthy." These phrases are cumbersome. A simple shorthand for the phrase "potentially healthy and actually sick" is "curable." So used, the phrase does not specify a distinct sort of potentiality—a potentiality whose goal is a change—but a potentiality for being in the end state possessed by a subject that is actually deprived. Thus, expressions like "curable," "changeable," and so on are ambiguous; they may designate a potentiality for change, but they may also designate in shorthand a potentiality for an end state possessed by a subject that is presently deprived.

I shall analyze Aristotle's definition using the three principles of change from *Physics* I. The following reconstruction will indicate that the definition is inadequate because it fails to specify change as a dynamic and directed entity. The essential nature of change cannot be captured without appeal to its cause, and for this reason Aristotle turns to the topic of agency in the next two chapters, *Physics* III.2–3. First, then, the definition in III.1; the analysis will take several steps.

The Definition of Change: A Reconstruction

Using a pair of opposites *not-ϕ* and *ϕ* and a subject *x*, I start with the following minimal analysis:

(1) Change is the actuality of *x*, which is potentially *ϕ*.

Obviously this statement will not do. The actuality of *x*, which is potentially *ϕ*, could be either of two items, *x* (the subject itself) or *ϕx* (the product). This reconstruction is inadequate, too, because it gives no indication about the actual state of x. If x fails to be actually ϕ, the actuality could be not-ϕx (the subject in its actual privative state); if, on the other hand, x is actually ϕ, then not-ϕx is not among the possible actualities. But unless not-ϕx is among the possible actualities, Aristotle's definition cannot capture the concept of change because change is a transition from a state of privation to a state of possession. If x already is ϕ, it will undergo no change with respect to ϕ.

On two occasions in *Physics* III.1 Aristotle indicates that the subject for change must have a potentiality that is first level—that is, a subject's potentiality for ϕ must coincide with the actual absence of ϕ. Early in the chapter Aristotle distinguishes things that exist only in actuality from others that exist in potentiality and actuality (200^b26–28). Presumably items in the first group are forms, and those in the second, material objects. Later in the chapter he reconsiders the group of things that exist in potentiality and actuality and makes a further differentiation, saying that, among the things that exist in potentiality and actuality, some are not potential and actual at the same time and in the same respect—for example, something hot in actuality is cold in potentiality (201^a19–22). This item is apparently being contrasted with something that is potentially cold and actually cold at the same time; such an entity, whose potentiality for coldness is second level, cannot undergo a change in respect of coldness because it already possesses the property. Aristotle's point is that, unless an object belongs to the group whose potentiality for a goal ϕ coincides with its actual absence, the object will not experience a change with respect to ϕ.[38]

The second passage is one to which I have already referred. Aristotle claims near the end of III.1 that the actuality of the buildable is either the building or the house, and he points out that, once the house exists, the buildable no longer exists (201^b9–13). Since the buildability is lost once the house exists, "the buildable" should be shorthand for "what is potentially a house and actually deprived." The buildable is lost once the house exists, not because the building materials have lost their potentiality, but because they have ceased to be actually deprived. Change, then, is the actuality of a subject whose potentiality is first level.

The original analysis can be modified to indicate that the subject's potentiality is first level. For some goal ϕ, privation not-ϕ, and subject x:

(2) Change is the actuality of x, which is potentially ϕ but actually not-ϕ.

This version allows three items to count as the actuality: the actuality of x could be x (the subject), not-ϕx (the subject deprived), or ϕx (the prod-

---

[38] I thank Paul Matthewson for suggestions concerning the interpretation of this passage.

uct). For example, the actuality of the bronze, which is potentially a statue but actually a nonstatue, could be the bronze (the subject itself), a nonstatue (the actual compound of privation and bronze), or a statue (the compound product). Part of the problem with this reconstruction is its failure accurately to reflect Aristotle's definition. He adds an important qualification: "Change," he says, "is the actuality of what is in potentiality, *as such*," and later he explains the function of the "as" phrase. The completion of the "as" phrase indicates how the subject is to be regarded. The subject is not to be regarded as what it is in itself (e.g., as bronze) because change is not the actuality of bronze as bronze (201^{a}30–31); bronze is the actuality of the subject conceived as what it is in itself. Instead the subject is to be regarded as potential. "Change," he says, "is the actuality of the potential, as potential" (201^{b}4–5).

The analysis might be modified in the following way. For some goal ϕ, privation not-ϕ, and subject x:

(3) Change is the actuality of x, which is potentially ϕ but actually not-ϕ, as potentially ϕ.

One could say, for example, that the being built is the actuality of bricks, which are potentially but not actually a house, as potentially a house. Although this version excludes one of the previous three actualities, namely, the actuality of the subject as what it is in itself (e.g., bricks), the interpretation of the "as" phrase will not do as it stands. Since the interpretation fails to indicate that the subject is conceived as potentially a house yet actually deprived, the phrase fails to exclude the product, which is the actuality of a subject that is potentially the product, whatever the subject's actual state. The actuality that Aristotle needs to isolate is the actuality of a subject that is potential and actually deprived, and considered *as* potential and actually deprived. Thus, not only must the subject's potentiality be first level, it must also be considered in respect of its first-level potentiality. For this reason Aristotle on one occasion spells out the "as" phrase to mean "as changeable" (201^{a}29) and later points out that, even though the process and the product are both candidates for the actuality of the buildable, once the house exists the buildable no longer exists. The "as" phrase excludes the product by stipulating that change is the actuality of the subject, which is potentially the product and actually deprived, and considered as such.

To make this meaning clear, I modify the analysis once more. For some goal ϕ, privation not-ϕ, and subject x:

(4) Change is the actuality of x, which is potentially ϕ but actually not-ϕ, as potentially ϕ but actually not-ϕ.

This definition should specify the subject-state complex at all moments up to but excluding the moment at which the subject starts to be ϕ. Since the subject passes though an entire series of states on the way to ϕ, and "not-ϕ" designates that series, the actuality should be the compound not-ϕx. The definition should therefore capture the change and exclude the product.

But the definition does not really capture the change. The specification picks out a subject at any stage of its journey, including its starting position and up to but excluding its final position. This sequence is not a change but simply the subject in a series of states. Thus, the definition picks out the bricks and stones lying in a heap but fully prepared for production into a house; it picks out the half-built house, the nearly completed structure, and any other intermediate stage in the process.[39] The inadequacy of the definition is its failure to capture the connectedness of the series into a dynamic whole—the change.

Clearly Aristotle wants a definition that captures the dynamic aspect of change, since he says, as quoted above, "It is evident that change is the actuality ($\grave{\epsilon}\nu\tau\epsilon\lambda\acute{\epsilon}\chi\epsilon\iota\alpha$) of the potential, as potential ($\mathring{\hat{\eta}}\ \delta\upsilon\nu\alpha\tau\acute{o}\nu$). It is clear then that [change] is this, and that [something] is changed just when the actuality ($\grave{\epsilon}\nu\tau\epsilon\lambda\acute{\epsilon}\chi\epsilon\iota\alpha$) is this, and neither earlier nor later; for it is possible for each thing sometimes to be active ($\grave{\epsilon}\nu\epsilon\rho\gamma\epsilon\hat{\iota}\nu$) and sometimes not, for example, the buildable, and the actuality ($\grave{\epsilon}\nu\acute{\epsilon}\rho\gamma\epsilon\iota\alpha$) of the buildable, as buildable, is building" (201^b4–10). Change is not the actuality of the subject that is potentially other than it is, as potentially other, and presently at rest, but the actuality of the subject once it has become active and only while it remains active. How can Aristotle capture this dynamic quality?

L. A. Kosman, in his influential paper "Aristotle's Definition of Motion,"[40] suggests that Aristotle defines change as the actuality that is the activity of a subject that is potentially other than it actually is. The definition avoids circularity because Aristotle carefully distinguishes activities from changes. Since activities exist only once a subject has ceased to be idle, a definition of change as activity captures the dynamic quality of change. Let me pursue this suggestion.

In a celebrated passage in *Metaphysics* Θ.6 Aristotle contrasts such actions as seeing, thinking, living well, and being happy, which he calls $\grave{\epsilon}\nu\acute{\epsilon}\rho\gamma\epsilon\iota\alpha\iota$ ("activities"), with removing fat, becoming healthy, building, and learning, which he calls $\kappa\iota\nu\acute{\eta}\sigma\epsilon\iota\varsigma$ ("changes") (1048^b18–35). Changes differ from activities in a number of ways, and critically in their relation to ends. A change is not an end but concerned with an end—it leads to an end, but the end lies beyond it. A change is incomplete because its end, its completion, is achieved only at the expense of its own termination:

[39] I am grateful to William Charlton, Paul Coppock, and Johanna Seibt for their suggestions about Aristotle's definition in III.1.

[40] Kosman 1969, esp. 54–58.

when the goal of the change is reached, the change is over.[41] One cannot say of a person that at the same time he is building a house and has built it, for while the building is still under way, the house is not yet finished, but once the house is finished—once the person has built the house—he is no longer building it. The process of building has ended because the project has been completed.

Activities, on the other hand, are ends in themselves. And because the end of an activity lies not beyond but within the action, an activity is complete at any moment for as long as it lasts.[42] Since completion is in this case simultaneous with performance, one can say of a person that at the same time she both sees and has seen, for the person's action of seeing is complete as soon as it starts. An activity is not aimed at a goal beyond itself. Aristotle typically treats activities as the exercise of a capacity possessed by a subject. The capacity itself is regularly acquired by means of a change, as in the example discussed in *De Anima* II.5. The person who theorizes is one who has acquired the ability; and such a person can exercise his knowledge at will, if not prevented (417^a27–28). An individual whose potentiality for the capacity is second level need not exercise the acquired capacity continuously, and someone with knowledge, but presently asleep or engaged in conflicting activities, retains the knowledge. So the knower can be idle or can manifest the capacity and theorize.

Kosman's provocative suggestion is that change is the activity expressed by a subject at the *first* level with respect to its goal—the activity of an object that is potentially other than it actually is. If Kosman is right, Aristotle's definition of change does not apply to the subject at rest because, when resting, the subject does not exercise its potentiality to be other than it is. While resting, the subject no more manifests its potentiality for otherness than does the knower, now sleeping, manifest his capacity for theorizing. Like the second knower described in *De Anima*, who exercises his knowledge only once he begins to theorize, the deprived subject of *Physics* III.1 exercises its potentiality only while it is moving.

Although Kosman's thesis enables Aristotle to characterize change as a dynamic entity, the proposal still seems inadequate because change is not only dynamic but also directed toward a goal that the subject fails to possess. The problem is that a subject can manifest its potentiality for otherness simply by expressing its lack. The flaunting of ignorance, and of other privations, is an occurrence with which we are all too familiar, and such exhibitions are typically not stumbling steps toward improvement but exactly what they appear to be: the display of a lack. A positive

[41] Cf. *E.N.* x.4, 1174^a19–$^b5$.
[42] See *E.N.* x.4, 1174^a14–19 and 1174^b5–9.

change is the constructive removal of a privation, not merely the expression of it, and since the subject that undergoes the change lacks, as such, the positive character that would guide the removal, the subject cannot account for the directedness of its change. The direction of change must be provided by an agent that leads the patient to the positive goal. Thus the change that unites a patient with its goal presupposes a mover, something that imposes the goal on the object changed.

Aristotle's treatment of change in *Physics* III.1 is a partial account that finds its completion in the next two chapters, III.2–3. *Physics* III.3 demonstrates that change is the mutual actuality of an agent and a patient, which is located in the patient. Since change is the mutual actuality of the mover and the moved, but located in the moved, the change exists while, and only while, the agent imposes the goal on the patient and the patient responds by developing toward it. At the end of III.3 Aristotle offers a full definition of change in terms of both the agent and the patient. By mentioning the agent, he can show that change is a sustained progression toward a goal. Since Aristotle's project in *Physics* III.3 presupposes his theory of agency, let me start by indicating some of the main features of his general theory: first, his doctrine of contact between mover and moved, second, the classification of movers and the nature of the first mover; and finally, his statement of the conditions under which a mover acts and a moved responds.

AGENCY

An agent possesses an active potentiality, one described in *Metaphysics* Θ.1 as an "active principle of change in another thing or in the thing itself qua other." In *Physics* III.2 Aristotle describes how an agent brings about a change.

> As we have said, every changer too is changed, [i.e., every changer] that is potentially changeable and whose failure to change is rest (for the failure to change is rest for that which admits change). For to act in relation to this (πρὸς τοῦτο) [the changeable], as such (ἧ τοιοῦτον), is to change it; and [the changer] does this by touching (θίξει), so that at the same time it also suffers (πάσχει); hence change is the actuality of the changeable, as changeable, and this happens by touching the changer, so that at the same time [the changer] also suffers. And the changer will always bring a form, either substantial (τόδε) or qualitative (τοιόνδε) or quantitative (τοσόνδε), that will be the principle (ἀρχή) and cause (αἴτιον) of the change, when [the changer] produces change. For example, the man in actuality produces a man from what is potentially a man. (202ᵃ3–12)

194

This passage makes two main points. First, every mover, if it is the sort of thing that can be changed, suffers a change when it causes a change in something else. This statement excludes unmoved movers from among the things that are changed when they cause change, because unmoved movers are not changeable (κινητόν), and their lack of motion is not rest. Rest, Aristotle says both here and in *Physics* VIII. I, is the failure or privation of motion (251ª26–27); properly speaking, then, only movable things can rest.[43] Aristotle suggests that the agent suffers a change by its contact with the object changed; since the agent touches the patient, the agent simultaneously suffers when it produces a change. Second, the agent imposes a form (substantial, qualitative, or quantitative) on the patient, and the form that the agent imposes is the principle and cause of the change. Thus, for example, a man in actuality—an entity that possesses the substantial form that makes him a man—generates another man by imposing his own form (the principle and cause) on something that is potentially a man. The male agent accomplishes the generation by contact with the material that has the appropriate passive potentiality. By its action, the male agent transforms the female material, which is potentially but not actually human, into an actual human.

Contact

In *On Generation and Corruption* I.6–7 Aristotle discusses the notion of contact and his theory of movers. In I.6 he claims that contact in the strict sense occurs between distinct located magnitudes that have their extremities together (322ᵇ32–323ª12). If contact occurs in this sense, the agent and patient experience direct physical contact with their extremities together, and the agent not only produces a change but also suffers a reciprocal reaction caused by the entity acted upon; for instance, a knife that cuts is blunted by the object cut, and something that heats is cooled by the object heated. But many causal productions do not involve contact in this strict sense. The example on which Aristotle dwells in *Physics* III.3, the action and passion of teaching and learning, requires contact between the teacher and student, but not (we trust) contact demanding that the two have their extremities together.

On Generation and Corruption I.6 loosens the requirements for contact. Aristotle offers a general account of contact, which preserves only the requirement that mover and moved are located, and he contrasts the general account, not with the earlier strict definition, but with one that stipulates that mover and moved stand "in relation to one another" (πρὸς

---

[43] In *Phys.* VIII, however, Aristotle sometimes speaks of unmoved movers as always resting; cf. VIII.3, 253ª28–32 and 254ᵇ4–6.

ἄλληλα) in such a way that doing (τὸ ποιεῖν) and suffering (τὸ πάσχειν) are attributable to them. He says, "The definition of contact is on the one hand 'general' (καθόλου), which applies to entities that have position and are capable, the one of moving, and the other of being moved, but [the definition of contact is] on the other hand 'in relation to one another' (πρὸς ἄλληλα), which applies to mover and moved in which doing (τὸ ποιεῖν) and suffering (τὸ πάσχειν) are present" (323ᵃ22–25).

The notion of relational contact (πρὸς ἄλληλα) is crucial for Aristotle's account in *Physics* III.3. Some scholars will claim, however, that Aristotle here introduces a single new notion, namely, general (καθόλου) contact, which requires only that the mover and moved have position, and contrasts it, not with relational contact, but with the strict notion requiring that mover and moved be distinct located magnitudes that have their extremities together.[44] Thus every mover, unless it is an unmoved mover, will be reciprocally moved by the object moved. This suggestion misses the significance of the phrase πρὸς ἄλληλα. In *On Generation and Corruption* Aristotle has three expressions that are commonly translated "reciprocal," unless the translation is obviously excluded by the context: ὑπ' ἀλλήλων ("by one another"), εἰς ἄλληλα ("into one another"), and πρὸς ἄλληλα ("in relation to one another").[45] In fact, only the first expression indicates the reciprocality of action and passion. For example, in describing contact in the strict sense, Aristotle says, "So it is clear that these things naturally touch one another, which, being separate magnitudes, have their extremities together and are able to move and able to be moved by one another (ὑπ' ἀλλήλων)" (323ᵃ10–12). Use of the preposition ὑπό with the genitive and the passive voice is a usual means of indicating agency in Greek, and the standard grammatical practice is pervasive in Aristotle's treatments of agency.[46] Thus, if two entities are said to be moved "by one another," each is moved by the other, and the change is reciprocal.

One need not suppose that the other two expressions have the same meaning.[47] In *Physics* III.1 Aristotle identifies the agent and the patient and generally the mover and the moved as things that are πρός τι (in relation to something) (200ᵇ28–31) and gives this reason: "For that which is able to move is able to move the moved and that which is able to be moved is able to be moved by the mover" (200ᵇ31–32). Although he explicitly says that the moved is moved by the mover (ὑπὸ τοῦ κινητικοῦ), he does not

---

[44] See Joachim 1922, 147; and Williams 1982, 117–19. The objection was put to me by Sarah Broadie and William Charlton.

[45] In his Clarendon translation of *G.C.*, Williams (1982) usually renders the phrases with the word "mutual," but at least in this context he takes "mutual" to indicate reciprocal action and passion (117).

[46] See, e.g., *Phys.* VIII.4–5.

[47] On the meaning of εἰς ἄλληλα as "reversible," see above, chapter 2, n. 43.

say that the mover is reciprocally moved by the moved. He merely alludes to the active relation of the mover toward the moved. And when in *Physics* III.2 he says that every movable mover is moved, he explains, "For to act in relation to this (πρὸς τοῦτο) [the changeable], as such, is to change it; and [the changer] does this by touching (θίξει), so that at the same time (ἅμα) it also suffers" (202ᵃ5–7). Again Aristotle says nothing about the agent's being reciprocally changed by the patient but speaks only of the active relation of the mover toward the moved, such that the agent also suffers. A few lines later he says, "Hence change is the actuality of the changeable, as changeable, and this happens by touching (θίξει) the changer, so that at the same time (ἅμα) [the changer] also suffers" (202ᵃ7–9).

If one assumes that the contact between mover and moved is contact in the strict sense, then the conclusion will be that the agent's suffering is a distinct change caused by the patient. But *Physics* III.2 does not indicate the sort of contact at issue and does not claim that the patient causes the agent's suffering. Instead the text says that the agent's suffering is caused by the touching and that the suffering is simultaneous with the change that the agent produces. Although many reciprocal reactions are simultaneous with the change that an agent produces, some certainly are not. The doctor who cures a person of fever and is infected himself does not suffer the fever at the same time as the cure. Aristotle's emphasis on the simultaneity of the agent's and patient's suffering, his claim that the agent's suffering takes place by the touching, and his failure to say that the agent's suffering is caused by the patient all tend to suggest that the issue is not reciprocal reaction. And it is crucial for his argument in *Physics* III.3 that the change of the agent is one and the same as (though different in being from) the change that takes place in the patient. Aristotle emphasizes the simultaneity of the agent's suffering with the patient's suffering in III.2 because he is preparing to argue in III.3 that the two changes of the two objects are one actuality, which is located in the patient (202ᵃ13–16). By arguing that action and passion are one actuality, he can finally show that change is a connected and dynamic event.

Aristotle thus needs a notion of contact less strict than the central notion of reciprocal contact, yet less broad than the general notion that, as he says in *On Generation and Corruption* I.6, relates an object moved to a mover that is totally unaffected by the motion it causes. Thus, starting with the focal notion of contact requiring that two distinct located magnitudes have their extremities together such that they are affected by one another (ὑπ' ἀλλήλων), he loosens the conditions first to a notion of contact that he describes as πρὸς ἄλληλα. Contact in this sense does not require that the two objects have their extremities together and does not entail that the mover is moved by the object moved. Two objects are in contact in this way if they are distinct located magnitudes and if "that which is able to move is able to move the moved and that which is able to be moved is able to be moved by the mover,"[48] such that the mover simultaneously suffers, not by the moved, but in relation to it or, as Aristotle puts it in *Physics* III.2, by the contact. In *On Generation and Corruption* I.6 he relaxes the conditions for contact still further to include a general (καθόλου) notion requiring only that two objects are located and that the one is mover and the other moved (323ª22–23). When contact occurs in this sense, the mover is unchanged by its contact with the object moved. It is possible, Aristotle says, for that which causes a motion only to touch what it moves, but not to be touched in return, and he mentions a grieving man who "touches" those near him but whom they do not "touch" (323ª28–33). Movers like the grieving man are unmoved.

Armed with three notions of contact, Aristotle proceeds in *On Generation and Corruption* I.7 to describe three sorts of movers. Typical changes often involve movers of all three sorts.

Movers

Generation and Corruption I.7 opens with a review of earlier opinions on the topic of action and passion, and Aristotle points out that, although most people think that action and passion occur between things that are unlike, Democritus claimed that agent and patient are like. He declares both sides to be partly right. Things totally like or totally unlike cannot act on one another: agent and patient must be like in kind, but unlike and contrary in form; for example, body is affected by body, flavor by flavor, and color by color (323ᵇ29–324ª5). So agent and patient act and suffer in respect of contrary properties within the same genus. If the agent's action succeeds, the agent assimilates the patient to itself (324ª10–11). Thus, once the change has been accomplished, agent and patient are not only like in kind but also like in form because the agent has successfully imposed the form that it possesses on the entity acted upon, fire making something cold to be hot, and something cold making something hot to be cold. By means of a change the agent guides the patient from a state unlike its own to one like its own.

Aristotle's treatment of causal action relies on the three sorts of contact specified in I.6. He calls attention to three sorts of movers, and each, in causing a change, is in contact with the moved in one of the ways earlier outlined. He describes the agent as that "in which [one finds] the principle of change," "because the principle is the first of the causes" (324ª26–28). For example, the doctor is the agent of health because he possesses the art

---

[48] *Phys.* III.1, 200ᵇ31–32.

of medicine; the art, which the doctor possesses, is the first cause or principle of health (324^{b}3). Both the doctor and his art are movers. In addition, changes often include a cause that Aristotle calls the "last" mover
(324^{a}28–29); for instance, the wine or bread prescribed by the doctor in
effecting a cure (324^{b}3–4). The last mover comes into direct physical contact with the entity moved and is itself moved by the moved; thus the
bread, in causing a change in the invalid, is itself heated or cooled (324^{b}1–
3).[49] In contrast with the last mover, the first mover is unaffected by the
moved (324^{a}35–^{b}1). The art of medicine, for example, located in the soul
of the doctor, "touches" the invalid, but the invalid does not "touch" the
art; the contact between the art and the invalid is "general." And the doctor's contact with the patient is πρὸς ἄλληλα because the doctor acts on
the patient, the patient is changed by the doctor, and the doctor is simultaneously affected in relation to the patient. There are, then, three sorts
of movers: a first mover, whose contact with the object moved is general,
that is itself unmoved by the contact; an agent, whose contact with the
entity moved is relational, that is affected by the contact; and a last mover,
whose contact with the entity moved satisfies the strict definition, that
suffers a reciprocal reaction caused by the moved.

All changes can be traced to a first unmoved mover.[50] Often the unmoved mover is located in a self-moving (living) agent, as in the case of
the medical art discussed in *On Generation and Corruption* I.7. The first
mover is the entity that Aristotle calls in *Metaphysics* Z.7 the "by something" (ὑπό τινος) and identifies as the form in the soul of the craftsman
in artificial productions and as the form of the generator in natural productions.[51] The first mover is in fact the agent's active principle. The
medical example is paradigmatic of artificial production in general: the
art in the agent's soul is the agent's active principle for producing some
definite result. Aristotle describes the first mover vividly in Z.7, saying,
"Indeed, the maker (τὸ ποιοῦν) and that from which the motion of becoming healthy begins (ὅθεν ἄρχεται ἡ κίνησις τοῦ ὑγιαίνειν), if the
production is artificial, is the form (τὸ εἶδος) in the soul" (1032^{b}21–23).
The art is the form or active potentiality that enables the agent to produce
a change. In natural contexts the agent's own form is the active potentiality and first mover; for example, a man's soul is the active potentiality
that enables him to replicate his kind.

Active potentialities are movers—efficient causes of change. But in
what sense are they efficient, if they experience no change at all? The

---

[49] In fact, food undergoes a more drastic change: it is transformed into blood and then
turned into the various bodily parts. See *De An.* II.4, 416^{a}29–^{b}9; *G.C.* I.5, 321^{b}35–322^{a}28;
P.A. II.3, 650^{a}34–^{b}13; II.4, 651^{a}14–15; and *G.A.* II.6, 744^{b}11–745^{a}18.

[50] See *Phys.* VIII.5.

[51] See above, pp. 120–21.

question is important because Aristotle appeals to first movers to explain both becoming and persistence.

Active Potentialities

Typical efficient causes are entities that bring about changes. Causal agents, in acting, experience strict or relational contact with the object changed and are themselves changed either by suffering a reciprocal re-action caused by the object moved or by some simultaneous change in relation to it. Active potentialities, however, do not initiate changes, yet Aristotle plainly regards them as efficient causes.[52] If such movers do not bring about changes, in what sense are they efficient?

De Anima II.4 gives an answer. Aristotle takes Empedocles to task for suggesting that organic growth is fully explained by appeal to material factors. According to Empedocles the roots of plants grow downward because earth naturally tends in that direction, and their stems and branches grow upward because fire naturally tends in that direction. Ar-istotle protests: If this were the answer, plants should fly apart, their roots in one direction, their stems and branches in another. What prevents this dissolution? It is prevented, he counters, because soul is the cause of nour-ishment and growth (415^b28–416^a9). Next he remarks that some people regard fire as the simple cause of nourishment and growth because fire appears to be the only simple body that is nourished and grows. To this proposal he responds: "[Fire] is in a sense the helping cause (συναίτιον), but it is certainly not simply responsible. Rather the soul [is responsible]; for the growth of fire is unlimited (εἰς ἄπειρον), as long as there is some-thing that can be burned. But all things constructed naturally have a limit (πέρας) and proper proportion (λόγος) of magnitude and growth. And these things are [the responsibility] of soul, but not of fire, and of the formula (λόγος) rather than matter" (416^a13–18).

Soul is a set of active capacities that directs the life activities, including nourishment and growth, for organisms. Fire contributes to the realiza-tion of these ends as an instrumental (last) cause, but fire on its own can-not accomplish them because fire grows without bounds as long as there is material for it to burn. The natural behavior of fire must be constrained and directed so that its natural behavior subserves a particular end. With-out direction the unbridled action of fire will not yield the appropriate outcome. Soul plays a supervisory role, and in this sense soul is the first efficient cause of nourishment and growth. An organism's soul deter-mines its particular identity. Thus, the particular bodily changes that

[52] See, e.g., *Met.* Λ.4, 1070^b28–35; *Phys.* II.3, 195^b21–25. Cf. *Phys.* II.7, 198^a24–27; *De An.* II.4, 415^b8–12.

constitute nourishment and growth—changes that fire as helping cause (συναίτιον) may well effect—occur when they do, where they do, and in the way that they do because the organism is the sort of thing that it is.

Active potentialities determine the goal of a change. For example, the doctor's medical art is knowledge of what health is, a knowledge that enables the doctor to direct his efforts toward the appropriate end when faced with the actual task of effecting a cure. The doctor's knowledge of health provides additional guides as well, by enabling him to recognize the sorts of objects for which his art is beneficial (organisms, but not, for example, bricks and stones); and, since the knowledge determines a range of possible procedures for organisms that suffer from a range of possible ailments, that knowledge provides a general guide to the sorts of procedures and instruments that he can expect to use on a given occasion. *Parts of Animals* I.1 claims that the final cause—the end for which the craftsman possesses the active potentiality—determines the sort of matter required and the procedural steps that lead to the goal.[53] The necessity imposed by the goal is called "hypothetical."[54] If some end is to be realized, then such and such materials are needed and such and such steps must be taken. So knowledge of the end equips the craftsman to work out a plan of action or to justify the course that he actually pursues.[55] Aristotle insists that what is true in artificial production is even truer in natural.[56] Although in this case no rational agent works out a plan of action, it is in virtue of the agent's active potentiality that a certain kind of matter is acted upon, that the change displays a certain pattern and concludes at a certain limit. As a first mover, the agent's active potentiality fixes the goal of the change, determines the sorts of things needed for its achievement, and directs production to that goal.

Consider an analogy. Suppose that a company is run by a single director who determines the company aims, decides the best means for accomplishing them, chooses the best individuals to do the work, and coordinates the actual proceedings—but does none of the physical labor himself. Such a person is comparable to Aristotle's first efficient cause because the director manages the whole enterprise.[57] Still, the analogy is somewhat misleading because the leader is the same order of entity as those led; and although the leader's efforts may be strictly mental, the job is still of the typically causal type. So instead the active potentiality might better be

---

[53] See *P.A.* I.1, 639ᵇ27–30.

[54] See *P.A.* I.1, esp. 639ᵇ12–640ᵇ4; 642ᵃ2–13; 642ᵃ32–ᵇ4; *Phys.* II.9; and *G.C.* II.11. References to recent work on hypothetical necessity are cited above, chapter 4, n. 49.

[55] See *Met.* Z.7, 1032ᵃ32–ᵇ21; *E.N.* III.3; and Cooper 1975, 10–46.

[56] *P.A.* I.1, 639ᵇ19–21.

[57] Cf. *Met.* Λ.10, 1075ᵃ11–15.

viewed as a set of operating rules for performing some complex task.[58] Such rules are productive because they enable their possessor to recognize his goal; to determine what materials, instruments, and procedures are needed for its realization; and to coordinate his efforts in order to achieve it. The active principle, proper to the agent, is the first efficient cause of becoming because it determines the goal of a change and sustains the progression toward that goal. What the active principle cannot do, and be unmoved, is to initiate motion in an object at rest. Let us now consider how Aristotle explains the beginning of motion.

Initiation of Motion

In simple contexts of action and passion, if an agent with an appropriate active potentiality and a patient with a corresponding passive potentiality come into direct physical contact, and if there is no external interference, the agent necessarily activates its active potentiality and the patient responds. Aristotle explains in *Metaphysics* Θ.5, "In the case of such potentialities [so-called nonrational active potentialities], when that which can produce (τὸ ποιητικόν) and that which can suffer (τὸ παθητικόν) associate (πλησιάζωσι) as potential (ὡς δύνανται), the one must produce and the other suffer (τὸ μὲν ποιεῖν τὸ δὲ πάσχειν)" (1048ᵃ5–7). For example, if fire, which has the active potentiality to make things hot, comes into contact with wood, which is combustible, and if nothing external interferes, the fire must act in accordance with its power, and the wood must respond by becoming hot and finally burning. Thus, in many cases it appears that, appropriate conditions obtaining, the sheer physical contact of an agent and patient with corresponding potentialities necessitates the activation of the agent's active and patient's passive potentialities.

Many situations of action and passion are not as straightforward as this. In *Metaphysics* Θ.2 and 5 Aristotle distinguishes the so-called nonrational active potentialities, to which I have just referred, from rational ones. Nonrational powers are directed toward a single end; for example, the active potentiality of fire, its power to heat, is for a single result—the production of heat. Rational powers, on the other hand, are directed toward a pair of contrary ends; the doctor's power to heal enables him also to injure, and the builder's power to build enables him also to tear down. If the active potentiality is a type of knowledge, the agent can determine both the positive end and the privation.[59] So a doctor at the bedside of

---

[58] Cf. the analogy at *M.A.* 10, 703ᵃ29–ᵇ2, according to which an animal is like a city governed by good laws, so that there need be no separate monarch because all the individuals do their own task. On form, cf. S. Mansion [1971] 1979.

[59] Cf. *Met.* Z.7, 1032ᵃ32–ᵇ6.

someone stricken with fever faces a choice. Given his art, the doctor knows what health is. Suppose that health is a balance of elements in the body.[60] The doctor can determine by observing the invalid's symptoms that restoration of health in this case requires cooling the person to reduce the fever. But the doctor also recognizes that he can increase the fever (impairing the invalid's condition still further) by inducing more heat. Since the doctor's knowledge enables him to recognize the negative as well as the positive end, mere association with the patient, or relational contact, is not enough to activate the doctor's power in the positive direction. In addition the doctor must choose which of the alternative ends to pursue (1048ᵃ7–11). Aristotle says of this sort of case, "Whichever [of the two ends] the agent desires decisively, this he will do, when, as potential (ὡς δύναται), he is present and associates with that which can suffer; so that in the case of everything that is potential in the rational sense, when [the agent] desires that of which he has the potentiality and is potential in the relevant sense, he must do this" (1048ᵃ11–15).

Metaphysics Θ.5 does not treat all the complexities of action and passion,[61] but the text does suggest that, unless there is interference, contact between an agent with an appropriate active nonrational potentiality and a patient with a corresponding first-level passive potentiality necessitates the action and passion. And in the case of rational potentialities, unless there is interference, contact between an appropriate agent and patient, together with the agent's choice between contrary ends, necessitates the action and passion. If the conditions are adequate, then an agent that comes into contact with a suitable object will act unless there is interference.[62] The important point is that action and passion occur in the appropriate conditions unless certain overriding factors obtain. One therefore needs to appeal to additional factors only to explain the failures of action and passion in particular cases and not the occurrences. This point must be stressed because the explanation of change always leads to a first mover. If Aristotle had to appeal to a first mover to explain how motion starts from a state of rest, the first mover would need to give the initial prod. Yet the first mover can provide no impetus and be unmoved. Given Aristotle's view that all changes can ultimately be traced to an unmoved mover, he cannot hold that a first mover explains why motion starts. Instead he must hold that what needs explanation is why motion sometimes fails to occur when a mover and its object are in contact. I shall return to this topic.[63] If change occurs automatically, barring interference, then the

---

[60] Cf. *Met.* Z.7, 1032ᵇ6–8; 1032ᵇ18–20.
[61] On these issues, see esp. Charles 1984.
[62] On this topic I have profited especially from Mourelatos 1967.
[63] See below, pp. 209–10.

contact (whether strict or otherwise) between an appopriate agent and patient should necessitate the change.

To summarize, Aristotle's theory of agency includes three sorts of movers: a first mover, which is the agent's active potentiality for a particular form; the agent itself, which imposes the form; and a last mover, which is typically an instrument used by the agent. Each mover is in contact with the moved in one of three ways. The first mover's contact is general ($\kappa\alpha\theta\delta\lambda\omega$), such that the moved responds to the mover but the mover is wholly unaffected; the contact between a typical (living) agent and patient is relational ($\pi\rho\delta\varsigma$ $\check{\alpha}\lambda\lambda\eta\lambda\alpha$), such that the moved responds to the mover and the mover simultaneously suffers by the contact; and the contact between the last (often inanimate instrumental) agent and patient is strict ($\kappa\nu\rho\iota\omega\varsigma$), such that the mover is reciprocally moved by the moved. In situations in which the agent's power is nonrational, the agent acts and the patient responds if, barring interference, the agent and the patient are in the appropriate state, the agent having an active potentiality for the same form for which the patient has a first-level passive potentiality, and the two are in contact. If the agent's active power is rational, the agent must, in addition, choose between contrary ends.

Using this theory of agency, Aristotle undertakes to show in *Physics* III. 3 that the change that takes place in the patient is a connected progression toward a goal.

AGENCY AND THE DEFINITION OF CHANGE

The definition of change in *Physics* III. 1 fails to capture the nature of change because, if actuality is interpreted as a static notion, the definition can apply to a series of objects at rest, and if actuality is interpreted as activity, the definition can apply to an entity displaying its lack. In *Physics* III. 2 Aristotle introduces the notion of agency in order to argue in III. 3 that change is the actuality of both the mover and the moved, but located only in the moved. If change is the actuality of both the agent and patient, change will be the coordinated expression of the agent's active and the patient's passive potentialities.

Aristotle claims in *Physics* III. 2 that every mover subject to motion is moved by touching the moved. He explicitly excludes unmoved movers by restricting the claim to apply only to those movers whose lack of motion is rest (202^a3-5). His argument concerns proper agents that bring about changes, and his focus is not an instrumental (last) agent, which is reciprocally changed by the moved, but an agent that "will always bring a form, either substantial, qualitative, or quantitative, that will be the principle and cause of the change" (202^a9-11). Thus, his topic is a mover whose contact with the moved is $\pi\rho\delta\varsigma$ $\check{\alpha}\lambda\lambda\eta\lambda\alpha$, in relation to the moved, such that the moved is moved by the mover, and the mover simultaneously suffers by the relational contact.

The Revised Definition of Change

In *Physics* III.3 Aristotle argues that the change, which the patient undergoes, is the actuality of both the agent and the patient. Although the change occurs in the patient and not in the agent, there is a single actuality of both. He presents a number of analogies to illustrate the way in which the change of the agent and the patient is a single actuality. He suggests that the change is like a road, which can be regarded as two journeys: a road from Athens to Thebes, and a road from Thebes to Athens (202ᵃ18–21).[64] Although the journeys are one because they follow the same path, they are not the same in being or account. The unity of the road differs from that of a mantle and a cloak (202ᵇ10–16). A mantle and a cloak are one in number and being, and so a particular garment can be called either a "mantle" or a "cloak" with no difference in implication; since the names are synonymous, the object to which the names apply has the same properties under either description. In the case of the road, the journey from Athens to Thebes and the journey from Thebes to Athens start and end at different locations, and they feature signposts in a different order—for example, one journey might be uphill and the other downhill. So Aristotle claims that, although there is one road, different properties belong to it depending upon whether it is described as "the road from Athens to Thebes" or as "the road from Thebes to Athens."

Action and passion are one in the way that the road from Athens to Thebes and the road from Thebes to Athens are one. In Aristotle's example of teaching and learning, there is one entity—the change—that can be described in two nonsynonymous ways as "teaching" and as "learning." Both expressions pick out the transition that takes place in the student, but they apply to that transition for different reasons. Described as "teaching," the change is "the actuality of this [the agent] in this [the patient]"; described as "learning," the change is "the actuality of this [the patient] by this [the agent]" (202ᵇ19–22). And so, depending upon which specification is used, the change has different properties: under one description it is the actuality of the *agent* as subject that occurs *in* the patient, and under the other description it is the actuality of the *patient* as subject *caused by* the agent. Depending upon whether it is viewed with reference to the agent or with reference to the patient, the change is an active production or a passive response. But there is, Aristotle insists, only one

---

[64] Note that ὁδός can mean "journey" as well as "road" (see Liddell, Scott, and Jones 1968, 1199).

actuality—the change—which is both the production (by the agent) and the response (in the patient).

Aristotle's claim in III.2 that the mover simultaneously suffers by touching the moved does not concern a possible reaction that the agent may experience by its direct physical contact with the object moved. Reactions are changes distinct from the one that the agent produces, and they occur in the agent. Furthermore, the claim does not concern any bodily movement displayed by the agent in the act of producing; the teacher's waving of the arms, the nervous pacing, the vibration of the vocal cords are again motions in the agent and so are not the issue when Aristotle claims in *Physics* III.2 that the agent suffers by its contact with the moved or when he argues in III.3 that the change of the agent is the same as the one that occurs in the patient. And furthermore, the claim does not concern the agent's proper activity or self-motion. This motion, again, occurs in the agent; self-motion is distinct from the motion that takes place in the moved, and such motion is an activity, not a change. Aristotle's point is that the agent's producing is a change of the agent as well as the patient. He insists that there is nothing strange about locating the actuality of one thing in another; the teaching "is the actuality of the teacher, in something certainly, and not separated off, but *of* something *in* something" (202ᵇ5–8).[65] The teaching, which is the actuality of the teacher, takes place in the one who learns.[66] The teaching and the learning are the same actuality.

Although a causal action takes place in the patient, the action qualifies as a change of the agent because it satisfies the criteria for being a change (κίνησις) laid down in *Metaphysics* Θ.6. Building, teaching, and other productions are directed toward a goal and are incomplete until the goal is reached. Since attainment of the goal terminates the change, an agent cannot have attained the goal while still undertaking to achieve it, and so it is not true to say of a builder that he simultaneously "is building" and "has built" a particular house (1048ᵇ31); once the builder has built the house, the task is finished, and he is no longer building it. Teaching is similar; the teacher has not taught the student unless he has communicated the lesson in such a way that the student has absorbed it.[67] The fundamental point is that only if the agent has completed the change has he successfully induced in the patient the form for which he has the active, and the patient the passive, potentiality. Only then has the agent achieved

---

[65] My earlier discussion of this topic in Gill 1980 has been criticized by Heinaman (1985 156–57). The present treatment preserves the main thesis of my earlier paper, while attempting to avoid Heinaman's objection.

[66] Cf. *Met.* Θ.8, 1050ᵃ23–34.

[67] Cf. *Met.* Θ.8, 1050ᵃ15–19.

his goal. And so the change that takes place in the patient is a change of the agent as well.

By introducing the notion of agency and arguing that change is the joint actuality of the agent and patient, Aristotle can define change as a continuous process toward a goal. The actuality that change is starts to exist when the agent and patient enter into relational contact and continues to exist while the contact lasts. The change is a directed progression because, during their association, the agent gradually induces in the patient the form for which the agent has the active potentiality and the patient a first-level passive potentiality. Once the change has been completed, the patient and the form are unified. The patient does not lose its potentiality once the change has been completed, but its potentiality has become second level rather than first; that is, the potentiality for the goal coincides with its actual possession. At the end of III. 3 Aristotle states the definition of change "more intelligibly" (γνωριμώτερον). Speaking first of alteration but then generalizing, he defines change as "the actuality of that which is potentially productive (τοῦ δυνάμει ποιητικοῦ) and of that which can be affected (παθητικοῦ), as such" (202ᵇ26–27). Both the agent and patient are specified as potential in a first-level sense; change is the joint actuality of a mover and a moved that together must still achieve their common goal.

The point of arguing that the production by the agent and the suffering of the patient are the same actuality is that Aristotle can thereby show that change is not merely a disconnected series of states informing the patient but a continuous and directed progression, and thus a dynamic entity. The connectedness of the process is due to the mover and is captured by a definition that specifies change as the joint actuality of the mover and the moved.

Self-Motion

Two questions might be asked about the account of change in *Physics* III.3. First, how can Aristotle accommodate self-motion within the theory? Self-motion seems problematic because, in this case, the mover and the moved are the same individual, and proper self-motions involve a mover that is unmoved. If this case fits the theory in III.3, then the unmoved mover is changed, since Aristotle has argued that the mover suffers by producing a change. If, on the other hand, self-motion does not fit the theory in III.3, what accounts for the fact that the moved part of the self-mover experiences a continuous motion, rather than remaining at rest? Second, if the interpretation of *Physics* III.3 is correct, how can one actually explain the change that takes place in the patient, since the production described in III.3 is in fact one and the same as the change that takes place in the patient?

The answer to both questions lies in Aristotle's theory of self-motion. One reason why self-motion seems puzzling is that there are two sorts of self-motion: first, proper self-motion, which is not a change but an activity; and second, self-change, as when a doctor cures himself. The second case is, in fact, simply a special instance of ordinary action and passion—the only difference being that the agent and patient coincide in the same individual. This example fits the model in *Physics* III.3 because the self-changer as patient undergoes a real change toward a goal imposed by the self-changer as agent, and the agent is changed in producing the change. The self-changer as doctor is not an unmoved mover but a proper agent. This special case of self-motion, like ordinary action and passion, is explained with reference to a proper self-motion, which is an activity—the joint expression of an unmoved mover and a moved within the self-moving agent.

Whether the real change takes place in a distinct patient or, in the case of self-change, in the mover itself considered as other, the agent's production is in fact two motions: first, a change that takes place in the patient (which is a change of, though not in, the agent), and second, an activity that takes place in the agent. Thus, the doctor who cures himself both experiences a self-change by acting as doctor on himself as curable and engages, as doctor, in the activity of doctoring. These motions are distinct. The patient of the self-change is the doctor's ailing body and its immediate cause is the doctor as agent; the doctor's production is a change of (but not in) the doctor as agent because the process is incomplete until the goal of health in the patient is realized. On the other hand, the patient of the self-motion—the activity of doctoring—is the doctor as doctor and its cause is the art of medicine, a first mover; and this first mover, which is unmoved, cannot be changed by the motion it causes. The person as doctor engages in a motion—an activity—that is genuinely distinct from the change that takes place in the ailing body, and this distinct self-motion explains the change that takes place in the patient. The question, then, is whether Aristotle can account for self-motion, which is responsible for ordinary changes, without admitting that the first mover is changed.

Aristotle waits to treat self-motion until *Physics* VIII.5, but he has prepared for this question on several occasions in III.1–3. In III.1 he distinguishes things that exist in actuality alone from things that exist in potentiality and actuality ($200^{b}26$–28); unmoved movers exist in actuality alone and so are not subject to change. Later in the chapter he sets the stage for the argument in III.3 by pointing out that even movers, as movers, are potential in a first-level sense and are therefore changeable ($201^{a}19$–25). But he quickly corrects a possible misunderstanding, saying, "So it seems to some people that every mover is moved, but the truth about this will be clear from other considerations (for there is something that moves and is unmoved)" (201ᵃ25–27). In III.2 he carefully excludes unmoved movers from among the things that are changed by their contact with the moved by stipulating that the claim applies only to those things whose lack of motion is rest (202ᵃ3–5). His account concerns proper agents whose contact with the moved is relational; such agents possess an unmoved principle but are themselves moved movers (202ᵃ9–12). Finally, in III.3 Aristotle argues that the change of the moved and that of the mover cannot be distinct processes, one located in the moved, the other in the mover, because if this were so one of two impossible results would follow: either there would be a mover that is both changed and unchanged (a contradiction), or there would be no such thing as an unmoved mover (and hence no change could be finally explained) (202ᵃ28–31). The change of the mover and of the moved are one and the same but are located only in the moved.

Self-motion is not a change but the joint activity of a mover and a moved; therefore neither the mover nor the moved is changed by the motion. These motions will be discussed in chapter 7. The present puzzle does not concern the activity itself—Aristotle readily attributes activities to unmoved movers. The puzzle concerns, instead, why self-motion occurs at all—that is, why a self-mover engages in a connected activity, rather than remaining at rest or interrupting its motion with intervals of rest. The sheer fact of motion and its continuity might seem problematic because Aristotle appeals to the agent in his account of change in order to show that the change that takes place in the patient is a connected progression rather than a series of disconnected states of the patient. He introduces the agent to show why the patient abandons its position of rest and why its motion toward the goal is sustained; and he calls the sustaining of motion a change of the agent. If, in the case of self-motion, a similar appeal must be made to the unmoved mover to show why the agent acts rather than failing to act, then the first mover will be called to account for the initiation of motion. But if the first mover must originate motion in an entity at rest, then, in starting the motion, the first mover will be moved. There will then be no such thing as an unmoved mover.

An unmoved mover cannot explain why something starts moving because, if it could, it would have to supply an impetus. Given that Aristotle explains all motions by final appeal to an unmoved mover, his view should be the following: If an appropriate mover and moved are in contact in one of the ways that he has explained, motion will occur unless there is interference; since the mover and the moved within the self-mover are always in general (καθόλου) contact, the moved responds to the mover unless it is prevented. Therefore, the natural state of the self-mover is motion rather than rest. If a self-mover starts moving from a position of rest, the explanation must accordingly lie not in the first mover but in the surrounding circumstances.[68] If these circumstances cease to interfere with the motion, the self-mover will automatically move. To return to the doctor: the doctor does not constantly engage in the activity of doctoring because, without a suitable patient in need of a cure, his activity is impeded. Given a suitable patient and his desire to cure, however, and barring other interference, the doctor will act, and the patient will be changed. Both the activity that occurs in the agent and the change that occurs in the patient are explained by the unmoved mover proper to the agent. As Aristotle says at the end of *Physics* III.2, the agent will always bring to the moved a form that is the principle and cause of the change (202ª9–12).

Let me spell out the account a bit further. A self-mover acts in response to its unmoved component unless there is interference. In the case of activities directed toward external objects, such as teaching, curing, and building, interference is frequently due to the absence of an appropriate object. But if the agent comes into strict or relational contact with a suitable patient, the agent automatically acts, barring other interference and, in cases of relational contact, involving the agent's choice between contrary ends. The agent's action is an activity, which takes place in the agent, and that activity causes a change, which takes place in the patient. Aristotle argues in *Physics* III.3 that the change in the patient is also a change of (but not in) the agent and uses this argument to show that the change in the patient is a sustained progression toward a goal. It is the agent's activity, however—a motion distinct from the change in the patient—that explains the change. The agent, in responding to its active potentiality for a particular goal, imposes that goal on the object moved, and (barring interference) the action persists until the goal is realized in the patient. Since the realization of the goal deprives the agent of a suitable object, the agent's activity is once more impeded, and the activity stops. Such action, though requiring for occurrence an appropriate object, explains the change that takes place in the patient because its own cause—the agent's active potentiality—both determines the end to be achieved and limits the progression once the goal is reached. The first mover thus accounts for the fact that a change displays a sustained direction and concludes at a certain limit.

TRANSITION TO THE SECOND MODEL

In contexts of change an agent conveys to a patient a property that the patient lacks but potentially has. Initially agent and patient are unlike be-

---

[68] See *Phys.* VIII.2, 253ª11–21; VIII.6, 259ᵇ1–16, and the discussion in Furley 1978; cf. Nussbaum 1978, 117–20.

cause the goal of the agent's active potentiality is opposed to the present actual state of the patient. By means of the change the agent "assimilates" the patient to itself; the agent imposes on the patient the property that is the goal of its own active potentiality. So, once the change has been completed, agent and patient are like. Very often the resulting likeness does not concern the type of potentiality possessed by the agent and the patient but concerns only the property that relates the active and passive pair. Thus, if a doctor cures a patient, he conveys to the patient the property for which he has the active potentiality: health. But the patient does not thereby acquire an active potentiality for health but only shifts from a first-level passive potentiality for health to a second-level passive potentiality.[69] The healthy person can respond to his surroundings in particular ways in virtue of his health, but his potentiality is not of the type that enables him to produce health in something else.

Sometimes, however, an agent conveys to a patient an active potentiality. A teacher can, and sometimes does, pass on to a student more than the specific content of a discipline. If a teacher conveys the rules by which to organize the content and the rules by which to extend the field—if he passes on the sorts of guidelines that make possible the student's independent research and further development—then the teacher will have conveyed an active potentiality because the rules enable their possessor to direct and coordinate his own (and sometimes others') further advance in the subject.

Nature is like a good teacher. In natural generation the agent conveys an active principle to the offspring. Man generates man (to use Aristotle's favorite example): the male parent induces in appropriate matter, not merely the form whose presence determines a passive potentiality as second level, but an active δύναμις as well. And this active δύναμις enables the offspring to act and develop on its own without an external active source. This is the situation for which Aristotle's second potentiality-actuality model is primarily designed. I now turn to this second model.

[69] See *G.C.* 1.7, 324^{b}14–18; cf. *Cat.* 8, 9^{a}21–24.

CHAPTER SEVEN

THE CAUSE OF PERSISTENCE

One might think that a product, once generated, remains the product that it is until something deprives it of its identity. Just as the acquisition of a positive character requires a productive agent, so the removal of that positive character might seem to require a destructive agent. But Aristotle had a different vision. Although he recognized violent destruction as one means of perishing, he also believed in internal decay due to an entity's matter.[1]

In chapter 5 I argued that the four elements are most themselves when in a state of uncombined simplicity. Earth, air, fire, and water do not express their fullest being when worked up into complex physical objects; when combined they exist only potentially, contributing their properties to some higher goal. If such service were good for the elements, the persistence of generated objects would not be problematic. But, in fact, the elements' potential existence in combination is not fulfilling for them. They realize their own natures most perfectly when they carry out their own business of finding their proper places. Recall that Aristotle criticizes Empedocles in *De Anima* II.4 for suggesting that the roots of plants grow downward because earth naturally moves in that direction and that the plants themselves grow upward because fire naturally moves in that direction. Aristotle protests, Why are plants not torn apart, their upper parts in one direction, their roots in another, if this is the true account of organic growth? Empedocles' account is mistaken because the soul of the plant prevents the elements from doing what they would naturally do (415^b28–416^a9). Despite his disagreement with Empedocles on the question of natural growth, Aristotle would presumably agree that, if the soul were not present to prevent dispersion, the parts of composite bodies would scatter according to the natures of their elemental ingredients. In *De Caelo* II.6 he declares: "All incapacities in animals are contrary to nature, for example, old age and decay. For the whole structure of animals is probably constituted out of things that differ in their proper place; for none of the parts occupies its own place" (288^b15–18). And in *De Caelo* I.12 he says, "Natural things are destroyed by the same things out of which they are constituted" (283^b21–22). Thus the

---

[1] See *De Iuv.* 4–5 on the physiological differences between these two means of destruction.

deterioration and destruction of organisms is caused by their own constituents, which tend to move off to their proper places, if given a chance.

Given the behavior of the elemental constituents, a product once generated cannot quietly enjoy the unity that it has achieved, and no external
destroyer is needed to bring about its destruction. Instead, composites are
always on the verge of annihilation on account of their own lower material properties, and the project of remaining the same and avoiding decay
is one that demands considerable exertion. The lower matter of a generated object is that to which Aristotle attributes the potentiality both to be
and not to be. Although, once a product has been generated, the material
genus has been actually differentiated by the form of the construct, and
although the differentiation actualizes the matter's potentiality to be the
higher construct, the generic matter retains a potentiality not to be the
higher object but to be something simpler instead. I argued in chapter 5
that the potentiality to be in the lower state determines the nature of the
material genus, while the potentiality to be in the higher state is accidental
to what the genus is;[2] for this reason the matter tends to reject the higher
form. In order to survive, the higher object must reassert its hold on the
form, and this control demands sustained work.[3] Since exertion is essential to avoid degeneration, an active cause is required not only in contexts
of becoming but also in contexts of persistence. The active cause enables
an entity to retain a high degree of complexity and to offset the process
of internal decay.

If an active cause is vital for maintenance, there is a critical line to be
drawn between those entities whose source of maintenance is internal and
those whose source is external. And this is the chief line that Aristotle
draws between organisms and artifacts.[4] Artifacts are not self-preserving
systems but depend on external agents both for the full realization of their
being and for their maintenance. Artifacts lack autonomy, and for this
reason they are ontologically dependent on other more basic entities.
Chapter 1 alluded to a deeper meaning of simple separation, which per-
mits Aristotle to identify certain composite substances as ontologically
primary. This separation is autonomy, or separation from an external
mover. Autonomous entities rely on themselves both for the realization
of their capacities and for their persistence. Living things achieve autonomy because their active potentiality—their soul—is their immanent
form.

Aristotle's second potentiality-actuality model explains the persistence
of composites that have been generated. The second model resembles the

---

[2] See above, pp. 163–67.

[3] In developing my views on this topic, I profited from discussion with Julius Moravcsik.

[4] See *Phys.* II.1, 192^{b}8–23; *G.A.* II.4, 740^{a}15–17; *Met.* Θ.7, 1049^{a}8–18.

first in all of its basic components. Like the first scheme, the second employs an active potentiality and a passive potentiality; and like the first, the second concerns two main actualities—a motion and a product. But unlike the first, the second system involves an agent and patient that act and suffer in respect of the same properties, and unlike the first, the second concerns a motion that is not a change but an activity (ἐνέργεια). Activity is the motion by which a generated product remains the same. On the second model no new product is generated; instead, by means of activity, a product that has already been generated is conserved as the product that it is. This dynamic preservation is the joint manifestation of an active and a passive δύναμις. For organisms, whose generic matter has been differentiated into a functional matter and whose soul is a set of active functions, persistence consists in the joint realization of the form and the functional matter in the activity of living. Since the properties in virtue of which the organism acts and suffers are δυνάμεις for activities, I shall translate δύναμις in this connection as "capacity" or "function." The soul is an active capacity, and the functional matter has a corresponding passive capacity.

THE SECOND POTENTIALITY-ACTUALITY MODEL

In *Metaphysics* Θ.6 Aristotle turns from the model that concerns change to the second model, the one that he suggests in Θ.1 is more useful for the project at hand. The second model concerns the being and persistence of an entity that has been unified by means of a change. Instead of defining the new notions of potentiality and actuality by their role in the second scheme, however, Aristotle presents a list of examples and says that his meaning will be clear from the analogies.

> What we mean to say is clear in each case by induction, and it is not necessary to seek a definition of everything but enough to understand by analogy, that it is as (1) what is building is to what can build, and (2) what is awake to what is asleep, and (3) what is seeing to what has its eyes shut but has sight, and (4) what has been separated out of the matter to the matter, and (5) what has been worked up to the not thoroughly worked.[5] Let actuality be set down as one side of this division, and let the potential be the other. (1048ª35–ᵇ6)

The passage concludes by summarizing the relations between the actuality and potentiality illustrated by the examples. "We do not call everything 'in actuality' in the same way, but rather by analogy: as this is in this

---

[5] Instead of "not thoroughly worked," translators usually render ἀνέργαστον as "unworked." See below p. 216.

or to this, so this is in this or to this. For some are related as change to potentiality (ὡς κίνησις πρὸς δύναμιν), and some as substance to a certain matter (ὡς οὐσία πρός τινα ὕλην)" (1048ᵇ6–9).

Since a number of puzzles surround the analogies, it is difficult to know what exactly Aristotle is trying to show. His conclusion might suggest that some of the preceding examples exhibit the first scheme, the model for change, and some the second, the model for substance.[6] Yet Aristotle does not say that some of the examples are κατὰ κίνησιν ("concerning change"), the phrase used on other occasions to refer to the first model;[7] instead he says that some of the actualities are related to the potentialities as change πρός ("in relation to") potentiality. In the examples themselves the same preposition (πρός) is repeated throughout. So if some of the analogies reflect the first model, they should be those mentioning a change as the actuality. But among the first three examples, (1) what is building to what can build, (2) what is awake to what is asleep, and (3) what is seeing to what has its eyes shut but has sight, only the first seems to mention an actuality that is a proper change. The so-called changes listed in examples (2) and (3) are paradigmatic activities. Later in Θ.6, when Aristotle spells out his distinction between changes and activities, he lists seeing as an activity,[8] and in De Anima he similarly regards being awake.[9] So at least two of the three "changes" do not belong to the model that concerns change. And the status of building too is questionable. Although building is listed later in the chapter as a paradigmatic change,[10] on one occasion in De Anima II.5 building itself seems to count as an activity.[11] It seems possible, then, that all three examples that display the relation of change to potentiality illustrate the second system rather than the first.

It has been suggested that the last two examples belong to the first model because Aristotle mentions the products of change and matter.[12] But the actualities, though products of change, are the outcome of changes that have been completed, a fact plainly displayed by the perfect participles used to describe both products: Aristotle speaks of "what has been separated out of the matter" (τὸ ἀποκεκριμένον) and "what has been worked up" (τὸ ἀπειργασμένον).[13] These examples presumably illustrate

[6] See Kosman 1984, 135–36.

[7] See Met. Θ.1, 1046ᵃ1–2; Θ.6, 1048ᵃ25–26; cf. B.1, 996ᵃ11.

[8] Met. Θ.6, 1048ᵇ22–23; 1048ᵇ33–35; cf. E.N. x.4, 1174ᵃ14–16; and De An. II.1, 412ᵇ27–413ᵃ1.

[9] De An. II.1, 412ᵃ25–26 and 412ᵇ27–413ᵃ1.

[10] Met. Θ.6, 1048ᵇ29–33; cf. E.N. x.4, 1174ᵃ19–29.

[11] De An. II.5, 417ᵇ8–9. On this passage, see below, pp. 224–25.

[12] See Kosman 1984, 135–36.

[13] Just before the analogy passage Aristotle gives three other examples to illustrate the relation between actuality and potentiality. "We call something in potentiality, e.g., (1) the

the second relation stated in the conclusion, the relation of substance to matter. So the decision about the relevant model turns on the status of the matter to which the products stand as actuality to potentiality. Is the matter the preexisting stuff out of which the product has been generated, or is it the generic or functional matter that belongs to the generated product? Example (4) could specify either the preexisting or the generic matter; there was some preexisting matter out of which the product was separated, but there is also, now that the product has been separated, some generic matter, which modifies the product. Example (5), on the other hand, especially if translated as it usually is, as "the worked-up to the unworked,"[14] seems to refer to the preexisting material. If so, then at least this example belongs to the first scheme.

Even this assumption is disputable, however. *Metaphysics* Θ.7, whose treatment of artifacts I have already discussed, also asks when the matter for a living thing is potentially the organism, and Aristotle argues that only once an entity has its own principle of generation is it potentially human.[15] Evidently this item is not "unworked," since it already has the formal principle that guides its further development; but presumably it is not "thoroughly worked" either, since it needs to develop further. Given the account of organic generation in Θ.7, it seems possible that even example (5) belongs to the second scheme.

Although some of the examples resist an easy interpretation, it may be that all five examples exhibit the second scheme.[16] The assumption at least seems plausible, since Aristotle presents the analogies in order to clarify the new notions of actuality. It also seems possible that the reason why some of the examples are hard to classify is that, although all five examples belong to the second system, they are meant to be analogous to examples proper to the first. Recall that the first potentiality-actuality model concerns two sorts of actualities—a complete actuality, or product, and an incomplete actuality, or change that yields the product. The summary in Θ.6 of the relations between actuality and potentiality could, in fact, describe examples proper to Aristotle's first model. On the first scheme, some of the actualities stand to potentiality as change to poten-

---

Hermes in the wood and (2) the half-line in the whole, because it might be taken out, and [we call] (3) a knower even the one who is not theorizing, if he is able to theorize. But [we call] the thing [contrasted in each case] in actuality" (1048ᵃ32–35). Notice that these examples treat the actuality, not as completed, but as a future possibility. Thus, in examples (1) and (2), which concern changes, the change to the actuality must still occur. It seems significant, then, that the last two examples in the analogy passage, though specifying actualities that are products of change, treat the products as already completed.

[14] Cf. the translation of 1048ᵇ3–4 in Ross (in Barnes 1984, 1:1655), Tredennick (1933, 447), and Furth (1985, 67).

[15] *Met.* Θ.7, 1049ᵃ13–16.

[16] This idea was first suggested to me by James Lennox.

tiality (κίνησις πρὸς δύναμιν) and some as substance (the product) to a certain (preexisting) matter (οὐσία πρός τινα ὕλην). For example, becoming a house is the incomplete actuality of bricks viewed as potentially a house but actually deprived (the relation of change to potentiality), and the house is the complete actuality of the bricks, which are ready to be put into service (the relation of substance to a certain [preexisting] matter). Aristotle's conclusion could, then, apply to his first scheme. I suggest that he clarifies the second model by exploiting the analogy with the first; like the first model, the second too involves two sorts of actualities—one related to a potentiality as change to potentiality (e.g., what is seeing to what has its eyes shut but has sight), the other as substance to a certain (generic or functional) matter (e.g., what has been separated out of the matter to its [generic] matter).

Most interpreters agree that the use of κίνησις in Aristotle's conclusion cannot refer to change in the technical sense because the word evidently refers to a thing awake and a thing seeing, and being awake and seeing are paradigmatic activities.[17] I agree with this assessment; Aristotle uses κίνησις as a general expression that applies both to change in the technical sense (the motion proper to his first scheme) and to activity (the motion proper to his second scheme). If indeed Aristotle clarifies his second model by indicating the parallel with the first model, then he has chosen the word κίνησις for a particular reason. His point is that, like the first model, the second too concerns one actuality that is a κίνησις and another that is a product. And if Aristotle uses κίνησις in a nontechnical sense in order to exploit the analogy between the two models, then there is an obvious reason for him to spell out the distinction between changes (in the technical sense) and activities, as he does at the end of the chapter. For the κίνησις proper to the second model is not a change in the strict sense but an activity.

I propose that Aristotle clarifies his second model by giving a series of examples, all of which belong to the second scheme. He then points out that, like the first model, some of the actualities are related to potentiality as change to potentiality, and some as substance to a certain matter. Thus Aristotle suggests that the structure of the second model parallels that of the first. The first model involves an active potentiality, a passive potentiality, a motion, and a product. Since the second scheme too involves a motion and a product as actualities, it too presumably involves two sorts of potentiality—one active and one passive. This is not the only possible interpretation of the analogy passage, and fortunately my proposal con-

---

[17] See Ross (1924, 2:251) and cf. *Rhet.* III.11, 1412ᵃ10 for a parallel use. Cf. Scaltsas 1985, 237 n. 37.

cerning Aristotle's second potentiality-actuality model need not rely on this text. In *Metaphysics* Θ.8 Aristotle offers the key to his second system.

Active Capacity and Activity

Metaphysics Θ.8 describes a δύναμις that Aristotle contrasts with the active potentiality familiar from Θ.1. "I mean by δύναμις not only the one that has been defined, which is called an active principle of motion in another thing or qua other, but generally every active principle of change and rest. For nature (φύσις) is also in the same genus as δύναμις; for it is an active principle of change but not in another thing but in the thing itself qua itself" (1049^{b}5–10). An entity's nature (φύσις) is an active δύναμις, but one that differs crucially from the active δύναμις described in Θ.1: an entity's nature is a source of change in the thing itself qua itself. This is not the active potentiality involved when a doctor cures himself qua knowing what health is and is cured qua deprived of health; in this case the doctor cures himself qua other. The doctor's motion is a self-change, not a proper self-motion. The situation that Aristotle here envisages is one in which the same subject is agent and patient and acts and suffers in virtue of the same positive character. The structure of the second model matches that of the first; there is an active δύναμις, a passive δύναμις, a motion, and a product. But the single modification, that the agent acts on itself qua itself, yields a system entirely different from the earlier one.

To use Aristotle's terms, in contexts of change, the patient has a property that is unlike and opposed to that for which the agent has the active potentiality, and the patient is changed in respect of that property. By means of a change, the agent "assimilates" the patient to itself. So once the change has been completed, once the patient has the property imposed by the agent, the agent and patient are like. The patient actually has the character for which it has the passive, and the agent the active, potentiality. The property acquired is itself a δύναμις: a passive capacity for some activity. To exercise its newly acquired capacity, the patient still depends on an active cause. But the active cause needed in order to exercise the capacity is not unlike and opposed but like.

Consider an ax. Suppose that a smith makes an ax out of bronze and wood. The craftsman's active potentiality is his knowledge of axes, and that knowledge is simply the form of an ax that he has in mind. The bronze and wood have a first-level potentiality for being an ax; they are suitable materials to be made into an ax, but they lack the properties that make an object an ax. Still, the active potentiality of the craftsman and the passive potentiality of the materials are related to the same end: the form of an ax. Since the form of an ax is its function, I will call the form "the capacity to chop."[18] The craftsman and his materials are unlike and opposed because the smith has in mind the capacity to chop, but the materials lack this capacity. In the course of production the craftsman transforms the bronze and wood into an ax by carving the handle, casting the bronze, sharpening its edge, and fastening the parts together. The resulting object, if the production succeeds, now has the crucial capacity to chop. So, once the production is finished, the smith and the ax are like. The materials that constitute the ax now have a second-level potentiality for the same form for which the smith has the active potentiality. And the ax itself, whose identity is determined by its function, has the capacity to chop. But the form of the ax is merely a passive capacity. If the ax is to exercise its capacity, there must be an agent who has an active capacity for the activity of chopping; the ax depends upon an ax user, who has an active capacity for the same activity for which the ax has the passive capacity. The action and passion of user and implement involve the action of like on like. The user does not alter the nature of the ax when he employs it to chop. Instead, the user enables the ax to manifest its full being in the activity for which it was made: chopping. The activity is the joint expression of an agent and patient whose active and passive δυνάμεις are like.

The important difference between artifacts and organisms is that, in living things, user and implement are the same individual. As Aristotle says in *Metaphysics* Θ.8, a nature (φύσις) is an active principle of change, not in another thing, but in the thing itself qua itself. The individual acts on itself qua itself, as like on like; it acts and suffers in respect of the same properties. But unlike the ax, which has merely a passive capacity for the activity of chopping and depends upon an external user with an active capacity for that activity, an organism is both the user and the implement. The creature's nature is an active capacity for living, and the implement is its functional body.[19] Like the ax, the organism's body has a passive capacity for the same activity for which the user has the active capacity. But unlike the ax, the user is an internal principle proper to the organism itself—the organism's soul. Thus an organism acts on itself qua itself, as soul on functional body, and the resulting motion is the activity of living.

An organism's activity is much more than an expression of what it is; it is also the means by which the organism preserves itself from deterioration. Let me explain by fitting together the parts of Aristotle's second potentiality-actuality model, beginning with actuality. In *De Anima* II.1 Aristotle distinguishes two levels of actuality—one illustrated by knowl-

[18] Cf. Ackrill [1972–1973] 1979, 66–68.
[19] On the instrumentality of the organic body, see Kosman 1987, esp. 376–82.

edge, which is a positive state that enables an activity, the other illustrated by theorizing, which is an activity enabled by the state of knowledge (412ᵃ9–11). Knowledge is a first actuality, theorizing a second actuality. Aristotle uses this distinction to clarify the nature of soul, which he says is an actuality in the way that knowledge is (412ᵃ21–23). Like knowledge, soul is a first actuality, and it can be described both as a positive state and as an active capacity (or nature [φύσις]) for some activity. As active capacities, knowledge and soul can also be described as first movers. These active capacities regulate the type and amount of activity appropriate for the entity whose active capacities they are. Thus, in *De Anima* II.4 Aristotle argues that the soul is the efficient cause of nourishment and growth because the soul determines the proper limit of these activities (416ᵃ9–18). In the case of organisms the second actuality, comparable to theorizing, is the activity of living. This second actuality is the final cause that identifies the goal of the active capacity.

Aristotle's second potentiality-actuality model involves two sorts of passive potentialities—a passive capacity for activity, and a second-level potentiality for form. The first is proper to the functional matter, the second to the material genus. In *De Anima* II.1 Aristotle specifies the soul as "the first actuality of a natural instrumental body" (412ᵇ4–6). The natural instrumental body is the organism's functional matter, which has a set of passive capacities that correspond to the active capacities that constitute the creature's form. Thus, the identity of both the form and the functional matter is determined by the final cause, or second actuality, which is the common goal of the active and passive pair;[20] and the goal—the activity—is the joint realization of the form and the functional matter. The properties of the form and the functional matter are like, but those proper to the form are active, while those proper to the functional matter are passive.

Besides the functional matter, there is also the lower generic matter that has been differentiated into the functional matter, and this lower matter has a second-level potentiality for the form of the higher object. The potentiality is second level because it is realized; the generic matter is actually differentiated into the functional matter (or, in the case of nonliving things, into the object itself). It is crucial for Aristotle's account of perishability that perishability be due, not to the nature of the higher object, but to the material genus or—to put the same point in another way—to the object in respect of its lower material properties. The composite, viewed as what it is in itself, does not have the potentiality to be and not

[20] See *De An.* II.4, 415ᵃ14–20; Aristotle says that, in order to understand what a capacity is, one must first examine the corresponding activity, since the actuality is prior to the potentiality in definition (κατὰ λόγον); cf. *Met.* Θ.8, 1049ᵇ4–17.

to be what it is, for the simple reason that the potentiality not to be what it is could never be realized by it. The material genus, in virtue of its nature, has the potentiality both to be and not to be the higher object. Composites decline and perish, and their generic matter is responsible for this perishability. Matter tends to drag the higher object out of existence because the potentiality to be in the higher state is accidental to what the generic matter is. On the other hand, the potentiality not to be in the higher state but to be in a simpler state instead constitutes the very nature of the material genus.

Recall that Aristotle solves the problem of horizontal unity by arguing that the matter from which a composite is generated survives in the object potentially. The preexisting matter survives in the higher object potentially because matter of that sort can be recreated if the material properties are allowed to express themselves without restraint. Such expression must be prevented if the higher object is to survive as the unified thing that it is. But repressing the tendency for this unnatural, yet seductive, expression demands considerable exertion on the part of that higher object. Activity consistent with an object's proper nature is the means by which the object prevents deterioration. Thus activity is not only the expression of what an entity is, it is also the means by which an object restores its form—reconfirms the differentiation of the material genus—and thus preserves itself as the thing that it is. The motion proper to the second potentiality-actuality model (i.e., activity) is thus vital for self-preservation. And given the vital role of activity in self-preservation, an entity that possesses an active capacity for such activity can maintain its own unity.

In *De Anima* II.I Aristotle points out the important difference between artifacts, whose active capacity is external, and organisms, whose active capacity is internal. Consider again an ax. "Suppose that some instrument, such as an ax, were a natural body. The being for an ax would be its substance, and this would be its soul. And if this were removed, there would no longer be an ax, except homonymously. As it is there is an ax. For the soul is not the essence and formula of such a body, but of the sort of natural body that has in itself a principle of motion and rest" (412^b11–17). If an ax were a living body, the essence of an ax would be its soul, an active capacity; and if the active capacity (the soul) were removed, the ax itself would be destroyed. As it is, the "soul" of the ax belongs not to the ax but to the person who uses the ax, and this soul, the active capacity, can be removed and the ax remain intact. The ax remains unharmed as long as it preserves its passive capacity, the capacity to chop. So the ax can remain unused and later serve perfectly well as an ax. On the other hand, because the ax lacks an active cause, which would enable it to preserve itself as an ax, it naturally deteriorates unless an ax maker regularly restores it into a usable ax.

Organisms, whose form is an active capacity or nature, cannot survive the loss of that capacity. But because they possess an active nature, they rely on no external mover for the exercise of their capacities; more important, by means of that exercise, they can preserve themselves as the complex entities that they are. Aristotle treats this topic in *De Anima* II.5, the text in which he outlines the levels of passive potentiality. I now return to that text to focus on the knower who can theorize when he wishes, if not prevented, and so become the one "who is in actuality and in the strict sense knows this particular A" (417ᵃ28–29).

Activity and Preservation

De Anima II.5 spells out the difference between the motion proper to the first model and the motion proper to the second. The first is a change, the second an activity. Aristotle claims that the first transition, that experienced by the first knower, is "a certain destruction by the contrary" (417ᵇ2–3), because agent and patient are unlike. The second transition, that experienced by the second knower, is different. Of this transition Aristotle says, "But the other is rather a preservation (σωτηρία) of what is in potentiality by what is in actuality and like it, in the way that potentiality is [like] actuality" (417ᵇ3–5). Here agent and patient are like. The entity acts in virtue of its active capacity, or first actuality, and responds in virtue of its corresponding passive capacity, and the result is a preservation of the entity as a thing that actually has those capacities. Aristotle continues, "For the thing that has knowledge comes to be theorizing, which is either not a being altered (for the development is into itself and into actuality) or it is another kind of alteration (θεωροῦν γὰρ γίνεται τὸ ἔχον τὴν ἐπιστήμην, ὅπερ ἢ οὐκ ἔστιν ἀλλοιοῦσθαι [εἰς αὐτὸ γὰρ ἡ ἐπίδοσις καὶ εἰς ἐντελέχειαν] ἢ ἕτερον γένος ἀλλοιώσεως)" (417ᵇ5–7). Alteration in the strict sense takes place when a subject acquires a character that it previously lacked or loses a character that it previously had. So theorizing is not an alteration in that sense because the knower neither gains a property previously lacked nor loses a character previously possessed; instead, the knower, when he theorizes, develops into himself (i.e., into what he already is)—a knower. The second actuality, or activity, reconfirms the presence of the first actuality—the active capacity or form.

My reading of these lines differs from the usual reading. Scholars typically take Aristotle to describe the transition from inactivity to activity, from latency to manifestation.²¹ On this view the antecedent of ὅπερ

---

²¹ Among recent commentators, see esp. Kosman 1984; cf. Kosman 1969, 55.

("which") is not θεωροῦν ("theorizing"), as I have supposed, but θεωροῦν γίνεται ("comes to be theorizing"). So construed, the sentence denies that the shift from inactivity to activity is a change. Aristotle does reject the idea that a shift from rest to motion is a change and argues in *Physics* v.2 that, if such a shift were a change, an infinite number of changes would be needed simply to start moving.[22] He is taken here to deny, perhaps for similar reasons, that the shift from idleness to activity is a change.[23]

It seems doubtful, however, that this shift is the issue because Aristotle contrasts the motion proper to the second model with that proper to the first, and the two situations are comparable in respect of the shift; in neither case is the switch to the motion a change. The crucial difference lies in the sort of motion in which the two switches result: the first is a transition to a state *other* than the one that the subject is presently in; the second is a transition to the *same* state that the subject is already in. The decision about these lines has important implications for the interpretation of Aristotle's second potentiality-actuality model. Since my reading challenges a widely accepted view, I will defend it first on grammatical grounds, then respond to a possible objection, and finally indicate a theoretical problem for the standard reading.

Consider, then, the grammar. First, if Aristotle is following the ordinary rules of Greek syntax, the phrase θεωροῦν γίνεται ("comes to be theorizing"), which is customarily taken to describe the switch from inactivity to activity, is a periphrastic construction equivalent to the finite verb θεωρεῖ ("theorizes").[24] If the construction is periphrastic, then the topic is not the shift to the activity but the activity itself. Second, the relative pronoun ὅπερ evidently refers to some sort of motion, since whatever it refers to is said not to be an alteration or at least another kind of alteration. The antecedent of ὅπερ is probably the whole preceding clause, since Aristotle regularly regards both changes and activities as compound entities that include the subject as well as the states traversed.[25] But the question still remains whether, within the whole clause, the transition specified is the switch, which commentators take θεωροῦν γίνεται to describe, or the activity itself, which could be indicated by θεωροῦν alone or periphrastically by the longer phrase. If θεωροῦν γίνεται is periphrastic, then ὅπερ refers to the activity. But even if the phrase is not

[22] *Phys.* v.2, 225ᵇ33–226ᵃ6.

[23] Cf. *E.N.* x.4, 1174ᵇ9–14.

[24] See Smyth 1920, 437, §1964.

[25] Recall that the analysis of change requires three principles, of which one is the subject; notice, too, that earlier in *De An.* ii.5 Aristotle includes the subject in his concept of activity (417ᵃ28–29); cf. *Met.* Θ.6, 1048ᵃ37–ᵇ2. On changes as composite entities, cf. Gill 1984, 17–18.

periphrastic, the emphasis on θεωροῦν as the first word in the sentence recommends it as the antecedent rather than γίνεται, which follows.

Furthermore, the next sentence, whose opening conjunction διό indicates a consequence based on the preceding discussion, more naturally supports my reading than the alternative. "So it is incorrect to say that the one who thinks is altered when he thinks (ὅταν φρονῇ), just as it is incorrect to say that the builder is altered when he builds (ὅταν οἰκοδομῇ)" (417ᵇ8–9). Aristotle's use of the temporal adverb ὅταν with the present subjunctive suggests that the actions of the thinker and the builder are ongoing rather than completed.[26] Given the present subjunctives, one could translate the passage, "So it is incorrect to say that the one who thinks is altered *while* he thinks. . . ." Were Aristotle describing the inception of motion, that point would be crucial to his argument, and a precise formulation would be expected, for instance, "It is incorrect to say that the thinker is altered when he *begins* to think. . . ." Aristotle's point is not carelessly put. His focus is not the shift from inactivity to activity but the activity itself, and this, he claims, is not an alteration.

Still, one could object to my reading, if not on grammatical grounds, at least on the basis of the examples mentioned in the passage just quoted. Why does Aristotle compare the person who thinks with the person who builds and claim that neither is altered by his action?[27] Although thinking is an activity, building is elsewhere treated as a paradigmatic change.[28] In *Physics* III.2–3 Aristotle argues that the agent's producing is a change of the agent, though located in the patient. Building a house counts as a change of the builder because the goal of the action, the finished product, lies beyond the action, and the action is incomplete until the project is finished. Because completion of the project terminates the action, one cannot at the same time correctly say that the builder "is building" and "has built" the house. The builder's action thus satisfies the conditions spelled out in *Metaphysics* Θ.6 for being a change. Given the treatment of building elsewhere, it is curious that Aristotle compares the thinker to the builder and claims that, like the builder, the thinker is not altered when he acts, since the builder is altered when he builds, if building is a change. Thus, on the assumption that the act of building is a change, one could argue that the point of Aristotle's comparison is to call attention to precisely the point of similarity between the two examples, namely, that just as the builder is not altered when he starts to build, so neither is thinker altered when he starts to think. And this is the defense needed for the traditional view.

[26] See Smyth 1920, 543, §2400.
[27] Sarah Broadie raised this objection.
[28] See references cited above in n. 10.

Even so, the grammar of the passage more naturally suggests an ongoing motion than the inception of motion, and there is another way to understand the comparison between the thinker and the builder. When the thinker thinks, he acts on himself qua himself; he expresses his knowledge in episodes of theorizing that preserve him in the state that he is already in. The action of the builder, which is typically viewed as the action of the builder on his materials, and hence as a change, can also be viewed as an action of the builder on himself, apart from its external object. Thus, as I argued in chapter 6, to explain the motion that takes place in the building materials, one must first explain the builder's action as a self-motion that involves a first mover and an object moved. The first mover, or active capacity, is the builder's knowledge of building, and the object moved is the builder himself, who acts in response to his active capacity. When the builder acts on himself qua himself, his action expresses his positive character, his capacity to build; and whether or not his action yields an ultimate product, the action's completion does not depend, inasmuch as it expresses the builder's knowledge of building, on its external outcome. When the builder acts on himself qua himself, the exercise preserves his capacity to build and develops him into what he already is—a builder. If the action is considered with reference to the builder's character and not with reference to the external goal, the builder is not altered by what he undergoes but rather preserves, and even improves, the state that he is already in. He not only retains his skill but becomes a better builder by using it.

So the passage can be read in the way that I am proposing. Furthermore, there is reason to question the alternative view. Aristotle contrasts the motion proper to the second model with that of the first, saying that it is "rather a preservation of what is in potentiality by what is in actuality (ὑπὸ τοῦ ἐντελεχείᾳ ὄντος) and like (ὁμοίου) it, in the way that potentiality is [like] actuality" (417ᵇ3–5). If the mentioned preservation is a shift to activity, as commonly assumed, then the actuality, or first mover, causes the activity to start. The burden falls on those who defend this view to explain how a first mover can do this. If a first mover explains why activity starts, then it must provide an impetus. But first movers are unmoved and therefore cannot give that initial push. Thus, an unmoved mover cannot explain why activity starts.²⁹ If Aristotle's topic had been

²⁹ Michael Wedin (1988, 16–17, 162–77) argues that the relevant actuality in II.5 is the object of thought. But my objection that a first mover, to initiate motion, must provide an impetus holds equally if the first mover is the object of thought. It seems more likely, however, that the actuality in II.5 is the active cause (in the case of thinking, the active intellect) rather than the object of the faculty. In *De An.* III.5 Aristotle compares the active mind to light and suggests that it makes things in potentiality to be in actuality (430ᵃ15–17). This comparison suggests that the active mind accounts for the fact that potential objects are

the inception of motion, then (as we saw in chapter 6) the relevant cause would be, not the actuality or first mover, but the removal of interference. Since Aristotle mentions the actuality as the cause of the preservation, his topic is not the inception of motion but the activity itself.

The difference, then, between the two sorts of motion proper to the first and second potentiality-actuality models is that, whereas the motion proper to the first model results in a state other than the one that the patient was previously in and is caused by an agent that acts in respect of a property opposed to and unlike the initial state of the patient, the motion proper to the second model results in the same state that the patient was previously in and is caused by an agent that acts in respect of a property like the initial state of the patient. Thus, the motion proper to the second model yields the same product that was there at the outset; the motion preserves the patient in the state that it is already in.[30]

The theory presented in *De Anima* II.5 is applied in the previous chapter. In II.4 Aristotle uses the second potentiality-actuality model to explain the operation of the lowest soul faculty—nutritive soul. Nutritive soul is shared by all living organisms, plants and animals alike, and it is the most vital capacity for living things because it controls organic growth, self-preservation, and reproduction.[31] Reproduction occurs when an organism directs its nutritive powers to something else and im-

---

actual objects of thought; if so, the active mind should be causally prior to the object of thought, and hence a likelier candidate to be the actuality at issue in II.5. Aristotle discusses a much simpler application of the scheme—involving nutritive soul—in *De An.* II.4; see below.

[30] In the next part of *De An.* II.5, Aristotle treats the two transitions and then mentions two types (δύο τρόπους) of alteration, one to a privative state, the other to a positive state and nature (417b9–16). Defenders of the traditional view sometimes suggest that the distinction concerns two types of changes proper to the first scheme: (1) a transition to an inferior state, and (2) a transition to a positive state (see, e.g., Hicks 1907, 357). This interpretation was pointed out to me by Sarah Broadie. On this reading, ὥσπερ εἴρηται at 417b14 should presumably be excised, since Aristotle now introduces a new distinction within the first scheme. Someone adopting the standard view might alternatively argue that all transitions proper to the first scheme (whether the goal is positive or not) are transitions to a privative state (since the goal is opposed to the present state of the subject) and that the switch to activity is a transition to the positive state and nature. This appears to be Hamlyn's view (1968, 102). Although, of the two interpretations, the second may be preferable because it follows more naturally from what precedes, the terms ἕξεις ("states") and φύσις ("nature") usually apply to positive states rather than to activities. The advantages of both interpretations can be preserved, without the disadvantages, by understanding the later distinction as I interpret the earlier one: (1) all transitions proper to the first scheme are toward a privative state (whether the goal is positive or not) because the goal is opposed to the present state of the object changed, and (2) all transitions proper to the second scheme are toward a positive state and nature because activities lead to the positive state that the subject is already in.

[31] *De An.* II.4, 416b11–17.

226

poses on a suitable material its own form. Reproduction is proper generation involving a distinct agent and patient whose active and passive potentialities relate to the same end and whose actual states are initially unlike. Nutritive soul can, however, be self-directed as well as other-directed, and when it is, the organism imposes on itself the nature that it already has. Such self-directed action results in self-preservation. Aristotle says, "[When] its substance (οὐσία) already exists, nothing generates itself, but preserves (σώζει) [itself]" (416ᵇ16–17).

Self-maintenance is the preservation that results from an organism's self-directed behavior. Aristotle mentions three items engaged in this activity: that which feeds (τὸ τρέφον), that which is fed (τὸ τρεφόμενον), and that by which the thing is fed (ᾧ τρέφεται). That which feeds is nutritive soul, that which is fed is "the body having this," and that by which the thing is fed is food (416ᵇ20–23). There is thus a first mover (the nutritive soul), a last mover (the food), and an object moved (the functional body). The nutritive soul, as first mover, oversees the proceedings by determining the sort and amount of food appropriate for the organism whose body is fed. The food is an instrumental last mover, which comes into direct physical contact with the body and is itself affected by the body acted upon. In fact, the food is transformed by the body into blood, which will then replenish the various bodily parts and produce the useful residues employed in reproduction. The nutritive body, the entity fed, has various instrumental parts, such as the mouth, the esophagus, the stomach, and so on, whose natures are determined by their role in nutrition.[32] The nutritive body provides the foundation for all the higher functions, such as perception and reason, and is regularly in need of fortification. Failure to provide it inevitably results in the loss not only of the nutritive body but of all the higher functions as well, since all depend on a viable body.

Bodily restoration is a precondition for the maintenance of the higher life functions. Although perception and reason are the special province of higher parts of the soul, nutritive soul regulates the organism as a whole and preserves its life; should this capacity fail, the creature dies. The organism begins to exist when it acquires nutritive soul and dies with its loss. Let us now consider when these significant moments occur.

THE LIFE CYCLE

The Matter for Organic Generation

Metaphysics Θ.7 asks at what point the matter is potentially some definite product. Aristotle's answer for artifacts was discussed in chapter 5,

---

[32] For Aristotle's account of some of the nutritive parts, see *P.A.* II.3, 650ᵃ3–32.

but he also asks when the matter for a living thing is, in the strict sense, potentially that creature, and his answer differs in a number of respects from the one that he gives for artifacts. He opens the chapter as follows: "We must consider when each thing is in potentiality and when not, for it is not at just any time. For example, is earth potentially a human being? Or not, but rather when it has already become seed, and perhaps not even then?" (1048ᵇ37–1049ᵃ3). Earth is the ultimate matter from which a human being is generated. Chapter 4 outlined the way in which earth enters the life cycle through the nutritive process.³³ Since earth is food for plants, and plants are food for animals; and since food becomes blood, and blood the residues; earth, which is the final outcome of organic destruction, is also the starting point of organic generation. The beginning of Θ.7 relies on the construction model of H.5 and the question asked is whether the ultimate matter from which organic generation begins is potentially the organism. The answer is no; the earth must first be worked up into seed. Aristotle then asks, Is the seed potentially human, or must the seed itself undergo a further change?

After raising his opening question about matter and organisms, Aristotle turns to those entities whose principle of generation is external (ἔξωθεν ἡ ἀρχὴ τῆς γενέσεως [1049ᵃ12]). This group includes the artifacts that we have discussed. He then returns to the things whose principle is internal and denies that the seed is potentially human. "And as for the things whose [principle of generation] is in the thing itself that has [the principle], when nothing external interferes, the thing will be [the product] through itself. For example, the seed is not yet [potentially a human being], for it must be in something else³⁴ and change. But when already through its own principle (διὰ τῆς αὐτοῦ ἀρχῆς) [something] is such [e.g., a human being], this is already in potentiality" (1049ᵃ13–16). What entity succeeds as potentially human? The first question is why the seed fails, and the answer to this question depends on what Aristotle means by σπέρμα ("seed") in Θ.7.

In *Generation of Animals* Aristotle often uses σπέρμα for the male contribution in sexual generation.³⁵ Semen is an instrumental agent, like a carpenter's tools,³⁶ or like the wine that the doctor prescribes in effecting a cure. Semen is a "last" mover, which comes into direct physical contact with the material and reacts in response to the material acted upon; the body of the semen dissolves and evaporates once its job is done.³⁷ But semen is an efficient, not a material, cause of the new creature. Semen

---

³³ See above, pp. 128–29.
³⁴ I omit πεσεῖν ("[must] have fallen"), which Ross (1924, 2:256) inserts at 1049ᵃ15.
³⁵ Cf. *Met.* H.4, 1044ᵃ35.
³⁶ *G.A.* I.22, 730ᵇ4–23; cf. I.21, 729ᵇ1–21.
³⁷ *G.A.* II.3, 737ᵃ11–12.

transfers the father's form in generation,[38] but it provides no matter—that provision being left to the mother. Since Aristotle's question in Θ.7 concerns the matter for a product, some commentators are troubled that he uses σπέρμα here.[39] But there is a straightforward explanation.

Although Aristotle frequently uses σπέρμα for the male contribution in generation, he does not reserve the word for that use only; in fact, in *Generation of Animals* he has a technical term γονή ("that which engenders") that he prefers in specifying the male factor. Recall that *Physics* I.7 uses σπέρμα for the preexisting entity from which a plant or animal proceeds. *Generation of Animals* often uses the word for the combination of male and female factors in situations in which the two are not separate, as in the asexual generation of plants.[40] He typically uses κύημα ("embryo") for the combination in situations in which the factors are initially separate, as in the sexual generation of most animals. It is not entirely clear whether σπέρμα can be applied to the embryo. It is clear, however, that the female contribution to generation, the καταμήνια, can be called σπέρμα because in *Generation of Animals* I.20 Aristotle says, "The καταμήνια is σπέρμα that is not pure but in need of being worked up (ἐργασίας)" (728ª26–27). The female material is impure σπέρμα because, in formal terms, it lacks the principle of soul (II.3, 737ª27–30), and in material terms, it is less concocted and therefore cooler than semen (I.19, 726ᵇ30–32). Although impure, the καταμήνια can be called σπέρμα, and the term is appropriate because καταμήνια shares with semen the same material constitution and serves the complementary role in reproduction.[41]

Since the καταμήνια can be called σπέρμα, despite its impurity, there should be no serious objection to referring to the κύημα as σπέρμα as well, since the κύημα is what the καταμήνια becomes when it has been heated by the action of the male. But, whatever one decides about the κύημα, the important point is that the word can apply to the preexisting entity, since it does apply to the female contribution alone. And the word is likely to refer to the preexisting material in *Metaphysics* Θ.7 because Θ.8 uses the word in this way, applying it both to the matter for plants (1049ᵇ19–23) and to an earlier stage in the generation of a human being (1050ª4–7). Although the text does not indicate whether the σπέρμα is the female blood or the embryo, the context does make clear that the earlier stage is not the semen.[42]

---

[38] On this topic, see Code 1987.

[39] See Ross 1924, 2:255–56.

[40] *G.A.* I.18, 724ᵇ4–21; and I.20, 728ᵇ32–729ª1.

[41] Both semen and καταμήνια are products of blood, which is itself a compound of earth, water, and air; see *Meteor.* IV.10, 389ª19–20; cf. *G.A.* II.2.

[42] Two examples are given to show that actuality is prior to potentiality in substance—a

In Θ.7 Aristotle denies that the seed is potentially human on the grounds that it must be "in something else and change." In the generation of a new human being, the καταμήνια and, at a later stage, the κύημα exist inside the mother's body; in this sense the seed is "in something else."[43] The seed must also change before it is potentially human. Although in one sense the καταμήνια is already potentially human, since it has a first-level potentiality to be actually human, this is evidently not the sense at issue here. The relevant passive potentiality is one that belongs to the second potentiality-actuality model.

I have pointed out that the second model involves two types of passive potentialities—first, a second-level potentiality for form, which applies to the generic matter that has been differentiated, and second, a passive capacity for activity, which applies to the functional matter that results from the differentiation. The entity that succeeds as potential in the appropriate way is something that has already been differentiated to the extent that it can be a human being "through itself" (δι' αὐτοῦ) and "through its own principle" (διὰ τῆς αὐτοῦ ἀρχῆς). Thus, in some sense the entity already is a human being, since it possesses the active human principle that enables it to act on itself qua itself. But the entity has evidently not yet been perfected, since it must still generate itself. What entity satisfies the description in Θ.7? Aristotle gives his answer in *Generation of Animals*, where he distinguishes generation proper, caused by an external agent, from self-generation, caused by an entity's own active principle.

Generation, Development, and Decline

Generation of Animals II gives a careful account of the reproduction of living creatures, and Aristotle argues that an organism takes charge of its own generation at the moment it acquires a heart or an analogous central organ. Before the heart has taken shape, the generation is caused by the male parent.

At conception the semen "sets" (συνίστησι) the female material by imparting to it its own motions (II.3, 737ᵃ18–22). Aristotle describes the initial process as a whole series of motions initiated by the male. "It is possible for this to move this, and this this, and for [the process] to be like the automata of the 'marvels.' For the parts, while at rest, somehow contain a potentiality; and when something outside moves the first of them, immediately the next comes to be in actuality" (II.1, 734ᵇ9–13).

---

mature man to a boy and a human being to σπέρμα. Just as a boy is a stage in the development of a grown man, so σπέρμα is a stage in the generation of a human being.

[43] I owe this suggestion to Anna Greco.

Apparently the early motions that take place in the embryo derive from the initial impulse caused by the male parent. Like automatic puppets, which display a complex series of motions issuing from a single external prod, so early embryonic development consists in a chain of events set off by the original act of the male parent.[44] The domino effect is externally caused in a way that parallels other typical changes.

Aristotle characterizes the process with another analogy, the action of rennet on milk.

When the secretion of the female in the uterus is set by the semen ($\gamma o\nu\acute{\eta}$) of the male, the semen acts like rennet on milk; for in fact rennet is milk that has vital heat, which unifies the similar stuff and sets it. And the semen is related in the same way to the nature of the $\kappa\alpha\tau\alpha\mu\acute{\eta}\nu\iota\alpha$, for milk and $\kappa\alpha\tau\alpha\mu\acute{\eta}\nu\iota\alpha$ have the same nature. So, when the bodily stuff comes together, the moist separates out, and when the earthy parts dry, membranes form around it [the bodily stuff] in a circle. This happens both from necessity and for a purpose. (II.4, 739^{b}20–28)

The first stages of generation occur as mechanically as the action of rennet curdling milk. But the process happens not only from necessity, in virtue of the nature of the materials, but also for a good and positive end, for the motions result in the first organ, the heart.[45] The vital heat induced by the semen into the $\kappa\alpha\tau\alpha\mu\acute{\eta}\nu\iota\alpha$ guides the mechanical operations so that the embryo is heated to the right extent, at the right times, and in the right places. Given such direction, the mechanical processes yield the central organ. Generation proper thus conforms to the pattern of other changes brought about by an external agent and ultimately explained by a first mover proper to the agent.

Once the heart has been formed, the embryo takes control of its own further development. Although, obviously, at this early stage the unborn creature still depends on its mother for nourishment, it no longer depends on its father or mother to direct its continued development and growth. Aristotle claims that, with the formation of the heart, the organism becomes separate from both parents.

So too, since in a certain way all the parts are present in the embryo potentially, the principle is furthest on the road to [actual] presence. Therefore the heart is separated in actuality first. And this is clear not only to perception (for it happens in this way) but also to reason. For when the generated thing has been separated from both [parents], it

[44] On Aristotle's analogy, see Nussbaum 1976, 146–52. Cf. *M.A.* 7, 701^{b}2–10.

[45] On Aristotle's appeal to both material necessity and purpose in his explanation of natural outcomes, see Cooper 1985.

must manage itself, just as the child must set up house when he is sent away from his father. So it [the embryo] must have a principle from which also later the ordering of the body takes place for animals. (II.4, 740ᵃ1–9)

As soon as the heart or analogous organ has taken shape, the organism can make itself grow (II.1, 735ᵃ13–26); and as soon as it can make itself grow, it is independent of its external source because its own principle directs its further development. Aristotle recognizes the heart as responsible for growth, and as the source of the uniform and nonuniform parts (II.4, 740ᵃ17–19). Since perception and locomotion depend upon the uniform and nonuniform parts, the heart is the bodily foundation for all human functions with the exception of intellect (νοῦς), which is realized in no material part.[46] But even νοῦς depends, in order to function, on an adequate state of the body, and this state is regulated by nutritive soul, whose central location is in the heart.

The entity that *Metaphysics* Θ.7 identifies as potentially human is the embryo once it has acquired a human heart. This entity differs critically from the σπέρμα,[47] since the potential human already is human in virtue of its active principle. I will call the potential human a "fetus." The fetus is complete in one respect but incomplete in another. It is complete in respect of its heart, its first functional part, which enables it to act on itself qua itself, and so to live a rudimentary sort of life. But the fetus is incomplete because it still lacks the range of bodily parts needed to realize the functions distinctive of human beings. Thus the lower-level matter, though it has been differentiated into a heart, must still be worked up into the other functional parts. Therefore the fetus not only acts on itself qua itself, it also acts on itself qua other and develops its generic matter into the complex body of the perfected creature. In *Physics* II.8 Aristotle describes natural generation as follows: "If the shipbuilding art were present in the wood, [the art] would produce the result in the way that it happens by nature. So if the final cause is present in art, it is also present in nature. The situation is especially clear when someone cures himself. For nature is like this" (199ᵇ28–32). The nature, or active capacity, of the fetus resembles the shipbuilding art. Just as the goal of the shipbuilding art is a complete ship, so the goal of the fetal nature is a complete human being. And although the fetus is complete in respect of its heart, it is not complete in respect of the other functional parts. So the fetus resembles the

---

[46] See references cited above, chapter 4, n. 8.

[47] Given the account of generation proper, the term σπέρμα should presumably be applicable not only to the καταμήνια but also to the κύημα before the active principle has been internalized.

doctor who cures himself because, like the doctor, the fetus, too, acts on itself qua other and thus differentiates its generic matter into an adequate functional body.

Organic development is both an activity and a self-change. In one way an organism's entire life, beginning at the moment at which the creature acquires a heart and ending at the moment at which the heart fails, is a single continuous activity due to the entity's action on itself qua itself.[48] As soon as the heart exists and the active principle has become internalized, the creature already is the creature that it will later more perfectly be. And the organism persists as that organism as long as its heart continues to operate.[49] Even if the other parts give out, the animal survives if its heart can still perform.[50] In *On Youth and Old Age* Aristotle puts the point in this way: "So when the other parts become cold, life remains, but when [warmth is destroyed] here [in the heart] the whole [body] is destroyed, because the principle of heat for all [the parts] depends on this, and the soul is as it were set on fire in this part, which is the heart in blooded creatures and the analogous part in bloodless creatures. So life must be present simultaneously with the preservation of this heat, and so-called death is the destruction of this" (4, 469^{b}13–20). But in another way the organism's life consists of a series of changes. When it develops, the creature acts on itself qua other and progressively differentiates the lower matter into the complex functional body; during decline the creature attempts to act on itself qua itself, and thus to preserve itself in its present state, but finds itself acting on matter that is increasingly other. As long as life continues at all, there is an activity; but stages of life are plainly changes.

During development an organism's nutritive soul is entirely self-directed. Aristotle points out that a boy cannot concoct seed (σπέρμα) for reproduction because he uses up all the nourishment for growth.[51] Fat animals fail to reproduce because they use up all their nourishment increasing themselves.[52] Females never successfully transcend the self-centered stage because, unlike the male, the female cannot adequately divert her nutritive soul from herself to another and so cannot reproduce offspring that share her species. Females of some species can produce wind eggs, but wind eggs lack the soul principle contributed by the male and

[48] Cf. *Met.* Θ.6, 1048^{b}25–27; both living well and simply living are listed as activities.
[49] Cf. Aristotle's claim at *Met.* Z.10, 1035^{b}25–27, that the central organ, whether heart or brain, is simultaneous with the creature.
[50] See *G.A.* II.5, 741^{b}15–24.
[51] *G.A.* I.18, 725^{b}19–25.
[52] *G.A.* I.18, 725^{b}29–726^{a}6; cf. *P.A.* II.5, 651^{b}8–18.

so never acquire the mother's form.[53] Although Aristotle sometimes calls females deformed males,[54] he does not mean that females lack any of the vital functions proper to members of their species; it is only in respect of their nutritive bodies that females fail to attain the degree of perfection that enables them to display the munificence characteristic of the mature male.[55] Only the mature male achieves the degree of perfection that enables him to redirect his active powers from himself to another and successfully to replicate his kind.

Yet even those organisms that achieve nutritive perfection grow weary, and weariness is a regular reminder to them of their humbler origins and humbler end. Organisms suffer from weariness on account of their generic matter.[56] Once a creature has died, its material properties will characterize a simpler body, but while the creature lives, the material properties must be coordinated to serve the higher purpose. And this task is tiring. So organisms become weak from their exertions and must frequently sleep. The main function of nutritive soul is to regulate the full range of higher activities so as to maintain the delicate balance of life. If there is too much proper activity or too little, a balance is upset that is only with difficulty restored. And, of course, the time comes when the exertion is simply too much effort. Behavior becomes erratic, the body becomes more and more difficult to control, and finally the heart itself ceases to operate. The functional matter gives way, reverting back to a simpler stuff. At the moment at which nutritive soul fails, something quite different remains: a corpse, a merely homonymous organism.

Wearying, decline, and natural destruction are the unfortunate lot of generated composites, even the most perfect. This tendency to lapse into a simpler state is the profound problem that the elements, which are worked up into unities, pose for the survival of those unities. Given the disruptive effect that the elements have on the life of higher bodies, it is striking that they themselves suffer no such internal disruption. The four elements do not tire of their activity, they do not decline, and they do not degenerate into simpler stuff. Their unity seems to be entirely unproblematic. Since they are not composites, they seem to be straightforward vertical unities. Why does Aristotle deny that the elements are substances? Why do they have less claim to be genuine substances than complex organisms, which tire and decline so easily?

[53] See *G.A.* II.3, 737^{a}27–34; cf. I.21, 730^{a}4–32; and II.5, 741^{a}13–32.

[54] *G.A.* II.3, 737^{a}27–30; cf. IV.3, 767^{b}5–9.

[55] Note that in *Met.* I.9 Aristotle states that sexual differences are proper features of animal, not in respect of the substance (form), but in respect of the matter and body (1058^{b}21–23). Apparently such differences are accidental to an animal's essence.

[56] See *Met.* Θ.8, 1050^{b}24–28.

THE STATUS OF THE ELEMENTS

Metaphysics Θ.8 contrasts perishable sublunary bodies with the celestial bodies in the superlunary sphere. The matter for perishable bodies is a potentiality for contradictory states, a potentiality for both being and not being (1050ᵇ8–16). We have seen that, because generated bodies are worked up out of simpler matter, because many properties of the simpler matter survive as a material genus, and because the material genus retains the potentiality not to be in the higher state but to be in the simpler state instead, complex bodies tend to decay into the elements and so to perish. The form that differentiates the generic matter can, and ultimately will, fail to be actualized; and so the higher complex will be reduced to something lower. The matter of the heavenly bodies is not a cause of perishability because celestial matter is not a potentiality for being and not being. The matter of heavenly bodies is merely responsible for motion from one place to another (πόθεν ποῖ) (1050ᵇ16–22). Because of their distinctive matter, which is not a source of perishability, the sun, moon, and stars are always active (ἀεὶ ἐνεργεῖ); there is no danger that they might stop moving—tire of their endless circular transit—because the cause of wearying is the potentiality for contradictory states, a potentiality from which the heavenly bodies are wholly free (1050ᵇ22–28). Since the heavenly bodies are not generated, their matter does not offer the sort of resistance that causes wearying, decline, and final destruction. And so the heavenly bodies are always active.

Constant activity and freedom from wearying are not, however, confined to the celestial bodies. The four sublunary elements share with the heavenly bodies the special immunity. Earth, water, air, and fire resemble the sun, moon, and stars in being always active. "And the things in transformation, for example, earth and fire, imitate the imperishable things. For these too are always active (ἀεὶ ἐνεργεῖ); for they too have change in themselves in virtue of themselves (καθ᾽ αὑτά)" (1050ᵇ28–30). The elements never tire of their proper activity, their natural motion—earth toward the center, fire toward the periphery, and water and air to the intermediate regions.[57] And the elements engage in their natural motion in virtue of themselves (καθ᾽ αὑτά), independently of an external mover.

Aristotle has reason to be impressed by the analogy between the elements and the celestial bodies. Unlike all other generated bodies, the elements are not generated out of simpler matter but come to be from one another. And since their generation is structurally linear rather than con-

---

[57] For a similar interpretation of this passage, see Kahn 1985, 189. The London Seminar (Burnyeat et al. 1984, 145) suggests that the constant activity concerns elemental transformation. Ross (1924, 2:265–66) mentions both alternatives but does not decide between them.

structive, the elements have no tendency to decay into simpler stuff. The elements are the simplest bodies, and because they perish into entities no simpler than themselves, their mutual transformations should require an external agent to enforce the change and not result from internal weakening.[58] Since the elements do not decay, they are exempt from wearying too, since no elemental feature offers the sort of resistance that could make their natural activity tiring. And so the elements are always active, like the heavenly bodies.

Perhaps their freedom from weariness and decay explains why in *Physics* VIII.4 Aristotle describes the elements as continuous, naturally unified, and one (255ª12–13). In the same discussion, he also portrays their natural motions, not as changes, but as activities, like a knower's theorizing. But if the elements are natural unities, and if their motions are activities for which they are themselves responsible, why should they not have the best claim of all sublunary bodies to be genuine substances? Aristotle's discussions of natural motion in *Physics* VIII.4 and *De Caelo* IV.3 help to explain why the elements are not genuine substances.

Natural Motion

Physics VIII.4 recalls the doctrine of potentiality presented in *De Anima* II.5.

> The reason why it is unclear by what such things [the elements] are moved, for instance, fire upward and earth downward, is that "in potentiality" is said in many ways. The person who learns is a potential knower in a different way from the person who already has knowledge and is not exercising it. But always, when the thing that can produce (τὸ ποιητικόν) and the thing that can be affected (τὸ παθητικόν) are together (ἅμα), the thing that is potential comes to be in actuality; for instance, the one learning, from being in potentiality, comes to be another thing [i.e., an actual knower] in potentiality (for the person who has knowledge but is not theorizing is in some sense a knower, but not as he was before he learned). But when he is in this condition [i.e., has knowledge], if nothing prevents him, he acts and theorizes, or else [if he does not act when unimpeded] he will be

---

[58] Note, however, that at *Meteor.* IV.1, 379ª12–16, Aristotle says that all the elements decay except fire, since earth, water, and air are matter relative to fire. In the subsection "Natural Motion and Elemental Form" below, I discuss a sense in which each element is matter in relation to its higher neighbor, but the claim that the elements decay is obscure because there is no simpler stuff into which an element can decay.

in the opposite state and in ignorance [i.e., his potentiality will be merely first level].[59] (255ª30–ᵇ5)

Aristotle then applies the doctrine of levels of potentiality to the elements and suggests that elemental transformation corresponds to the shift from a first-level potentiality to a second, and that elemental natural motion corresponds to the activity made possible by the property that renders a potentiality second level.

> The situation is similar also in the case of the natural bodies. The cold thing is potentially hot, but when it has changed, [there is] already fire, and it burns, if nothing prevents or hinders it. And the situation is similar also concerning the heavy and the light. For the light comes to be from the heavy, for instance, air from water (for this [water] is the first thing in potentiality), and [air] is already light, and will straightaway (εὐθύς) act, if nothing prevents it. The actuality of the light is to be somewhere, namely up, and it is prevented when it is in the contrary place. (255ᵇ5–12)

Aristotle's thesis seems to be the following. Water, which is actually heavy (i.e., tends naturally downward), has a first-level potentiality to be light because, in virtue of its wetness, it can be transformed into the light element air. Once the water has been transformed into air, the emergent air has a second-level potentiality to be light. Air already is light, regardless of its location in the cosmos. And the lightness of the air is a capacity for upward motion. If the newly generated air happens presently to be in the place of water (the region above earth), the air moves upward directly, if nothing prevents it; and this upward motion is an activity expressing the nature of air. The upward motion of air resembles the knower's theorizing. All the air needs in order actually to move is the removal of external interference; if the impediment is removed, the air "straightaway acts," that is, the air moves unless something interferes with its motion. No external agent is needed to initiate the motion; air moves upward in virtue of itself (καθ᾽ αὑτό).

If this is the theory, the elements' independence from an external mover seems to give them even the special autonomy that had seemed to be the prerogative of living things alone. But Aristotle does not grant them that autonomy, for he denies that the elements have an active principle of motion and attributes to them only a passive source (255ᵇ30–31). He suggests that the elements are moved accidentally by whatever removes an impediment to motion (e.g., the person who removes the supporting pillar accidentally allows the object supported to fall) (255ᵇ24–29; 256ª2); he also

---

[59] This interpretation of the final lines (255ᵇ3–5) was suggested to me by Christopher Hitchcock.

suggests that the entity that generated the element might cause the natural motion (256ª1). Thus, if some water transforms some air into water, the water that turned the air into water counts as the cause of the downward motion of the newly generated water. Both sorts of movers are, however, merely accidental causes of the elements' motion, and we are left asking what counts as the proper active cause.

Aristotle's conclusion seems strangely unsatisfactory. What justification does he have for denying to the elements, which are responsible for their own motions, an internal active cause? Is it simply that he must deny them an active principle in order to exclude them as substances? Aristotle's problem is that, if the elements have such a principle, they deserve to be substances; and if they deserve to be substances at all, they threaten to be the substances par excellence in the sublunary sphere, since their simple unity is unproblematic. But it is not enough that he must exclude the elements in order to save the highest honor for organisms; he needs a warrant for refusing the elements an active principle.

He does have such a warrant. First, the elements have no need for an active principle or indeed for any intrinsic form at all. If an entity displays any degree of complexity, it tends to behave in conflicting ways. For example, the simple metals, which are compounds of earth and water, would behave like their constituents, whose behaviors differ, if their own coordinating form did not differentiate them from, and regulate their behavior in respect of, those constituents. Since the elements are not complex, they experience no conflict between divergent behaviors, and so their behavior calls for no regulation. Thus the elements need no intrinsic form. Furthermore, if the elements were informed, their behavior would have some intrinsic limit.[60] In *De Anima* II.4 Aristotle contrasts the behavior of fire, which would burn indefinitely as long as there is anything to burn, with that of all things naturally constructed (τῶν φύσει συνισταμένων πάντων), whose size and growth have a certain limit and proportion because of their form (416ª15–18). The natural motion of composites is *internally* limited. The simple elements, on the other hand, which are constantly active, would move upward or downward indefinitely, except for the fact that their motion is *externally* limited. In *De Caelo* IV.3 Aris-

[60] Note that in *Phys.* II.1 Aristotle identifies the nature (φύσις) of a thing as its internal principle of motion and rest (192ᵇ13–15; 192ᵇ20–23) and that he attributes such a principle to the elements and the parts of animals as well as to whole plants and animals (192ᵇ8–13). In *Phys.* VIII.4 he recognizes that, if the elements could stop their natural motion, they should count as self-movers (255ª5–11). If the elements were self-movers, they would be proper substances; so their inability to limit their motions is a crucial reason why they are not substances. *De Cae.* I.2 defines a φύσις as a principle of motion (rest is not mentioned) (268ᵇ16). This restriction on φύσις, as applied to the elements, is an important modification of the doctrine of *Phys.* II.1.

totle returns to this topic and makes a remarkable suggestion about elemental form and about the status of the elements themselves.

Natural Motion and Elemental Form

De Caelo IV.3 ends by rehearsing the conclusions of Physics VIII.4, but De Caelo probes more deeply into the question of elemental natural motion and, in its final summary, lists the causes of Physics VIII—the generator and the remover of impediments—as movers in addition to some other cause (311ᵃ9–12). Early in the chapter Aristotle suggests that the motion of a simple body to its proper place is a motion to its own form (εἶδος) (310ᵃ31–ᵇ1). Again he treats natural motion as a motion proper to the second, not the first, potentiality-actuality model, for he claims that the motion reflects the old saying that "like moves to like" (310ᵇ1–2). Since motion toward its place is movement of like to like, a dislocated element already has the character that it will have when it reaches its own location; it is not changed by its motion. The progress of fire upward resembles the knower's theorizing, which—to recall the description in De Anima II.5—is a development (ἐπίδοσις) of a thing into itself and into actuality. Natural motion develops an element into what it already is.

Besides mentioning the periphery and the center of the cosmos as elemental forms, Aristotle also speaks of the element above as form to the next below (310ᵇ14–15). The elements move automatically upward or downward according to their natures, but they stop moving only because they are compelled to stop. Fire is not programmed to stop at the periphery; if there were no boundary contained by the fifth element, fire would continue its upward progression. Similarly, the downward progress of earth is limited when it reaches the center because it can proceed downward no further. And although no cosmic boundaries mark the intermediate regions, the motion of the elements is confined at the top by the dominant element that fills the adjacent region. So there is a certain hierarchy among the elements, by which each containing element is superior to the one contained.[61] But more important, each containing element is *conceptually* prior to the one contained, since the limiting of an element's motion is explained with reference to its higher neighbor.[62] Earth, water, air, and fire are not, after all, vertical unities because each higher element is conceptually prior to the one below.

De Caelo IV.3 still has in view the question about the principle of motion proper to the elements themselves, and Aristotle does not alter the

[61] A hierarchy is also suggested in De Cae. IV.4; G.C. I.3; and Meteor. IV.I, and fire is regularly given priority. The hierarchy described in Met. Θ.7, which puts fire at the bottom of the scale, is purely illustrative.

[62] I thank Sarah Broadie for this suggestion.

conclusion of *Physics* VIII.4. Instead he makes a provocative claim about the status of the elements. He repeats that the elements seem to have in themselves a principle of motion (ἐν αὑτοῖς δοκεῖ ἔχειν ἀρχὴν τῆς μεταβολῆς) (310ᵇ24–25), and he contrasts the elements with entities that change in response to a slight external prod, such as living organisms that regain health if barely stimulated by an external source (310ᵇ25–31). Even more than things requiring bare stimulation, the elements seem responsible for their own motions. He says, "More than these the heavy and the light appear to have in themselves the principle because their matter is closest to substance (διὰ τὸ ἐγγύτατα τῆς οὐσίας εἶναι τὴν τούτων ὕλην)" (310ᵇ31–33). This is not a revision of *Physics* VIII. The elements do seem to have an active principle, but in fact, since they are totally simple, their passive principle adequately explains their natural motion. The elements need no external mover to set them in motion but move "straight-away" if unimpeded. All that requires explanation is why the elements stop moving, and to explain this Aristotle says that their motion is confined by the adjacent element. In a certain way, then, the confining element is the form for the element confined, since it limits and thus regulates the motion. But what is truly interesting about the passage just quoted is the claim that the matter of the elements is "closest to substance." In fact, the elements simply are their material natures, and it is presumably because those material natures alone can sustain natural motion that Aristotle suggests that elemental matter is closest to substance. Unlike all other generated bodies, the elements need no active cause to direct their activity or to preserve them. All this their material nature can do on its own.

Of all material bodies that seem to be substances and fail, the elements come closest to succeeding. Aristotle can exclude the elements precisely because they lack form and must therefore each be defined with reference to something else. Recall that *Metaphysics* Z.16, which revises the list of substances from Z.2, ranks the elements as mere potentialities (δυνάμεις) rather than genuine substances and gives the following reason: "None of these [the elements] is one, but like a heap, until it is worked up and some unity comes to be from them" (1040ᵇ8–10). The elements are heaps because they are formless matter. And although, as pure matter, the elements nearly succeed as genuine substances, substancehood is fairly awarded to the autonomous organic unities that the elements serve.

THE PARADOX OF UNITY

I opened this book with a paradox that seems to undermine the claim of living organisms and other composites to be primary substances. The unity of composites is problematic because every generated object, with the exception of the elements, contains matter from which it was generated and that survives in it as a constituent. Aristotle insists upon horizontal unity through generation and destruction to avoid the Parmenidean objection against sheer emergence; horizontal unity, however, as straightforwardly interpreted, deprives the composite of vertical unity. A generated composite cannot be a vertical unity if the preexisting matter from which it was generated remains within it as a definite subject to which the form of the composite belongs. On this conception of generation, the composite lacks vertical unity because its nature is determined in two ways—by its form and by its matter. Since the composite lacks vertical unity, it is not a conceptually primary entity because its form and its matter are conceptually prior to it.

Aristotle solves the paradox of unity, not by weakening the demand for vertical unity, but by reinterpreting the demand for horizontal unity. He argues that the matter from which a composite is generated survives in the product potentially but is actually destroyed. This single modification within the theory of generation allows him to argue that composites whose constituent matter is potential are vertical unities. The preexisting matter survives in a product potentially, in the sense that its essential properties (as well as some nonessential properties) survive to modify the higher construct. Since these properties are accidental to the nature of the higher body, there is room for composites to be vertical unities, definable with reference to their form alone. But in fact these lower properties, accidental though they are to the higher construct, constantly threaten its vertical unity. This is because, unlike nonsubstantial properties, which can modify a body only accidentally, the material properties can determine the essential nature of a simpler body. The essential properties of the elements—the hot, the cold, the wet, and the dry, and the elemental principles of motion—are actual, though accidental, properties of higher bodies. Because they are essential properties of the elements, however, the elements can be readily recreated as separate actual bodies. For this reason the vertical unity of the higher object, though a genuine vertical unity, is easily destroyed. Aristotle appeals to a cause of unity—an active principle—to explain how composites are maintained as the composites that they are. An active cause directs and coordinates the behavior of a composite so that the composite itself survives. Given the vital role of the active principle in conservation, there is a decisive line to be drawn between those entities whose active principle is internal and all others. Inanimate bodies, with the exception of the elements, depend on external movers both to express their capacities and to avoid degeneration. Living organisms are truly primary substances because they are autonomous self-preserving systems. That they cannot finally resist deterioration is their tragic weakness.

The traditional scheme of the Aristotelian cosmos is orderly and austere, with God (pure form and actuality) at the top of the scale, and prime matter (pure matter and potentiality) at the bottom. Between these extremes are composite bodies, which find their place in a great chain of being. All things are arranged by degrees of perfection, and all strain upward toward a common goal. The elements occupy the lowest rung of the ladder, followed by other inanimate objects; then come living organisms and man, who is honored by his central place on the scale; higher still are the heavenly bodies. Motions within the cosmos are coherent and regular, and the behavior of all things is governed by the highest good for which they all strive to the extent of their limited powers.

I have suggested a different picture, though in some ways it resembles the traditional scheme. At the top of the system is God, pure form and actuality, and at the bottom is pure matter. But, contrary to the traditional scheme, the pure matter at the foundation is not an indeterminate potentiality but a set of simple elements—earth, water, air, and fire in the lower cosmos, aether in the higher sphere. Although the elements have definite natures, they are not composites of matter and form. A composite consists of simpler ingredients that can exist as separate bodies or be structured into a higher complex. The nature of the higher whole is determined entirely (in the case of vertical unities) or partly (in the case of lesser unities) by the organizing form. The great ladder of being does not accurately describe the status of entities within the Aristotelian cosmos. I have not discussed Aristotle's theory of separately existing forms. These are primary substances, whose eternal existence marks them off from other substances whose life is limited. Although their life is brief, all living organisms, including the simplest plants, are primary substances, whose unity and autonomy guarantees them both a conceptual and ontological independence from other things. Furthermore, the elements, although failing to be substances, cannot be relegated to the lowest rung of the cosmic ladder. Instead, among all material bodies that seem to be substances and fail, the elements come closest to being genuine substances. The Aristotelian cosmos is a world of tension and commotion—ordered and preserved by form, disordered by matter. Yet within this world of conflict and opposing forces, living organisms emerge and, for a short time, display a perfect balance and harmony, comparable in quality, if not in duration, to that of the eternal beings in the higher sphere.

APPENDIX

PRIME MATTER AND
ON GENERATION AND
CORRUPTION

I consider here three passages from *On Generation and Corruption*. Two of the passages (II.1, 329ᵃ24–ᵇ3; and II.5, 332ᵃ26–ᵇ5) are important because the one introduces and the other summarizes Aristotle's account of elemental transformation in Book II. The third (I.3, 319ᵃ29–ᵇ4) directly precedes *On Generation and Corruption* I.4, the chapter that distinguishes elemental generation from alteration, which was discussed in detail in chapter 2. Since all three passages have been taken to show Aristotle's commitment to prime matter, they might be cited as evidence against my proposal about the elements.

The passage from *On Generation and Corruption* II.1 is regarded by many scholars as decisive evidence for Aristotle's belief in prime matter, and it has proved the stumbling block for those critics who doubt that he held the doctrine. Previous skeptics have usually argued that, by elemental matter, Aristotle means the elements themselves, which he calls "matter" because, in their transformations, the elements serve as matter for one another.[1] This view is difficult to square with what Aristotle says about matter in II.1, but my account does not face the same difficulties. I have argued that the elements are not composite but simple bodies; unlike composite bodies, there is no further matter out of which the elements are made. So elemental matter is not an ingredient (or set of ingredients), and elemental form is not an organization of the ingredients. When Aristotle speaks of elemental "matter" and "form," he uses these notions simply to specify the item that plays the role of matter and the item that plays the role of form in an elemental transformation. Thus the item that persists through an elemental change can be called "matter," and the item that results from the replacement can be called "form." And so, on my account, one contrary (the σύμβολον that persists) can be called the "matter" for the pair of contraries exchanged, and the contraries exchanged can be called "privation" and "form."

[1] See King 1956, 383; Charlton 1970, 135–36; 1983, 201; cf. Jones 1974.

On Generation and Corruption II. 1, 329ª24–ᵇ35

> But we say that there is a matter of perceptible bodies, but that this [matter] is not separate but always together with a contrariety, from which [matter] the so-called elements come to be. A more precise account about them [matter and contrariety] has been given elsewhere. However, since the primary bodies are also from the matter in this way, we must explain about these [the primary bodies] too, assuming that the matter that is not separate but underlies the contraries is a principle and primary; for the hot is not matter for the cold nor the cold for the hot, but what underlies [is matter] for them both. So first, the potentially perceptible body is a principle; second, the contrarieties, e.g., hotness and coldness; and then third, fire and water and such things. For these change into one another . . . , but the contrarieties do not change. (329ª24–ᵇ3)

Any interpretation of this passage must decide about the ambiguous reference of various pronouns. My decisions are displayed in the square brackets, and in every instance I have followed Joachim (1922).[2] There is also disagreement about the location of the more precise account that Aristotle claims to have given, and again I agree with Joachim that Aristotle refers to *Physics* I.6–9 and that this account concerns the three principles of change for which he argues in that work, here specified as "matter" and "contrariety"—the latter concept including privation and form.[3] But I do not agree with Joachim that Aristotle, in alluding to *Physics* I, refers to an account of prime matter. Many scholars, including some who are prepared to find the concept in *On Generation and Corruption*, now believe that prime matter is not to be traced to the first book of the *Physics*. That text investigates the principles required for change in general and argues that there must be three: a pair of contraries identified as "privation" and "form" and a persisting subject (ὑποκείμενον) identified as "matter." The text does not treat elemental change or the question of what sort of continuant exists in that situation. In any case, had Aristotle meant to refer in *On Generation and Corruption* II. 1 to some account of prime matter and the contrarieties, he should have used the genitive plural of "contrariety" (ἐναντιώσεων) at 329ª26 to specify the two pairs hot/cold and wet/dry. He uses the singular (ἐναντιώσεως) instead, thereby specifying the pair of principles privation and form.

Aristotle recalls the general account of change and indicates that the general theory can be extended to the analysis of elemental transformation. So he promises an account of the elements that will employ three

---

[2] For a discussion of the ambiguities, see Williams 1982, 154–56.
[3] For a different view, see Williams 1982, 154–56.

principles—a pair of contraries, one of which replaces the other, and a persisting matter. He points out that, since the elements conform to the general theory, an account must be given of them too, on the assumption that "the matter that is not separate and underlies the contraries (ὑποκει-μένην τοῖς ἐναντίοις) is a principle and primary" (329ᵃ29–31). One might think that, if this remark accords with the *Physics*, Aristotle's elemental theory should involve a pair of contraries predicated of an underlying subject; and such reasoning has persuaded many commentators that, in his account of the elements, Aristotle appeals to prime matter as an ultimate subject and regards the contraries as properties of it. But if so, then this passage contradicts his claim in *On Generation and Corruption* I.4 that generation occurs when *nothing* remains of which the resulting item is a property (πάθος) or generally accidental (319ᵇ33–320ᵃ2). So, unless Aristotle now rejects his position in I.4, he must envisage some relation between the contraries and the underlying matter other than an accidental relation between πάθη and a subject they modify. Aristotle's reference to the *Physics* recalls his argument that all changes involve three principles. The account of change in the *Physics* is discussed in chapter 3, where I argue that Aristotle does not defend a particular model for change but simply defends the claim that all changes involve three principles.[4] Different groups of changes are described by different models.

The first part of the passage does not provide evidence for Aristotle's commitment to prime matter. There Aristotle recalls his general discussion of matter, form, and privation in the first book of the *Physics* and indicates that the general account of change provided in that work can be extended to elemental transformation as well. The second half of the passage, however, has been regarded as decisive. Having said that the matter that is not separate and underlies the contraries is a principle and primary, Aristotle offers this explanation: "For the hot is not matter for the cold nor the cold for the hot, but what underlies [is matter] for them both" (329ᵃ31–32).

Now why should Aristotle deny that the hot is matter for the cold or the cold for the hot if this were not the sort of error that one might possibly make? If Aristotle were presupposing a doctrine of prime matter, why should he say this? If the hot and the cold were not the sorts of entity that could serve as the matter for something, his statement is bizarre. Given his doctrine of yokes in II.3, however, he has a reason to insist that one contrary cannot underlie its own contrary. He claims that, although the four contraries could theoretically form six yokes, only four yokes are actually possible because contraries contrary to each other cannot be yoked. The pairs of contraries come in two sorts—temperature (hot/cold)

[4] See above, pp. 98–108.

245

and humidity (dry/wet)—and the acceptable yokes consist of one contrary of each sort. Both temperature and humidity contribute to an object's tangibility,[5] and Aristotle evidently thinks that to be actually tangible a body must have features of both sorts. So the hot (or the cold) can underlie the dry or the wet and can therefore count as the "matter" for them, and the dry (or the wet) can underlie the hot or the cold and can therefore count as the "matter" for them. The only item that the hot cannot underlie is its own contrary, the cold; nor can the cold underlie the hot. Prime matter is still irrelevant.

Commentators claim, however, that the end of the passage specifies prime matter. Here Aristotle states three principles: first, "the potentially perceptible body"; second, the contrarieties, for instance, hotness and coldness; and third, fire and water and such things. One should ask, Is the specification of the first principle a definite description of the entity that serves as elemental matter, or is it a general description of whatever serves as elemental matter? Notice that, in specifying the second principle, Aristotle first offers a general description ("the contrarieties") and then names one relevant contrariety ("hotness and coldness"). So his description of the first principle as "the potentially perceptible body" is just as likely to be a general description on a par with "the contrarieties" as it is to be a definite description on a par with "hotness and coldness." And if the phrase is a general description, then whatever underlies a contrariety such as hotness and coldness should count as "the potentially perceptible body." If the contrariety is hotness and coldness, then "the potentially perceptible body" should be the item later called a σύμβολον, the feature shared by two adjacent elements, namely, the dry (if the adjacent elements are fire and earth) or the wet (if the adjacent elements are air and water).

Still, someone might object that the description "the potentially perceptible body" is inappropriate for the hot, the cold, the wet, and the dry because Aristotle identifies them as the differentiae of bodies in respect of tangibility; thus the contraries should be actually perceptible features of the bodies they differentiate. But the fact that the contraries are perceptible features of actual bodies does not make the description unsuitable. First, Aristotle must characterize the role of the continuant in an elemental change; if in fact the hot, the cold, the wet, and the dry are the intended continuants, then he needs a label that identifies them as continuants and not as contraries. In the later discussion he fixes upon the label σύμβολον ("tally"), but he has not yet introduced the term; more important, if this passage is designed to link his elemental theory to the more general account of change in the *Physics*, Aristotle needs a description that applies

---

[5] See *G.C.* II.2, 329^b7–20; *De An.* II.11, 423^b27–29.

generally to the material continuant in contexts of substantial change. As chapter 5 indicates, Aristotle often refers to the continuant in substantial changes as "potential," and in fact does so in *Physics* I.9.[6] So his choice of expressions here calls attention to a connection between elemental transformation and typical examples of generation treated in the *Physics*.

Second, the actually perceptible bodies are the four elements, whose generation and destruction he means to explain. The σύμβολον, which survives an elemental change, does not itself determine a perceptible body because no contrary on its own can do so. Recall that in *On Generation and Corruption* II.4 Aristotle excludes a mechanism for elemental change that would yield a body that is hot-hot (331^b26–33); the mechanism is impossible because no actual body can exist that is simply hot. Each contrary contributes part of the tangibility of the two adjacent elements whose transformation it underlies (e.g., the hot determines part of the tangibility of fire and air, and the wet, part of the tangibility of air and water). Thus the contrary that survives a transformation of adjacent elements, though on its own unable to determine either element, determines the tangibility of both elements potentially. If the surviving contrary is yoked with either member of the contrariety that it underlies, the resulting yoke of contraries differentiates a single actual element. Thus, for this reason too, it is appropriate to call the contrary that survives an elemental change "the potentially perceptible body."

The first two principles that Aristotle mentions—"the potentially perceptible body" and the contrarieties—thus specify the persisting item and the items replaced in an elemental change, and both roles are played by the contraries. The elements themselves—the actually perceptible bodies, such as fire and earth—are listed as the third principle. The preface to Aristotle's account of elemental transformation mentions only those entities employed in the actual theory, first, the contrarieties, which play two roles; and second, the elements, which are differentiated by pairs of contraries. Aristotle's final claim in the passage, that the elements change into one another but the contrarieties do not (329^a35–$^b3$), does not then omit one principle discussed in the foregoing passage. Prime matter is not mentioned in the conclusion because prime matter was not mentioned earlier and plays no part in the theory.

On Generation and Corruption II.5, 332^a26–$^b5$

Defenders of prime matter have another text that might seem to support their case, a passage from *On Generation and Corruption* II.5 in which Aristotle summarizes his theory of elemental transformation. This pas-

---

[6] See *Phys.* I.9, 192^a25–29.

sage seems important because here, finally, he speaks of elemental matter both as not separate and as imperceptible. On the traditional view, imperceptibility is the feature of prime matter that authorizes the distinction between generation and alteration. Since I argue above (see pp. 48–51) that *On Generation and Corruption* 1.4 says nothing about an imperceptible material component, a critic might regard the present passage as vital confirmation of the traditional view.

In *On Generation and Corruption* II.5 Aristotle argues that there must be exactly four elements. He first objects to theories positing a single element as primary and restates the objection that he had leveled in Book 1 against the early materialists, such as Thales and Anaximenes. If, as some people think, any one of the four elements underlies the others and the others are generated by modifications of it, elemental transformation will be alteration rather than generation because the same thing will remain and change merely in its accidental properties ($\pi\acute{\alpha}\theta\eta$) (332^{a}6–9).[7] No single element can be primary because, if it were, all generation would reduce to alteration. Nor, he goes on, can there be anything else besides the four elements from which they all derive, for example, a mean ($\mu\acute{\epsilon}\sigma o\nu$) between air and water or between air and fire, because the mean will simply be air and fire with their contrariety (wet-dry). Since one of the contraries is the privation of the other, no such entity could ever be isolated (332^{a}20–26). Evidently no such entity could ever be isolated because something differentiated by incompatible essential properties cannot exist. Aristotle ruled out such a possibility earlier when he denied the viability of a yoke of contraries contrary to each other and when he excluded a mechanism that might yield such a yoke (331^{b}26–33). There can be no body that is essentially wet and dry. Aristotle's target in this passage is Anaximander's $\check{\alpha}\pi\epsilon\iota\rho o\nu$ ("boundless") (332^{a}25), and he finds this item even less acceptable than the materialists' more familiar substrata, such as Thales' water or Anaximenes' air. Aristotle insists, against Anaximander, that a first principle must either be one of the elements or nothing at all.

Aristotle now argues that there are four elements and does so on the basis of his earlier account of elemental transformation.

> So if there should be nothing, at least perceptible, prior to these [the elements], these would be all there is. Therefore, either they [the elements] must always remain without changing into one another, or they must change—either all or some only, as Plato wrote in the *Timaeus*. Now it was shown earlier that [the elements] must change into one another, and that they do not [come to be] one from another equally quickly—since those having a common factor ($\sigma\acute{\upsilon}\mu\beta o\lambda o\nu$) come to be from one another more quickly, while those lacking [a

[7] Cf. *G.C.* 1.1, 314^{a}8–11; 314^{b}1–4.

σύμβολον] come to be more slowly. So if the contrariety according to which they change is one, they [the elements] must be two [rather than three]; *for the mean (τὸ μέσον) is the matter that is imperceptible and not separate.* But since the elements are seen to be more than two, there would be at least two contrarieties. But if there are two contrarieties, there cannot be three but are four elements, as is evident; for there are that many yokes (συζυγίαι) [i.e., four], for although six yokes are possible, two cannot occur because [the features] are contrary to each other. (332ᵃ26–ᵇ5)

Someone might urge that, in recalling his theory of elemental transformation, Aristotle now mentions the invisible player. In addition to the contrariety, one member of which replaces the other, there is the "matter" or "mean," which is "imperceptible and not separate." Thus Aristotle replaces Anaximander's perceptible mean with one of his own, which is imperceptible. Aristotle's imperceptible mean is then taken to be prime matter.[8]

But consider the point of the passage.[9] Aristotle is arguing that there are exactly four elements. He first considers a situation in which there is a single contrariety and argues that there would be two elements (332^a34–$^b1$); he then says that, since there are evidently more than two elements, there are at least two contrarieties (332^b1–2). And if there are two contrarieties, then there cannot be three but are four elements (332^b2–3). This result follows from the fact that there are exactly four yokes of contraries; although six yokes of contraries are possible, yielding a total of six elements, two are excluded because they consist of contraries contrary to each other (332^b3–5). The passage containing the clause about imperceptible matter occurs in the first step of the argument, which concludes that there are two elements. In this section Aristotle excludes a third element consisting of an impossible yoke.

Suppose that there is a single contrariety, for example, hotness and coldness. If there is a single contrariety, then the number of elements is two, for instance, air and water. According to Aristotle, Anaximander would say that this situation involves a third element that serves as the material continuant. Thus, if the transformation occurs between the contraries hot and cold, the continuant is the mean, which is both hot and cold. Against Anaximander Aristotle objects that there is no third element because the mean that Anaximander calls the matter is imperceptible and not separate. Anaximander's mean is imperceptible because perceptibility depends upon two sorts of tangible properties, temperature and humidity, and his mean has two features of the same sort; his mean

[8] See Joachim 1922, 226; and Williams 1982, 214.

[9] I thank Tim Maudlin for his insight into this passage.

is not separate because, as Aristotle said earlier, an entity whose nature is determined by mutually exclusive essential properties cannot be isolated (332^a23–24). Thus in calling matter "imperceptible" and "not separate," Aristotle is not describing his own material continuant but is attacking Anaximander.

If he were describing prime matter, his description would, in any case, be extremely odd. Although prime matter may be imperceptible and not separate, it is scarcely a mean—that is, an intermediate between two extremes. Prime matter is not a mean for the simple reason that there are no comparable entities for it to be a mean between: prime matter is one of a kind. This passage, then, provides no evidence for prime matter and so is irrelevant to the question about imperceptible matter.

On Generation and Corruption I.3, 319^a29–$^b4$

Although there are many passages in which commentators find references to prime matter, it should be evident from my treatment of the passage from On Generation and Corruption II.5 that many of these texts can be explained by examining the surrounding context. There are, however, several important passages in which Aristotle says that there is a single or common matter of the elements but one that is "not the same in being." I conclude this Appendix by indicating how these passages can be interpreted, and I shall focus on one text cited in the discussion of alteration and generation in chapter 2 above: On Generation and Corruption I.3, 319^a29–$^b4$. This passage directly precedes Aristotle's treatment in I.4.

Aristotle claims in On Generation and Corruption I.3 that the generation of one thing is the destruction of another, and he considers why people tend to regard one terminus of the change as positive and the other as negative, so that, for example, in describing a transformation of air into water, they tend to speak of the generation of water rather than the destruction of air, whereas in describing a transformation of water into air they tend to speak of the destruction of water rather than the generation of air. Aristotle's own elemental theory treats both termini as positive terms. At the end of the chapter he suggests that perhaps the item properly designated as negative is neither of the termini (e.g., neither fire nor earth) but the underlying matter, which he then describes.

> But someone might question whether this unqualified not-being is one of the two contraries, for example, earth and the heavy not-being, and fire and the light being, or whether instead earth too is being, while not-being is the matter of earth and fire alike. And again [one might ask], Is the matter of each different, or [in that case] would they [the elements] not come to be from one another and from con-

traries (for to these—fire, earth, water, air—the contraries belong)? Or is [the matter] in a sense the same, and in a sense different? *For what underlies, whatever it is, is the same, but the being is not the same.* (319^a29-^b4)

Aristotle has a common idiom: "*x* and *y* are one (or the same) but not one (or the same) in being (form or account)." He regularly uses the phrase to describe a single subject that has distinct properties, and often distinct functions, depending upon its being viewed as *x* or *y*. For example, in *Physics* I.7, in discussing a man who comes to be musical from having been unmusical, he says that the unmusical man is one in number but not one in form or account. The unmusical man fails to be one in form because the being for man is not the same as the being for the unmusical; furthermore, the one (namely, the man) survives the change, and the other (namely, the unmusical) does not survive (190^a13-21). In this example there is one object, the unmusical man, but that object can be identified either as a substance of a particular sort (a man) or as something qualified in a particular way (the unmusical); described as "man," the object survives the change, while described as "the unmusical," the object is destroyed. There are many comparable examples.[10] If Aristotle invariably used the idiom as he does in the example from *Physics* I.7, one might reasonably conclude that, when he speaks of elemental matter as one but not one in being, he has in mind a single object (prime matter) that can be identified by distinct properties.

But Aristotle does not always use the phrase in the same way. For example, in *Nicomachean Ethics* v.1 he says that the two qualities virtue and justice are the same but not the same in being: justice is a certain character relative to someone else, while virtue is the character simply (1130^a10-13). This passage suggests that there is a single general character, virtue, which is called "virtue" when viewed simply but called "justice" when the virtue is applied between persons. He treats practical wisdom and political wisdom similarly in *Nicomachean Ethics* vi.8. Since Aristotle does not always use the idiom in the usual way, there is no need to understand it in that way in *On Generation and Corruption* I.3.

One could interpret the claim in I.3 as follows: whatever underlies an elemental change is the same in the role that it plays (since it is the item that persists), but its being is not the same because a different item persists through different changes.[11] For instance, the dry survives a transformation of earth into fire, and the hot survives a transformation of fire into air. Alternatively, Aristotle could be saying that whatever underlies an

[10] See, e.g., *Phys.* III.3, 202^a18-20; IV.13, 222^a17-20; VIII.8, 263^b12-14; *De Mem.* 1, 450^b20-27. Further references are given in Bonitz 1870, 221^a50-61.

[11] I owe this suggestion to James Lennox.

elemental change is the same in *kind* (since all four contraries are tangible properties) but not the same in *being* because the specific identity of each is different.[12] The second interpretation is likely to be appropriate in the various instances in which Aristotle speaks of a "common" matter of the elements;[13] the matter is common because all four contraries are generically the same. Because the elements are generically the same but specifically different, they are able to act on, and to be transformed into, one another. In fact, Aristotle insists that action and passion regularly involve an agent and patient that are like in kind and unlike in form.[14]

I argue in chapter 2 that prime matter finds no place in Aristotle's elemental theory, and if I am right, allusions to prime matter should not be littered throughout the corpus. References to prime matter have been found in Aristotle's writings because his theory was thought to require the doctrine. If, as I have argued, his theory does not require it, these passages should all admit another interpretation.

[12] Cf. *G.C.* I.7, 324^{b}6–9.
[13] See, e.g., *G.C.* II.7, 334^{a}15–18; 334^{a}23–25; *De Cae.* IV.5, 312^{a}28–^{b}2.
[14] See *G.C.* I.7, 323^{b}29–324^{a}14; and see above, chapter 6, p. 198.

BIBLIOGRAPHY

EDITIONS OF ARISTOTLE

Categories and *De Interpretatione*

L. Minio-Paluello. 1949. *Aristotelis Categoriae et Liber De Interpretatione*. Oxford.

Prior and *Posterior Analytics*

Ross, W. D. 1964. *Aristotelis Analytica Priora et Posteriora*. Oxford.

Topics and *Sophistici Elenchi*

Ross, W. D. 1958. *Aristotelis Topica et Sophistici Elenchi*. Oxford.

Physics

Ross, W. D. 1936. *Aristotle's Physics*. A revised text with introduction and commentary. Oxford.

Wicksteed, P. H., and F. M. Cornford, 1929. *Aristotle: The Physics*. 2 vols. Loeb Classical Library. Cambridge, Mass.

De Caelo

Allan, D. J. 1936. *Aristotelis De Caelo*. Oxford.

Guthrie, W.K.C. 1939. *Aristotle: On the Heavens*. Loeb Classical Library. Cambridge, Mass.

On Generation and Corruption

Forster, E. S. 1955. *Aristotle: On Coming-to-Be and Passing-Away*. Loeb Classical Library. Cambridge, Mass.

Joachim, Harold. 1922. *Aristotle: On Coming-to-Be and Passing-Away*. A revised text with introduction and commentary. Oxford.

Meteorology

Lee, H.P.D. 1952. *Aristotle: Meteorologica*. Loeb Classical Library. Cambridge, Mass.

De Anima

Hett, W. S. 1936. *Aristotle: On the Soul, Parva Naturalia, On Breath*. Loeb Classical Library. Cambridge, Mass.

Hicks, R. D. 1907. *Aristotle De Anima*. With translation, introduction, and notes. Cambridge.

Rodier, G. 1900. *Aristotle: Traité de l'âme*. 2 vols. Translation and commentary. Paris.

Ross, W. D. 1956. *Aristotelis De Anima*. Oxford.

————. 1961. *Aristotle: De Anima*. A revised text with introduction and commentary. Oxford.

BIBLIOGRAPHY

De Iuventute et Senectute, De Memoria, and *De Sensu*

Ross, G.R.T. 1906. *Aristotle: De Sensu and De Memoria.* Text and translation with introduction and commentary. Cambridge.

Ross, W. D. 1955. *Aristotle: Parva Naturalia.* A revised text with introduction and commentary. Oxford.

Parts of Animals

Peck, A. L. 1937. *Aristotle: Parts of Animals.* Loeb Classical Library. Cambridge, Mass.

Movement of Animals

Nussbaum, Martha. 1978. *Aristotle's De Motu Animalium.* Text with translation, commentary, and interpretive essays. Princeton.

Generation of Animals

Lulofs, H. J. Drossaart. 1965. *Aristotelis De Generatione Animalium.* Oxford.

Peck, A. L. 1942. *Aristotle: Generation of Animals.* Loeb Classical Library. Cambridge, Mass.

Metaphysics

Frede, Michael, and Günther Patzig. 1988. *Aristoteles, Metaphysik* Z. 2 vols. Text, translation, and commentary. Munich.

Jaeger, Werner. 1957. *Aristotelis Metaphysica.* Oxford.

Ross, W. D. 1924. *Aristotle's Metaphysics.* 2 vols. A revised text with introduction and commentary. Oxford.

Tredennick, Hugh. 1933. *Aristotle: The Metaphysics. Books I–IX.* Loeb Classical Library. London.

Nicomachean Ethics

Bywater, I. 1894. *Aristotelis Ethica Nicomachea.* Oxford.

Rhetoric

Ross, W. D. 1959. *Aristotelis Ars Rhetorica.* Oxford.

EDITIONS OF OTHER ANCIENT AND MEDIEVAL AUTHORS

Alexander of Aphrodisias

Hayduck, Michael. 1891. *Alexandri Aphrodisiensis In Aristotelis Metaphysica Commentaria.* Berlin.

Aquinas, St. Thomas.

Maggiòlo, P. M. 1965. *S. Thomae Aquinatis In Octo Libros Physicorum Aristotelis Exposito.* Turin.

BIBLIOGRAPHY

Heraclitus and Parmenides

Diels, Hermann, and Walther Kranz. 1972. *Die Fragmente der Vorsokratiker*. 16th reprint. 3 vols. Zürich.

Philoponus

Vitelli, Hieronymus. 1897. *Ioannis Philoponi In Aristotelis Libros De Generatione et Corruptione Commentaria*. Berlin.

Plato

Burnet, John. 1900–1907. *Platonis Opera*. 5 vols. Oxford.

Simplicius

Diels, Hermann. 1882. *Simplicii In Aristotelis Physicorum Libros Quattuor Priores Commentaria*. Berlin.

MODERN AUTHORS

Ackrill, J. L. 1963. *Aristotle's Categories and De Interpretatione*. Clarendon Aristotle Series. Oxford.

———. 1965. "Aristotle's Distinction between *Energeia* and *Kinesis*." In *New Essays on Plato and Aristotle*, edited by Renford Bambrough, pp. 121–41. London.

———. [1972–1973] 1979. "Aristotle's Definitions of *psuchê*." *Proceedings of the Aristotelian Society* 73: 119–33. Reprinted in *Articles on Aristotle*, vol. 4, *Psychology and Aesthetics*, edited by J. Barnes, M. Schofield, and R. Sorabji, pp. 65–75. London.

Albritton, Rogers. 1957. "Forms of Particular Substances in Aristotle's *Metaphysics*." *Journal of Philosophy* 54: 699–708.

Annas, Julia. 1976. *Aristotle's Metaphysics. Books M and N*. Clarendon Aristotle Series. Oxford.

Anscombe, G.E.M., and P. T. Geach. 1961. *Three Philosophers*. Ithaca.

Balme, D. M. 1972. *Aristotle's De Partibus Animalium I and De Generatione Animalium I*. Clarendon Aristotle Series. Oxford.

———. [1980] 1987. "Aristotle's Biology Was Not Essentialist." *Archiv für Geschichte der Philosophie* 62: 1–12. Reprinted in *Philosophical Issues in Aristotle's Biology*, edited by A. Gotthelf and J. Lennox, pp. 291–302. Cambridge.

———. 1984. "The Snub." *Ancient Philosophy* 4: 1–8. Also appears in *Philosophical Issues in Aristotle's Biology*, edited by A. Gotthelf and J. Lennox, pp. 306–12. Cambridge, 1987.

———. 1987a. "Aristotle's Use of Division and Differentiae." In *Philosophical Issues in Aristotle's Biology*, edited by A. Gotthelf and J. Lennox, pp. 69–89. Cambridge.

———. 1987b. "Note on the *aporia* in *Metaphysics* Z." In *Philosophical Issues in Aristotle's Biology*, edited by A. Gotthelf and J. Lennox, pp. 302–6. Cambridge.

Barnes, Jonathan. 1975. *Aristotle's Posterior Analytics*. Clarendon Aristotle Series. Oxford.

——, ed. 1984. *The Complete Works of Aristotle*. The Revised Oxford Translation. 2 vols. Princeton.

Bogaard, Paul A. 1979. "Heaps or Wholes: Aristotle's Explanation of Compound Bodies." *Isis* 70: 11–29.

Bolton, Robert. 1987. "Definition and Scientific Method in Aristotle's *Posterior Analytics* and *Generation of Animals*. In *Philosophical Issues in Aristotle's Biology*, edited by A. Gotthelf and J. Lennox, pp. 120–66. Cambridge.

Bonitz, H. 1870. *Index Aristotelicus*. Berlin.

Bostock, David. 1982. "Aristotle on the Principles of Change in *Physics* I." In *Language and Logos: Studies in Ancient Greek Philosophy*, edited by Malcolm Schofield and Martha Nussbaum, pp. 179–96. Cambridge.

Brunschwig, Jacques. 1979. "La form, prédicat de la matière?" In *Etudes sur la métaphysique d'Aristote*, Proceedings of the Sixth Symposium Aristotelicum, edited by P. Aubenque, pp. 131–66. Paris.

Burnyeat, Myles et al. 1979. *Notes on Book Zeta of Aristotle's Metaphysics*. Oxford.

——. 1984. *Notes on Eta and Theta of Aristotle's Metaphysics*. Oxford.

Chappell, Vere. 1973. "Matter." *Journal of Philosophy* 70: 679–96.

Charles, David. 1984. *Aristotle's Philosophy of Action*. London.

Charlton, William. 1970. *Aristotle's Physics: Books I and II*. Clarendon Aristotle Series. Oxford.

——. 1972. "Aristotle and the Principle of Individuation." *Phronesis* 17: 239–49.

——. 1983. "Prime Matter: A Rejoinder." *Phronesis* 28: 197–211.

——. 1987. "Aristotelian Powers." *Phronesis* 32: 277–89.

Chen, Chung-Hwan. 1956. "Different Meanings of the Term Energeia in the Philosophy of Aristotle." *Philosophy and Phenomenological Research* 17: 56–65.

Code, Alan. 1976. "The Persistence of Aristotelian Matter." *Philosophical Studies* 29: 357–67.

——. 1986. "Aristotle: Essence and Accident." In *Philosophical Grounds of Rationality: Intensions, Categories, Ends*, edited by R. E. Grandy and R. Warner, pp. 411–39. Oxford.

——. 1987. "Soul as Efficient Cause in Aristotle's Embryology." *Philosophical Topics* 15: 51–59.

Cohen, Sheldon. 1984. "Aristotle's Doctrine of the Material Substrate." *Philosophical Review* 93: 171–94.

Cooper, John M. 1975. *Reason and Human Good in Aristotle*. Cambridge, Mass.

——. 1985. "Hypothetical Necessity." In *Aristotle on Nature and Living Things*, edited by Allan Gotthelf, pp. 151–67. Pittsburgh.

——. 1988. "Metaphysics in Aristotle's Embryology." *Proceedings of the Cambridge Philological Society* 214:14–41.

Dancy, Russell. 1978. "On Some of Aristotle's Second Thoughts about Substances: Matter." *Philosophical Review* 87: 372–413.

Driscoll, John. 1981. "ΕΙΔΗ in Aristotle's Earlier and Later Theories of Substance." In *Studies in Aristotle*, edited by D. J. O'Meara, pp. 129–59. Washington, D.C.

Fine, Gail. 1984. "Separation." *Oxford Studies in Ancient Philosophy* 2: 31–87.

————. 1985. "Separation: A Reply to Morrison." *Oxford Studies in Ancient Philosophy* 3: 159–65.

Frede, Michael. [1978] 1987. "Individuen bei Aristoteles." *Antike und Abendland* 24: 16–39. Reprinted and translated in *Essays in Ancient Philosophy*, by Michael Frede, pp. 49–71. Minneapolis.

————. Forthcoming. "The Definition of Sensible Substances in *Metaphysics* Z." Typescript.

Freeland, Cynthia. 1987. "Aristotle on Bodies, Matter, and Potentiality." In *Philosophical Issues in Aristotle's Biology*, edited by A. Gotthelf and J. Lennox, pp. 392–407. Cambridge.

Furley, David. 1978. "Self Movers." In *Aristotle on Mind and the Senses*, Proceedings of the Seventh Symposium Aristotelicum, edited by G.E.R. Lloyd and G.E.L. Owen, pp. 165–79. Cambridge. Also appears in *Essays in Aristotle's Ethics*, edited by Amélie Rorty, pp. 55–67. Berkeley, 1980.

————. 1983. "The Mechanics of *Meteorologica* IV: A Prolegomenon to Biology." In *Zweifelhaftes im Corpus Aristotelicum: Studien zu einigen Dubia*, Proceedings of the Ninth Symposium Aristotelicum, edited by Paul Moraux and Jürgen Wiesner, pp. 73–93. Berlin.

Furth, Montgomery. 1985. *Aristotle's Metaphysics: Books VII–X.* Indianapolis.

————. 1988. *Substance, Form, and Psyche: An Aristotelean Metaphysics.* Cambridge.

Geach, P. T. 1969. *God and the Soul.* London.

Gill, Mary Louise. 1980. "Aristotle's Theory of Causal Action in *Physics* III.3." *Phronesis* 25: 129–47.

————. 1984. "Aristotle on the Individuation of Changes." *Ancient Philosophy* 4: 9–22.

————. 1987. "Matter and Flux in Plato's *Timaeus*." *Phronesis* 32: 34–53.

————. 1988. "Aristotle on Matters of Life and Death." In *Proceedings of the Boston Area Colloquium in Ancient Philosophy*, vol. 4, edited by John J. Cleary and Daniel Shartin, pp. 187–205. Lanham, Md.

Gotthelf, Allan. 1985. "Notes toward a Study of Substance and Essence in Aristotle's *Parts of Animals* II–IV." In *Aristotle on Nature and Living Things*, edited by Allan Gotthelf, pp. 27–54. Pittsburgh.

Graham, Daniel W. 1987. "The Paradox of Prime Matter." *Journal of the History of Philosophy* 25: 475–90.

Grene, Marjorie. 1963. *A Portrait of Aristotle.* Chicago.

Hamlyn, D. W. 1968. *Aristotle's De Anima: Books II and III.* Clarendon Aristotle Series. Oxford.

Happ, Heinz. 1971. *Hyle: Studien zum aristotelischen Materie-Begriff.* Berlin.

Hartman, Edwin. 1977. *Substance, Body, and Soul: Aristotelian Investigations.* Princeton.

Heinaman, Robert. 1985. "Aristotle on Housebuilding." *History of Philosophy Quarterly* 2: 145–62.

Hussey, Edward. 1983. *Aristotle's Physics: Books III and IV.* Clarendon Aristotle Series. Oxford.

Jaeger, Werner. 1948. *Aristotle: Fundamentals of the History of His Development.* 2d ed. Translated by Richard Robinson. Oxford.

Jones, Barrington. 1974. "Aristotle's Introduction of Matter." *Philosophical Review* 83: 474–500.

Kahn, Charles. 1985. "The Place of the Prime Mover in Aristotle's Teleology." In *Aristotle on Nature and Living Things*, edited by Allan Gotthelf, pp. 183–205. Pittsburgh.

King, Hugh R. 1956. "Aristotle without *Prima Materia*." *Journal of the History of Ideas* 17: 370–89.

Kirwan, Christopher. 1971. *Aristotle's Metaphysics: Books Γ, Δ, and E.* Clarendon Aristotle Series. Oxford.

Kosman, L. A. 1969. "Aristotle's Definition of Motion." *Phronesis* 14: 40–62.

———. 1984. "Substance, Being, and *Energeia*." *Oxford Studies in Ancient Philosophy* 2: 121–49.

———. 1987. "Animals and Other Beings in Aristotle." In *Philosophical Issues in Aristotle's Biology*, edited by A. Gotthelf and J. Lennox, pp. 360–91. Cambridge.

Kostman, James. 1987. "Aristotle's Definition of Change." *History of Philosophy Quarterly* 4: 3–16.

Kung, Joan. 1978. "Can Substance Be Predicated of Matter?" *Archiv für Geschichte der Philosophie* 60: 140–59.

Lacey, A. R. 1965. "The Eleatics and Aristotle on Some Problems of Change." *Journal of the History of Ideas* 26: 451–68.

Laycock, Henry. 1972. "Some Questions of Ontology." *Philosophical Review* 81: 3–42.

Lear, Jonathan. 1987. "Active Episteme." In *Mathematik und Metaphysik*, Proceedings of the Tenth Symposium Aristotelicum, edited by A. Graiser, pp. 149–74. Bonn.

Lennox, James. 1985. "Are Aristotelian Species Eternal?" In *Aristotle on Nature and Living Things*, edited by Allan Gotthelf, pp. 67–94. Pittsburgh.

———. 1987a. "Divide and Explain: The *Posterior Analytics* in Practice." In *Philosophical Issues in Aristotle's Biology*, edited by A. Gotthelf and J. Lennox, pp. 90–119. Cambridge.

———. 1987b. "Kinds, Forms of Kinds, and the More and the Less in Aristotle's Biology." In *Philosophical Issues in Aristotle's Biology*, edited by A. Gotthelf and J. Lennox, pp. 339–59. Cambridge.

———. Forthcoming. "The Matter of *Meteorology* IV." Typescript.

Lesher, James. 1971. "Aristotle on Form, Substance, and Universals: A Dilemma." *Phronesis* 16: 169–78.

Leszl, Walter. 1970. *Logic and Metaphysics in Aristotle.* Padua.

Liddell, H. G., Robert Scott, and H. S. Jones 1968. *A Greek-English Lexicon.* 9th ed., with a Supplement. Oxford.

Lloyd, A. C. 1981. *Form and Universal in Aristotle.* Liverpool.

Lloyd, G.E.R. 1962. "Right and Left in Greek Philosophy." *Journal of Hellenic Studies* 82: 56–66.

————. [1964] 1970. "Hot and Cold, Dry and Wet in Early Greek Thought." *Journal of Hellenic Studies* 84: 92–106. Reprinted in *Studies in Presocratic Philosophy*, vol. 1, edited by David J. Furley and R. E. Allen, pp. 255–80. London.

————. 1968. *Aristotle: The Growth and Structure of His Thought.* Cambridge.

Loux, Michael. 1979. "Forms, Species, and Predication in *Metaphysics* Z, H, and Θ." *Mind* 88: 1–23.

Mabbott, J. D. 1926. "Aristotle and the ΧΩΡΙΣΜΟΣ of Plato." *Classical Quarterly* 20: 72–79.

McDowell, John. 1973. *Plato: Theaetetus.* Clarendon Plato Series. Oxford.

Mansion, Augustin. 1945. *Introduction à la physique aristotélicienne.* Louvain.

Mansion, Suzanne. 1969. "Tὸ σιμόν et la définition physique." In *Naturphilosophie bei Aristoteles und Theophrast*, Proceedings of the Fourth Symposium Aristotelicum, edited by Ingemar Düring, pp. 124–32. Heidelberg.

————. [1971] 1979. "Sur la composition ontologique des substances sensibles chez Aristote (*Métaphysique* Z 7–9)." In *Philomathes: Studies and Essays in the Humanities in Memory of Philip Merlan*, edited by R. B. Palmer and R. Hamerton Kelly, pp. 75–87. The Hague. Reprinted and translated in *Articles on Aristotle*, vol. 3, *Metaphysics*, edited by J. Barnes, M. Schofield, and R. Sorabji, pp. 80–87. London.

Maudlin, Tim. 1988–1989. "Keeping Body and Soul Together: The Z.3 Puzzle and the Unity of Substances." *University of Dayton Review* 19: 121–33.

Miller, Fred D. 1978. "Aristotle's Use of Matter." *Paideia* 7: 105–19.

Modrak, D. K. 1979. "Forms, Types, and Tokens in Aristotle's *Metaphysics*." *Journal of the History of Philosophy* 17: 371–81.

Morrison, Donald. 1985a. "Χωριστός in Aristotle." *Harvard Studies in Classical Philology* 89: 89–105.

————. 1985b. "Separation in Aristotle's Metaphysics." *Oxford Studies in Ancient Philosophy* 3: 125–57.

————. 1985c. "Separation: A Reply to Fine." *Oxford Studies in Ancient Philosophy* 3: 167–73.

————. 1988. "Commentary on Gill." In *Proceedings of the Boston Area Colloquium in Ancient Philosophy*, vol. 4, edited by John J. Cleary and Daniel Shartin, pp. 206–12. Lanham, Md.

Mourelatos, A.P.D. 1967. "Aristotle's 'Powers' and Modern Empiricism." *Ratio* 9: 97–104.

Nussbaum, Martha. 1976. "The Text of Aristotle's *De Motu Animalium*." *Harvard Studies in Classical Philology* 80: 111–59.

Nussbaum, Martha, and Hilary Putnam. Forthcoming. "Changing Aristotle's Mind." Typescript.

Owen, G.E.L. [1960] 1979. "Logic and Metaphysics in Some Earlier Works of Aristotle." In *Aristotle and Plato in the Mid-Fourth Century*, Proceedings of the First Symposium Aristotelicum, edited by I. Düring and G.E.L. Owen, pp. 163–90. Göteborg. Reprinted in *Articles on Aristotle*, vol. 3, *Metaphysics*, edited by J. Barnes, M. Schofield, and R. Sorabji, pp. 13–32. London.

————. [1961] 1975. "*Tithenai ta Phainomena.*" In *Aristote et les problèmes de méthode*, edited by Suzanne Mansion, pp. 167–90. Louvain. Reprinted in *Articles on Aristotle*, vol. 1, *Science*, edited by J. Barnes, M. Schofield, and R. Sorabji, pp. 113–26. London.

———. [1965] 1975. "The Platonism of Aristotle." *Proceedings of the British Academy* 50: 125–50. Reprinted in *Articles on Aristotle*, vol. 1, *Science*, edited by J. Barnes, M. Schofield, and R. Sorabji, pp. 14–34. London.

———. 1978–1979. "Particular and General." *Proceedings of the Aristotelian Society* 100: 1–21.

Owens, Joseph. 1963. "Matter and Predication in Aristotle." In *The Concept of Matter in Greek and Medieval Philosophy*, edited by Ernan McMullin, pp. 79–95. Notre Dame, Ind. Also appears in *Aristotle: A Collection of Critical Essays*, edited by J.M.E. Moravcsik, pp. 191–214. Notre Dame, Ind., 1967.

———. 1978. *The Doctrine of Being in the Aristotelian Metaphysics*. 3d ed. Toronto.

Pellegrin, Pierre. 1982. *La classification des animaux chez Aristote: Statut de la biologie et unité de l'aristotélisme*. Paris.

———. 1987. "Logical Difference and Biological Difference: The Unity of Aristotle's Thought." In *Philosophical Issues in Aristotle's Biology*, edited by A. Gotthelf and J. Lennox, pp. 313–38. Cambridge.

Penner, Terry. 1970. "Verbs and the Identity of Actions—a Philosophical Exercise in the Interpretation of Aristotle." In *Ryle*, edited by Oscar P. Wood and George Pitcher, pp. 393–460. New York.

Polansky, Ronald. 1983. "*Energeia* in Aristotle's *Metaphysics* IX." *Ancient Philosophy* 3: 160–70.

Robinson, H. M. 1974. "Prime Matter in Aristotle." *Phronesis* 19: 168–88.

Scaltsas, Theodore. 1985. "Substratum, Subject, and Substance." *Ancient Philosophy* 5: 215–40.

Schofield, Malcolm. 1972. "*Metaph*. Z 3: Some Suggestions." *Phronesis* 17: 97–101.

Sellars, Wilfrid. [1957] 1967. "Substance and Form in Aristotle." *Journal of Philosophy* 54: 688–99. Reprinted in *Philosophical Perspectives: History of Philosophy*, by Wilfrid Sellars, pp. 125–36. Reseda, Calif.

Sharples, Robert. 1983. "Alexander of Aphrodisias: Problems about Possibility II." *Bulletin, Institute of Classical Studies* 30: 99–110.

Smith, J. A. 1921. "ΤΟΔΕ ΤΙ in Aristotle." *Classical Review* 35: 19.

Smyth, Herbert Weir. 1920. *Greek Grammar*. Cambridge, Mass.

Solmsen, Friedrich. 1958. "Aristotle and Prime Matter: A Reply to Hugh R. King." *Journal of the History of Ideas* 19: 243–52.

———. 1960. *Aristotle's System of the Physical World: A Comparison with His Predecessors*. Ithaca.

Sorabji, Richard. 1980. *Necessity, Cause, and Blame: Perspectives on Aristotle's Theory*. London.

Stahl, Donald. 1981. "Stripped Away: Some Contemporary Obscurities Surrounding *Metaphysics* Z 3 (1029a10–26)." *Phronesis* 26: 177–80.

Waterlow, Sarah. 1982. *Nature, Change, and Agency in Aristotle's Physics*. Oxford.

Wedin, Michael. 1988. *Mind and Imagination in Aristotle*. New Haven.

White, Nicholas. 1971. "Aristotle on Sameness and Oneness." *Philosophical Review* 80: 177–97.

———. 1972–1973. "Origins of Aristotle's Essentialism." *Review of Metaphysics* 26: 57–85.

Whiting, Jennifer. Forthcoming. *Aristotelian Individuals.* Oxford.

Wieland, Wolfgang. 1970. *Die aristotelische Physik.* 2d ed. Göttingen.

Williams, C.J.F. 1972. "Aristotle, *De Generatione et Corruptione* 319b21–4." *Classical Review*, n.s., 22: 301–3.

———. 1982. *Aristotle's De Generatione et Corruptione.* Clarendon Aristotle Series. Oxford.

Woods, M. J. 1974–1975. "Substance and Essence in Aristotle." *Proceedings of the Aristotelian Society* 75: 167–80.

Zeller, Edward. 1897. *Aristotle and the Earlier Peripatetics.* 2 vols. Translated by B.F.C. Costelloe and J. H. Muirhead. London.

form (εἶδος) (cont.)

as cause of persistence, 213–14, 222–27, 241–42

controls matter, 169–70, 171, 212–13, 238, 242

as definable unity, 4–5, 7, 35–36, 111–14, 131–33, 136–41, 145, 171; problem of matter for, 115–16, 126, 127–28

differentiates matter, 143–44, 159–60, 213

directs and limits activity, 238

directs and limits changes, 200–202

distinguished from species, 119n.17, 120n

as efficient cause, 120–21, 199–202

as essence, 17, 116–20

as first actuality, 139–40, 143, 176–77, 182

as first cause of change, 195, 198–202

as function. See form: as capacity

as goal of potentiality (active and passive), 173–74, 176–81, 184, 204, 210–11, 218–19, 230

immaterial, 111, 126, 127

individual, 32–34

and matter, unity of, 139–40, 141–44. See also composite: as definable unity

as nature, 9, 121

ontological dependence of, on matter, 35, 37, 112, 116, 126, 131–33, 138, 145

ontological notion, 66–67

particular, 32–33

parts of, 36

as potentiality (active), 9, 199–202, 218. See also change: explained by potentiality and actuality (model 1)

proximate matter for, 131–33

relation of, to composite, 66

separation of, 16–17, 35–36, 38, 83, 86–87, 112, 131–33

separately existing, 4, 5, 35, 242

and snub analogy, 4–5, 112, 127–28, 131–32

substantiality of, as subject, 15–19, 30–31, 38, 56, 86–87, 127, 167–68; problem of matter for, 39, 83, 109, 133

thisness of, 16–17, 31, 32–34, 38, 83, 86–87

transmission of, 33. See also agent: and transmission of form

ungenerated, 111, 120, 121–22, 126, 127, 138, 145

See also capacity

Forster, E. S., 71nn.43, 44

Frede, M.: on definition, 4n.5, 36n.52; on genus, 15n; on Met. Z.1, 37n.56; on Met. Z.3, 16n, 17n.5, 18n.9, 22n.14, 23n.18, 26nn.24, 26, 29nn.30, 31; on Met. Z.4, 117n.12; on Met. Z.7–9, 10n.18, 111n.2, 120n, 121n.21, 125n.26; on Met. Z.10–11, 128n.32, 133nn.50, 51, 134n.54, 135n.56, 136nn.59, 60, 137n.61, 137n.62; on Met. Z.12, 140n.66; on thisness, 31n.33

Freeland, C., 150n.10, 178n

function. See capacity

Furley, D., 96n.22, 162n.36, 210n

Furth, M.: on Cat., 10n.19; on elemental theory, 43n.2, 76nn.48, 50; on Met. Z, 20n.10, 111n.2, 117n.12, 136n.59; on Met. H and Θ, 88n.13, 216n.14

Geach, P., 53n

generation (γένεσις):

analogy of, with nonsubstantial change, 6, 122–25

Aristotle's criticism of predecessors on, 45n.9, 53–54, 248–50

constructive, 63–64, 85, 86, 94–97, 146

continuant in, 6, 57–60, 92, 145, 146–49, 163–65, 240–41

distinguished from nonsubstantial change, 45–67, 86, 90–94, 248

implications of, for definition, 6–9, 85–86, 105–6, 111, 120–26

irreversible, 92, 96–97

linear (nonconstructive), 64–65

linguistic conventions concerning, 28–29, 101–2

opposed terms in, 47, 54n, 54–60, 91–92, 93–94

path of, 92, 93–94, 95–97, 108, 128–29, 164–65

product of, as composite, 103–7

qualified, 93, 94–95. See also change: nonsubstantial

relation of opposed terms to continuant in, 57–60

relation of opposed terms to subject in, 48–57, 61–62

requires "horizontal" unity, 6–9, 44–46

requires preexisting subject, 43–44